NASSER
AND
HIS GENERATION

P. J. VATIKIOTIS

ST. MARTIN'S PRESS   NEW YORK

Copyright © 1978 P.J. Vatikiotis

All rights reserved. For information write:
St. Martin's Press Inc., 175 Fifth Avenue, New York, N.Y. 10010
Printed in Great Britain
Library of Congress Catalog Card Number: 78-9765
ISBN 0-312-55938-0
First published in the United States of America in 1978

Library of Congress Cataloging in Publication Data

Vatikiotis, Panayiotis J   1928-
    Nasser and his generation.

    Includes bibliographical references and index.
    1. Egypt – Politics and government – 1952-   2. Nasser,
Gamal Abdel, Pres. United Arab Republic, 1918-1970.   I. Title.
DT107.83.V29   320'.962'05   78-9765
ISBN 0-312-55938-0

Printed in Great Britain by offset lithography by
Billing & Sons Ltd, Guildford, London and Worcester

Contents

Contents

Acknowledgements

My debt in preparing this book to the writings of many Egyptian, other Arab, European and American authors is clear from the detailed references and notes. But I was also assisted by many Egyptian friends, colleagues and acquaintances, who gave me generously of their time, attention and hospitality. They were prepared to discuss Nasser, his generation and his régime in the light of their experience and understanding of them. Some of them knew Nasser and his closest associates in power personally; others had worked for his régime; still others had suffered under it. I am grateful to all of them. Even though most of them must remain unnamed, I wish here to record a special debt of gratitude to Louis Awad, Tawfiq al-Hakim, Muhammad Heikal, Muhammad Sid Ahmed, Boutros Boutros Ghali, Tahseen Bashir, Abdel Malek Auda, Yusef Idris and Galal Amin for their tolerating my persistent questioning over the years.

Some of my colleagues in America and Britain shared with me their knowledge and views of post-1952 Egypt: Malcolm Kerr, John Waterbury, Roger Owen and Elie Kedourie. The last two mentioned read an early draft of the book manuscript and made valuable suggestions for its improvement. I am indebted to all of them. Miss Janet Marks and Miss Ann Mackintosh typed and reproduced various sections of the manuscript. Finally, I am particularly grateful to my publisher, David Croom, for his valuable assistance throughout the preparation of the book for the press.

For what is finally presented here, I am solely responsible.

Chronology

1918 Nasser born in January. Other Free Officers, members of the RCC, also born this year: Zakariyya Muhieddin, Anwar Sadat, Gamal Salem, and Hussein Shafei.

1919 National uprising demanding complete independence and a constitution led by Saad Zaghlul, leader of the Wafd. Free Officer and RCC member Abdel Hakim Amer born.

1922 Unilateral British Declaration of Egyptian independence in special relationship with Britain based on the Four Reserved Points. Split in the original Wafd and the formation of the Liberal Constitutional party.

1923 Sultan Fuad proclaimed King Fuad I; constitution promulgated.

1924 First elected Parliament and government led by Saad Zaghlul. Assassination of Sir Lee Stack Pasha, Sirdar of the Egyptian Army, by Egyptian nationalist extremists.

1927 Death of Zaghlul and succession of Mustafa Nahhas to the leadership of the Wafd. Foundation of the Young Men's Muslim Association (YMMA).

1928 Foundation of the Society of Muslim Brethren by Hasan al-Banna in Ismailiyya.

1930 Abrogation of the 1923 constitution by Ismail Sidqi and the promulgation of a new one providing for a stronger executive. Economic depression; introduction of protective tariffs.

1933 Resignation of Sidqi as Prime Minister. Foundation of *Misr al-Fatat*, the Young Egypt Society, by Ahmad Hussein and Fathi Radwan.

1935 Widespread demonstrations for the restoration of the 1923 constitution and against Palace-appointed governments.

1936 Ali Maher, strong man of Egyptian politics and close to the Palace, appointed Prime Minister. Death of King Fuad and succession of Faruq. Successful negotiation of Anglo-Egyptian Treaty; Wafd back in power. Nasser matriculated from secondary school.

1937 Montreux Convention ending the Capitulations in Egypt. Nasser entered military academy; so did other Free Officers, members of the RCC: Abdel Hakim Amer, Abdel Latif Boghdadi, Zakariyya Mohieddin, Anwar Sadat, Gamal and Salah Salem, and Hussein Shafei. Conference of Arab States at Bludan, Syria, over the Palestine Question.

1938 Free Officers listed above graduated from Military Academy and commissioned. Young Egypt Society transformed into a political party. General Aziz Ali Masri appointed Inspector-General of the Egyptian army. Saadist party formed by dissidents Ahmad Maher and Mahmud Fahmi Nuqrashi, who split from the Wafd.

1939–40 Ali Maher, Prime Minister, formed nationalist, anti-British government. Young Egypt transformed to the National Islamic party. Crisis in relations with Britain and dismissal of Ali Maher government.

1940–2 Independent, Palace-appointed governments, and deepening crisis in Anglo-Egyptian relations over position of Egypt in the war, culminating in Lampson's ultimatum to Faruq in February 1942 (the Palace Incident); Nahhas forms an all-Wafd government. Spying cases in summer 1942 and the arrest of Anwar Sadat along with German agents. Ali Maher exiled within Egypt and General Aziz Masri arrested.

1944–5 Dismissal of Wafd from power, Ahmad Maher, Saadist party leader, forms government and declares war on the Axis powers; assassinated.

1946 Assassination of Amin Osman; heightened activity of the Muslim Brethren. Massive student and worker demonstrations; new left groups in evidence. Sidqi-Bevin talks on Anglo-Egyptian relations; Sidqi government anti-Communist campaign.

1947 UN Partition Resolution for Palestine. British military withdraw in Egypt to the Canal Zone; Egypt brings the question of Anglo–Egyptian relations before the UN. Frequent bombings of public places.

1948 Involvement of Muslim Brethren volunteers, including army officers, in Arab guerrilla operations against the Jews in Palestine; proclamation of the state of Israel and the outbreak of the Palestine War. Assassination of Prime Minister Nuqrashi by a Muslim Brother, and the Commandant of Cairo Police.

1949 Reported formation of the Constituent Committee of the Free Officers. Egypt signs armistice with Israel in Rhodes. Assassination of Hasan el-Banna, Supreme Guide of the Muslim Brethren. Military *coup d'état* in Syria led by Colonel Husni Zaim. Serious strikes in Egypt, including a general one by the police.

1950 The Wafd returns to power. Free Officer leaflets distributed. Executive committee of Free Officers formed.

1951 Anglo–Egyptian negotiations fail, Wafd government unilaterally abrogates 1936 treaty with Britain. Egyptian sabotage operations against British installations in the Canal Zone. Free Officers challenge the King over Officer Club elections. Wafd government allusions to a policy of neutralism.

1952 Clashes between British forces and Egyptian police in Ismailiyya; massive demonstrations and the burning of Cairo on Black Saturday; deterioration of political situation; a succession of governments unable to stem the tide. Army *coup* on 23 July, RCC formed, abdication and exile of Faruq. Ali Maher briefly Prime Minister, disagrees with RCC over agrarian reform and General Naguib assumes premiership of a civilian government; Agrarian Reform Law decreed. Labour clashes at Kafr el Dawar textile factory; ringleaders executed.

1953 Liberation Rally formed with Nasser as its secretary-general. Committee to draft a new constitution appointed. Extensive purge of army officers; political parties ordered to purge and reorganise themselves, later dissolved. Revolutionary tribunals set up. Abolition of the monarchy and proclamation of Egypt as a republic with General Naguib as first President. Voice of the Arabs begins broadcasting. The Permanent Council for National Production formed, and a provisional constitution proclaimed. Anglo–Egyptian agreement over the Sudan signed.

1954 Struggle for power between Nasser and Naguib leading to widespread political unrest in the country and near-mutiny in the officer corps. Initialling and signing of evacuation agreement with Britain, followed by the attempted assassination of Nasser by a Muslim Brother during an Alexandria rally; Muslim Brethren proscribed, and Naguib ousted from office. Nasser becomes Prime Minister of a mixed civilian-military government.

1955 Signing of Baghdad Pact. Egyptian-trained Palestinian *fedayeen* incursions into Israel, and Israeli retaliatory raid on Gaza. Nasser attends Bandung Conference and subsequently announces Soviet arms deal.

1956 Last British troops leave Egypt; RCC abolished by Nasser. Nasser nationalises Suez Canal; proclaims new Egyptian constitution. Sinai War and Anglo–French landing in Port Said—the Suez war; Nasser confiscates and nationalises British and French assets in Egypt; concludes a temporary alliance with Saudi Arabia. Sudan becomes independent; King Hussein dismisses General Sir

John Glubb from command of the Jordanian Army (Arab Legion).

1957 Further nationalisations of foreign assets in Egypt; expansion of public sector, formation of the Economic Organisation and the beginning of economic planning. Increased Egyptian involvement in the affairs of Arab states; abortive *coup* against King Hussein in Amman. Political crises in Syria and Lebanon; the Eisenhower Doctrine; continued Egyptian–Iraqi rivalry. National Union formally established in Egypt, replacing the Liberation Rally; elections to a National Assembly. Israel quits Gaza.

1958 Union of Egypt and Syria, formation of the United Arab Republic (UAR); 1956 Egyptian constitution abolished and replaced by a provisional constitution for the new UAR. Preliminary negotiations with Soviet Union for the financing of the Aswan High Dam. Civil war in Lebanon.

1959 Trouble between Nasser and the leadership of the Syrian Baath in the UAR; Nasser quarrels with Qassem of Iraq and Khrushchev; fierce anti-Communist campaign at home; Shawwaf uprising in Mosul, Iraq, allegedly fomented and financed by Egypt from Syria.

1960 Second stage Soviet loan arrangements for the Aswan High Dam; tightening of Egyptian control over Syria (the Northern Region of UAR) under direction of Field Marshal Abdel Hakim Amer as Nasser's gauleiter and pro-consul in Damascus; first Five Year Plan. Egyptian involvement in Africa—the Congo—"Nasser's African Policy." Strain in Egyptian–Belgian relations and eventual nationalisation of Belgian assets in Egypt.

1961 Secession of Syria from the UAR led by military *coup* of Syrian officers; break-up of Egyptian–Syrian union; first "socialist decrees" in Egypt promulgated. Rumours of Nasser's illness and rift between him and Amer.

1962 Further crisis in Egyptian–Syrian relations. National Congress of Popular Forces in Egypt part of political reorganisation and retrenchment and the introduction of socialism into the country; National Charter proclaimed. Missile race with Israel; parading of home-grown rockets and missiles with help of expatriate German scientists and engineers. Sallal *coup* in Yemen overthrows the Imam; Egypt declares her support for the rebels and the new republic. Algeria becomes independent.

1963 Expanded Egyptian military involvement in Yemen in support of Republicans against royalist forces supported by Saudi Arabia;

new Cairo–Riyadh rivalry in the region. Abortive tripartite talks on Arab unity between Egypt, Iraq and Syria.

1964 Further reorganisation of Egyptian armed forces under vastly expanded Soviet military and technical assistance; Khrushchev visits Egypt; friction with the United States; new provisional constitution and reorganised government; Amer appointed First Vice-President, Zakariyya Mohieddin, Hussein Shafei and Hasan Ibrahim appointed Vice-Presidents, Ali Sabri appointed Prime Minister; Arab Socialist Union in full swing as single state political organisation. Cairo Arab summit to counteract Israel's division of Jordan river waters; Palestine Liberation Organization formed under Shuqairi. Armistice in the Yemen.

1965 Nasser re-elected President for another six years. Zakariyya Mohieddin appointed Prime Minister; economic difficulties. Mustafa Amin, ex-publisher of *Akhbar*, convicted as US spy. Nasser meets Feisal of Saudi Arabia in Jedda. Crisis in relations between Egypt and Federal Republic of West Germany over the latter's relations with Israel. Rumours of Nasser suffering a mild heart attack.

1966 Strident anti-US policy; US stops wheat shipments to Egypt, and USSR replaces them. Announcement of the uncovering of a Muslim Brethren conspiracy against the régime; over 220 members of the organisation arrested, seven sentenced to death; among those executed Sayyid Qotb, leading ideologue of the Brethren. Mounting tension between Israel and Arab states, especially Syria. Islamic bloc formed by Saudi Arabia; cold war between Arab revolutionary camp led by Nasser and conservative Arab rulers led by Faisal of Saudi Arabia worsens.

1967 Middle East crisis leading to Six Day War; Israeli forces conquer all of Sinai, West Bank of Jordan and Golan Heights; Nasser resigns for one day and returns to office by public "furore"; Field Marshal Amer commits suicide; Khartoum Arab summit; withdrawal of Egyptian forces from Yemen; Soviets re-arm Egyptian forces; fighting renewed in the Canal.

1968 Trial by military tribunal of high-ranking air force officers in Cairo; demonstrations of workers and students in Helwan, Cairo and Alexandria; Nasser assumes premiership of government and proclaims his "March 30 Manifesto" for political reform; more riots in Alexandria, Cairo and other towns; Israeli spy ring uncovered; increased Israeli shelling across the Canal. Nasser undergoes hydrotherapy treatment in the Soviet Union for arteriosclerosis caused by his advanced diabetic condition.

1969 War of attrition on Canal. Senusi monarchy in Libya over-thrown by army *coup d'état* led by Colonel Muammar Qadhafi. Nasser suffers serious heart attack. Arab summit in Rabat; Egyptian–Libyan–Sudanese federation project announced.

1970 Israeli deep penetration air raids on Egypt; Nasser requests missile defence system from Soviet Union; Soviet pilots fly operational missions in defence of Egyptian air space. Nasser accepts American Rogers Plan for cease-fire on Canal; Soviet SAM missiles installed on West Bank of Suez Canal. Palestinians clash with Jordanian Army in Amman; Jordanian forces crush the Palestine Resistance Movement; Nasser holds urgent meeting of Arab heads of state in Cairo to settle the crisis in Jordan; dies of a heart attack.

Author's Note

Unless otherwise indicated, all quotations from and references to Nasser's speeches and public statements in this book are from the Arabic texts published periodically in his *Collected Speeches* by the Egyptian Department of Information. The full texts of his major speeches were also as a rule published in the newspaper, *al-Ahram*. References to articles in Arabic weeklies are confined to name of the author and date.

Transliteration of references in Arabic sources, names and places is in simple phonetic form. Diacritical marks are used only where necessary in order to avoid mis-reading.

The rather extensive references and notes are necessary in view of the fact that Western readers usually have no access to statements made by Egyptians or Arabs themselves about the Nasser régime.

FOR DAPHNE

Introduction

Any attempt to sketch a political portrait of Gamal Abdel Nasser of Egypt is a controversial undertaking. It is difficult, in any case, to reconstruct his life without disfiguring it, and there are those who consider it an audacious exercise. There are also those who prefer a cosmetically embalmed hero; others who desire a sculpted restoration of his hidden warts in sharp relief. To strike a balance between these two extremes may be an ideal rarely attained. There will be, to be sure, as many versions of Nasser's life as there are students who are prepared to write about it.

This is not, however, a biography of Nasser in the conventional sense. Nor is it a psycho-biography in the sense of linking the man's words and actions to the pathology of his organic or psychic make-up. Nor is this study a detailed history of the Nasser régime. Such histories abound already. Rather it is an interpretation of Nasser as a ruler of Egypt at a particular period and juncture of that country's history. Moreover, it considers Nasser to be representative of a *generation* of Egyptians, many of whom rode on his bandwagon to power, served him and then, more or less, promptly forgot him. To this extent this is not only an attempt to sketch a political portrait of Nasser, but of a whole Egyptian generation.

It is for this reason that particular attention is given to the new radical political forces which arose in Egypt in the 1930s, such as the Young Egypt Society, the Society of Muslim Brothers, the younger vanguard wing of the Wafd party, the lesser, violence-prone youth formations of the old National party, the several Marxist and Communist groups, and the various small terrorist cabals of pro-Axis Air Force officers. Most of Nasser's generation of army officers, that is, the group that came to constitute the core of the Free Officer movement in 1949–52, were either members, collaborators or sympathisers of one or more of these radical groups. These organisations provided the officers with some of their earliest political notions and experience, and in general helped their political formation. They were all opposed to the British presence in Egypt in particular and the West in general. They were at the same time alienated from their own rulers, consisting of the monarch and politicians.

By the end of the Second World War Nasser's generation of middle- and lower-ranking army officers was pitted against that of senior officers, often associated or identified with the political establishment. They came mainly from lower-class, or petit bourgeois, families, not from rich land-owning or other upper bourgeois backgrounds. Conservative by upbringing in the main, they had been radicalised by a process of alienation, and sought to avenge the injustices they believed had been inflicted by Egypt's "haves" against them, the "have-nots".

The conditions and circumstances in which Nasser's generation of army officers became politically conscious are set out in Part I. The Free Officers' road to power and the eventual emergence of Nasser as the sole ruler, the autocrat, of Egypt are considered in Part II. These two parts set the scene for the emergence of the military régime, outline its main characteristics and course in general and Nasser's career at the top in particular. They also highlight in passing the disintegration of the old political order which the Free Officers overthrew in 1952.

Part III deals with Nasser in his several capacities as absolute ruler of Egypt, his relations with the Arabs, Israel and, in passing, the rest of the world. Part IV provides a depiction of Nasser as the absolute ruler of Egypt. Part V attempts a general assessment of Nasser's personality and his impact on Egypt.

I am not interested in extracting moral or ethical lessons from the life and political career of my subject, or that of his contemporaries. What does interest me is the impact of a personality like Nasser's on the course of events affecting his country in the midst of all the impersonal economic, social and other forces of history. His person and personality were so central to Egypt—indeed the very focus of an entire region of the world—that there were those for whom Egypt in the period from 1954 to 1970 was synonymous with Nasser. Even certain wider Arab attitudes, postures and policies of the last twenty years were readily identified by outsiders as constituting Nasserism.

The emphasis therefore is on the importance of studying Nasser as an Egyptian phenomenon, since what we seek is to understand the kind of political experience he constituted for the Egyptians. In this connection, his formative years, especially the period from 1933 to 1937, and his military career (1937–52) are crucial. It is in the context of these years that we can deal with such personality manifestations as despair, disgrace, romantic notions of justice, epic and nostalgic

ideas of heroism, caution and dissimulation, loneliness and conspiracy, aspirations to modernity and tenacious personal
conservatism, ambition on one hand, ambivalence and cynicism on
the other; or the characteristics of puritanism accompanied by
callousness, public activism contrasted to a quiet family life,
romantic mythologising countered by a cynical monopoly of power,
preoccupation with dignity while humiliating others, retention of the
baladi, or lower-class native, culture in the face of a professed desire
for modernity.

As regards Nasser in power, I consider the fact that, unlike
Zaghlul and Nahhas before him, both of whom were great popular
leaders, he came closest to being an Egyptian "Kingfish". The
population seemed to assume he was the answer to all their problems.
They were convinced he was the miracle-working idol and the
romantic idol-prince. How Nasser responded to this indigenous
adulation is important, because it affects any assessment of his
vision of a new Egypt, his perception of governing, his relations with
colleagues and associates, his response to external influences, his
political style, his handling of real and imagined opponents, his
attitude to members of certain strata of society which he had
passionately rejected since adolescence, viz. the upper bourgeoisie
and the "middle classes" of intellectuals, bureaucrats and professionals.

There are those who observed in Nasser, from the outset of his
career, an inordinate obsession with power. But this must be judged
in terms of the pathological situation in which Nasser came to
prominence, not simply as a pathological condition in him. That is,
was he a typical Arab demagogue, a modern mass leader, a *duce*, or
a thoroughly native *sultan-amir-ma'bud*[1] with extraordinary political
talent? Was he a leader of *futuwwat*,[2] the typically Egyptian–
Islamic populist heroes? This may have in great measure constituted
the social-ideological basis of his national leadership because it lay
deep in his experience in the native crowded and poor urban quarters
with their manners, values and idiom, and in the populist Islamic
national socialist movement of the 1930s, the Young Egypt Society,
that he joined, with its paramilitary organisation and aspiration to
mobilise the masses.

If Nasser, then, was steeped in this tradition, was he simply a
leader of the masses and the chief, *rayyes*, of an authoritarian state?
Or did he also wish—and had a vision for that purpose—to lead them
somewhere? Or did he merely drug them into unconsciousness as

Tawfiq al-Hakim has argued?[3] Was he, as a *futuwwa*, a man of violence who generated an atmosphere of violence? Was he in addition an introspective politician who paused to contemplate the power he had grasped and how best to use it? Or was he simply a secretive, lonely conspirator? Did his cynical contempt for politicians derive from a personality trait, or was it a by-product of his charisma which permitted him to destroy his opponents? Did Nasser covet and prefer arbitrary power, and was this a deviation from the Egyptian norm?

The difficulty in dealing with all these matters derives largely from the dearth of biographical material on Nasser. Much of it is extrapolated and inferred from his milieu, career, utterances, behaviour and policies when he was in power. Despite the vast Egyptian paper bureaucracy, the recording of contemporary historical events is not popular among Egyptians (those who might otherwise indulge in it consider it politically unsafe), and particularly the Free Officers. There are hardly any genuine diaries, critical private papers—only *ex post facto* ones for polemical purposes, so-called revelational tracts—that are readily available to the student.[4] All one can hope for at this stage is a political portrait, perhaps only a cameo; and in this book I hazard to suggest what the possible ingredients for its construction might be.

Notes

1. In the sense of "sultan-prince-idol".
2. *Futuwwa* (pl. *futuwwāt*) refers to folk, neighbourhood heroes, feared and respected for their physical prowess. See C. Cahen and Fr. Taeschner, *Encyclopedia of Islam*, 2nd ed., Vol. 2, pp.961–9. See also P. J. Vatikiotis, "The corruption of futuwwa: a consideration of despair in Nagib Mahfuz's Awlād Hāritna", *Middle Eastern Studies*, Vol.7, No.2, May 1971, pp.169–84.
3. This is one of the themes in al-Hakim's tract, '*Awdat al-Wa'i (The Return of Consciousness)* (Beirut, 1974). The tract caused a stir, and it was criticised by other Egyptian writers. Al-Hakim published a second tract, partly in order to reply to his critics, *Wathāiq fi tariq 'awdat al-wa'i (Documents on the road to the return of consciousness)* (Cairo and Beirut, 1975).
4. Examples of these tracts are Sami Gohar, *Al-sāmitun yatakallamūn (The silent ones speak)* (Cairo, 1975); Husein Karum, *Abdel Nasser bayna Haikal wa Mustafa Amin (Nasser between Heikal and Mustafa Amin)* (Cairo, 1975); Musa Sabri, *Wathāiq harb Oktobar (Documents of the October War)* (Cairo, 1974), reprinted in 1974 and 1975; Ahmad Hussein, *Kayfa 'araftu Abdel Nasser was 'ishtu ayyāma hukmihi (How I knew Abdel Nasser and lived the days of his rule)* (Beirut, 1973); Kamal al-Din Hussein, "Qissat thuwwār yulio" ("The story of the July 1952 rebels"), *al-Musawwar*, Cairo weekly, series of interviews, Nos.2671–6, 19 December 1975–23 January 1976; Fathi

Radwan series in *Rose el-Youssef*, Cairo weekly, Nos.2462 and 2464, August 1975; Hussein Dhu'l-Fiqar Sabri, *Rose el-Youssef*, No.2549, 18 July 1975, and other prominent figures of the Nasser régime. See also Nāsir al-Din al-Nashāshibi, *Al-hibr aswad . . . aswad (The ink is black . . . black)* (Paris, 1976).

PART I

Political Formation

CHAPTER 1

Nasser before the Revolution

. . . extraordinary individuals by their own self-centred
manoeuvres and through the prodding of the charismatic
hunger of mankind become (auto)biographies. Erik Erikson,
Young Man Luther.

Gamal Abdel Nasser's grandfather, Sheikh Hussein Khalil Sultan,
claimed descent from an Arab tribe, Āl Sultan. In 1880 he built a
one-room brick house near a mosque in the village of Beni Murr,
Abnub province. His eldest son, Abdel Nasser, father of Gamal,
was born in that house on 11 July 1888. In 1898 or 1900, Sheikh
Hussein endowed a *kuttab,* or village school, on the roof of the
nearby mosque, where his son became the first pupil. His second
son, Khalil (who features prominently in Nasser's school years in
Cairo and who, later in 1957–8, was elected Deputy for Abnub
province in his nephew's first National Assembly) attended it too.

Abnub province is populated partly by descendants of Arab tribe
settlers, has a relatively large concentration of Copts, and is
historically associated with sporadic outbursts of dissidence,
rebellion and plain crime. Beni Murr today is a village of about
5,000 inhabitants, who farm about 2,000 *feddans* (one *feddan* =
1.038 acres). Of these people, 3,500 are Muslims and 1,500 Christians
(Copts). It has three mosques, one church and a monastery, an
elementary school and an agricultural co-operative. The largest
landowner at any time owned a hundred *feddans.*

In 1903 Sheikh Hussein's in-laws emigrated to Alexandria as
merchants, and Abdel Nasser was sent along in March 1904 to
attend *Madrasat al-Najah al-Ahliyya* elementary school. His younger
brother Khalil also attended the school. In 1908 or 1910 (it is not
quite clear when) Abdel Nasser entered the postal service. Early in
1917 he married Fahima Hammad, daughter of a minor Alexandria
merchant. Gamal, their first child, was born on 15 January 1918 in
their home at No. 18 Anawati Street, Bakos (near Ramle),

Alexandria. Two other boys, 'Izz al-'Arab and al-Leithi, followed in quick succession.

The years 1925 to 1930 were most unsettling for Gamal and, in retrospect, rather traumatic. His father was transferred to the post office in Khatatba, and Gamal was sent to his uncle Khalil in Cairo where he attended *al-Nahhasin* elementary school for a year. Meanwhile, his mother died in the spring of 1926, when Gamal was just over eight years old, and his father remarried before that year was out. It is reported that Gamal, who was very attached to Fahima, resented not only his father's quick remarriage, but also felt humiliated because he was not told of his mother's death immediately. The trauma at that age may have been superficial, in the sense that it could have been easily overcome. The fact remains though that Gamal never had a close relationship with his father, or his brothers, throughout his life. Most of my informants, who were closely associated with Gamal over the years, assert that he was never close to his father.[1]

In 1928, Gamal returned to Alexandria where he attended the *'Attarin* elementary school, but lived with his maternal grandfather, Muhammad Hammad. This may not be significant in itself, for his father with his new wife and other children (a third boy, Shawqi, Gamal's half-brother, had already been born) was still in Khatatba. He was not posted back to Alexandria until 1930. Gamal spent the school year 1929–30, however, as a boarder in Helwan, a suburb of Cairo, but was back again in Alexandria after that at *Ras el-Tin* school.[2]

Even though his father and his family were back in Alexandria in 1930, Gamal attended only the first year or two (1930–2) of secondary school at *al-Faridiyya* (although this is obscure) and *Ras el-Tin* in Alexandria. In 1933, we find him back in Cairo with his uncle Khalil, and as a pupil in the notorious *al-Nahda* school (notorious for the political involvement of its pupils in nationalist agitation from the days of Mustafa Kamil, founder and leader of the extremist National (Watani) party) in Bab al-Sha'riyya.[3] Uncle Khalil's home was in the native quarter of Khamis al-'Ads, Khoronfish, and so was the school in a native quarter. Unlike Darb al-Ahmar, which has hardly any immigrants or transients from the countryside, Khamis al-'Ads and Bab al-Sha'riyya are conglomerations of villagers and provincials who have moved from the country to the city.

From 1925 to 1933 Nasser was shunted back and forth between

Cairo and Alexandria to live with relatives and attend a string of different schools. This experience at a young age may have contributed to several personality traits and behaviour characteristics evident in Gamal throughout his secondary school days, his attendance at military academy, and in his military and political career. It must have made him feel uneasy, secretive and cautious. The secretiveness, caution, enigmatic dissimulation and intensely puritanical feeling of shame and sense of dignity observed and reported by so many of his colleagues later could well have denied Gamal, in later life, the capacity for loyal personal relations and a less ruthless concern with others. Reminiscing about their early days as subalterns in Manqabad in 1938, Anwar Sadat reported:

> Gamal nursed many painful personal disappointments which he remembered since his mother died when he was very young. Her death greatly affected his life. Thus he was inordinately shy . . . Alongside his shyness and quiet disposition, he had a typical Saidi personality. He was tender and loyal, full of compassion . . . But he quickly turned into a ferocious lion the moment he felt that anyone even simply thought of insulting or hurting him. [4]

Australian Prime Minister Sir Robert Menzies, reporting to Eden after his meeting with Nasser over the Suez Crisis in 1956, described the Egyptian ruler as follows:

> I was told that Nasser was a man of great personal charm who might beguile me into believing something foreign to my own thought. This is not so. He is in some ways a likeable fellow but so far from being charming he is rather gauche . . . I would say that he was a man of considerable but immature intelligence. He lacks training or experience in many of the things he is dealing with and is, therefore, awkward with them . . . His logic does not travel very far. [5]

Whereas Nasser's youth may appear to have been unhappy, there is no evidence that he suffered material deprivation. Throughout his school years until 1936 when he matriculated in the Baccalaureat, Arts Branch, Gamal was not one of the deprived poor. Photographs of him in his teens show a handsome, tall, well-dressed and well-fed lad. There is no evidence that he was treated in any, except a good, way by his uncle Khalil. His father, it has been reported, was a £12 per month sub-postmaster in Alexandria in 1933. Similarly, his uncle Khalil, at that time an employee of the Ministry of Waqfs, earned an equally adequate salary for the early thirties.

The potted biographical sketches of Nasser which were penned by Egyptians and other Arabs in the fifties suggest that he became involved in school political agitation and demonstrations during the Ismail Sidqi régime (1930–3) and the Palace-appointed governments of 1933–5.[6] According to his Arabic master, Ahmad Husein al-Qarni, in al-Nahda school, Gamal was already politically involved in 1934, a possible reference to his membership in the Young Egypt Society. In his famous speech in Alexandria on 26 October 1954, celebrating the conclusion of the Evacuation Agreement with Britain, Nasser himself said:

> When I began addressing this popular rally in Manshia Square today, my memory went back to those days in 1930 when I was a boy of twelve and shared with the sons of Alexandria their struggle against tyranny and oppression, shouting with them for the first time for freedom and Egypt . . . and I remember how I escaped the bullets of Imperialism.

But this sort of political involvement for the overwhelming majority of youth rarely has a lasting impact. On its own, it does not constitute the foundations of a sustained political education and experience.

The political climate of Egypt in the thirties was, however, turbulent. Not solely because of the contest between the King, the Wafd and the British, but significantly because of the widespread reaction against the recently adopted Western European political forms and ideas. The reaction and reappraisal themselves were matters of political conflict between the institutions and men of power in the country. Conservative Islamic political currents were represented by the Muslim Brothers.[7] Fanatically religious, xenophobic national socialist and romantic idealist trends motivated the Young Egypt Society.[8] A scent of muted though clear hostility to the foreign, i.e. Christian, influences of European domination was emitted by the Young Men's Muslim Association (YMMA), founded in 1927. Prominent liberal writers with a European education were reconsidering the sources, strengths and advantages of their Arab–Islamic culture, while other equally prominent writers entertained the civilisational force of their country's Pharaonic antecedents.[9] The audience, clientele and potential recruits of these diverse movements and proffered formulae of national salvation were the students. By 1935, they had become an identifiable political group which was alternately wooed and punished by the Palace, the political parties and the new radical movements on the right and the left of the national political spectrum.

The world was in the grip of an economic depression. At home, an autocratic régime was trying, amidst great unpopularity, to cope with its effects. The great democracies were being seriously challenged by Fascism and Nazism in Europe, and their prestige was at a low ebb. British and French imperial power was being eroded. All of these developments contributed to the rapid radicalisation of Egyptian political life, and the undermining of the authority of existing political arrangements, made by those leaders who, fifteen years earlier, had spearheaded the movement for independence. In these conditions, disenchantment and disillusionment, especially among the frustrated and aspiring young, were not surprising. Their political involvement derived in part from such feelings. The romanticism of Wafdist nationalism had spent itself with the Anglo–Egyptian Treaty of 1936. The economic sophistication of the Sidqi régime did not stir the masses. A new romantic fever for power and glory had seized the aspiring outside the political élite. As Muhammad Subeih put it in 1971, "In the thirties there appeared certain revolutionary youth movements trying to change the course of the national movement, among them the Young Egypt Society and the Muslim Brethren."[10] Gamal was no different in this respect from his contemporaries. Nostalgic invocation of Egyptian national hagiology was common: Omar Makram against Napoleon,[11] Orabi against the Turks and the British, Mustafa Kamil with his hypnotic oratorical haranguing of secondary school pupils and the electrifying cry, "Egypt for the Egyptians", Zaghlul, "the father of the nation" and hero of the struggle for independence. Gamal was not the only pupil in 1933 or 1935 who wondered, "There is in Egypt a government based on bribery and corruption; where is the one who will change all this?" His desperation was not unique.

Most secondary school students of that period read the best-selling books of Mahmud 'Abbas al-'Aqqad, Tawfiq al-Hakim and others. In the early thirties, these constituted a peculiar combination of romantic Islamic epic and Egyptian renaissance literature. There were also Muhammad Hussein Heikal's essays on Voltaire,

Rousseau and other leading figures of the European Enlightenment
and French Revolution. The Islamic reformer Sheikh Rashid Rida
(d. 1935) kept the Islamic nationalist 'Abd al-Rahman al-Kawakibi's
Taba'i' al-istibdad (*The Nature of Tyranny*) and *Um al-qurā* (*Mother
of Cities*) in circulation. Amin al-Rafi'i's Watanist newspaper *al-
Akhbar* was popular. So was the poetry of the Egyptian nationalists
Hafez Ibrahim and Ali al-Ghayati. Translations of Hugo's *Les
Misérables* and the speeches of Mustafa Kamil were easily accessible
too. The multitude of party newspapers, most of them recipients of
Italian subventions through, among others, Ugo Dadone, a Fascist
agent in Egypt, poured out a stream of anti-British invective. Ahmad
Hussein's and Fathi Radwan's *al-Sarkha* and *Wadi al-Nil*, and
al-Qadir Hamza's *al-Balagh*, the Wafd's *al-Jihad* and others kept
the youth of the country inflamed, and the tension between the King
and politicians high.

Another of his teachers, Naguib Ibrahim, reports that Gamal read
al-'Aqqad's *'abqariyyat* series, such as *Sirat'Omar ibn al-Khattab*
(*Life of the Caliph Omar*) and later *Sa'ad Zaghlul, sira wa tahiyya*
(*A biography of Zaghlul*), al-Hakim's *'Awdat al-ruh* (*The return of
the soul*), Taha Hussein's *al-Ayyām* (*Stream of days*), potted biographical sketches of Voltaire and Rousseau, biographies of
Napoleon, Alexander, Caesar, Garibaldi, Gandhi and Hannibal.
There is little doubt he was greatly influenced by al-'Aqqad's and
al-Hakim's writings. The former concentrated on the rehabilitation
of Muslim heroes, the latter ploughed the theme of Egypt's eternal
resurrection in the person of an idolised, charismatic leader.[12] When
Nasser was President he gifted his tract, *Philosophy of the Revolution*
(1954), to both these leading men of Egyptian letters with appropriate
inscriptions of gratitude, in recognition of their influence on the
formation of his own nationalist ideas. He bestowed the Medal of
the Republic (*wisām al-jumhuriyya*), second-highest state decoration,
on al-Hakim.[13] When his confidant Muhammad Hasanein Heikal
erected the magnificent Ahram building in Cairo, a literary wing on
the sixth floor was set aside for al-Hakim, his colleagues and
protégés. Another aspect of this relationship with 'Aqqad and
al-Hakim may be noted. Several of Nasser's associates, as well as
al-Hakim himself, have suggested that he was very much taken by
journalism and writers. He is reported to have tried his hand at
writing a novel, emulating al-Hakim's *'Awdat al-ruh* (*Return of the
soul*, first published in 1933) and using the same name, "Muhsin",
for its hero.

And he [Nasser] wrote several pages of a novel, *Fi sabil al-hurriyya* (*In the cause of freedom*), the hero of which he called Muhsin, which is also the name of the hero in '*Awadat al-ruh*. Circumstances, however, transformed him from the author of Muhsin on paper to Muhsin in real life. And he lived like Muhsin and behaved according to the dictates of his emotional, reactive nationalist passions [i.e. his nationalist impulses].[14]

His introduction in 1946 or 1949 to Ahmad Abul Fath, editor of *al-Misri*, and his avid reading of newspapers and magazines throughout his life—he hardly read any books—increased his fascination with journalism and scribblers.

Nasser took an active part in the November 1935 demonstrations which resulted in serious clashes with the police, and was wounded in one of them. But he also got into trouble with the school authorities. He was in danger of being refused permission to sit for his Baccalaureat examinations because he had attended a mere three months of school in his last year. Apparently, he had written letters to a few of his schoolmates during the summer vacation, urging them to organise massive demonstrations jointly with other schools, such as the well-known Madrasat Fu'ad and colleges of the university.

Like the poorer class of petit bourgeois Egyptian secondary schoolboys, Nasser sought solace, balsam for his wounded pride and dignity, fire for his nationalist passion and hope for the future in the resurrectionist themes of al-Hakim's writings; in the vitriolic columns of Young Egypt's newspaper *al-Sarkha*, with its passionate attacks against Britain and its new "theology of justice" essential to the restoration of a glorious Egypt; in the uncompromising anti-British views of the National party. The conjunction of economic-political conditions in the period from 1933 to 1937 and the activities of a new radical right in Egyptian politics—Young Egypt, the Muslim Brethren, the Blue Shirts of the Wafd—became the main source of Nasser's ideas about himself, Egypt and the world.

Immediately after graduating from secondary school, the Anglo–Egyptian treaty was concluded in August 1936, and Gamal sought entry into the military academy. He was rejected. His application for a place in the police academy was also turned down. He then proceeded to enrol in the law faculty of Fuad I University (a popular faculty with university students throughout the Middle East and the Mediterranean), where he remained until March 1937 when, upon re-application, he gained a place in the military academy. Fifteen years after entering the Academy Nasser led the *coup* against the monarchy. Some twenty years later he became President of the Republic and absolute ruler of Egypt.

The turbulent environment of Nasser's youth, in particular the years when he was a secondary school pupil, is vividly reported in the British records of the time. Arthur Yencken, Acting High Commissioner, in a despatch to Sir John Simon, dated 30.i.1934, regarding the formation of Young Egypt, wrote,[15]

> it is a fascist organization of anti-foreign and extreme nationalist complexion. Instigators appear to be Abd al-Hamid Said, Watani deputy and President of the YMMA and certain young journalists working on *al-Sarkha* [meaning Ahmad Hussein and Fathi Radwan]. It has a strong appeal particularly to the student class.

Only the preceding summer Ronald Campbell was reporting from Ramle about the activities of the opposition, including a review of its press, whose message was "England is responsible for all our troubles."[16] Sir Miles Lampson's report on Young Egypt suggested, "The movement appears to be Watanist in kind if not in origin." Its appeal was to

> The patriotic idealism of youth, with a strong religious bias, which is said to attract some of the students of the University of Al-Azhar . . . It attempts to awaken in its members admiration of the military spirit and of physical fitness . . . Politically, it declares . . . that the ultimate goal of Egypt is the leadership of Islam in alliance with the Arab Powers. It is not inconceivable that the ardent young patriot will find the ill-led Wafd no longer so emotionally satisfying as in Zaghlul's days[17].

Sir Percy Loraine, in his despatch, added, "This movement being based on Moslem fanaticism and aggressive xenophobia, provides an inflammable element in the situation."[18]

In 1935, Kelly's despatches from Cairo and Keown-Boyd's (Director of the European Department, Egyptian Ministry of Interior) reports refer not only to the activities of Young Egypt, but to more widespread political agitation among students, and youth organisations of all parties. Italian agents sought to enlist the Young Egypt Society in a pro-Italian, anti-British campaign through a certain Anis Dawud. So were journalists and members of other parties including the Wafd, most of whom received Italian money. The fact remains that the Palace-appointed government of Nessim Pasha was very unpopular, the influence of the Royal Chamberlain, Ibrashi Pasha, was widely resented and the general political climate was highly inflamed.

In a meeting of the Young Egypt Society on 17 August 1935, its leader Ahmad Hussein urged violence and political assassination upon his followers, especially against the police and Nassim Pasha himself. The society was reported "to be making endeavours . . . to persuade young officers within the Egyptian Army to join its ranks". Ali Maher, the King's *chef de cabinet*, was reported to be in close contact with all these activities, but as reported by Sir Alex Keown-Boyd, this was because "Ali Maher wishes to use Young Egypt and its Green Shirts as a counterpoise to the Wafd and its Blue Shirts[19]." By that time, "Young Egypt was calling for the end of the Capitulations and Mixed Courts, and Ali Maher . . . was restraining them."[20]

Generally, since 1933, despatches from Cairo report a mounting anti-British tone in Egyptian politics, adopted even by the Liberal newspaper, *al-Siyāsa*, and the moderate Wafd. Partly aimed at discrediting Nahhas Pasha and partly used as a campaign against the Sidqi régime, it also coincided with a campaign against Christian missionaries in the country.[21] The political agitation of students in the turbulent year 1935 was analysed and reported in detail by Sir Alex Keown-Boyd. In his "Note on the Student Movement in Egypt", dated 23 January 1936,[22] he wrote,

the primary causes of their discontent can be traced to several months back . . . and can be summarized under the . . . headings: (a) the difficulty of graduates of university and other government schools in obtaining employment, and the low salaries offered; (b) the rivalry amongst different political parties in their efforts to gain control of students with a view to utilizing them for party purposes; (c) Italian propaganda.

In fact, all political parties as well as the Palace, were involved in organising and inciting the students, each for its own purposes. The venomously anti-British pens of al-'Aqqad and Mahmud 'Azmi[23] added fuel to the fire. 'Aqqad especially was "a popular writer . . .

amongst the students, and his daily outbursts found a welcome echo in the hearts of many ardent youths, who began to doubt whether their blind confidence in Wafd was not after all misplaced."[24] 'Aqqad was officially a Liberal, yet intellectually and emotionally a sort of Fascist Watanist who ended up a Wafdist. The Young Egypt Society encouraged this phase. Even the Liberal leader, Muhammad Mahmud Pasha, joined with them in inciting the students against the government of the Wafd. Italian propaganda concentrated all efforts among the students, distributing money, arms and anti-British propaganda leaflets.

On 13 November 1935, university and secondary school students marched from Giza to Cairo armed with missiles, screaming "Down with England", "Death to Samuel Hoare", "Down with Nessim Pasha", "We want the 1923 constitution." They clashed with police and there were casualties on both sides. Next day, there occurred the famous clash on Abbas Bridge when police were forced to open fire on the students. On 19 November, the student Mahmud Abd al-Hakim died of his wounds, and was given a hero's public funeral which was attended by Nahhas and other political leaders. A demonstration in front of *Beit al-Umma*, Wafd headquarters, on 21 November resulted in further clashes with the police. On 7 December, some 8,000 students clashed with police on Abbas Bridge again. "The students, especially in Cairo," Keown-Boyd wrote, "displayed a very determined, bitter and aggressive spirit. They were much more difficult to deal with than in the past . . . The University undergraduates showed particular bitterness and tenacity in their clashes with the Police . . ."[25] The Young Egypt Society was most active in these disturbances. "Its policy," Keown-Boyd suggested, "is a diehard anti-Imperialist one. Its membership is not very large, but it contains a number of convinced revolutionaries who have been very active in the recent troubles and continue to advocate revolution against the British."[26] In fact, Young Egypt was claiming categorically in 1935–6 that[27] "it represented the youth of Egypt and new generation . . . it expresses both the spirit and aspirations of the entire Egyptian nation." In attacking the old political parties and the British, Young Egypt referred to the shock "to our dignity". Their aims were to Egyptianise industries, end illiteracy, raise the status of the working classes, reorganise the village, educate the fellah. All this so that "Glory be to Egypt."[28]

By nature and upbringing the anti-foreign, vaguely reformist, conservative Islamic national socialism of Young Egypt appealed to the pupil Gamal, and at one point he joined the society. Addressing an Egyptian overseas student mission before it left the country about the role of youth, Nasser reminisced on 5 May 1970,

> In 1935 or 1936 I joined the Young Egypt Society by sheer coincidence. I was walking in the Manshia quarter of Alexandria when I came upon a clash between the crowds and the police. I naturally joined the crowd against the police and I was arrested and taken to the Manshia police station where I was detained. I asked those with me what the clash was all about, and they told me that the police had tried to prevent a meeting of the Young Egypt Society. Next day, the *sheikh el-hara* [local mayor] came and freed me on surety, and I went out looking for the Young Egypt Society, and found it had in it Ahmad Hussein and Fathi Radwan. I joined it . . . later of course the authorities persecuted us and we were arrested and imprisoned several times until I entered Military Academy.[29]

Other evidence suggests Nasser joined the Society in 1934. He became an active Green Shirt in Bab el-Sha'riyya.[30]

In the two year period 1935–7, between Nasser's last year in secondary school and entry to military academy, the conclusion of the Anglo–Egyptian Treaty caused the disillusionment of the young with national leaders, especially the Wafdists. The latter, once back in power, proceeded to entrench themselves with a vengeance in all central, provincial and local institutions of power—and privilege. The young King, surrounded by anti-Wafdist advisers and courtiers, guided chiefly by Ali Maher and later Ahmad Hasanein, soon clashed with the leaders of the majority party and the British Embassy. The Wafd sought to strengthen their position further by pampering the security forces, army and police. The King, however, was at that time very popular with the army. Nevertheless, the situation upon emancipation from more direct British control became perilous:[31]

> the acephalous state of the army, suddenly deprived of the British officers on whom it leant for guidance and now exposed to the competing intrigues of the Wafd and Palace, is obviously very dangerous if the British Military Mission [BMM] cannot steady matters in time. Armies infested with politics easily become the prey of unscrupulous military adventurers, with

results often disastrous to all, including the politicians who have been intriguing to make use of the soldiers.

Military Career

Nasser entered military academy in March 1937, two months before a convention in Montreux abolished the extraterritorial privileges of foreign powers and their nationals in Egypt under the Capitulations. Together with the Anglo–Egyptian Treaty signed the previous summer, these measures constituted the two most important steps in Egypt's emancipation from foreign control. But they also inaugurated a period of violent, ultimately chaotic, domestic political conflict. Lampson, for instance, singled out three dangers: (1) a chaotic educational policy—too many unemployed graduates; (2) miserable finances; and (3) lack of a proper civil service. He commented ruefully,

> Looking back on the period of British control, it is evident that what we provided was a scaffolding around a rickety building and not an entire foundation for the house. Now that the scaffolding has been taken away, it can be clearly seen that the house is still far from secure.[32]

Two months later, commenting on the splits in the Wafd, Kelly remarked, "The general tendency of the present development is to create a petit bourgeois party dictatorship of Nahhas and Makram [Ebeid], and to exclude from the Wafd the former elements within it drawn from the semi-aristocratic families and the intelligentsia."[33]

The radicalism of the thirties was, in part, forcing the Wafd, especially through its Blue Shirt youth organisation,[34] to lower the quality of its membership as well as of its political style. It now adopted a more demagogic approach that would appeal to the masses. It was partly successful in so far as it was able, for a while, though losing the more genteel intelligentsia, to attract large numbers of school and university graduates, army and public security officers to its ranks, and so overshadow Young Egypt and the Muslim Brotherhood at least until 1942. Still, as Kelly perceptively noted, "it is difficult in the East to run parliamentary machines without dictatorial methods, as Turkey and Persia illustrate."[35] Meanwhile, the spurious Turco–Egyptian Palace aristocracy, with their *salon-Fähigkeit*, already showed strains of degeneracy and a complete lack of moral fibre.

By October 1937, the Embassy in Cairo was reporting that "In the last five years the Wafd has gradually shed its intellectual elements . . ." Many of these, incidentally, moved to the left, forming a vanguard Wafd group; others drifted to the several Marxist and Communist groups. "The composition of the Wafd has now become so primitive that it cannot be taken seriously by the intelligentsia."[36] Significantly, though, many young educated Wafdists, including army officers, reverted to supporting the Palace, while Blue Shirt clashes with the police pushed them further into the anti-Wafd camp. What remained behind the Wafd were the "masses of unsophisticated provincial propertied classes. Nahhasist Wafd is doomed." In a telegram on 29 November 1937, Lampson foresaw: "HM by all indications is shaping for the role of traditional oriental despot . . . His ultimate overthrow will occur when Nahhas goes . . . Wafd now on the downgrade and a bad horse to back indefinitely."[37] On 28 November 1937, Green Shirt 'Izz al-Din 'Abd al-Qadir tried to assassinate Nahhas outside his home. In December relations between the King and the party were very strained. A deputation of forty army officers, including seventeen brigadiers and generals, called at the Palace to promise unswerving loyalty to the crown, and renew their personal oath of allegiance to the King.

Nasser's future constituency and the conditions propitious to the success of the military conspiracy he was to lead fifteen years later were already taking shape when he embarked upon his military career at a time of great political unrest in Egypt. The euphoria engendered by the Anglo–Egyptian Treaty was short-lived. On the contrary, Egyptian politicians turned against each other, while the new young monarch, egged on by unscrupulous courtiers, harboured inordinate and foolish ambitions of his own. The shrill voice of a new radical Egyptian nationalism, with overtones of an Arab–Islamic restoration and Pharaonic resurrection, xenophobia and Fascist tendencies, was heard. The vast majority of city-dwellers were alienated from their leaders; a new urban proletariat and petite bourgeoisie with rural connections—students, petty officials, under-employed itinerant types—"those who work, eat, laugh and sleep"—swarmed into the cities. They were no longer moved by the political establishment; soon they became alienated from the King. Egypt's soul, which was thousands of years old, needed a "mover". But it did not require any prior revolutionary organisation: simply a mover, a *rayyes* who, according to al-Hakim, "thought with his heart, not his mind". The Egyptian altar was vacant, the *ma'bad* was uninhabited, awaiting the *ma'bud*, the idol, to appear.

On 26 May 1938, a young Egyptian visited Hamilton at the British Embassy in Cairo. He emphasised his immediate political objective: ". . . to get rid of the 'old gang' of Egyptian politicians and replace them by members of the younger generation, pledged to make every sacrifice for the wellbeing of the Egyptian people."[38] The young Egyptian could well have been Nasser. But it was Ahmad Hussein, leader of the Young Egypt Society. The similarity, however, between the aims and views of the two men does not end there.

According to Brigadier Muhammad Fawzi,[39] Commandant of the Military Academy in 1957, Nasser enrolled in March 1937, after having attended five months of law school from October 1936 to February 1937. There were 43 other entering cadets in the course, which lasted sixteen months, five of which were preparatory. In the final stage of his training course, Nasser was a squad leader. The late Field-Marshal Abdel Hakim Amer joined the Academy a few months later, early in 1938. Nasser was commissioned a second lieutenant, infantry, on 1 July 1938, graduating with a total mark of 71 per cent. His highest mark, 95 per cent, was significantly in administration. He was posted to the 5th Battalion in Manqabad and later to Gabal Awlia and Khartum in the Sudan. His routine promotions came at normal intervals: First Lieutenant in September 1940, Captain in September 1942, during which year he served for several months on the Western Desert frontier. In February 1943, he was appointed Instructor at the academy where he remained until July 1946, when he was assigned to the 6th Rifle Battalion. He entered Staff College in May 1948 and was promoted Major in July of the same year. After a tour of combat duty in the Palestine War, he was made Instructor in the Army Administration School in July 1949. In November 1951 he became Instructor in the Staff College, having been promoted Lieutenant-Colonel.

It is difficult to evaluate the little information there is about Nasser's sixteen months in the military academy. Its Commandant at that time was a Brigadier Abel Wahid'Ammar who, in 1957, reminisced to an interviewer: "Nasser exhibited early manhood . . . rarely smiled, was firm and strong in personality, proud and showed no signs of fatigue from duty."[40] While a cadet, he held the rank of Corporal. He was taught however by a Watanist–Muslim Brother, Colonel Ahmad 'Abd al-'Aziz, who had some influence over him.

Nasser's years as Instructor in the academy and Army Administration School were routine and uneventful. In 1944, he married

Tahiyya Khazem, daughter of a merchant of Persian origin, whose forefathers had come to Egypt via Iraq. Between 1944 and 1946, while still Instructor at the Academy, he met three people who were to influence his career: the *marxisant*, and later member of the Communist party, Khalid Mohieddin (military academy, 1940; BA Commerce, 1951), and, through him, the Communist lawyer, member of HADETU, Ahmad Fuad (who was later to draft the so-called socialist laws and decrees of 1961; he became subsequently an official of Bank Misr). Sarwat Okasha introduced Nasser to his brother-in-law, Ahmad Abul Fath, editor of the mass circulation Wafd daily *al-Misri* (founded in 1938). Through other fellow-officers he had met in Manqabad, the Sudan, Alexandria and the Western Desert (e.g. Anwar Sadat, Zakaziyya Mohieddin, Abdel Hakim Amer, Abdel Latif Boghdadi, Hasan Ibrahim, Kamal al-Din Hussein)[41] he came in contact with members of the Muslim Brotherhood and the Communist party. It is also reported that he even established links with members of the British Intelligence front organisation, the Brotherhood of Freedom (*Ikhwān al-hurriyya*), a wartime British operation to counter Axis propaganda in the Middle East.[42]

One may assume that before 1945 Nasser, the young army officer, was politically inactive. There was no evidence (other than subsequent embellishments by his colleagues)[43] of his involvement even on the periphery of political life. On the contrary, Nasser appeared serious and purposeful about his military studies. Throughout the Second World War, he seemed to behave and deport himself correctly towards the authorities and his superiors in contrast, say, to the activities of Sadat, Boghdadi, or the Sabri brothers.

Undoubtedly the political crisis of 1940-2 over the wartime relationship of Egypt to the belligerents affected him, as it did all other members of the officer corps. The Egyptian protagonists in that crisis were the King and his men, especially Ali Maher, their agents such as General Saleh Harb Pasha who had succeeded the deceased Abd al-Hamid Sa'id Bey as President of the YMMA, Ahmad Hussein, leader of Young Egypt (now renamed the Islamic National party), and that inveterate though ineffectual rebel, General Aziz Ali al-Masri who had just been sacked as Army Inspector-General on the insistence of Britain. Another leading Palace figure was the King's mentor, Ahmad Hasanein Pasha.[44]

The matter of Egypt's position in the war became the major bone of political contention. The Palace harboured pro-Axis sympathies, which became more pronounced as the British military position in the Western Desert and the Mediterranean deteriorated and became more precarious in 1941–2. In a minute to a despatch from Cairo, dated January 1942, the otherwise remote and caustic permanent head of the Foreign Office, Sir Alexander Cadogan, remarked, "We must try to secure that both palace and people are never united against us." It is here where the Wafd, in opposition at the time, became useful to Britain. Moreover, the activities of Axis agents in Egypt had to be kept under surveillance and countered.

On 4 February 1942 British armoured units surrounded Abdin Palace. Sir Miles Lampson, HM Ambassador in Cairo, accompanied by General Stone, GOC Land Forces, Middle East, marched into King Faruq's office and read to him an ultimatum demanding that he either appoint a government headed by Nahhas Pasha, leader of the Wafd party, or abdicate. The way the ultimatum was delivered was seen by Egyptian nationalists as a usurpation of the country's sovereign independence. The 1936 treaty was now seen as a sham; the national leadership of the Wafd as a group of traitors. The temporary sympathy of Egyptians for their hard-pressed and humiliated monarch did not long conceal the fact that he could not in future command their undivided loyalty. His own behaviour in the next decade hastened the evaporation of any such public feelings of goodwill towards him.

There were reports of meetings in the Officers' Club to consider ways of protesting against the incident, as well as of general unrest and disaffection in the officer corps. Stiffened by British support, the new Wafd government threatened courts martial and effected transfers of troublesome officers—measures not designed to win the party the sympathy of the army. The King no doubt was active on his own behalf among the corps through his senior officer appointees and protégés. He encouraged the formation of an Iron Guard largely from among officers of his own Palace guards. At the same time as the Germans advanced towards the Egyptian frontier, the Muslim Brothers increased their political agitation among Azharites and students of other religious institutions.[45]

Nasser's tour of combat duty in the Palestine War, where he was wounded, ended in March 1949, when he returned to Ismailiyya. Before that, he had established contact in December 1947 with the Mufti of Palestine who was ensconced in his family compound in Zeytoun, a suburb of Cairo. He had also been in touch with volunteer units of the Muslim Brotherhood through the intermediary of his friend Captain Kamal al-Din Hussein and his old Academy instructor, Colonel Ahmad abd el-Aziz, an old protégé of General Aziz Ali al-Masri. On the front itself he had, according to his own admission, tried to recruit officers of the line into an organisation—not yet formed except in his own mind—to combat political corruption at home.

> I grew restless at HQ and went out on tour of our positions in order to ascertain the mood of the officers. I will not deny that I was really trying to enlist some of them in our Free Officers' Organization. In my conversations with the officers I did not come directly to the point. My method at that time aimed at two things. First to win the confidence of those I met and secondly to strengthen my personal relationship with them as much as possible. I was certain . . . that trust and personal friendship were certain to turn into something deeper when the opportune moment arose.[46]

This was probably the reason for his questioning by the Army Chief of Staff General Osman Mahdi and Prime Minister Abdel Hadi in Cairo on 22 May 1949.

By then too the terror campaign of the Muslim Brotherhood and other radical groups had claimed the lives of Amin Osman Pasha, Prime Minister Nuqrashi, the Chief of Cairo Police Salim Zaki, and was soon to claim the life of a High Court Judge, Ahmad al-Khazindar. The Muslim Brotherhood's Supreme Guide Hasan al-Banna himself had been assassinated by government agents in February. Elements of Young Egypt and an army group in which Sadat was involved committed other acts of terrorism, especially the bombing of public places.[47] The perennial conflict between King and Wafd was on with renewed vigour and bitterness, while, crucially, the British military presence had, since March 1947, contracted to the Suez Canal zone. Ahmed Hussein's Young Egypt, now renamed the Egyptian Socialist party, was more active than ever. Its extremist agitation and reckless incitement to sedition constituted the prelude to the burning of Cairo on 26 January 1952; the smashing of the Communist party's cadres by Ismail Sidqi in 1946 and Ibrahim Abdel Hadi in 1949 had been followed by the emergence of new, native Marxist groups in the university and among the workers.[48] Significantly, a large group of younger members of the Wafd were critical of the party's established leadership. Chief among these was Ahmad Abul Fath, editor of *al-Misri*, and now friend of and adviser to Nasser and his small band of officer friends.

Within the army itself it was the division between the pro-establishment High Command, willing to accept British advice—and dictation during the war—on one hand, and the pro-Axis abortive rebellions of General Aziz Ali al-Masri (Army Inspector-General 1938–40), supported by Ali Maher and the one-time Minister of Defence, the Muslim fanatic General Saleh Harb Pasha on the other, which influenced most of Nasser's generation of army officers. The Muslim Brothers too had infiltrated the officer corps through Abdel Monein Abdel Rauf (Nasser wanted him liquidated soon after the 1952 *coup*, and he escaped to Lebanon), Colonel Rashad Mehanna, Kamal el-Din Hussein, Major Mumammad Labib and others. Generally, the anti-British *ambiance* appealed to these officers of lower-class background with a strong attachment to the religious values of Islam. Whether or not there was, as has been suggested, a secret organisation in the corps led by General Masri is immaterial.[49] Rather it was Masri's personality, chequered pseudo-heroic career in Arabia, Libya and Spain and his implacable enmity of Britain which influenced these young officers. Muhammad Subeih, for instance, emphasised General Masri's great influence over dissident and rebellious officers since the war when he wrote, "There is no doubt that Aziz Masri was the inspiration for these ideas . . . and his students among the officers were the staunchest elements in this movement . . ."[50] Here it is interesting to recall Lampson's prophetic remarks a year before the outbreak of war. With the clouds of a world war overhead, Sir Lancelot Oliphant of the Foreign Office requested a general appreciation of the situation in Egypt and a projection of British options. Lampson in his reply complained that Oliphant's request "sets me a proper teaser: What attitude should we adopt?" He suggested three possibilities:

(1) the loss of popularity of Faruq was due to his own behaviour; parliament and parties could ask him to abdicate; (2) there could be a constitutional struggle between Palace and Parliament in which Faruq would be backed by the conservative elements and the army, but that there could be bloodshed if town mobs were stirred up by Parliamentary leaders; (3) there could be a military revolt against Faruq on Orabi lines with a view to installing a military dictatorship and expelling the house of Muhammad Ali.[51]

Nasser's meagre political re-education and shift away from his earlier association with Young Egypt began in 1946, when he befriended Khalid Mohieddin and through him Ahmad Fuad. His relations with the left, however, were not as close as those with the right and left-of-centre Wafdist group as represented by Ahmad Abul Fath. He thus visited Ahmad regularly, consulted him on the role of the press, the state of play within the Wafd, the state of Anglo–Egyptian relations. Through Kamal al-Din Hussein, Anwar Sadat, Kamal Rifaat (a Royal Guard officer since 1944 and an acolyte of General Masri, who met Gamal in Isdud during the Palestine War)[52] Nasser established closer contacts with the Muslim Brethren and other radical groups. He forged links with the *Akhbar el Yom* newspaper establishment of the Amin twins. His friend Abdel Hakim Amer provided Nasser with a pipeline to the Palace through his acquaintance with Yusuf Rashad, a naval officer physician attached to the King and thus information about the King's Iron Guard organisation within the army. Hakim was also a nephew of General Haidar, GOC, Armed Forces, in 1950–2. Abdel Moneim Abdel Rauf, Abdel Latif Boghdadi and Gamal Salem provided Nasser with additional links with the Muslim Brethren.

From Young Egypt Nasser and his colleagues had learned as early as 1938 that working closely with the army a *coup* could "wipe out the 'old gang', suppress the Constitution and run a régime modelled on that of the totalitarian states".[53] In fact, they could not realise at the time with what ease they would sweep away the "old gang".[54] Vague notions of agrarian reform, social justice, the suppression of all titles and privileges, Egyptianisation and the establishment of a single social class[55] were ideas frequently bandied about by Young Egypt.[56]

With the exception of Boghdadi, none of the officers in Nasser's group had been abroad to Europe; few among them knew a European language well; none of them had studied overseas. The native Egyptian, "local type" (*baladi*) quality was overwhelming. They were moreover single-mindedly dedicated to the aim either of imposing a new leadership on the country or of overthrowing the existing political edifice, King and all. It was perhaps Nasser's consuming obsession with this single objective which gave him paradoxically an extraordinary tactical flexibility, such as his instrumental contacts, alliances and co-operation with all anti-establishment groups, as well as with external forces, such as the

CIA, if Miles Copeland is to be believed.[57]

It seems—and Muhammad Hasanein Heikal as well as several of Nasser's closest associates in the Free Officer movement agree— that Nasser acquired his motive to power in the period from 1946 to 1949. Nor was this a random or haphazard development: it was linked to his formative experience in the thirties and forties. The earlier period of his life was permanently influenced by his feelings of rejection, loneliness and despair; his adolescent years and his early military career by the stabilising force of his innate and native autocratic conservatism against the dilettantism and apparent irresponsibility of the politicians; his post-Palestine war career by his disgust with the King and establishment, and his humiliation by the defeat in Palestine. The kind of adolescent publicity he craved as a writer and journalist *manqué* in the thirties and forties had been transferred into an aspiration to power. Together with his conviction, partly derived from al-Hakim's criticism of corrupt parliamentary government and his call for a charismatic reformer who would be idolised by the Egyptians, this was a potent mixture. Mustafa Kamil and Saad Zaghlul became model precedents of the populist potential. Thus Ahmad Hussein in May 1938 may have remonstrated with Hamilton of the British Embassy in Cairo about how he would "get rid of the 'old gang' ". For Nasser in 1949 this prospect was not a remote, or unattainable, one.

Notes

1. Nasser's eldest son, Khalid, reports that in fact it was the stepmother who caused frequent rifts between father and son.
2. The Egyptian historian Abdel Rahman al-Rafii, who attended Ras el-Tin school, describes it as "one of the most important schools in the country". *Mudhakkirati (My Memoirs)* (Cairo, 1952), p.7.
3. Ibid., pp.10–14.
4. Quoted by Muhammad Subeih, *Ayyām wa ayyām (Days and Days)* (Cairo, 1966), p.273, from Anwar al-Sadat, *Safahāt majhūla*, p.25.
5. Anthony Eden, *Memoirs, Full Circle* (London, 1960), p.471.
6. For example, the weekly Cairo magazine *al-Musawwar*, Special Issue, August 1957; Abdel Moneim Shumais, *al-Za'im al-thā'ir (The rebellious chief)* (Cairo, 1954); Taha Abdel Baqi Surur, *Gamal Abdel Nasser, rajul ghayyara al-tarikh (Nasser, a man who changed the course of history)* (Cairo, 1957); Saniya Qara'a, *Hāris al-majd, Gamal Abdel Nasser (Guardian of glory: Nasser)* (Cairo, 1959); Anwar al-Jundi, *Hādha huwa Gamal (This is Gamal)* (Beirut, 1960); Suleiman Mazhar, *'Imlāq min Beni Murr (A force from Beni Murr)* (Cairo, 1963); Muhammad Rabi', *Shakhsiyyat Abd al-Naser (The personality of Nasser)* (Cairo, 1966); and many others. Nasser's letters to his classmate Ali Hasan al-Nashar were never fully reproduced. Excerpts from one or two appeared here and there. See Abdel Qadir al-

Bindari and Najib Ilyas Barsum, *Thawrat al-hurriyya* (*The revolution of freedom*) (Cairo, 1961), pp.28–31 and 43–4. Subsequent letters written in 1942 are quoted in ibid., pp.46, 47–8. See also Shumais, *al-Zā'im al-thā'ir*, pp.14–22.

7. On the Muslim Brothers generally, see Richard P. Mitchell, *The Society of Muslim Brothers* (London, 1969). See also J. Heyworth-Dunne, *Religious and Political trends in Modern Egypt* (Washington, 1959).

8. On the Young Egypt Society generally, see James P. Jankowski, *Egypt's Young Rebels: 'Young Egypt': 1933–1952* (Stanford, 1975).

9. For example, Tawfiq al-Hakim in his writings, especially his play *Ahl al-kahf* (*The dwellers of the cave*) (Cairo, 1933), and his romance, *'Awdat al-rūh* (*Return of the soul*) (Cairo, 1933).

10. Al-Hakim, *'Awdat al-rūh*, p.252.

11. Nasser had a monument erected in Alexandria honouring Omar Makram for his role in the history of the Egyptian national resistance movement against European domination.

12. As developed in his famous novel *'Awdat al-rūh*. Also, in his *Praska aw mushkilat al-hukm* (*Praska, or the problem of government*) (Cairo, 1939), al-Hakim affected a prophecy about a "blessed revolution" which would sweep away corruption. Al-Hakim was a consistent critic of the failings of the parliamentary system in Egypt from 1936 to 1939. In fairness to al-Hakim it should be noted, however, that he considered the solution offered by military dictatorship (*Praska*, 1939) and rejected it; he later entertained the Nazi and Fascist solutions and rejected them too (*Sultān al-zalām*) (Cairo, 1941). Earlier, in 1937, in '*Usfūr min al-sharq* (*A bird from the East*), he had discussed the Communist way and rejected it. It should be recalled that in 1939–40, a "strong-man" government came to power, headed by Ali Maher (also the first Prime Minister after the July 1952 army *coup*). General Aziz Ali al-Masri was made Inspector-General and Army Chief of Staff. It is reasonable to suggest that his government represented the Ottoman or Turkish style of politics, with Ataturkist proclivities and Axis sympathies. But it is probably a mere coincidence that al-Hakim opined in his *Shajarat al-hukm* (Cairo, 1939); "Model rule, in fact, is not based on ideal principles, but on the excellence and virtue of individuals. The miracle of prophets does not lie in their teachings, but their personalities . . . What is new in a prophet is his personality." Can one say that al-Hakim provided Egyptians generally and Nasser in particular with a native conception of legitimacy? His ideal rule, as expressed in most of these writings, consisted of a great leader who combines the three essential elements of freedom, power and reason. But his ideal ruler emerges not as a prophet, but a magician who, according to Louis Awad, can juggle these three "golden apples" as the "gula-gula" man juggles the egg and the stone. See the brilliant volume of essays by Louis Awad, *al-Hurriyya wa naqd al-hurriyya* (Cairo, 1971), esp. pp.57–109.

13. See al-Hakim's own version of this epsiode in his '*Awdat al-wa'i* (*The return of consciousness*) (Beirut, 1974).

14. Ibid. This is also reported by Ahmad Abul Fath, *L'Affaire Nasser* (Paris, 1962).

15. Public Record Office, FO 371/17977.

16. August 1933, FO 371/217.

17. 7 May 1934, FO 371/17997.

18. November 1933, FO 371/217.

19. Report dated 1 July 1936, FO 371/20114.

20. Lampson to Eden, 2 March 1936, FO 371/20101.

21. Campbell to Simon, 28 July 1933, FO 407/217.

22. FO 371/20098.
23. On Mahmud Azmi's interesting and chequered career, see despatch no. 59, dated 7 August 1937 from Gilbert Mackereth, HM Consul-General in Damascus, to Eden, FO 371/20786. For Azmi's Arab nationalist propaganda, see his *Jabha min al-shu'ub al'arabiyya (An Arab people's front)* (Cairo, 1938).
24. Sir Alex Keown-Boyd, 'Note on the Student Movement in Egypt'.
25. Ibid.
26. Ibid.
27. Ibid.
28. Later on, reference is made to the similarity between the ideas and programme of Young Egypt since 1933 on one hand and those of Nasser and the Free Officers on the other. Reference is also made to leading members of Young Egypt and other radical youth organisations of the thirties who assumed Cabinet and senior administrative posts in the Nasser régime.
29. Quoted by Ahmad Hussein in *Kayfa 'araftu Abdel Nasser, was 'ishtu ayyāma hukmihi* (Beirut, 1973), pp.100–1.
30. See Fathi Radwan in *Rose el-Youssef,* 18 and 25 August 1975. A correspondent commenting on these articles in the same magazine of 19 September 1975 wrote in to correct Radwan's statement concerning Nasser's Young Egypt activities in Bab al-Sha'riyya,: under the leadership of Muhammad Subeih. Cf. Subeih, *Ayyām wa ayyām.* In his speech to the opening session of the National Assembly on 22 July 1957, Nasser himself said:

> During the formative years . . . I was interested in all the political parties which aimed to restore to the Egyptian people its freedom. I joined the Young Egypt Society but I left it after I discovered that despite its message it would not achieve anything concrete.

See *al-Mawsū'a al-nāsiriyya (The Nasser encyclopedia)* (Beirut, 1973), Vol.1, pp.112–130.
31. Lampson to Eden, 16 February 1937, FO 407/221. In the same despatch Lampson described the Anglo–Egyptian Treaty as the "beginning of Egypt's emancipation from British control as hitherto exercised by the Residency and the British elements in the Egyptian Administration and forces of public order".
32. Lampson to Eden, 29 July 1937, FO 407/221.
33. 16 September 1937, FO 407/221.
34. Regarding its leaders, finances and party control, see the report by Keown-Boyd, 'Note on the Student Movement in Egypt'. See also Lampson's despatches dated December 1935, FO 371/19080 and 20096. Kelly's despatches of January and November 1936 are also informative; so is Lampson's dated 15 July 1937, FO 407/221. See also J. P. Jankowski, 'The Egyptian Blue Shirts and the Egyptian Wafd', *Middle Eastern Studies,* Vol. 6, 1970, pp.77–95.
35. Kelly, despatches of January and November 1936.
36. Despatch dated 28 October 1937, FO 407/221.
37. Telegrams 706–740, FO 407/221.
38. Lampson to Oliphant, FO 371/21947.
39. After the June 1967 Six Day War, Nasser appointed him Commander of the Armed Forces and Minister of Defence. He was related to the then Minister of Information, Muhammad Fa'iq, and soon became a member of the inner clique of Nasser's "courtiers". He was imprisoned for his part in the conspiracy against President Sadat in May 1971.

40. See *al-Musawwar*, August 1957.
41. All of them original members of the Revolution Command Council (RCC). See Anwar Sadat, *Revolt on the Nile* (New York, 1957).
42. See Freya Stark, *Dust in the Lion's Paw* (London, 1961), pp.67ff. I am indebted to Miss Elizabeth Monroe for this reference. Ahmad Abdul Fath, *L'Affaire Nasser*, refers to Nasser's connections. Kamal Rifaat has claimed subsequently that it was a Nasser tactic to associate himself with a variety of groups. However, in view of other references in this text, it is clear Nasser was a member of Misr al-Fatat before he entered military academy.
43. See, for example, Anwar al-Sadat, *Hadha ʿammak Gamal* (*This is your uncle Gamal*) (Cairo, 1955). But cf. his *Asrar al-thawra al-misriyya* (*The secrets of the Egyptian revolution*) (Cairo, 1965).
44. On the role of Ahmad Hasanein, see Muhammad al-Tabiʿi, *Min asrar al-sasa wa al-siyasa al-misriyya* (*Secrets of Egyptian politics and politicians*) (Cairo, n.d.).
45. See FO 371/31424 (1942).
46. See his *Palestine War Memoirs* serialised in the Cairo weekly magazine *Akhir Saa*, March–April 1955, and reproduced in Subeih, *Ayyam wa ayyam*, pp.305–68. An unpublished English translation in typescript by Professor Walid Khalidi of the American University of Beirut was never published to my knowledge. See pp.19–20 of this translation.
47. See Sadat, *Asrar al-thawra*, and Saad Zaghlul Fuad, *al-Qital fi'l qanal* (*The Fighting in the Canal*) (Cairo, 1969). See also Tariq al-Bishri, *al-Haraka al-siyasiyya fi misr, 1945–1952* (*The Egyptian political movement*) (Cairo, 1972).
48. See Walter Z. Laqueur, *Communism and Nationalism in the Middle East* (New York, 1956); Rauf Abbas, *al-Yasar al-misri* (*The Egyptian left*), *1925–1940* (Beirut, 1972); and Rifaat Said, *al-Sahafa al-yasariyya fi misr, 1925–1948* (*The leftist press in Egypt*) (Beirut, 1974).
49. See Major A. Sansom, *I spied spies* (London, 1965). See also Muhammad Anis, *Arbaʿ fibrayer fi tarikh misr al-siyasi* (*4 February in the political history of Egypt*) (Beirut, 1972), pp.42–51. For a personality profile of General Aziz Masri, see FO 371/19076.
50. Muhammad Subeih, *Batal la nansahu: Aziz al-Masri wa ʿasruhu* (*A hero we shall not forget: Aziz al-Masri and his age*) (Beirut, 1971), p.298.
51. 23 July 1938, FO 371/21948.
52. See his autobiographical interview recorded orally and reproduced in Abdel Tawwab Abdel Hayy, *ʿAsir hayati* (Cairo, 1966). See also Kamal al-Din Rifaat, *Harb al-tahrir al-wataniyya, mudhakkirat Kamal al-Din Rifaat* (*The war of national liberation: the memoirs of Kamal al-Din Rifaat*) (Cairo, 1968), Vol.1.
53. Lampson to Oliphant, 25 May 1938, FO 371/21947.
54. Tawfiq al-Hakim describes this case and its impact on the people in his tract, *ʿAwdat al waʿi*, cited earlier.
55. See Nasser's later speeches in the early and mid-sixties. Thus addressing the National Assembly on 25 March 1964 he said, among other things, "We must at any cost prevent the emergence of a new class which assumes that privilege is its heritage from the old class . . ." or "the socialist society means self-sufficiency and justice, the eradication of differences between classes." Later in a speech to a trade union congress at Helwan on 4 April 1968, he said, "Full democracy means the dissolution of differences between classes, which is the same as equality."
56. See Young Egypt's programme publicised in Cairo on 18 March (including

al-Ahram) when the Society had been proclaimed the National Islamic party. The same programme was publicised two years before that in 1938 (See *Oriente Moderno*, Rome (1938), pp.491–4). See also Noel Charles to Halifax, 1 August 1938, FO 371/21948, reporting on Ahmad Hussein's visit to Italy and the splash in *Il Messaggero* with overtones of Mazzini's "God, people and country". See also the articles of Ahmad Hussein in his newspapers *al-Sarkha* and *Wadi al-Nil*, some of which are cited or reproduced in his *Qadiyyat al-tahrid* (Cairo, 1957).

57. Miles Copeland, *The Game of Nations* (London, 1969).

CHAPTER 2

Nasser's Political Roots

In looking at the youth of today, one is apt to forget that
identity formation, while being "critical" in youth, is really
a generational issue. Erik Erikson, *Identity.*

Egypt's military academy was only sixteen years old when some of
its graduates grabbed power by *coup d'état* in July 1952. Before
1936, it had been a military school. For nearly one hundred years,
until 1928, it was very rare for any of its entering cadets to possess a
secondary school certificate. Entrants after 1936, however, had to
be secondary school graduates. They came into the academy
therefore with a higher standard of literacy and general education.
But they also arrived with four years of adolescent political involvement in those schools, and sharing the extreme nationalist orientation
of a rapidly increasing number of secondary school-leavers in the
country.

The military academy graduates of the years 1938 to 1942
constituted a critical group of army officers, for they had entered
the academy with some experience in street politics and a smattering
of undigested nationalist views which they had acquired from
conservative Islamic and radical quasi-Fascist groups in the turbulent
years 1933–6. They had joined the riots and demonstrations against
Palace-appointed minority governments, agitated in 1935 for the
reinstatement of the 1923 constitution that had been abrogated by
Ismail Sidqi in 1930 and replaced by his own, which favoured a
reinforced executive.

Significantly, the reduction—in certain cases total remission—of
fees for attending the academy enabled a greater number of young
men from lower-class background—sons of small-holding farmers,
government employees, minor provincial officials, merchants and
teachers—to enter the academy. Then, the absence of an aristocratic
military tradition, as in England or France, or feudal recruiting
ground for professional soldiers, as in Germany, meant that the

47

Egyptian officer corps was not fashioned by an élite with a corporate ethos and links with a parallel civilian class in society. On the contrary, the rapidly increasing numbers of secondary school-leavers, university students and graduates appeared dispossessed and crushed by economic and other difficulties in a rapidly changing society, and felt alienated from a political establishment they considered avaricious, callous and hostile. They had grown up as incipient native industrial, financial and commercial enterprise was growing, as a greater awareness of the economic requisites of national independence expanded, as a competition with foreigners for the control of trade and commerce sharpened. They became politically conscious in a period of population growth, rapid urbanisation, the expansion of lay education and the founding of secular universities.

The post-1936 crops of academy graduates were then both in terms of social background and early political experience part of the generation which produced a variety of new radical nationalist formations and movements, such as the Young Egypt Society, the Muslim Brethren, the Marxist Partisans of Peace, the Communist HADETU (National Democratic Liberation Movement), all of them opposed to the traditional political parties whose leaders belonged mainly to the native "bourgeoisie" of landowners, senior government officials, politicians and men of affairs.

The Free Officers who assumed power in 1952 were not therefore the only vanguard group capable of leading a reformist or revolutionary movement in the country. They constituted a miniscule section of the new, post-Second World War younger radical nationalist élite of the country. Yet when they grabbed power they did so alone, without the participation of any of the other radical political forces in Egypt. However, as a radical movement within the army the Free Officers had been much influenced in their political formation and behaviour by the radical youth "political culture" of the 1930s which rejected the *ancien régime* of the monarch and the traditional political parties, and sought to overthrow it by force.

Writing in 1966, Muhammad Subeih, a leading member of the Young Egypt Society, argued that one of the trends in the thirties was the appearance of

> youth movements, aiming at leading the national struggle against the colonialists . . . The two most prominent of these

were Young Egypt and the Muslim Brethren . . . Together they showed that old party politics were no longer able to satisfy the desires and aspirations of an emerging nationalist youth vanguard and the masses.[1]

Beginning in 1937 members of Young Egypt and the Muslim Brethren "infiltrated the Military Academy and the Army . . . They became the nucleus of the Free Officer Movement."[2] For Subeih the 1952 revolution "was a nationalist youth revolution inspired by the moral and national principles of the youth of the thirties";[3] that is, it was an extension of the youth movement of that period. Indeed, sometime after the 1952 *coup*, Wagih Abaza, a prominent air force officer and member of Young Egypt, told Subeih that Nasser, the leader of the *coup*, was an old Young Egypt colleague. "Suddenly", Subeih reports, "I remember this quiet young man who led Young Egypt's branch in Bab el Sha'riyya";[4] that is, in al-Nahda Secondary School where Nasser was a pupil.

Leading members of the Revolution Command Council (RCC: 1952–6), who took an active part in the 23 July 1952 *coup*, thus constituted a generation that grew up in the violent atmosphere of the 1930s. They were young officers during the Second World War, saw active duty in the Palestine War, participated in or collaborated with various underground terrorist groups in the decade preceding their assumption of power. Anwar Sadat, Abdel Latif Boghdadi, Zakariyya and Khaled Mohieddin, Salah and Gamal Salem, Hasan Ibrahim, Kamal el-Din Hussein, Abdel Hakim Amer, Hussein Shafei, Kamal el-Din Rifaat, Hasan 'Izzat, Wagih Abaza, Hasan al-Tuhami, Nasser and many others were all born in the period between 1917 and 1922, were either contemporaries or overlapped in military academy. Several of them attended Staff College together, were assigned to the same units on active duty, or served together in the Palestine War, 1948–9.

Exposed to the same influences of radical nationalist organisations and anti-British terrorist groups, seasoned by a common pattern of experiences in their military careers, and affected by the same political forces and events—the British ultimatum to their monarch on 4 February 1942, the world war, the guerrilla and sabotage campaign against British troops in the Canal, the Palestine War— these officers constituted an 'historical generation'. Although they did not subscribe to a common ideology, the affinity between them derived from a uniform educational preparation, as well as social and economic background—the lower urban and rural classes. They also harboured similar aspirations, suffered common frustrations, and shared vague plans for the overthrow of the existing order. They were anxious for a break, a radical departure from the *status quo*, which was dominated by the generation of political leaders who had emerged under the protection of Britain in the years from 1907 to 1919 to become the rulers of Egypt in 1923.

The Wafd, the standard-bearer in the struggle for independence, undoubtedly played a major role in making them politically conscious at an early age. For a variety of reasons that will become clear later in this narrative, the Wafd never quite succeeded in infiltrating the officer corps, let alone controlling it. It was the more activist, extreme nationalist and less secular political formations of the thirties and forties which suggested to the young officers a more direct and economical, albeit violent, way to power.

The political atmosphere of the 1930s in Egypt, as well as the Arab states in the Fertile Crescent, spawned the kind of ultra-nationalist movements which favoured youth's adoption of violent politics. The leading exponents of this trend in Egypt were the Young Egypt Society (*Jam'iyyat Misr al-Fatat*), the Society of Muslim Brethren, and the small terrorist groups within the old National party. Not only Nasser, but Sadat and other Free Officers became members of one or another of these groups in the 1930s. Before and during the war some of them came under the influence of the eccentric and violently anti-British General Aziz Ali al-Masri, who was briefly Inspector-General of the army in 1938–40, and before that time Commandant of the police academy. All of them were impressed by the apparently overwhelming power of Nazi Germany, while briefly succumbing to the propaganda of Italian Fascist agents in Egypt.

Young Egypt was founded in 1933 by a group of law school graduates in Cairo headed by Ahmad Hussein and Fathi Radwan. Its emphasis on the role of youth in the struggle for independence and the regeneration of a powerful Egypt naturally appealed to Nasser and his contemporaries. A year earlier, Fathi Radwan, who became its secretary and later in the 1950s Minister of Communications and subsequently propaganda Minister under Nasser, was in the news as secretary of an organisation calling itself the "Preparatory Committee of the Congress of Students from the East". In a publication[5] calling for the co-operation between students from the East, he proposed the convening of an annual congress in different eastern capitals to discuss economic and political co-operation between eastern states. Listed among the advisers to Radwan's committee were some well-known academics, men of letters and nationalist leaders: Dr Abdul Wahhab Azzam, Professor of Oriental Languages in Cairo, Khalil Bey Mutran, famous poet, and Dr Abdul Rahman Shahbandar, prominent Syrian Arab nationalist, assassinated in 1940. Prominent among the members of the Committee were Ahmad Hussein, co-founder with Fathi Radwan of the Young Egypt Society the following year, the Palestinian nationalists Musa al-Husseini and Abdel Qadir al-Husseini, who was killed in the decisive battle of Kastel for the control of the road to Jerusalem during the Palestine War in 1948; Mustafa al-Wakil, who became a leading member of Young Egypt and its main agent in Iraq in 1939–41, after which he escaped to Berlin to collaborate with the Nazis, and Nur al-Din Tarraf, a medical student, who became Prime Minister for a brief period in the Nasser régime.

The emergence of Young Egypt at that time was not, however, an isolated phenomenon in the Middle East. Youth movements calling for the revival of Arab power and glory and for the deliverance of the Arab nation from foreign control and local oppression proliferated in the Fertile Crescent too. In addition to the better-organised and enduring Syrian National Social Party (Parti Populaire Syrienne), founded by the Christian Lebanese Antun Saadeh in 1932,[6] there were the League for Arab (National) Action in Syria, founded by the Alawite from Iskenderun (Alexandretta) Zaki al-Arsuzi,[7] and the Muthanna Arab Club and Futuwwa organisation in Baghdad.

In 1935, Futuwwa, for instance, published in Baghdad[8] its first pamphlet, *Youth Movements in the World* (*Harakat al-shabab fi'l-'alam*). Its opening statement is interesting, for it reflects a general mood of political disaffection, an inclination to violence and a preference for national social, paramilitary organisation:

> The world is overwhelmed today with various youth movements which aim at the fundamental reform of the social, political and economic bases of their life, and aspire to build a powerful nation capable of facing the world with its various currents.
>
> These movements are distinguished from all others by their nationalism, their action in rousing the spirit of public service and their activation of the effectiveness of youth. And all of

this by way of the glorification of the history of the nation, of its heroes, and the preservation of its social bonds such as language, culture and customs.

The tract goes on to assert that the First World War and its aftermath awakened this national spirit in youth largely in order to counter Communism. It cites examples of such youth movements as the Red Shirts of India led by Abdel Ghaffar Khan and the Green Shirts of Young Egypt.

In the same year, the Muthanna Club published "The Arab National Programme" (*Al-manhaj al-qawmi al-arabi*) in Baghdad. After identifying imperialism as the source of all the ills in the Arab countries and the main cause of their division and disunity, material and moral poverty, the tract calls for a new Arab ideology to activate the struggle against imperialism and towards Arab unity. "Since the movement is one of revival and struggle to secure the future, it is natural that it depend primarily on Arab youth." It, incidentally, also advocated the state ownership of the major sources of national wealth.

Two years later, in October 1937, a Customs Service Captain, Muhammad Mahfuz, published a tract, "The Blue Shirt" ("Al-qamis al-azraq"). A clear reference to the Wafd party's youth organisation by that name, Mahfuz argued that "shirt organisations" were a very old phenomenon, going back in Islamic history to Abu Muslim al-Khurasani. Shirt organisations were part of the nationalist movements in India and Italy. In the case of Egypt, Mahfuz asserted that the Blue Shirts were not linked to European Fascism, but were the progeny of the 1919 national independence revolt.[9]

When the Free Officers attained power and later at the height of Nasser's own popularity, most students of Egypt, including this writer, were unduly preoccupied with the question whether he and the Free Officers had an ideology. The preoccupation obscured from them the fact that the new régime of soldiers produced a programme of national reform almost immediately they came to power, and implemented it in the first six to eight years of their rule. After that, there was hardly any further movement in that direction. What the origins or antecedents of this programme were, which allowed an agrarian reform law to be decreed 45 days after the *coup*, is a question that was not seriously considered.

There are several clues in Nasser's own public statement, *Egypt's Liberation, the Philosophy of the Revolution*, first published in 1954, which point to the possible background of the Free Officers, as well as his own, political orientation. There are also the writings of other active members of the Free Officer conspiracy, such as Anwar Sadat and Kamal al-Din Rifaat, which shed further light on this background.[10] A careful examination of these allows a fresh interpretation of the beginnings and development of the officers' movement and demonstrates its roots in the general drift of political events in Egypt from 1933 to 1943.

A careful reading of Nasser's tract rewards one with some major findings. There is in it a frank assertion that the Free Officers, especially Nasser himself, had no common ideology ("philosophy"), or political belief (*'aqida*). Rather their political ideas were blurred by religious faith and the confused admixture of Islamic-Fascist notions of the pamphlets of the 1930s.

It is significant, none the less, when Nasser states in this connection: "I had sentiments [*mashā'ir*] which took the form of a vague hope, then that of a definite idea, and finally that of practical arrangements [i.e. planning a conspiracy] until midnight of 22nd July".[11] In addition to these "sentiments", which gradually were translated into political action, Nasser refers to "experiences" (*tajārib*). These consisted of his participation in political demonstrations during the 1930s and membership in certain organisations as his subsequent frequent eliptical allusions suggest. An integral part of these "experiences" were his active service in the Palestine War, his contacts with like-minded brother officers who participated in the anti-British campaign during the Second World War under the inspiration and preceptorship of General Aziz Ali al-Masri, General Saleh Harb Pasha, later of the Young Men's Muslim Association (YMMA), and Ali Maher Pasha, "the strong man of Egyptian politics, of the Atatürkish style".

One infers from these admissions that the Free Officers had no common political ideology. Rather Nasser and his army colleagues shared certain "sentiments" which propelled them towards vague hopes, such as the one of ridding Egypt of the British connection, or of co-operation with Arab states and Egyptian leadership of them once the colonial powers had retreated from the Middle East. Similarly, they shared certain "experiences" within the framework of political events in Egypt which ultimately pushed them to revolt by mounting a *coup d'état*.

Neither the "sentiments" nor the "experiences" undergone by Nasser and his generation of fellow-officers were acquired in a vacuum. These were of a dual provenance: first, the general political mood of Egypt and some Arab states in the decade 1933–43, and the social and economic conditions which helped to produce it; and second, the specific political movements and organisations which were active in that period and later.

Nasser, for instance, asserts, "I have believed in soldiering (*al-jundiyya*) all my life." What he means by soldiering is not literally the life of the soldier. Rather he is referring to the notion of militancy in the national struggle, and his own participation in the political agitation of the 1930s. The term *jundiyya* itself, however, is of specific provenance. It was used primarily—perhaps exclusively—as will be recorded below, by one political group in the country, the Young Egypt Society.

A perusal of Young Egypt's earliest published statements of objectives and programmes in 1933, or when it was reconstituted into a party in 1938, or in its open letters addressed to King Faruq in July 1940, when it had transformed itself into yet another party, the National Islamic Party, or later in 1949/50 when it presented itself as the Socialist Party, suggests a vanguard role for the *jundiyya*, or militant Egyptian youth, in the struggle against Britain, the *status quo*, and for the restoration of national glory. The party's constitution and organisational manifestoes clearly describe its members as "soldiers of Egypt", and militarism as the

party's preferred system and style for strengthening the youth's determination in their struggle to realize the party's objectives [*viz*. independence], an Egyptian empire comprising Egypt and the Sudan, a powerful national army, social justice deriving from agrarian reform, industrialization and Egyptianization, a high dam at Aswan, cooperation and solidarity with the Arab countries, and Egypt's inevitable leadership of the Islamic world . . .[12]

In his own tract, Nasser repeatedly reminds his readers that 23 July was not an isolated incident, but the successful culmination of several Egyptian attempts at national liberation that failed in the past. It is "the fulfilment of a hope which the people of Egypt nurtured ever since, in the modern period, it began to think of self-determination and self-rule." Such was the attempt "the day Omar Makram led the popular movement to make Muhammad Ali the Great Governor of Egypt (1804–5) . . ., the day Orabi demanded a constitution in 1881–2 . . . , . . . the 1919 revolt led by Saad Zaghlul . . ."

He also rejects as real causes of the 1952 revolution the Palestine War, or the defective arms scandal, or the Officers' Club elections in 1951. Nasser insists "the matter was more complicated and due to deeper causes." The Officers' Club elections, the Palestine War, the arms scandal and the King's disgraceful behaviour in the years from 1948 to 1952 were all factors which speeded up the military *coup*. Yet Nasser reminds his readers the seeds of revolt go further back in time. Nasser wrote,

> The day I discovered in myself the seeds of revolt is earlier than the 4 February 1942 palace incident,[13] about which I wrote a friend at the time; 'What is to be done now that this has happened and we accepted it with surrender and servility? The truth of the matter is that I believe colonialism has one card in its hand with which it threatens us. But if it felt that some Egyptians intend to sacrifice their lives and face force with force it would retreat like a prostitute.'[14]

So that February 1942, which symbolised the humiliation of the Egyptian crown by Britain and, by implication, constituted the greatest insult to the national honour and dignity of all Egyptians, according to Nasser, had a lasting impact on his generation of army officers. It imbued them with a new purpose and determination. "This stab", Nasser wrote, "restored the spirit to some bodies. It made them realize there is a dignity to be retrieved and defended . . ."

> But even this day [in February] is more distant in my life than the excitement I experienced when I was a student participating in the demonstrations demanding the restoration of the 1923 Constitution in 1932 [*sic:* 1933–5] . . . of the days when I visited with student delegations the homes of leaders asking them to unite for Egypt's sake [referring to the call for a National Front of Egyptian opposition parties in 1935, when he led the Young Egypt Society branch in Bab al-Sha'riyya].

Nasser recalls that on 2 September 1935, in connection with these events, he wrote to a friend, "The house of despair has strong foundations. Where are those who can demolish it?" But he also states, "the seeds of rebellion were not in me alone; I found them especially in the depths of many others . . ."[15]

Nevertheless, Nasser explains in his tract, these seeds of revolt were no more than "sentiments", not clear ideas strengthened by "experiences". His generation of youth "dreamt of a strong liberated Egypt". At one stage, they considered the best way to this objective to be that of "political enthusiasm", and "I led demonstrations while a pupil in Nahda School." Later on,

> I confess . . . I considered political assassination a fruitful means for the attainment of our ends . . . By the end of the Second World War and shortly before it . . . *we moved, as a generation in its entirety moved, towards the adoption of violence.*[16]

"Our life", he recalled, "in that period resembled an exciting detective story. We harboured great secrets, concocted code-words, and hid in the dark, stashing away revolvers next to grenades."

Clearly, these fantasies of violent, apocalyptic action to deliver Egypt of its oppressors were in the context of the time's ever-spreading use of violence for political ends. But Nasser admits, "I felt confused, I was perplexed . . ." His nationalist feelings remained ambivalent, confused with religious faith; mercy was mixed with ruthlessness. Interestingly, though, he explains his obsession to do something, his drive for power, and justifies the use of violence to attain national objectives by saying, "My motives were for the sake of my country."

In short, there is in Nasser's tract a glimpse of his and his colleagues' early political formation in that period of violent politics, when relations with Britain were difficult, when the polarisation between the older generation of rulers and political leaders on one hand and a younger one of aspiring Egyptians on the other was occurring. The sharper the polarity the more intense became the feeling against the British, the foreigners and the régime. The antagonism between the establishment, the governing élite of the country and those who desired a greater say in the conduct of public affairs was, by 1945, explosive. The latter group represented a new generation that grew up shouting the slogan, "O dear God, the devil take the English." Thus, the reason Nasser gives in his tract for being unable to discuss the "philosophy of the revolution" in abstract terms is because "I was, myself, in the violent mainstream of the revolution."

The intersection between historic events and life histories is one of the most controversial concerns of political history and biography. But it may well have something to contribute in interpreting the confusion and ambivalence Nasser surveys in his tract. One could ascribe it generally to a crisis of ego-identity, "that critical moment in a young person's life". The tensions in Egyptian life were, in the 1930s, heightened by rapid change at a time of economic difficulty, social dislocation, political turmoil and cultural ambivalence.[17] One could also argue that this crisis of identity was shared by a significant section of Nasser's contemporaries; that is, by those constituting the "generation" that came to power in 1952, or that became dominant in the affairs of post-monarchy Egypt. It was even more widely shared by their contemporaries in other Arab countries, as has already been suggested. What Nasser and his Baathist rivals referred to in the mid-1950s as *masir al-umma*, "the destiny of the Arab Nation", was perhaps an expression of their search for a symbiosis between a personal and cultural identity. The one radicalised them as individuals and pushed them into secret, conspiratorial and violent political activities; the other impelled them to reject the "past" with all its domestic and foreign connections and associations.

The ideological unrest which Nasser expressed at that time of his life was not unrelated to the strained relations with his family, especially his father, and his uncertainty over his post-school plans. Membership in a movement passionately concerned with Egyptianity, religious morality and political power was not therefore extraordinary, for it allowed a symbiosis between Nasser's youth crisis and events in Egypt. The anxiety over post-school plans also reflected Nasser's identity crisis. Events and the political radicalism of the thirties in Egypt became a source of attractive ideologies and alternative formulae of political salvation for those seeking a resolution of their problems that derived in part from their identity crisis. The Young Egypt Society, the Muslim Brethren and the other diverse student organisations were particularly attractive to a sensitive and ambitious youth like Nasser, who had no plan of his own.

Ideologies provided by the Young Egypt Society or the Muslim Brethren offered members of Nasser's age group what Erik Erikson called "overly simplified yet determined answers to exactly those vague inner states, and those urgent questions which arise in consequence of identity conflict."[18] The medium of salvation for Ahmad Hussein, co-founder and president of Young Egypt, as we shall see below, was acting. Having failed twice to train for a career in the theatre, he opted for politics via law school. Hussein, incidentally, was despondent over this turn in his fortunes and, at one point, near utter despair. *He feared he might be nothing.* The intensity and passion with which he immersed himself in political activity while a law student attests to this fear. But it helped him create a world of his own in which he lived and acted most of his life. He devoted his life to reshaping the minds of his young contemporaries.[19]

Nasser's salvation lay in an army career, which provided as much a make-believe identity as Ahmad Hussein's paramilitary Young Egypt Society. Furthermore, an army commission placed him a notch above his unattractive father on the social ladder. His adolescent estrangement from the normal pattern of society in the early 1930s and from his father was overcome in the new avenue of rejuvenation, the radical Young Egypt Society, which also expanded his national consciousness as an Egyptian. Together with military academy later, it helped him reconstitute and restructure his ego-identity. The motivation for a military career, though, is more complex. Many of Nasser's generation sought an army career for very practical reasons of material security, social prestige and possible political involvement—in that order.

It is interesting to note that at one point in the crisis Nasser too almost surrendered. Failing to secure a place both in the military and police academies in 1936, he joined briefly Cairo University's law school. The moment there was a second chance to enter military academy, however, he grabbed it eagerly, suggesting a deep need to identify with an institution characterised by discipline, force and dominant-subordinate hierarchical relations. Yet neither membership in Young Egypt nor training in military academy seemed to shake Nasser's desire for privacy and anonymity, attributes which remained pronounced in his personality until 1952–3. It suggests a compulsive character, with a tenacious concentration on the means to a practical end, and the realisation of a consuming ambition.

The crisis, however, was not only Nasser's. It was a widespread, if not common, one among all his contemporaries. They felt the need for a system of ideas that could provide a convincing alternative *Weltanschauung*. The identity problem of Egyptian youth in the thirties was not only related to their ideological needs, but also to their sexual anxieties in a still segregated society. The problem is particularly well expressed and reflected in Egyptian fiction, especially the writings of Tawfiq al-Hakim and Naguib Mahfuz. These depict the changing tastes and life-styles of a particular class, the lower bourgeoisie, to which Nasser and most of his fellow army officers belonged.[20] Ahmad Hussein's Young Egypt Society, the Muslim Brethren and later the diverse Marxist groups on the left provided some of the political foundations and direction for the change.

If Nasser then reflects the biography of his age, his generation, with its anxieties, fears, hopes and conflicts, his political portrait becomes relevant. His egoism and will converged with wider communal desires and aspirations, so that he mirrored the age he belonged to. He and his associates emerged in 1952 from anonymity and turned on an older Egyptian political world that had for long ignored or rejected them, and whose representatives they no longer accepted as the rightful rulers of their country. Young Egypt attracted them in part because of its leader's grandiose schemes: the High Dam at Aswan, industrialisation, the nationalisation of the Suez Canal, agrarian reform, the redistribution of wealth, complete independence from Britain. The petite bourgeoisie of Cairo and Alexandria had been on the skids ever since the Great Depression and through the Second World War. Nasser, like Ahmad Hussein before him, could communicate with them on a level of common distress, despair, despondency and aspiration, share and shoulder everyone's hopelessness. The vast majority of Egyptians were "hicks, and he was a hick, and who did anything for a hick but another hick," to use Huey Long's favourite slogan in the Louisiana of the 1920s. He promised them dignity, self-respect —and revenge.

The years from 1933 to 1936 constitute, then, a watershed in recent Egyptian history. Student groups, as already noted, became an identifiable, pliable political group. Their political indoctrination and formation was fed by the epic writings of Mahmud Abbas al-'Aqqad about the heroes of Islamic history, by the national Pharaonic mythopoeia of Tawfiq al-Hakim, and the rhetoric of Ahmad Hussein. The last emphasised the need to make Egypt great again and denigrated despair: all Egyptian youth can become heroes who will change things. The only serious attempt to divorce Egyptian politics from the broader Islamic tradition of society by Ismail

Sidqi (1930–3) ended in autocracy, and provoked a thunderous return to a native, Islamic and populist idiom, first introduced by the massive Wafd, later developed by the Muslim Brethren and Young Egypt, and finally perfected by Nasser.

The Young Egypt Society was where Nasser received his early political education. It seems clear he joined in 1934 or 1935 when he was a pupil at Nahda School. "In these formative years", Nasser reminisced in his address to the opening session of the National Assembly on 22 July 1957, "all the political parties working for the liberation of the Egyptian people interested me. I joined Misr al-Fatat, but I left it later after I realized that, despite its aims, it was not achieving anything definite." But he remained attracted to its economic and social reform programme, including the demand for the nationalisation of the Suez Canal.[21] He was still listed as a member of the Society in 1938 in the reports of the political police investigating the attempt on the life of Nahas Pasha, leader of the Wafd, by Young Egypt member 'Izz al-Din Abd al-Qadir, on 28 November 1937. A consecutively numbered roster in the High Court Dossier 143/1938 lists Gamal Abdel Nasser Hussein as member number 20. His address is given as "The Post Office, Khamis al-'Ads, Khoronfish" (Cairo), where Uncle Khalil, with whom Nasser lived as a schoolboy, resided. Other members listed in the file include Muhammad Anwar el Sadat, Hassan 'Izzat and Wagih Abaza, all of them Free Officers, and all entrants to the military academy in 1937.

The popular and widely accepted story about Nasser's entry into the academy is that on his first application he was turned down by the Entrance Board as unsuitable on social grounds. It is also believed that on his second application influential friends interceded on his behalf and he gained a place. It should be noted, however, that both of Nasser's applications for a place in the academy were submitted when the popular Wafd, with its liberal policies, was in power; so that the matter of which party controlled the government does not arise. What is less widely known though, and which may have some bearing on Nasser's application, is the fact that Young Egypt had been trying, ever since its foundation in 1933, to secure places in the academy for some of its younger members.

Gamal Abdel Nasser was one of the first cadets to enter the

Military College, influenced by our teachings. It is possible he already had ambitious political plans . . . Among members of the RCC in July 1952, were Hasan Ibrahim, a Young Egypt member from Alexandria, Anwar Sadat who was in continuous touch with Young Egypt throughout his long political struggle with our member Hasan 'Izzat, and Gamal Abdel Nasser who was a Green shirt . . .[22]

The Executive Committee of Young Egypt, known as the "Council of Jihad", listed among its advisers and financial backers such prominent Egyptian politicians as Ali Maher, Muhammad Ali Alluba, Abdel Rahman 'Azzam, Baheiddin Barakat, Abdel Salam al-Shazli, General Saleh Harb, Mustafa Shorbaji and others. General Aziz Ali al-Masri, a close associate of Ali Maher, later Inspector-General and Army Chief of Staff, was listed as Honorary President of the Society. Ahmad Hussein, President of the Society, was throughout his political career in close touch with Ali Maher, while Generals Masri and Harb, staunchly conservative and anti-British, enjoyed some influence in the Egyptian army.[23]

In the first published statement of 21 October 1933, outlining the Society's programme and objectives, as well as in his other writings, Ahmad Hussein consistently called for the wider militarisation of society and urged young Egyptians to join the army. Then, on 24 January 1934, he published in the Society's newspaper, *Al-Sarkha* (No. 17), an open letter to the Minister of War, attacking the army's organisation and its control by the British who wished it to remain weak. He demanded the reduction of the term of military service from five years to one year so that more Egyptians could join. He also attached a petition to his letter signed by 50 young men indicating their readiness to join the army. This particular article led to his arrest and trial in April 1934.[24]

From Hussein's other writings too it is clear the Society was anxious to secure places for its members in the military academy.[25] The Society's executive council was interested in infiltrating the officer corps with a view to recruiting more members. Ali Maher, in the Palace, for his part, was equally anxious to use the Society and its military members in his struggle against the Wafd. His closest collaborators to this end were General Masri and General Saleh Harb. The Society solicited the assistance of all three in the selection of some of its members for places in the military academy. In 1937,

four Society members, Nasser, Sadat, 'Izzat and Abaza, secured
places in the academy, regardless of whether they did so as a result
of the Society's efforts or not.[26]

Nasser and his colleagues, therefore, did not begin their military
careers without any commitments or political notions. Hassan
'Izzat's and Anwar Sadat's subsequent chequered careers as serving
officers in the period from 1939 to 1942 may have been more
impulsive, adventurous, audacious and troublesome—even criminal
—than Nasser's.[27] The fact remains that after 1945 the old strands
of common aims, common hatreds and militancy inspired by Young
Egypt came together once again. They may have evolved in a somewhat different direction and form, culminating in the July 1952 *coup*.
But many of the objectives and perceptions, much of the political
idiom and style first articulated and developed by Young Egypt were
retained.

In addition to the information about the political situation in Egypt
in the decade 1933–43 which can be gleaned from official British
despatches, especially those relating to youth and student movements,[28] the founder and leader of Young Egypt himself has written
a great deal between that time and 1971. What is uncanny about his
writings is the astounding similarity in style, argument, idiom and
preoccupation between his movement and that of the Free Officers,
including Nasser's own utterances in later years.

Without suggesting that Nasser and his fellow-officers who
acceded to power in 1952 acquired all their political ideas and lifted
all their policies from Young Egypt, their view of power and their
approach to it, their attitude and policies towards the British, Europe
or the West, the Arab Middle East and the world, as well as their
perception of the Egyptian national problem and their remedy for it
all appear, upon careful examination, too close to those of Young
Egypt for the connection to be lightly dismissed as conjecture, or
over-reading. Moreover, the fears, sentiments, fantasies and heroic
conception of the political regeneration of Egypt, expressed by
Nasser and represented by his conspiracy and early days of his
régime are akin to those articulated by Ahmad Hussein in his earliest
writings and political activities over forty years. Or, again, how can
one ignore, let alone dismiss, the fact that many of the prominent
members of Young Egypt came to occupy, after 1952, senior posts
in the military régime's administration.[29]

As the military conspiracy underwent its evolution in various stages between 1939 and 1952, its leading participants, especially in the air force, happened to be Young Egypt members. There is ample evidence of the close links between the Nasser generation of army officers and the Young Egypt Society, for one not to consider the ideological, political and national influence of the latter on the former. This is not to say that after 1945 the military rebels did not forge new links with other groups, such as the Muslim Brethren and the Marxists (HADETU especially), or the so-called Vanguard of the Wafd (*Al-tali'a al-wafdiyya*), as well as other of the older political parties. On the whole, however, the longest, closest and most important connection was the one with the ultra-nationalist-Muslim, anti-British Young Egypt Society, the Muslim Brethren and the National Party.

Whether one is seeking antecedents to Nasser's Arab nationalism, Arab or revolutionary socialism, agrarian reform, rural co-operative schemes, industrialisation, Egyptianisation-nationalisation policies, the creation of a powerful national army, the abolition of privilege and class differences; or his ideal of free higher education for all, one may find them in the lifetime writings of Ahmad Hussein. Similarly, the intricate involvement of individual army officers in the assassination and bombing campaigns of the years from 1944 to 1952, organised and led by Young Egypt members, the Muslim Brethren and National Party, is further proof of the links between the Society and the army conspiracy. [30] Ahmad Hussein's vitriolic articles in 1951 and 1952, calling openly for the overthrow of the régime, were the most vehement manifestations of the campaign by all opposition groups in the country, including the Free Officers with their clandestine pamphlets and tracts, against the then rulers of Egypt.

Ahmad Hussein in a way was the prototype of the angry Egyptian youth that rebelled against the *status quo* in the early 1930s. To be sure, he and his movement were subvented and manipulated by that secretive, curious strong man of Egyptian politics, Ali Maher, and other known anti-British politicians of the time for their own purposes. The fact remains that when he was Prime Minister in 1939–40, Ali Maher was pro-Axis; so was the Army Chief of Staff General Masri, and both were considered by the Young Egypt Society and its young army officer members and sympathisers as mentors and protectors. Masri became involved in plain anti-Allied espionage and sabotage activities in the years from 1940 to 1942. It is therefore important for an appreciation of the sources of

Nasser's and his generation's political attitudes and aspirations to examine at some length the Ahmad Hussein episode, the phenomenon of the new radicalism, or radical romanticism, in recent Egyptian political history, as this was expressed in his movement and that of the Muslim Brethren.

Notes

1. Muhammad Subeih, *Ayyam wa ayyam*, 1882–1956 (*Days and days*) (Cairo, 1966), p.252.
2. Ibid., p.255.
3. Ibid., p.442.
4. Ibid., p.442–3.
5. Published by the Fuad Press, Cairo; copy in Abdin Palace Archives, Cairo.
6. Executed by the Lebanese government in 1949. On his party generally, see Labib Zuwiyya Yamak, *The Syrian Social Nationalist Party, an ideological analysis* (Cambridge, Mass., 1966). See also his own *Mabādi' al-hizb* (*The principles of the Syrian Nationalist Party*), 2nd English ed. (Beirut, 1949); *Al-muhādarāt al-'ashar* (*The ten lectures*), 3rd ed. (Beirut, 1956); and his theory on the rise of nations, *Nushū' al-umam* (Beirut, 1928), 2nd ed., 1951.
7. On his links with the early Baath party, see Sami al-Jundi, *Al-Baath* (*The Baath*) (Beirut, 1969), and his own *Baath al-umma al-arabiyya wa risālatuha ilā āl-'ālam* (*The resurrection of the Arab nation and its message to the world*) (Damascus, n.d.), *Mashākiluna al-ijtimā'iyya wa mawqif al-ahzāb minha* (*Our social problems and the attitude of the political parties towards them*) (Damascus, 1956), and *Al-umma al-arabiyya, māhiyatuha, risālatuha, mashākiluha* (*The Arab nation, its nature, mission and problems*) (Damascus, 1958). See also the perceptive despatch on pan-Arabism by Consul General Gilbert Mackereth in Damascus to Anthony Eden, 15 May 1936, FO 371/19980 (E3039/381/65).
8. Al-Karkh Press.
9. On the Wafd's Blue Shirts youth organisation, see Kelly to Eden, 31 August 1937, FO 371/20885, and J. P. Jankowski, "The Egyptian Blue Shirts and the Egyptian Wafd, 1935–1938", *Middle Eastern Studies*, Vol.6, No.1, January 1970, pp.77–95.
10. Anwar al-Sadat, *Qissat al-thawra kāmila* (English translation, *Revolt on the Nile*) (New York, 1957); *Hāda 'ammak Gamal* (*This is your uncle Gamal*) (Cairo, 1963); and *Al-thawra al-misriyya, asraruha al-khafiyya wa asbābuha al-bsīkolojiyya* (*The Egyptian revolution, its hidden secrets and psychological causes*) (Cairo, 1965). Another version of the story of Sadat's activities in the thirties and forties was published in *al-Musawwar*, Cairo weekly magazine, No.2529, 30 March 1973, pp.8–10. See also Kamal al-Din Rifaat, *Harb al-tahrīr al-wataniyya, mudhakkirāt Kamal al-Din Rifaat* (*The war of national liberation, the memoirs of Kamal al-Din Rifaat*), edited by Mustafa Tibah (Cairo, 1968), and Rifaat's reminiscences in an autobiographical interview in Abd al-Tawwab Abd al-Hayy, *'Asīr hayāti* (*Résumé of my life*) (Cairo, 1966); Tāriq al-Bishri, *Al-haraka al-siyasiyya fi misr, 1945–1952* (*The political movement in Egypt, 1945–1952*) (Cairo, 1971); and Muhammad Subeih, *Batal la nansāhu, Aziz al-Masri wa 'asruhu* (*A hero we shall not forget, Aziz al-Masri and his age*) (Beirut, 1971). Writing about the secret officer cabals in the forties under the inspiration of General Aziz al-Masri, Subeih refers to a book by the Muslim Brother Wasim Khalid, *Al-kifah*

al-sirri didd al-ingliz (*The secret struggle against the English*), a preface for which was written by Anwar Sadat. Wasim Khalid was, it seems, involved in the assassination of Amin Osman in January 1946. See Khalid, *Al-kifah al-sirri*, pp.280–1.

11. All quotations are from Nasser's Arabic original, *Falsafat al-thawra* (*Philosophy of the revolution*) tract, published by the Department of Information (Cairo, 1954). See English text also published by the Department of Information, and the glossier edition prepared by the Egyptian Embassy in Washington, published in 1955 with an introduction by Dorothy Thompson.

12. Incorporated and reproduced in Ahmad Hussein, *Īmānī* (*My faith*) (Cairo, 1936, 1946), pp.89–92 and 64–71; also to be found in *al-Tali'a* (Cairo), Vol.1, March 1965, pp.155–7. First programme and principles also in National Archives (Cairo, 1933); reiterated in 1938 when the Society became a political party, and in a letter to Faruq dated 18 March 1940 and a threat to pro-British politicians dated 22 June 1940, both in the National Archives, Cairo.

13. A reference to the episode when the British Ambassador in Cairo, Sir Miles Lampson, after issuing an ultimatum to King Faruq demanding the return to power of a Wafd government which the King ignored, marched into Abdin Palace backed up by troops and armour to demand Faruq's abdication. See an Egyptian version of the incident by Muhammad Anis, *Arbaa febrāyir 1942 fi tarikh misr al-siyāsi* (*4 February 1942 in the political history of Egypt*) (Beirut, 1972), and cf. Gabriel Warburg, "Lampson's ultimatum to Faruq, 4 February 1942," *Middle Eastern Studies*, Vol.11, No. 1,pp.24–32.

14. Also reproduced in Abdel Qadir al-Bindari and Najib Elias Barsum, *Thawrat al-hurriyya* (*The revolution of freedom*) (Cairo, 1961), p.47, and Abdel Moneim Shumais, *Al-za'im al-thā'ir* (*The rebel leader*) (Cairo, n.d.), p.20.

15. See also Shumais, *Al-za'im*, pp.14–15.

16. Emphasis added.

17. See generally Anouar Abdel Malek, *Egypt, military society* (New York, 1968), and P. J. Vatikiotis, *The Modern History of Egypt* (London, 1969 and 1976).

18. *Young Man Luther* (London, 1959), p.39, quoting an earlier article by him on "The Problem of Ego Identity".

19. Ahmad Hussein, *Imani*, pp.45–51.

20. See Tawfiq al-Hakim, '*Awdat al-rūh* (*Return of the soul*), 2 vols., first published in Cairo 1933, and Naguib Mahfuz's Trilogy: *Al-sukkariyya, Bayn al-qasrein*, and *Qasr al-shawq* (Cairo, 1956–7). See the full-length study on Naguib Mahfuz by Sasson Somekh, *The Changing Rhythm* (Leiden, 1973).

21. *Al-mawsū'a al-nāsiriyya* (*The Nasser encyclopedia*), Vol.1 (Beirut, 1973), p.112; see also pp.112–14.

22. Ahmad Hussein in a written answer to questions submitted by Mr. H. . Kopietz of the School of Oriental and African Studies, University of London, dated Cairo, 19 February 1973.

23. General Saleh Harb served as Minister of National Defence in Ali Maher's government of 18 August 1939 to 22 June 1940. He later became president of the Young Men's Muslim Association and was active in the Palestine conflict in 1947–9. On General Aziz Ali al-Masri, see FO371/19076 and 21396; Majid Khadduri, "Aziz Ali al-Masri and the Arab nationalist movement" in Albert Hourani (ed.), *Middle Eastern Affairs* (St Antony's Papers No. 17), London, 1965, pp. 140–63; and Subeih, *Batal la nansāhu*. See also Ahmad Hussein, "Aziz Ali al-Masri kama 'araftuhu" ("Aziz Ali al-Masri as I knew him"), *al-Gumhuriyya* newspaper, Cairo, 1 July 1965,

p. 8; Fathi Radwan, *Qabil al-fajr* (*At the break of dawn*) (Cairo, 1957); and A. Sansom, *I Spied Spies* (London, 1965).

24. Hussein, *Imani*, pp. 97–8.
25. See *Nisf qarn ma' al-'uruba wa qadiyyat filastin* (*Half a century with Arabism and the Palestine Cause*) (Saida, 1971), and *Kaifa 'araftu Abdel Nasser . . .*
26. Entry to the military academy was liberalised by the Wafd party that had returned to power with great popular support and had signed the Anglo–Egyptian treaty in August 1936. But it is also reported that in order to allow the easier entry into the academy of the sons of its party stalwarts and supporters in the provinces, i.e. village headmen and others, the Wafd made a deal with some of the leading conservative politicians such as Ali Maher, Saleh Harb and others which allowed some of their protégés from among the youth of the National party, the Young Egypt Society and the Muslim Brethren to enter the academy too. Although the report sounds plausible enough within the general context of political horse-trading in those days, I have not been able to locate any substantial documentary evidence about it.
27. See Chapters 3 to 5 below.
28. See Chapters 1 and 3.
29. Fathi Radwan, who became Minister of State and at one time Minister of Communications and Culture and National Guidance, was the most prominent among them, even though he had left Young Egypt sometime between 1943 and 1945 to join the National party. Among others were Major Wahid Ramadan, leader of the Youth Organisation in 1953, and Lieutenant-Colonel Ahmad Subeih, Director of Organisation for the Liberation Rally in 1953. Dr Hilmi Bahgat Badawi, brother of Free Officer and ex-Young Egypt member Mustafa Bahgat Badawi, for example, was involved in the plans for the nationalisation of the Suez Canal as early as 1954. See Subeih, *Batal la nansahu*, pp. 482–3. In the sixties Dr Hilmi Murad became Minister of Education. On the other hand, many other members of Young Egypt were imprisoned by the Nasser régime.
30. See Chapters 3 to 6 below. See also Subeih, *Batal la nansahu*, and Kamal al-Din Rifaat, *Harb al-tahrir al-wataniyya*.

CHAPTER 3

The Young Egypt Society

There are men who are by nature mirrors of what surrounds them. Jacob Burckhardt, *The Civilization of the Renaissance in Italy.*

In his *Half a Century with Arabism* (*Niṣf qarn maʿal-ʿurūba*), published in Saida in 1971, Ahmad Hussein refers to the early period of the Society, 1933–5, during which many of its members were imprisoned by the authorities for one reason or another. "It is during this period", he states, "that Gamal Abdel Nasser joined the Young Egypt Society, as he himself has said subsequently, mentioning that it was his first school in public life".[1] In his first book, *My Faith* (*Īmānī*), published in Cairo in 1936, Hussein reproduces a list of members arrested by the government for their political activities in Young Egypt in the period from October 1933 to October 1934, under the heading: "Page of glory and pride of Young Egypt's soldiers: fifty enter prison in a year, and hundreds of others have their homes searched and their persons interrogated by the state authorities." The forty-eighth on that list is a "Gamal al-Din Nasser". It could well have been Nasser.[2] It was common among Egyptians of that age (16–17) to give the simplest rendition of their name: first name and father's first name. Later in life, many adopted a fuller appellation by adding the father's second name.

Hussein's *Īmānī* is a crucial document for an appreciation of the personal and social difficulties faced by Nasser's generation. Hussein dedicates his book to "the symbol of the new generation and vanguard of glory, Faruq". The slogan of the Society is "Allah, Fatherland, King". A frontispiece photograph of the author in full dress uniform of the Young Egypt Society—green shirt, khaki breeches with boots and shoulder strap—is impressive for its look of vitality and purposefulness. Hussein, incidentally, throughout the book uses the terms belief, faith, creed, ideology interchangeably, all of them subsumed under the emotive word *Īmānī*.

At the very outset, Hussein suggests that his fervent Egyptian
nationalism was the result of his "conversion" during a scouting
trip to Upper Egypt—Valley of Kings and Karnak in Luxor, the
then Aswan Dam and Komombo.[3] He calls upon fanatic nationalism
to revive Egypt by an appeal to its Pharaonic civilisation. His simple
argument is, if our ancestors were able to attain such a great civilisation and immense power, then we can achieve the same. What was
needed was knowledge, militant organisation, inspiration and strong
sentiment. "I felt reborn," he wrote, "[that day in December 1928]
marked the transformation in myself and my entry into a new world
. . . I fell in love with Egypt . . . Life was meaningless without dignity,
patriotism and self-respect."[4] This was to become a familiar and
favourite incantation of Nasser's when in power: "*al-izza wa'l-
karāma*, self-respect and dignity".

Hussein then drew inspiration for patriotic action from the
preserved, the mummified past. He was filled with notions of
greatness and power. He imagined the military victories of an
Egyptian imperium of old, and believed these could be repeated in
the twentieth century. A touch of delusion, nostalgia for power,
riches and greatness became the key to the resolution of Hussein's
crisis of youth—and identity. Fantasy and the evocation of sentiment
were to become the trade marks of his political career. So were mass
rallies of uniformed, paramilitary youth, bellowing patriotic anthems
to the glory of Egypt, saluting flags and eventually fomenting
rebellion.

Hussein's admission of a sudden Saul-type conversion on the way
to the Karnak and its impact on his extemporaneous oratorical
powers, however, must be considered in the light of his Thespian
activities in the Khedivial School. "I was keen on acting", he
ruminated, "and president of the drama society in the Khedivial
School. I was enamoured and enchanted by the theatre."[5] In the
Karnak, he claims, he was "resurrected", "and so must every
Egyptian youth." But what must they do in order to retrieve the
glorious past? They must have *faith* in Egypt and her potentialities.
Faith without a programme of action however was not enough, and
Hussein suggested one which, in retrospect, is similar in its general
outline to the programme of the Free Officers. A High Dam at
Aswan to generate power for the industrialisation of Egypt was one
aim, for example. But Britain had demoralised the Egyptians and
cast doubts over their capabilities. "I returned from my visit to
Aswan full of anger towards the British occupation and our weak

governments, thinking of all Egypt could really be ... in the future."[6]

During his visit to the sugar plantations in Komombo Hussein was equally exercised by the foreign company's monopoly of that industry. He called it a

> foreign colony, a state within the state which enslaved thousands of fellahin ... They own everything ... even the land, which is our property and which we have cultivated for thousands of years ... Under the occupation and capitulations the foreigners know how to conscript us to their service ... Why should [the land] not be distributed to the poor peasants ... Why should these peasants work for the foreigners?[7]

On this occasion, too, Hussein addressed his mates extemporaneously with a violent harangue against foreigners, and exhorted them to fight for the liberation of the fatherland. Like Nasser, twenty years later, it was important for Hussein to discover he was an orator.

All these were sentiments and perceptions that were shared by Nasser and his generation: the revival of the glory of Egypt, the liberation from the British connection, the improvement of the life of the peasant through agrarian reform and a more equitable distribution of wealth, and industrialisation. Similarly, Hussein's call to all Egyptian youth to become familiar with their country's history and culture—the glorious past—was not simply a counter to European influence. It became the premise of a political renaissance, "so that they do not grow up believing there is no more to life than food, drink and sleep".[8]

Hussein, like Nasser and the Free Officers after him, was groping for ways to promote patriotism among the youth and raise their morale; to release their latent energy and power. Clearly, Hussein, like his acolytes and admirers later, could only direct his efforts towards the new generation. Hence the Green Shirts organisation, whose primary purpose was to teach youth how to love their country, and have faith in its greatness. The impact of paramilitary life, with its anthems and parades, would presumably help to resurrect the nation.

Ahmad Hussein's life history throws light on the personal crises faced by Nasser and his generation. It helps explain some of their predilections, prejudices and perceptions. Ahmad was born in Cairo in March 1911, just short of seven years before Nasser. His earliest schooling was in the Islamic charitable schools. At eight, in 1919, he had already heard about the exploits of the Germans in the First World War. He claims that at this early age he joined the demonstrations of the 1919 revolt in the Ibn Tahir mosque. But he was also given to fantasy, and his imagination was fertile when he conjured up air raids over the city. A temporary academic failure—he repeated the same year in elementary school three times—obliged his father to move him to a state school. There, in the Muhammad Ali School, he met Fathi Radwan, the man with whom he later entered law college, founded the Young Egypt Society and published its newspapers. Hussein claims that together they embarked upon their first ever political activity: they founded in school the "Society for the Triumph of Islam" for which they prepared and distributed leaflets. They were encouraged in this by their religious teacher, but stopped from further activity by the headmaster. At thirteen, in 1924, when Saad Zaghlul was Prime Minister, they went on strike in protest against the 28 February 1922 Declaration.[9]

This put an end to Young Ahmad's first excursion into social agitation. There now began a period in his school career when he was wholly occupied with his dramatic interests. He attended the rehearsals and performances of the Company for the Advancement of the Arabic Theatre, was greatly influenced by Hamlet and often acted the part at home in the privacy of his room. He was further influenced by Mahmud Murad who composed patriotic plays, operettas and musicals about Pharaonic themes, as for example, 'The Glory of Ramses', " . . . which resurrected the spirit and filled us with enthusiasm and power".[10] Murad had also written a play about Tutenkhamon, whose tomb had been discovered in 1922–4, and he was later a supporter of Young Egypt.

Ahmad Hussein states he joined the Khedivial School partly because it had the best dramatic group. He played the part of Ramses in Murad's Tutenkhamon play. With that, Hussein confesses, "I surrendered completely to the actor's vocation." By the third year in secondary school, Hussein asserted, "I did nothing else except act, and produced a play I wrote, *Abu Muslin al-Khurasani*."[11] Ahmad, however, decided to make a career in theatre. But his hopes in that direction were dashed. He failed twice to secure a place in the drama institute, and did not get a job with the Ramses Theatre. The trauma was shattering. "Failure was an affront to my dignity and I rebelled; I tended toward dissidence because acting was everything in my life."[12] As second best, he chose to do the Baccalaureat course and apply for a place in the law school.

Ahmad himself admits that his failure to gain admission into the drama institute marked a crossroads in his life. It constituted a turning-point. From acting in the theatre, he turned to acting on behalf of Egypt's liberation. He took on the school magazine and its debating society, and in his final year in school, 1927–8, he went on the scouting trip to Upper Egypt and to his "conversion". Henceforth, he was obsessed by one idea, "How to resurrect the glory of Egypt, and how to restore life to the country by transforming weakness into strength, despair into hope; in short, how to transform Egypt the serf into Egypt the mistress."[13]

Hussein read about Egyptian history and Islam, which,

in contrast to Christianity teaches power; and Egypt's central, leading position in it: she led the revolt against the third Caliph Othman, and quickly became independent—under Ibn Tulun ... I saw how Egypt was able to destroy all her conquerors and triumph over them at the end by transforming them into Egyptians in blood, flesh and thought.[14]

He found Muhammad Ali the Great (1905–49) most impressive, and admits to his having the greatest influence on his own historical perceptions. But he also realised that Muhammad Ali's imperial plans were frustrated by Britain. "Had it not been for the English, we would have had an empire." All of this embittered Hussein. He felt oppressed. But he also became determined to enlighten the younger generation about Egypt's glorious history.

While in law school, Hussein claims, he analysed the elements of weakness in contemporary Egypt, such as ignorance, and discovered a religious decadence deriving from these, as well as national degeneration. Other contributing factors to this state of affairs were the monopoly of foreigners over business and industry, and inflated bureaucracy, an inequitable distribution of wealth that left peasants very poor. But most deleterious of all was the British occupation and its control over Egyptian policy. At the same time, he was impressed by "the struggle of Italy" and urged Egyptians forward to action.[15]

In the last months of his secondary schooling, Hussein wrote a series of articles in the school magazine entitled "My Mission" (Vol.

8, No. 1, December 1928). "In them", he claims, "I sowed the first
seed of Young Egypt." Borrowing haphazardly from Nietzsche, he
argued that one theory prevailed in the world:

> the earth is the heritage of the strong, and the future belongs
> to the victorious people who have a right to life. The struggle
> for existence, that is, is also one for domination. Egypt will
> retrieve her ancient glory. Our duty, as students, is to construct
> a new country. Come let us erect our future greatness on a
> foundation of steel . . . Industry and commerce constitute the
> civilization of the twentieth century and spirit of modern nations
> . . . Let us preach the greatness, glory and history of Egypt. Let
> us support social, moral, cultural and economic innovation.[16]

A year later Hussein organised the "Society of Free Youth in
support of the Treaty" on the occasion of the 1928–9 Anglo–
Egyptian treaty negotiations, and found his first temporary political
patron, the then Prime Minister, the Liberal Muhammad Mahmud.
Hussein was perhaps well on his way to a political career. He called
on Egyptians to rise, and emphasised the need for a "leader of action,
who is not of Turkish or Circassian, but of Pharaonic blood".[17]
There is the implication here that so long as Egypt's rulers are not
native Egyptians, there is less of a chance for her development into a
great state. By March 1930, Hussein had published, with Fathi
Radwan, the first issue of *al-Sarkha* (*The Cry*) that was soon (in
1933) to become the organ of their Young Egypt Society.

Certain common ideas, preoccupations and values between
Hussein's youth movement and Nasser's generation are reflected in
the principles and programme of Young Egypt, published in 1933.
Among these, three are of particular interest. The Young Egyptian
was to scorn everything that is foreign and become a fanatic patriot.
His fatherland consisted of Egypt and the Sudan, united and
inseparable, allied to the Arab states. His aim was to make Egypt a
great state above all, and the leader of Islam. As for the purpose of
the Society's programme, it was to imbue youth with a martial
spirit. Moreover, it aimed at the nationalisation of all foreign
concerns by Egyptianising them; the introduction of agrarian reform
and establishment of co-operatives, the development of industry
and achievement of commercial autarky and free education for all;
combating vice and implementing military service, and the improve-

ment of public health. The means for the pursuit of these tasks was to be the potent mixture of faith and action.

The publication of the First Principles and Programme of the Young Egypt Society begins with a declaration of faith:

Egypt is at the centre of the Eastern World and the leader of Islam. It must be resurrected. The inflamed blood of youth is in need of faith and action. The task requires those who are prepared to die, suffer hardship and welcome sacrifice. These qualities cannot be found among the older generation. It is the youth, the new generation, soldiers of Young Egypt, upon whose shoulders falls the task of resurrecting our old glory. This is the faith of the Young Egypt Society.

The Society's programme and objectives are then enumerated:

Our slogan is God, Fatherland and King. Our objective is for Egypt to become . . . a great empire, comprising Egypt and the Sudan, allied to the Arab states, and leading the Muslim Community. Our overall struggle aims to put foreigners in their proper place as guests, not masters, of our country, and that by abolishing the Capitulations and Mixed Tribunals with the stroke of the pen, by the Egyptianisation of foreign companies and the making of Arabic the official language of commerce, and Friday the official day of rest, and the prohibition of foreigners to work in Egypt without special permission. [These demands were in the mainstream of Egyptian nationalism. Thus, the Capitulations were abolished by the Montreux Convention of 1937 on the heels of the 1936 Anglo–Egyptian Treaty; the Mixed Tribunals closed down in 1949; 1947 saw the beginning of the Egyptianisation of companies. Friday became the day of rest under the Free Officer régime.]

Our economic struggle aims at the expansion of arable land, the doubling of agricultural production, the extension of credit to farmers, the organization of co-operatives for the provision of fertilizer, seed, loans and farm machinery. In industry we aim to develop agricultural-based industries, chemicals and steel, and the generation of electricity from the Aswan Dam. In commerce we aspire to internal autarky and the control of export trade, the construction of a merchant navy, a transport infrastructure and a Central Bank for the issue of currency and the provision of capital. In education we intend to make higher education open to all, erect libraries and provide radio receiving sets in all the villages, and to organize a campaign for compulsory military service. In social legislation we seek the encouragement of savings and the establishment of state social insurance schemes.[18]

Without attributing any particular originality to Young Egypt, all of the above quoted aspects of its programme have a familiar ring. They are echoed in the Free Officers' and Nasser's own speeches and programme of reform twenty years later. There was agitation for a common struggle against Britain and the Egyptian régime in the intervening period. Links between Young Egypt and a number of Free Officers existed in the various underground army conspiracies in the period from 1938 to 1949.[19]

In 1939, Ahmad Hussein sent a letter to King Faruq in which he appealed to the monarch's youth as being crucial to the regeneration of Egypt and Islam. He complained of the loss of religious fervour, the dissolution of the family, the disorientation of the villager, the corruption in the city. As for the governing classes and their cohorts, "personal gain is their first and last aim," Hussein asserted. It is, he pointed out, futile to change ministries in succession. What is needed is to change values and principles by purifying Egyptian life on the basis of Islamic legislation and the recruitment of young men to the country's service. This is only possible if there were in Egypt a strong young government believing in God, confident in the rights of the fatherland and allowing no one to tamper with them.

A year later, Young Egypt changed its name to the National Islamic party. It submitted yet another letter to the King. The contents strike one as more ambitious, for by then the Muslim Brethren were gathering alarming strength, the war was close by in the Western Desert, Britain was at bay. The theme of youth recurs in this communication. In it Hussein deplores the failures of the older generation, and emphasises the need to strengthen the feeling of Egyptianity. But there is allusion to Egypt as the leader of an Arab bloc, because "the spirit that possesses the world today is that of struggle and conflict . . . the weak have no place in it . . . We cannot remain weak." The document goes on to suggest that power can be acquired only at the hands of the new generation. The new theme of Arab solidarity is introduced with a block of fifty million Arabs in mind, based on one religion, one culture, one language. Disunity amongst the Arabs is due to decadence and backwardness. Egypt is the natural leader of this bloc. The basis of strength in the new community is faith and law, and action against Europe. "Islam is the religion of dignity and strength." At the end of the communication, Hussein appeals to the King's pride in the achievements of his great ancestor, Muhammad Ali, and pleads for an end to foreign privileges. Above all, he pleads for the creation of a powerful army.

One notes here the evolution of the Society from its earlier insular, parochial Egyptian nationalist orientation to a wider Arab–Islamic preoccupation.

> Since our programme has evolved beyond the narrow limits of Egyptian nationalism, and as we believe that the basis of this nationalism to be Islam and its objectives the struggle to advance Islamic interests, we have added the word 'Islamic' to 'National' [statement in the communication regarding the change of the party's name].[20]

Now the party wishes to combat imperialism in all the Muslim lands, paramilitarise all public officials, and enact puritanical legislation. It demands a standing peacetime army of some 200,000 and a national armaments industry. It wants to close all foreign schools and provide free medical care and social insurance for all. It calls for the nationalisation of all foreign monopolies and the Suez Canal, and the prohibition of land ownership by foreigners. It urges the transformation of Egypt into an industrial country, the formation of an Arab alliance against imperialism in the region. It demands that Cairo acquire the most powerful broadcasting station in the world.

On 22 June 1940, on British insistence, the Ali Maher government was dismissed. With it also went General Masri, army chief of staff, Honorary President of Young Egypt, and one of its most ardent supporters. A pamphlet appeared, dated 5 July 1940, attributed to Young Egypt. It begins with the invocation, "Allah is with us: declaration of *jihad* against the English." The "quadrilateral leadership"—suspected to consist of Ahmad Hussein, Aziz Ali Masri, Ali Maher and Fathi Radwan—"of the Egyptian Islamic revolution declares in the name of God, the Fatherland and the King, war on the English and the traitors who support them."[21]

In fact, Young Egypt was protesting the dismissal of the Ali Maher government. But in declaring Holy War against the English, they also proclaimed a revolution. Among its objectives were "the reconstruction of Egyptian society on the basis of the redistribution of wealth . . . the raising of the standard of living of the working classes."[22] They also openly urged all army and police officers to actively promote this revolution. They called them to immediate action and required them to cease all co-operation with the British authorities and all those who served them; to impede and obstruct British army communications and supplies. Finally the Society issued a warning to those traitors who have disgraced and humiliated Islam and the Muslims, especially in Palestine. Equally, senior army officers who co-operated with the British Army were warned:

> We must point out to them that younger officers are looking out for them, and will deal with them if they dare tamper with this revolution, especially those responsible for the dismissal and exile of General Aziz Ali al-Masri. Politicians and careerists are similarly warned.[23]

Naturally, this kind of leaflet was prompted by the forcible retirement of the Ali Maher government and the dismissal of General Masri. Nor was it free of Italian endeavour to embarrass the British in Egypt in wartime. Yet the important fact remains that the tone and content of the memorandum to the King as well as the pamphlet reflect the attitudes and perceptions of disaffected youth, including the rebellious army officer generation of Nasser, who were confused by world events and ambivalent towards authority.

Eight years later, with the Muslim Brethren at the peak of their activity and height of their popularity, with the Palestine War on and anti-British sabotage operations in the Canal Zone in full swing, with the emergence of Soviet power and its corollary of heightened Communist activity in most countries, Ahmad Hussein changed yet again the name of his organisation to that of the Socialist Party of Egypt, and adapted its programme to meet new conditions. The old slogan, "Allah, Fatherland and King" was changed to "Allah, Fatherland, the People", in deference to a presumed class struggle and a mounting opposition to the monarchy. However, his socialism, Hussein insisted, derived from the heart of Islam and the core of its mission.[24] Still, the party's newspaper was re-named *Al-ishtirākiyya* (*Socialism*).

In its programme, the renamed party demanded the limitation of land ownership to 50 *feddans*. Landowners would be expropriated against long-term bond compensation and their land redistributed in five-*feddan* lots to peasant farmers, to be paid for in instalments. They sought the collectivisation of agricultural production, the nationalisation of industry and all public utilities. They proposed a social security scheme and the redistribution of wealth through graduated direct taxation on incomes and inherited wealth, as well as an incomes policy. One of its members, Ibrahim Shukri, was elected to Parliament on this platform in 1949. He introduced a Bill for agrarian reform, the abolition of titles and the organisation of peasant farmer and labour unions. [25]

There was a marked shift to the left in the party's external policy. Essentially, it retained the cardinal objective of the unity of the Nile Valley between Egypt and the Sudan. But it was now also for the unity of the Arab peoples under a "United Arab States". It rejected negotiation in principle as a means of attaining independence and the signing of treaties with imperialist states as well as joint defence agreements with them. It declared itself against the Atlantic Alliance and American imperialism that supported the British presence in Egypt. It demanded the immediate nationalisation of the Canal, and proclaimed its support for China over the Korean War. [26] This shift was most pronounced in Hussein's message to the Arab Socialist Congress in Lebanon in 1951 when the Egyptian delegate was prevented from attending by the Cairo government: "Capitalism, Imperialism and Reaction have ganged up on them [the Egyptian people] to rob them of their will and make them prisoners of ignorance, sickness and poverty . . . We are here to represent them". [27]

By 1951–2, Ahmad Hussein and his party were openly calling for the violent overthrow of the Egyptian régime. Streams of vitriolic articles poured forth from his pen as of May 1951 until the notorious Black Saturday burning of Cairo in January 1952. In these he developed the two stages of the so-called revolution: the struggle against the régime of "feudalists and capitalists" as an aspect of the struggle against imperialism. In this sense he also linked the struggle for national liberation with that of social justice, and defined Egyptian socialism in these terms. [28]

By that time the Wafdist Vanguard and all so-called progressive elements and groups called for similar action—the overthrow of the régime: *Al-malāyīn of HADETU, Al-jumhūr al-Masrī, Rose el-Youssef*, and *al-Kātib* of the Partisans of Peace.[29]

Though not wholly free of prodding by powerful politicians—Ali Maher, Saleh Harb, even the Palace—Ahmad Hussein, throughout his political career, remained consistent in his radical nationalist agitation. In fact, his view of Egyptian, Arab and international politics became progressively more radical with the passage of time. His Society, his party and their propaganda helped radicalise a whole generation of Egyptians, particularly some who were already, or later became, army officers, and who soon became involved in conspiracies against the *status quo* both within and outside the army. Such was the case of Anwar Sadat, Hassan Izzat, Wagih Abaza and others. Hussein helped them link the need to overthrow the régime and evict Britain from Egypt with the prospect of a leading role for Egypt in Arab and Middle Eastern affairs.

The British in Egypt were aware of these developments and their information about them was almost always accurate. Despatches from Cairo to the Foreign Office as early as July 1933 contain reports about the Young Egypt movement and its links with Egyptian politicians. An early *Sarkha* leaflet sent to the High Commissioner by post referred to "the catastrophe of the Suez Canal, the tragedy of the Mixed Courts, the stigma of the Capitulations, the separation of Jaghbub and the Sudan from Egypt, the farce of the Constitution and Parliament", all of which were considered links in the chain of conspiracy for the consolidation of British influence in the Nile Valley. Young Egypt no longer believed in British methods.[30]

Coinciding with a flurry of anti-missionary activity by the Young Men's Muslim Association and other groups, Young Egypt spread the belief about that "England is responsible for all our troubles," a slogan often repeated by Nasser twenty years later. Contrary to the advice of Sir Alex Keown-Boyd, Head of the European Department, Department of the Interior, the High Commissioner was convinced—and rightly so—that Palace forces, i.e. Ali Maher and King Fuad, were behind the Young Egypt Society.[31] By May 1934, Sir Miles Lampson was warning the Foreign Secretary about the potential danger of Young Egypt. He considered the movement "not important in itself . . .", but it "represents possible tendencies which will have to be watched". He felt the young in Egypt "may conceivably find in the Young Egypt Society political self-expression more satisfying to the realist, semi-Fascist mentality of the type of younger Nationalist devotee."[32]

During the Abyssinian crisis, the High Commissioner was reporting the Society's links with Italian agents, particularly Ugo Dadone of the *Giornale d'Oriente*. The sympathies of Palace men and newspaper publishers shown for the Society were also noted, as well as incipient links with Prince Abbas Halim's labour organisation. Hussein responded to Italian pressure and money by advocating Egypt's neutrality in the Abyssinian affair.[33] His and Fathi Radwan's visit to Europe and the UK in late 1935 was closely watched by British Intelligence and the Special Branch.[34] Sir Alex Keown-Boyd reported to Lampson on 1 July 1936 about Ali Maher's attempt to secure funds from the Ministry of the Interior for Ahmad Hussein. "Ali Maher wishes to use the Young Egypt and its Green Shirts as a counterpoise to the Wafd and its Blue Shirts." But Ali Maher could not always control or temper Hussein's activities. Upon his return from England in February 1936, Hussein addressed a welcoming rally in which he advocated the use of force as a means of securing the removal of Britain's hold over Egypt. He spoke of force as the one way to independence in the event of the treaty negotiations breaking down. Young Egypt was to become the nucleus of an army that would fight against the English. There were scuffles with the Wafd's Blue Shirts on that occasion.[35]

After the attempt on Nahhas Pasha's life on 28 November 1937 by Greenshirt 'Izz al-Dīn 'Abdel Qādir, there is a great deal of reporting from the High Commissioner on Young Egypt's expanded activities and diversified links. In May 1938, Lampson informed Oliphant,

Public Security Department, which I have reason to know maintains closest touch with Greenshirt organisation, further reports discussions have lately taken place among Greenshirt leaders of the possibility of later on working with the army and police a *coup d'état* to wipe out old gang, to suppress Constitution and to run a régime modelled on that of totalitarian states.[36]

For two years after his first trip to Europe, Ahmad Hussein's and Young Egypt's activities abated somewhat, for they were closely watched by Public Security under a Wafd government. Two events in 1937 further slowed down the Society's momentum: a court case against the Society's newspaper for libel against Nahhas Pasha and Makram Obeid of the Wafd, for which Hussein was given a three-month suspended sentence; and the attempt on Nahhas' life by Abdel Qadir. The new Muhammad Mahmud government in 1938, however, allowed Hussein a freer hand and, when legislation in April 1938 prohibiting the activities of shirt organisations came into force, he transformed his Society into a political party.

His heightened activities in 1938, prior to another tour of Europe that summer, included a visit to Hamilton of the High Commission on 26 May, during which Hussein protested the disgrace brought by politicians on the Egyptian people. At the same time he praised Ali Maher, Bindari Pasha (of the Palace), Aziz Ali al-Masri and Amin Osman. All of these, incidentally, were men of the Palace, and Amin Osman a friend of the High Commission. It is not altogether fanciful to assume some stirring both from the Palace and the High Commissioner.

Hussein's interview with *Il Messaggero* in Rome that summer however made quite a splash. He

likened his movement to the task accomplished by Mazzini in Italy: God, King and Country. Asked if the spirit of his movement was closer to that of the parliamentary democracies of France and England or to that of the "plebiscite" democracies of Italy and Germany, he replied indicating the latter two countries, which were, he said, the only true democracies in Europe today; one of the points in his programme was the suppression of all titles and privileges and *the establishment of a single social class.*[37]

Three things stand out in Hussein's renewed activities in 1938: his closer manipulation by the Palace and certain politicians, chief among them Ali Maher; his receiving funds from Italian agents, as well as from British Intelligence via Amin Osman Pasha;[38] his more frequent reference to dissatisfied young officers in the army, alluding specifically to links with members of the Society who were now commissioned officers, and his wider contacts with Fascist agents in the country and in Europe. His political fortunes of course rose under the Muhammad Mahmud government. Ten years before that Hussein had organised a student group in support of Mahmud's Anglo–Egyptian Treaty negotiations. But they rose even higher the following year, 1939–40, when his main political supporter, Ali

Maher, headed the Egyptian government, in which another supporter, General Saleh Harb Pasha, served as Minister for Defence,
and General Aziz Ali al-Masri as Army Chief of Staff. His
difficulties with the authorities increased once Ali Maher's government was dismissed under British pressure and some of his followers
in the officer corps became involved in anti-British conspiracies in
1941–2. That marked the separation of army conspirators from the
mainstream of Young Egypt activities and their eventual independence in the pursuit of power.

None the less until that time the Young Egypt Society effectively
projected an image of a movement that expressed the views and
reflected the aspirations of youth rebelling against Egyptian political
conditions, the moderation of the Wafd with regard to the Anglo–
Egyptian relationship and its collaboration with the British. In this
respect it was closer to the old National party. It became involved
once more in Egyptian politics during the Palestine War and
intensively so in the operations against British troops in the Canal,
especially during the months between the Wafd's unilateral abrogation of the Anglo–Egyptian Treaty in October 1951 and the 1952
military *coup d'état*. As a socialist party in 1949–52, it mounted a
massive attack on the régime in its entirety—king, politicians and
parliament. It advocated armed struggle against Britain after
October 1951, and organised so-called Liberation Brigades. It
preached death to the feudalists and capitalists.

Even though in the 1930s it attracted followers from among
students, government officials, army officers, merchants, workers
and a few rich Egyptians, the Society in all its guises remained one
man's political platform. As a party it lacked solid organisation and
therefore was incapable of assuming and holding power. Despite its
manipulation by powerful politicians throughout that period it
none the less purveyed a few attractive ideas concerning national
strength, economic reform and social justice. Even in 1951–2, when
the circulation of its newspaper *al-Ishtirakiyya*, now published
weekly, reached the improbable figure of 80,000, its main thrust
was that of inciting people against their rulers rather than one of
preparing them for systematic revolutionary action. The fact remains,
though, that by its propaganda and other activities it provided a
whole generation of Egyptians, particularly that of Nasser, with an
awareness and heightened consciousness of the need to change
political masters at least; to reject and overthrow the *ancien régime*.
Perhaps Ahmad Hussein's ties with Ali Maher and other politicians

proved too inhibiting and disabling a connection—as in fact they
did in January 1952 after Black Saturday in Cairo—and he was
hopelessly precluded from ever assuming power. Yet after the
military *coup* in July 1952 it was Ali Maher who was summoned by
Ahmad Hussein's old acolytes to lead the first civilian government
of the new military régime. Several of his closest associates and
collaborators found their way to high state office under the Free
Officer régime.[39]

The echoes of Ahmad Hussein's political teachings reverberated
within the Egyptian army officer corps. It is not so much that
several of the younger officers commissioned after 1936 were
members or sympathisers of the Society as it was the convergence
of the attitudes, beliefs and personalities of a whole generation of
young subalterns who had undergone similar social and economic
vicissitudes and psychological shocks in adolescence and secondary
school, particularly in the years from 1933 to 1936. The great
political agitation against the despised Sidqi régime (1930–3), for
example, had reached its climax when the popular Wafd was
returned to power in 1935. But even the latter's successful negotiation
of an Anglo–Egyptian Treaty in August 1936 did not arrest the
disillusionment of that generation with the political establishment.
Nor did it lessen its anti-British sentiment. At the same time, the
deeper resentment of European modernity had been encouraged for
a variety of reasons by rival politicians, the Young Egypt Society,
the Muslim Brethren and Fascist agents from Europe. In the meantime, the Palestine Question had also come on to the Arab political
scene. There were parallel radical movements in the Fertile Crescent,
all of which assumed an anti-British posture. Disaffection with the
slow processes of political negotiation led to the option for more
violent means, and for armed struggles.

It was in this general atmosphere that many of the future Free
Officers, including Nasser, received their commissions and first
postings, barely two years before the outbreak of a world war. In
social background and political formation, they were different from
the older generation of officers, particularly senior officers who, for
a long time, worked in close collaboration with the British Army in
Egypt. By 1940–1, moreover, the Muslim Brethren had infiltrated
the Egyptian officer corps and could boast of a chief recruiting officer,
Major Mahmud Labib, as well as several cells. Young officers were
also buffeted by the rivalries between the King, who sought to

dominate the officer corps on one side, and his rivals, the Wafd, who hoped to frustrate the monarch in his plans on the other.

Notes

1. Ahmad Hussein, *Nisf qarn ma'al-'uruba* (Saida, 1971), p.55.
2. Ahmad Hussein, *Imāni* (Cairo, 1936, 1946), pp.97–8. Nasser's eldest son, Khalid, asserts his father was never known as "Gamal al-Din".
3. *Imāni*, pp.21–3.
4. Ibid., p.21.
5. Ibid., pp.30–1.
6. Ibid., pp.35–6.
7. Ibid., pp.37, 38, 39.
8. Ibid., p.40.
9. British unilateral declaration, offering Egypt independence within the context of a special relationship with Britain based on four reserved points. The Declaration terminated the British Protectorate over Egypt. For the text of the Declaration, see J. C. Hurewitz, *Diplomacy in the Near and Middle East, A Documentary Record: 1914–1956* (New York, 1956), Vol.II, pp.100–3.
10. *Imāni*, p.45.
11. Ibid., pp.46, 47.
12. Ibid., p.48.
13. Ibid., p.49.
14. Ibid., p.55.
15. Ibid., p.57.
16. Ibid., pp.65–6.
17. Ibid, p.67.
18. The foundation of the Young Egypt Society was announced in *al-Sarkha* on 13 October 1933, accompanied by a Manifesto signed by twelve founding members. Its Principles and Programme were published in *al-Sarkha* on 21 October 1933. See *Imāni*, pp.82–3, and for text of programme, pp.84–92.
19. See earlier references, especially Muhammad Subeih, *Batal la nansāhu, Aziz al-Masri wa 'asruhu* (Beirut, 1971) and Kamal al-Din Rifaat, *Harb al-tahrir al-wataniyya, mudhakkirāt Kamal al-Din Rifaat* (Cairo, 1968).
20. The Islamic Nationalist party's (ex-Young Egypt) programme was published in the movement's newspaper *Misr al-Fatat* on 18 March 1940. A copy of the programme was sent by Ahmad Hussein to the Palace as an enclosure to a letter addressed to Faruq.
21. Subeih, *Batal la nansāhu*, pp.143–4, suggests the "quadrilateral leadership" consisted of Misr al-Fatat, the National party, the Muslim Brethren, and General Aziz al-Masri.
22. From text of leaflet attributed to Young Egypt, dated 5 July 1940, and marked No. 1, in National Archives, Cairo.
23. Ibid.
24. See *Al-ishtirākiyya allati nad'ū ilayha* (*The socialism we support*) (Cairo, 1951). Cf. *Al-ard al-tayyiba* (*The good earth*) (Cairo, 1951).
25. *Al-ishtirākiyya allati*. See also the party newspaper, *Al-ishtirākiyya*, Cairo, 20 April and 11 May 1951.
26. *Al-ishtirākiyya* (newspaper), Cairo, 11 May, 22 and 29 June, 8 and 23 August 1951.
27. *Al-ishtirākiyya allati*, pp.3–4.
28. Ibid., pp.16, 23–5.

29. See Ahmad Hussein, *Qadiyyat al-tahrid* (*The case of incitement*) (Cairo, 1957), *passim*.
30. Campbell to Simon, July 1933, FO 407/217 No. 731.
31. Sir Percy Loraine to Sir John Simon, 9 November 1933, FO 407/217, No.978.
32. Lampson to Simon, No.367 FO 371/17977.
33. See *Stefani Papers*, Archivio Centrale dello Stato, Rome, Carte Morganti, Scatola 13, fascicolo "Ugo Dadone". Dadone was recommended for a citation of distinction to Mazzolini by Morganti in Cairo in October 1938. See also, Kelly's despatches dated 31 August and 13 September 1935, FO 371/19097 and 19074, as well as Keown-Boyd's letter to the Oriental Secretary, dated 23 January 1936, enclosed in FO 371/20132 regarding the activities of Ugo Dadone and other Italians. See also Note dated 19 November 1935 in FO 371/19078.
34. See FO 371/20098 J 1104/2/16 and FO 371/19079 J 9029/110/16, Lampson despatch on Hussein's and Fathi Radwan's travels to Europe and the UK, dated 6 December 1935.
35. Lampson No.491, 2 May 1936, FO 371/20107.
36. Lampson to Oliphant, 25 May 1938, FO 371/21947.
37. Despatch from Rome Embassy, Noel Charles to Halifax, No.721, 1 August 1938, FO 371/21948, reporting on Ahmad Hussein's visit to Italy. Emphasis added. Twenty years later, in outlining the nature of Arab socialism, Nasser insisted on refuting the class struggle in favour of "national solidarity", or the establishment of a single class, a kind of corporatist vision for Egyptian society.
38. Lampson to Oliphant, 25 May 1938, FO 371/21947.
39. The only monograph in English on Young Egypt is James P. Jankowski, *Egypt's Young Rebels*, "*Young Egypt*": *1922–1952* (Stanford, 1975). A documentary presentation of Young Egypt's principles and programme is to be found in "Wathāiq: al-ahzāb wa al-tanzimāt al-siyāsiyya fi misr: hizb misr al-fatat", ("Documents: parties and political organizations in Egypt: the Young Egypt party"), *al-Tali'a*, Cairo, Vol.1, No.3, March 1965, pp.155–62. The most reliable information about the party's and its leader's activities is to be found in British despatches from Egypt, 1933–8.

CHAPTER 4

The Society of Muslim Brethren

> There remains the Third Circle ... the circle of our Brethren in Islam ... As I ponder over these hundreds of millions of Muslims, all welded into a homogeneous whole by the same Faith, I come out increasingly conscious of the potential achievements cooperation among all these millions can accomplish ... which will ensure for them and their Brethren-in-Islam unlimited power. Nasser, *The Philosophy of the Revolution.*

It is difficult to determine the full extent or precise nature of the connection between the Muslim Brethren and Nasser's generation of officers in the period from 1940 to 1952. Reports in various sources are spotty, confused and conflicting. Some Free Officers—Abdel Moneim Abdel Rauf and Rashad Mehanna, for example—were Brothers; others like Boghdadi, Nasser, Kamal el-Din Hussein and Anwar Sadat were sympathisers and collaborators of it.

In fact, the political involvement of many army officers who were later associated with the Free Officer movement occurred within the Brethren-led operations in the Palestine conflict (1947–9), and those against the British in the Suez Canal Zone (1946–53). The Brethren's network in the armed forces was extensive. They also co-ordinated certain operations with Young Egypt, the Mufti of Palestine and the Syrian Army against the British in Egypt and the Jews in Palestine. Politically more interesting was their co-operation in certain circumstances with Ali Maher, Saleh Harb and other Egyptian politicians.

The volunteer "Rovers" force of the Brethren (*Jawwalat al-ikhwan al-muslimin*) was already in Palestine in 1947 before any of the local Arab groups had organised their own volunteer forces. At the same time, the Arab League had despatched retired General Abdul Wahed Subul to organise local Palestinian Arab resistance to the Jews.

The Brethren formations constituted the backbone and mainstay of that early resistance. They had some experience of the Palestine scene in 1936, when the Arab revolt broke out there. Their leading agent (*dā'i*) in Palestine was no less a personality than Sa'id Ramadan. Major Mahmud Labib, their agent in charge of military affairs in the Egyptian Army, was also chosen to lead the struggle in Palestine.

The Brethren sent their first volunteer regiment to Palestine before 15 May 1948. It was financed by the Arab League, trained by volunteer and seconded Egyptian army officers at Huskstep Camp outside Cairo, and commanded by the legendary Colonel Ahmad Abdul Aziz, who was subsequently killed in action.

One day, Kamal el-Din Hussein was sitting near me in Palestine, looking distracted, with nervous, darting eyes [Nasser wrote in 1954]. "Do you know what Ahmed Abdul Aziz said to me before he was killed?" he said. "What did he say?" I asked. He replied with a sob in his voice and a deep look in his eyes, he said to me "Listen, Kamal, the biggest battlefield is in Egypt." [1]

According to Nasser, in April 1948, the Free Officer organisation "was lying low". "The eyes of the Political Police were trained in our direction." [2] He himself was completing his course at Staff College. Many officers were considering volunteering for duty in Palestine under Colonel Abdul Aziz's command. Nasser, who had only a month left to complete the Staff College course, chose not to volunteer. But, he reports,

About this time, a group of the Constituent Committee of the Free Officers' Organization met at my house and it was decided that some of us should proceed to Palestine as volunteers and that the rest should remain in Cairo. [3]

It was Kamal el-Din Hussein, a reputed sympathiser, if not indeed a member, of the Brethren, who volunteered. Meanwhile, the wider recruitment of volunteers for Colonel Abdul Aziz's force in the field was supervised by Major Labib and old General Saleh Harb of the YMMA. While Colonel Abdul Aziz commanded operations in the field, the training of fresh recruits back in Egypt was entrusted to another Muslim Brother, Lieutenant-Colonel Hussein Mustafa, an officer on active duty, seconded to this temporary, extraordinary task. The Brethren's Supreme Council meanwhile appointed Sheikh Muhammad Al-Farghali "Political Commissar", to supervise all operations and activities in Palestine. He was hanged in 1954 when the military régime in Cairo proceeded to proscribe and dissolve the Brethren.

It is clear then that the running in the battle for Palestine from Egypt was made in 1947–8 by the Brethren. Despite the government's reservation and caution, it could not very well prevent the Brethren from becoming involved in the Palestine cause. Hence the Arab League cover. Nor could the government easily exclude those army officers who wished to join in this venture without bringing upon itself charges of treason to the Arab cause. None the less, the government was duly alarmed. Not only because the Brethren could dispose of such vast organisational and manpower resources, but more ominously because the Brethren had clearly infiltrated the armed forces so successfully.[4]

Nasser, too, drew the appropriate lesson from this show of organisational capacity and strength by the Brethren. A measure of co-operation between the Free Officers and the Brethren was inevitable, even politic. In any case, many of these officers were either sympathisers or members of the Brethren. The careful use of their vast resources and extensive network was of some advantage to the conspiratorial aims of the Free Officer organisation. However loose the latter may have been at that point in time, it was quickly falling under Nasser's control. Furthermore, a degree of collaboration with the Brethren in the circumstances of the Palestine War— and soon in the anti-British operations in the Canal Zone—gave him the opportunity to observe at very close range their organisational and command structure, assess their actual and potential strength. It was this kind of information, acquired in the period from 1948 to 1952, which enabled Nasser later in 1954, and again in 1965, to successfully withstand and frustrate the Brethren's opposition to his régime, even though without necessarily eradicating their appeal, or following, in the country at large.

A great deal of the information about the relations between army officers and the Brethren in the crucial pre-*coup d'état* period, 1946–52, comes from the Brethren themselves. Therefore, it must be used with caution. The Brethren by 1948, however, were such a massive and far-flung organisation that their infiltration of most institutions in state and society can be safely accepted. As an Islamic movement, the level and idiom of the Brethren's discourse were closer to those of the vast majority of the public than that of any of the established political parties and groups on the left. The latter's notions and programme were articulated and debated by very small Westernised minorities anyway.[5]

In 1948 too the Brethren provided the most credible challenge and constituted the most immediate threat to the establishment. Their claim that they made the major contribution and greatest sacrifice in the struggle against the Jews in Palestine or the British in the Canal Zone cannot be lightly dismissed. Because of their readiness and ability to act in these directions, they easily attracted the sympathy, support and services of army officers in that turbulent period of Egyptian history.

Much of the information about these matters and events came to light after the open break between the Nasser régime and the Brethren in October 1954. Needless to say, the disagreement occurred earlier—in fact, at the very outset in July 1952—when the Brethren expected as of right a special role in the new military régime. Kamil Ismail al-Sharif finished the first draft of his *The Secret Resistance in the Suez Canal, 1952–54*,[6] ready for publication in late 1953, but he held up its publication because the Anglo–Egyptian Evacuation Agreement negotiations were still in progress. The first edition therefore appeared after October 1954, when the Brethren had expressed their disapproval of the Evacuation Agreement by attempting to assassinate Nasser in Alexandria on 26 October.

The Brethren objected to the Evacuation Agreement on two counts. First, because it retained a relationship with Britain that compromised Egypt's independence. Second, because no government, including that of the Free Officers, could have convinced Britain to evacuate the Canal "had it not been for the relentless struggle and costly sacrifice of Egyptian [read, Brethren] youth."[7] There is a note of bitter resentment at being denied the fruits of their endeavours over the years. Sharif refers to

the assassinations and abductions of British Army personnel, and the bombing of their installations as of 1945 by Brethren Death Squads as an expression of suppressed popular rage. The Government today embraces a cause the people have subscribed to for a very long time . . .[8]

These, incidentally, are the kind of terrorist activities in which some army officers were also engaged during the same period, and which are recounted in Sadat's, Rifaat's and Hamrush's writings. Only the link between the two remains unestablished, albeit more than a matter of conjecture. Similarly, the demonstrations in the late 1940s and in 1950–1 owe a great deal to the Brethren's organisation and leadership.

What probably attracted army officers who collaborated with the Brethren more than anything else is the existence of a Special Secret Organisation within that movement, consisting of dedicated volunteers and concerned chiefly with the gathering of intelligence information and the execution of sabotage and other terrorist acts. It is probable that officers active in the Egyptian "underground" after the Second World War and up to the Palestine conflict co-operated with them. Most of the available information suggests that the Brethren's *al-Gihaz al-Sirri* (Secret Organisation) was formed in 1946. Its agents infiltrated the Egyptian labour force working in British installations in the Canal Zone, the railways and other transport facilities, the army and the police, student groups and professional syndicates. The member of the Brethren's Supreme Council responsible for these special operations was Abdul Qadir Auda. He too was hanged by the Nasser régime in 1954.

Before considering the nature and extent of this Secret Organisation's operations and the direct or peripheral involvement of army officers in them, a brief assessment of the Brethren's transformation from an organisation dedicated to the spread of religious teaching and the promotion of Islamic morality to one of radical political pursuits, including the use of terror and violence, is in order. In doing so, a closer look at the peculiar relationship of the Brethren to the government and political establishment is essential.

A cogent analysis of this transformation and relationship was put forward by none other than Ahmad Hussein in 1949, when he published the record of his court defence of those accused of conspiring to assassinate Premier Nuqrashi in December 1948. The thrust of Hussein's defence brief was based on a single premise, in two parts: that the tragedy of political assassination was a consequence of peculiar party politics, and that the thirteen accused young men were the products of political circumstances. As university students, engineers, state employees and workers, they represented a cross-section of the community. At the same time, Hussein alluded to the peculiar relationship between the Brethren and the agencies of the state. Thus the army high command knew about the Supreme

Guide's activities throughout 1948. Yet when the organisation was suppressed on 8 December 1948, its Supreme Guide, Hasan al-Banna, was not arrested. Instead, he remained free until he was assassinated on the steps of the YMMA building in Cairo the following February.[9]

Hussein emphasised the strength of the Brethren which derived from their religious message and popular opposition to the Establishment. Thus the confessed assassin of Prime Minister Nuqrashi, Abdel Majid Ahmad Hassan, committed his crime with the sanction of a religious dispensation—*fatwa*—issued by a certain Sheikh Sayyid Sabiq. He assassinated the Prime Minister, that is, because the latter, in the view of the Brethren, had ceased, by his policy, to belong to the community of believers. Nuqrashi, in short, had deviated from *ijma'*, the consensus of the community of Islam.

One may accept Hussein's assertion that until 1940, the Brethren was primarily a religious organisation, opposed to acts of violence. The question, though, is why and how it was transformed?[10] The answer lies in part in the wooing of the Brethren by the government. By 1941 Banna had been released from internment. "He became richer and more powerful, assisted by his close association with government ministers, free to preach his mission and promote his cause."[11]

It will be recalled that the unstable political situation in Egypt in the years from 1940 to 1942 reflected the parlous military position of Britain in the Western Desert. The apparent British imposition of a Wafd government on the Palace and the country in February 1942 earned Britain and her Wafdist collaborators the resentment of the King and the minority parties, not to mention the widespread hostility of all radical groups, including younger army officers. There was good reason, therefore, for all of these to collaborate, albeit uneasily, in their common aim to destroy the Wafd. Many of them considered the further promotion and use of the Brethren in the prosecution of this aim most convenient, albeit as it turned out, dangerous.

The wooing of the Brethren in order to destroy the Wafd, especially from 1944 onwards, was interpreted by Banna as a green light for the furtherance of his organisation's interests, even for the pursuit of state power.

So in 1946, the Brethren degenerated and transformed themselves from a purely spiritual movement, friendly towards all

to one with a partisan political orientation . . . The Ikhwan
however were pushed and encouraged, even forced, along this
path and in this direction . . .[12]

At this juncture, the idea and duty of *jihad*, Holy War, to which the
Brethren subscribed, was institutionalised in a new Secret Army
organisation. They founded the *Jawwala* (Rovers), which from its
inception was an illegal paramilitary organisation. "Their number
at one time reached 2,000. The leadership of the Ikhwan could
mobilize them anywhere."[13] Within this Secret Army there was a
"special organisation" (*al-gihāz al-khāss*), later to be commonly
known as the Secret Organisation, consisting of *fedayeen*, death
squads. "Whereas the 'special organisation' was the Ikhwan's real
army, the Jawwala were its official army, recognized by the
authorities, and eligible for government assistance as the agency of
a registered charitable-religious association, and permitted to parade
publicly."[14] Some five hundred branches of the Brethren were
eligible for government assistance through provincial and municipal
councils by virtue of their being officially registered charitable
institutions.

To their own newspapers, factories, hospitals, commercial,
financial and insurance enterprises the Brethren now added a private
army. Little wonder, then, that the nature and style of their activities
underwent a fundamental change. The use of violence became an
accepted tactic, and a clash with the authorities became inevitable.[15]
The peak of the Brethren's political power in Egypt was reached
when the government used them in the Palestine conflict prior to
the committal of regular forces on 15 May 1948.

Until then Arab governments feared direct involvement in the
Palestine conflict. They therefore decided to act in an unofficial
manner via the Arab League. The latter, in turn, was to depend
for any action on the groups and organizations that had
expressed enthusiasm and a readiness to act in defence of
Palestine. Thus the volunteer force known as "The Army of
Liberation" came into existence.[16]

Meanwhile, the Arab Higher Committee of Palestine made Cairo
its headquarters, and requested arms from Egypt. The Egyptian
government officially rejected the request, but unofficially allowed
the Higher Committee to procure arms with the help of the Ikhwan,

especially in the Western Desert under the supervision of the Commanding Officer, Frontier Defence Force. The Ikhwan themselves opened machine and repair shops to render these arms serviceable, and provided, or arranged, transport for them.

Hussein refers to the great appeal the Brethren held for a cross-section of Egyptian society, including army officers. "The Ikhwan had been a popular organization of the first order, the likes of which was never seen in Egypt before. It mustered 500,000 members on a most conservative reckoning."[17] On the eve of their dissolution in October 1948,

> it was an organization occupying a privileged and prominent position in the country . . . It was not created in a day and a night, for its history went back twenty years, during which period it acquired an unprecedented amount of power and influence over the life of the country. It has no parallel in any Islamic country.[18]

What also helped the Brethren was not merely their own vitality, but the fact that succeeding governments encouraged them in their chosen course and range of activities. Nor did any government ever proceed to apply strict police measures against their leaders, commercial ventures or social programmes. It was therefore impossible, once the government decided to proscribe and dissolve them, to actually do so, for in twenty years they had "extended their tentacles everywhere, and joined their interests with those of the people."[19]

Between 1946 and 1948, the Brethren dominated the struggle against the régime and the British in Egypt. Their operations overshadowed those of all other opposition groups in magnitude, daring, audacity and effectiveness. Their decision to lead a guerrilla war against the British in the Canal Zone had an electrifying effect on Egyptians. The government became apprehensive; the rebels everywhere, but especially in the army, became excited, envious and worried over the possibility of their being left out of this "popular, national struggle".

The Brethren chose the province of Sharqiyya for the centre of their operations. Ismailiyya contained their strongest secret formation and was the administrative headquarters of their movement for the Canal Zone, headed by Sheikh Muhammad al-Farghali, a member of the Supreme Council. From that headquarters, Farghali directed the Brethren's oldest intelligence network. Sharqiyya, moreover, was strategically important; British installations were located there, and it was close to the Western Desert and the Sinai.

The Brethren devised a three-fold strategy, consisting of: (1) the infiltration of workers in British installations for spying and sabotage; (2) a campaign of religious propaganda to strengthen their ties with village headmen, tribal sheikhs and other local dignitaries; and (3) a campaign to raise money and procure arms and ammunition. Their chosen tactics were those of the boycott against British facilities and sporadic guerrilla war (*harb al-'iṣābāt*). Once they secured control over the labour force, the first became possible. Their Secret Organisation provided the second. By 1950–1, they were in a position to use their dominant role in this struggle to organise country-wide demonstrations as well as exploit those organised by others, and then simply exert pressure on the government. Their famous conference in Ismailiyya in 1951 considered further means of showing both the government and the British that the Canal base was untenable in that kind of hostile environment.

The Secret Organisation operatives underwent strict spiritual preparation, ready to sacrifice their lives in the national-religious cause. Landowners in Sharqiyya assisted the Brethren in setting up training camps, especially in the Faqus area. Training was provided by volunteer officers from the army, prominent among whom were Muhammad Ali Salim and Abdel Aziz Ali, the latter also mentioned by Sadat.[20]

The Brethren's ability to recruit ever-larger numbers and train them impressed and disconcerted both the government and the underground movement in the officer corps. In 1951 the government tried to counter these developments by appointing a military training command staffed by senior officers, some of them retired, such as Aziz Ali al-Masri, al-Mawawi of Palestine War fame, and the old warrior for Islamic causes, General Saleh Harb. They earmarked £E100,000 for that purpose. But little was done, and almost nothing achieved.[21]

The Brethren, in contrast, were able to set up training centres in universities under the overall supervision of their notorious agent, Hasan Doh, and do the same in the religious Azhar University. Some army officers volunteered to train these units. On the whole, that is, the Brethren were able to use the terrain (as in Sharqiyya) and the population at large for the purposes of cover and concealment, intelligence-gathering, paramilitary training and sabotage.

There were, though, dedicated Muslim Brother officers on active duty who provided training in remote areas. Abdel Moneim Abdel Rauf did so in el-Arish, for example. Colonel Rashad Mehanna kept an eye on the top army command on behalf of the Brethren by devising means of countering British influence in the army. When Abdel Rauf was in Ras Sudr, on the east bank of the Canal, opposite Suez, he rendered invaluable assistance with the procurement of arms and ammunition. "Abdel Moneim Abdel Rauf was among the first pioneers who carried the message of the Islamic mission inside the army and rallied some officers round it." [22] He also volunteered to serve with the Brethren's units in the Palestine War before the commitment of Egyptian regular army units to that battle. Meanwhile, Major Mahmud Labib remained the chief representative of the Brethren in the officer corps. Salah Salem and Abdel Hakim Amer, two prominent Free Officers, co-operated with the Brethren by supplying ammunition and transport for their guerrilla units in the Canal while both of them were stationed in Rafah after the Palestine War. Lieutenant-Colonel Mahmud Riad, currently (1976) Secretary-General of the Arab League, also sought involvement in the Brethren's Canal Zone operations. Captain Abdel Fattah Ghuneim served as liaison between some of these officers and the Brethren. Abul Mahasin Abdel Hayy, Maaruf al-Khidri and Hussein Hammuda participated too. Kamal al-Din Rifaat, Major Salah Hedayat, Hassan al-Tuhami (subsequently in Nasser's presidential office) and Nasser himself, all of them Free Officers, were involved with the Brethren through the latter's chief agent in the police, Major Salah Shadi, in a plot to prepare a mine with which to sink a ship and so block the Canal. The plot failed for technical reasons. [23]

Between 1946 and 1951 more officers became involved in anti-British underground operations which were politically, administratively and logistically controlled by the Brethren. The overwhelming prominence of the Brethren's well-organised and extensive political campaign forced a measure of co-operation between them and all other conspiratorial groups. Sharif, for instance, asserts that until then the army officers were isolated from this "popular resistance" movement. The Brethren's successful campaign pushed them, or forced them, into its mainstream. "The Suez Canal question united the army and the popular forces, and propelled them to embark upon the army movement [i.e. the *coup* of July 1952]." [24] He also contends that after the *coup*, Nasser used the Brethren in the Canal until the signing of the Evacuation Agreement with Britain in October 1954. Sharif complains that during the lean days of the Free Officer conspiracy the Brethren helped Nasser and his fellow-conspirators by stashing away arms for them. Later, when the Brethren fell out with the military régime over the terms of the Anglo–Egyptian Evacuation Agreement, Nasser used this knowledge and old association to discredit them.[25]

It would be ungenerous and unfair, whatever the exaggerated claims of the Brethren's spokesmen, publicists and apologists, to deny the fact that their activist organisation and programme constituted an attractive alternative formula of political salvation and avenue to power for many Egyptians and, particularly, many army officers. The Brethren were a native mass movement, perhaps the only one in modern Egyptian history, with tremendous popular appeal.[26] In the period 1946–52, its activities awed many and terrified even more, particularly the Establishment and those who aspired to overthrow it, the Free Officers. Thus Major-General D. K. Palit, Indian Military Attaché in Cairo, in his second half-yearly Report, 15 July–12 December 1950, reported the Brethren were active among the ranks of junior army officers. They were exploiting the demoralisation of the army after their unhappy experience in the Palestine War, the arms scandal and other episodes. He visited Manqabad, where troops returning from Faluja the previous year were in open discontent. There was open talk about the abolition of the monarchy, the collusion between the Wafd and the Brethren, allowing the latter a secret broadcasting station and considering their legalisation under a new name, the Islamic Union.[27]

When, in 1950–1, Nasser realised that the régime could be over-thrown by a military *coup d'état*, he also recognised the dangers of a successful mass religio-political movement on the loose. His conception of power, influenced as it was by the native idiom propagated by the Young Egypt Society of the thirties and com-plemented by the populist Islamic thrust of the Brethren's activism, was a highly personalised one. Its base could be only the teeming, politically amorphous masses, and a state controlled by the military that also dominated society to the exclusion of all others. He could not very well allow an extensive, highly organised hierarchical movement like the Brethren to compete for the loyalty of the masses. It would have been an uncomfortable, prickly intermediary—and rival. Intermediaries in the age of the radio, the transistor and television, as Heikal put it,[28] were not needed to reach a new military despot's power base.

Notes

1. Nasser, *Philosophy of the Revolution*, p.22 in the Washington 1955 edition.
2. *The Palestine War Memoirs*, unpublished English translation by Professor Walid Khalidi, Beirut, n.d., p.2. The Arabic original was serialised in the Cairo weekly magazine, *Ākhir Saa*, March–April 1955. They are also reproduced in Muhammad Subeih, *Ayyām wa ayyām* (Cairo, 1966), pp.305–68.
3. Ibid., English translation, p.3.
4. Premier Nuqrashi dissolved the Brethren in late 1948, a drastic act which cost him his life when a Muslim Brother assassinated him on his way to his office in December of that year. In defending those accused of plotting the assassination of the Prime Minister the following year, Ahmad Hussein alluded to the attraction of the Brethren for a cross-section of Egyptian society, including army officers, and outlined some of the practical reasons for their having attained the kind of political strength they disposed of at that time. See *Murāfaat Ahmad Hussein al-muhāmi fi qadiyyat ightiyāl al-marhūm Mahmud Fahmi al-Nuqrashi (The advocacy of Ahmad Hussein in the case of the assassination of Mahmud Fahmi Nuqrashi)* (Cairo, 1949).
5. See Elie Kedourie, *Arabic Political Memoirs and other studies* (London, 1974), pp.177ff.
6. Kamil al-Sharif, *Al-muqāwama al-sirriyya fi qanāt al-suweis, 1951–1954*, 2nd printing (Beirut, 1957). Cf. Saad Zaghlul Fuad, *Al-qitāl fi'l-qanāl (Fighting in the Canal)* (Cairo, 1969). See also "Asālib al-nidāl al-misri: min harb al-tahrir didd al-ghazu al-faransi 1798 ila al-muqawama al-sha'biyya didd al-'udwān al-thulāthi" ("Patterns and style of the Egyptian national struggle: from the liberation war against the French conquest 1798 to the popular resistance against the Tripartite Aggressive 1956"), *al-Talī'a*, Vol.3, December 1967, pp.7–55.
7. Kamil al-Sharif, *Al-muqāwama al-sirriyya*, p.9.
8. Ibid., p.31.
9. Ahmad Hussein, *Murāfaat Ahmad Hussein*, pp.17–20. Between 1944 and 1949 there was a spate of assassinations and bombings: Ahmad Maher in 1945, Amin Osman in 1946, Nuqrashi in 1948, the Commandant of the Cairo police, Salim Zaki, in the same year, Hasan al-Banna, the Supreme Guide of the Muslim Brethren, and an Appeals Court Judge in 1949. There were bombings of police stations and public places in 1947 and 1948. Kamal Rifaat has argued that the failure of the Wafd to "move the masses" led to confusion and disorientation among Egyptian youth. Some of them soon joined small underground Communist groups; others gravitated towards Fascist organisations; and still others embarked upon a campaign of terror and sabotage, including assassination. Kamal al-Din Rifaat, *Harb al-tahrir al-wataniyya, mudhakirāt Kamal al-Din Rifaat* (Cairo, 1968), pp.31–4. See the dramatisation of some of these events in Ahmad Hussein, *Wahtaraqat al-Qāhira (And Cairo Burned)* (Cairo, 1968).
10. Hussein, *Murāfaat*, pp.31–40. It has already been noted that Ahmad Hussein himself in 1940 transformed his Young Egypt party to the Islamic Nationalist party in keeping with the prevailing general political-cultural atmosphere of a return to the more native idiom and its use against Britain in the war.

11. Ibid., pp.40–41.
12. Ibid., p.42.
13. Ibid., p.44.
14. Ibid., p.46.
15. As, for instance, the clash with the police in Port Said on 6 July 1946. See Ahmad Hussein, *Wahtaraqat al-Qāhira*, pp.48–50. See also, Tāriq al-Bishri, "'Āmm 1946 fi al-tarikh al-misri" ("The year 1946 in Egyptian history") *al-Taliʻa*, Cairo, Vol.2, February 1966, pp.50–8.
16. *Murāfaat*, pp.56–7.
17. Ibid., p.62.
18. Ibid., p.61.
19. Ibid., p.67.
20. Kamil al-Sharif, *Al-muqāwama al-sirriyya*, pp.95–6.
21. Kamil al-Sharif, *Al-muqawama al-siriyya*, pp.95–130. See also Anwar al-Sadat, *Al-thawra al-misriyya, asraruha al-khafiyya wa asbabuha al-bsikolojiyya* (Cairo, 1965).
22. Ibid., p.191.
23. Kamal Rifaat, *Harb al-tahrir al-wataniyya*, pp.78–81. Rifaat also claims the Free Officers had laid a plan which was to be executed by Nasser to blow up all British camps and installations in the Suez Canal zone simultaneously. See pp.82–4. See also Subeih, *Ayyām wa ayyām*, pp.407–9.
24. Kamil al-Sharif, *Al-muqāwama al- sirriyya*, p.217.
25. Ibid., pp.303–15.
26. On the Muslim Brethren generally, see J. Heyworth-Dunne, *Religious and Political Trends in Modern Egypt* (Washington, DC, 1950); Ishak Musa Husaini, *The Moslem Brethren* (Beirut, 1956); Christina Phelps Harris, *Nationalism and Revolution in Egypt* (The Hague, 1964); and Richard P. Mitchell, *The Society of the Muslim Brothers* (London, 1969).
27. St Antony's College, Oxford, Private Papers Collection: Annual Half-Yearly and Monthly Reports.
28. Muhammad Heikal, *Nasser: The Cairo Documents* (London, New English Library, 1972), p.173.

PART II

Coming to Power

CHAPTER 5

*The Origins of the Free
Officer Conspiracy*

Several radical groups claim the honour of starting the first subversive cells within the Egyptian officer corps, though most seem
agreed that they began in 1939. Muhammad Abdel Rahman
Hussein claims that Abdel Aziz Ali of the National party established
a secret society, involving Sadat among other officers, and that it
had links with the air force by 1940.[1] Sadat himself hints at the
activity of the Muslim Brethren and the inspiration of the violently
anti-British General Aziz Ali al-Masri, who organised Air Force
officers in attempts to collaborate with the Germans and Italians
against the British.[2]

Ahmad Hamrush reports that a secret group was formed in 1939,
consisting of seven officers: Abdel Latif Boghdadi, Hasan Ibrahim,
Hussein dhu'l-Fiqar Sabri, Abdel Moneim Abdel Rauf, Wagih
Abaza, Ahmad Suudi and Hasan 'Izzat. Anwar Sadat joined them
later.[3] These officers were "dazzled and impressed by Nazi
organization and propaganda and considered the early war victories
of German arms as making German victory in the war a foregone
conclusion".[4]

However, their efforts on behalf of the Reich were not very
successful, although al-Masri allegedly did manage to pass on to
the Italians the British defence plan for Egypt. Sadat's subsequent
collaboration in Cairo with the two German intelligence agents,
Hans Eppler and "Sandy" Monkaster, was no more successful; all
three were arrested.[5] There were also isolated incidents of sabotage
by Egyptian officers in the Western Desert, such as the case of
Magdi Hasanein,[6] who hijacked Free French lorries loaded with
hand grenades, other explosives and detonators which he passed on
to Hasan 'Izzat of Young Egypt for use much later, in the 1940s,
in the bombing campaign in Cairo. Otherwise, the price of failure

for these subversive officers was imprisonment or dismissal from the
army, or transfer to distant parts in the Sudan.[7]

On 4 February 1942, the British Ambassador, Sir Miles Lampson,
delivered an ultimatum to King Faruq, demanding the appointment
of a government headed by Mustafa Nahas Pasha, leader of the
Wafd party. When the King did not comply, Lampson had Abdin
Palace surrounded with British armour units, marched into the
King's office, accompanied by General Stone, GOC Land Forces,
Middle East, and read him a note demanding his abdication. The
timely intervention of the Royal Chamberlain, Ahmad Hassanein
Pasha, led to the resolution of the crisis when the King agreed to
invite Nahas to form a government.[8] This episode came to be
known as the Palace Incident, and it led to a temporary revival of
seditious agitation in the officer corps. Muhammad Naguib
impressed his younger colleagues in those days, when, in protest
against the British ultimatum to the King, he considered resigning
his commission. Abdel Latif Boghdadi and one or two other officers
offered the king's *chef de cabinet*, Ahmad Hasanein Pasha, to
assassinate the "traitor" Nahas, leader of the Wafd. The more
lasting impact of that episode, however, lay in the growing mood of
disaffection among the officers. A pro-King cabal of officers, the
Iron Guard, emerged, among whose prominent members were
Captain Mustafa Kamal Sidqi, Anwar Sadat and Kamal al-Din
Rifaat. The King, for his part, as the injured party and supreme
symbol of national sovereignty, grabbed this opportunity to befriend
officers with frequent visits to the Officers' Club in Zamalek, in the
hope of increasing his popularity.

Although the officer cabals were under the influence of extreme
nationalist political groups (Young Egypt, the National party, the
Muslim Brethren), they were still oriented towards "King and
Country", so to speak; they were not as yet completely alienated
from the political establishment. By 1944, however, the imminent
German defeat in the war caused their disorientation and disarray.
There followed a period of civilian political agitation (1944–7), led
primarily by the Muslim Brethren and new formations of the left,
especially among students, workers and intellectuals.[9] Both these
extremes of the radical political spectrum became active in the
officer corps.

What emerges from the blur of Sadat's published statement is
the fact that before 1945 there were in the officer corps several
conspiracies. Officers involved collaborated with the youth forma-

tions of several anti-British organisations, as for instance that of the National party under Abd al-Aziz Ali, and also the Muslim Brethren.

The period between February 1942 and 1945, according to Sadat, was one of heightened revolutionary activity in the army and among youth organisations throughout the country. One group of officers, for example, met in a home in Zeitun, a suburb of Cairo, under the chairmanship of Kamal el-Din Hussein, a Brethren sympathiser. Another met with Captain Mustafa Kamal Sidqi. They planned sabotage and political assassinations. These groups included air force, cavalry (armour), signals and service corps officers. Sadat was chosen to liaise between them and civilian terrorist groups.[10] An old member of the Young Egypt party, air force Pilot Officer Ahmad Suudi, was among them. So were Wagih Abaza, Hassan 'Izzat, Abdel Latif Boghdadi and others. They also met in cafés. They recruited and trained pupils in the use of firearms and explosives from the Khedivial, Fuad (al-Awwal) and Sa'idiyya secondary schools, all three of them notorious for their involvement in nationalist agitation, as well as students from the law and engineering faculties of the university. They planned attacks on British camps and depots in Meadi, Heliopolis and Kasr el-Nil, as well as the abduction of British military personnel from the streets. They infiltrated the diplomatic service. Yet despite all this activity they lacked a clear political objective. They were simply committed to removing the British from Egypt. Nevertheless they all agreed with General Masri's admonition to Sadat, "There is no salvation except in a military *coup d'état.*" In fact, the general was viewed by them as a "military reformer and rebel who believed in German militarism and its technical superiority". His hatred of the British clearly appealed to them. They were also attracted by the mystique and romanticism surrounding his personality as a revolutionary soldier who, in his youth, had founded secret political organisations of Arab officers in the Ottoman army, and who always believed in political action by soldiers. Little wonder then that Sadat could assert to Banna in one of their meetings in 1940–1, "We all believe in what General Masri told me, and realize that Egypt cannot be freed from colonialism except by an army coup."[11]

During this period and in the political confusion of 1945–7 the most important long-term influence on the political orientation and perception of these officers was that of the Muslim Brethren. At about this time, for instance, with the Palestine crisis in the forefront, rebel officers such as Boghdadi, Hasan Ibrahim, Kamal el-Din Hussein and others collaborated closely with the Brethren and established contacts and links with the Mufti of Palestine and Fawzi al-Qawuqji, the Lebanese commander of the volunteer "Army of Rescue" in Palestine.[12] The Brethren, moreover, helped promote their dislike of and opposition to all political parties and nurture an anti-democratic predilection in them. It corroborated and strengthened some of their earlier radical national socialist views which they had acquired as secondary school pupils from the Young Egypt Society and the National party's militant wing. In general, it bred in them a conservative view of the world, and an extreme anti-Western orientation regarding Egypt's political destiny.

Sadat reports that he met Sheikh Hasan el-Banna, Supreme Guide of the Muslim Brethren, for the first time, at dinner in the Signal Corps Headquarters, Meadi, outside Cairo, in the summer of 1940. He was then a first lieutenant. Banna was brought in by a soldier of the corps, a fact that underlines the Brethren's infiltration of all ranks in the army. "That night," writes Sadat, "marked the start of a series of events about which Egyptians only partially heard. Some of them were secret, others reverberated loudly in the form of bombs and other acts of sabotage."[13] Sadat went to see Banna again at his home and reports that although Banna confined his remarks to religion, he also "alluded to other things". Most important, he arranged for Sadat to see General Aziz Ali al-Masri, then on forced leave as Army Chief of Staff, and in hiding with a Muslim Brother physician in the crowded Sayyida Zeinab quarter of Cairo.[14]

From 1940 the Muslim Brethren had expanded their recruitment within the officer corps, but they were never able to dominate it. They had placed key men like Abdel Moneim Abdel Rauf in the air force and Kamal el-Din Hussein in artillery, as well as Rashad Mehanna, but they lacked the power to co-ordinate all the various strands of the conspiracy. Their terror campaign and total support of an Islamic holy war against the Jews in Palestine in 1948–9 gained the Brethren more soldier adherents, but the Palestine War also marked the beginning of their decline. Defeat in the war led for the first time to the widespread distrust of the entire régime by the officers. Tension between younger officers and their superiors increased. The seeds of the Free Officer movement were then sown to the extent that officers with widely ranging views and links with different political groups came together to challenge authority.

Events between 1949 and 1952, when the Wafd could not challenge the monarch openly, when the Brethren grew too powerful, prompted a number of officers to consider a political movement of their own, independent of all other organisations in the country. A general undifferentiated *malaise* prevailed among their ranks after the Palestine War, mainly against the *status quo*, but not necessarily or clearly for something in particular. It was at this juncture, say, 1949–51, that Lieutenant-Colonel Gamal Abdel Nasser played a prominent personal role in welding together officers with different political views or orientation. [15]

Sadat suggests that Nasser had been involved in an army conspiracy in late 1944 and 1945, but only in a minor role. He says Nasser took over responsibility of the secret movement within the army in November 1944 but did not begin to exert his organisational efforts seriously until after the Palestine War in the spring of 1949.

Sometime in 1949 a Constituent Committee (Founding Committee) of five came into existence, comprising Nasser, Hasan Ibrahim, Khaled Mohieddin, Kamal el-Din Hussein and Abdel Moneim Abdel Rauf, all of them at one time or another connected with the Brethren, the Young Egypt Society or the National party. This committee was firmly under Nasser's control and, according to Sadat, Nasser insisted on its complete independence from all other groups within and outside the armed forces. Most particularly, Nasser was determined to insulate the movement from the Muslim Brethren, just at the time when the Brethren were trying to recruit an ever-greater number of army officers through their chief agent, Major Mahmud Labib. Early in 1950 Abdel Latif Boghdadi, Anwar Sadat, Abdel Hakim Amer, the brothers Saleh and Gamal Salem were brought into the Committee. [16] At the same time it was transformed into an executive committee of the Free Officer movement, a term which appeared for the first time in clandestine political handbills distributed in February 1950. These proclaimed the army belonged to the nation, and demanded radical reform of state and society. [17]

One can date the officers' formal "declaration of independence" from other political organisations from this period. The beginning of an officers' political organisation distinct from all civilian political groups was reflected in the new executive committee, even though some of its members retained their links with these groups, e.g. Khaled with HADETU, Kamal el-Din Hussein and Abdel Moneim Abdel Rauf with the Brethren, Sadat with the Palace. Nasser displayed his political instinct and versatility by maintaining contact with more than one organisation, especially the Brethren, the Wafd and the broad left through the HADETU lawyer, Ahmad Fuad, and others.

One can also assume that the general political discontent in the country immediately after the war which led to a period of massive demonstrations, frequent strikes and terrorism (1946–9), coupled with the anti-British campaign in the Canal Zone and the Palestine War, percolated down into the officer corps. Political discussion among groups of lower- and middle-ranking officers—lieutenants to lieutenant-colonels—became common. The Free Officer movement was to a great extent born of these events and influences.

After 1947, there was no British Military Mission to inhibit the political activities of Egyptian officers. With their growing alienation from the King and politicians, sedition became possible. Ideas of a *coup d'état* against authority gained ground with developments in other Arab states, particularly Syria, and the deteriorating, discredited political order. It was, moreover, difficult for a very small Egyptian military intelligence structure to keep every cabal under surveillance. The civilian or state security establishment, consisting mainly of the political police, was too busy with the seditious activities of the Ikhwan and other extremist groups. Soon military intelligence itself was infiltrated by the Free Officers.[18]

The liberalisation policy of the Wafd government in 1950–1 helped the Free Officer movement to strengthen its organisation and increase its clandestinely published propaganda, the chief message of which was "the army belongs to the people". Marxist influences soon became apparent in this propaganda campaign, with attacks on the King's excesses and demands for higher pay for soldiers. In the meantime, the Free Officers readily assisted any group operating against the British in the Canal by supplying them with arms, ammunition and training facilities,[19] without themselves, however, becoming directly involved in these operations.

These activities of the Free Officers elicited a response from the Palace and the government. A confrontation between them and senior army commanders and the King became inevitable. The clash occurred over the elections of the Officers' Club executive committee in late 1951, a contest which the Free Officers won with the triumph of their candidates, headed by Brigadier Muhammad Naguib. "The Officer Club Elections", wrote Hamrush in 1975, "marked the public confrontation between the King and the Free Officers."[20]

But these coincided with massive demonstrations in Cairo in November–December 1951 against the British after the Wafd government's dramatic and demagogic unilateral abrogation of the 1936 treaty. Attacks on public transport, places of amusement— bars, casinos and cinemas—were organised and led by the Ikhwan and Young Egypt in December, introducing a new factor in the deteriorating security situation, and giving everyone a foretaste of what was to come on Black Saturday, when the mob burned Cairo.

The impact of Black Saturday (26 January 1952) on the Free Officers was immediate and devastating. Some of them on the right of the political spectrum counselled immediate action. Others, especially those on the left, pressed for a tighter political organisation and a systematic campaign of agitprop. Khaled Mohieddin, for example, with the help of his civilian HADETU comrades (e.g. Ahmad Fuad) played a principal part in the drafting of the move- ment's famous Six Principles of the Revolution sometime in February or March 1952. The Free Officers at least now proclaimed the aims of their intended revolution, which were as follows: the destruction of colonialism and its Egyptian collaborators; the destruction of feudalism; the ending of the monopoly and control of the state by capital; the establishment of social justice; the construction of a strong national army; the creation of sound democratic life.

By this time the Free Officers were projecting an independent movement, and embarked upon the clandestine promotion of "progressive and radical" nationalist views, such as the linking of the régime in Egypt to Anglo–American imperialism. They also thought in terms of a *coup d'état*, especially after some officers associated with their movement had been arrested in connection with Black Saturday. Muhammad Naguib himself was under surveillance.[21] At this time too the Free Officers reorganised the structure of their movement with one centre of its activities in Cairo (consisting of Nasser, Khaled Mohieddin, Zakariyya Mohieddin, Hussein Shafei, Magdi Hasanein and Amin Shakir), and another in el-Arish, headquarters of the Egyptian army and air force in Sinai (consisting of Yusuf Siddiq, Abdel Hakim Amer, Salah and Gamal Salem). They also purged their ranks of ambivalent prominent members who remained divided in their loyalties between the army movement and civilian political groups. Thus Abdel Moneim Abdel Rauf was pushed to the periphery because of his links with the Ikhwan. What is relevant for an understanding of Nasser is that, at this juncture, he got his fellow-conspirators to agree that only he should continue maintaining contacts, on an expedient opportunistic basis, with political groups outside the army.

The seeds of a future controversy regarding the links between the Free Officers and US Intelligence were sown at this time. Were they encouraged in their preparation of a *coup d'état* by the Americans? In view of the escalating Cold War and the weakened British position in the Middle East, Washington was anxious to secure Western interests in Egypt. The spectacle of demonstrations, riots, assassinations and bombings carried out by extreme Egyptian political groups was, to put it mildly, disquieting. The Americans feared a popular uprising, or, worse still, a Communist-inspired revolt.

Normal, regular contacts between the intelligence services of friendly states, Egypt and the USA, existed at that time. But there were also para-intelligence connections between American diplomats in Cairo and Egyptian journalists (e.g. Mustafa Amin of *Akhbar El Yom*), as well as certain high state officials and Ministers (e.g. Hafez Ramadan, Murtada Maraghi, Mustafa Marei and Ahmad Hussein, Egyptian Ambassador to Washington). [22]

At first the Americans considered the possibility of a "peaceful revolution" under King Faruq in the hope of forestalling a more extreme popular uprising of uncertain orientation and direction. Early in 1952, Kermit Roosevelt, a senior CIA official, was assigned the task of planning and executing this particular project. [23] Roosevelt, however, soon found the policy not to be feasible or realistic. Yet by March 1952 he had established close contacts and conducted exploratory talks with emissaries of the Free Officer executive. By May, Roosevelt was convinced the Free Officers could and would execute a *coup d'état* with consequences *not* detrimental to American or Western interests in Egypt and the Middle East; that the officer corps represented the only credible alternative to the Faruq régime. The Free Officers for their part had ascertained America's benevolent neutrality towards their planned seizure of power. [24]

The 1952 *coup* brought a new generation of officers—as well as civilians—to power in Egypt. Significantly, it also carried with it the political influence of the radical agitation and terrorism generated by Young Egypt, the Ikhwan and National party in the preceding decade. It ousted from the command of the armed forces nearly every older senior officer. Naguib, 52 years old at the time of the *coup*, was the only senior officer associated with the junta. Equally significant was the fact that whereas military *coups* in other Middle Eastern countries—Iraq in 1936 and 1940, and Syria in 1949—were led by senior officers, the one in Egypt was prepared and led by captains, majors and lieutenant-colonels whose age ranged from 28 to 35. Yet members of the Free Officer Executive, subsequently the Revolution Command Council (RCC), had, within the limits and by the standards of the Egyptian armed forces, several achievements to their credit, such as exceptional field promotions in the Palestine War, other high state decorations for meritorious service and appointments at a fairly early age to the teaching cadre of the Staff College. On the whole, they had better academic and practical training in service schools than their senior officers. But there were hardly any among them from rich families or, with the exception of Naguib, from families with a military tradition. They were, on the whole, diligent military bureaucrats, or as Copeland dubbed them, "good organization men".

What is perhaps extraordinary is their seizure of power barely three years after their executive came into being (1949–52). More incredible to the uninitiated is the fact that the members of the executive and their disparate followers in the various arms of the services held different political views, that is, lacked ideological cohesiveness or uniform political consciousness. But the generational links, comprising their social and economic backgrounds, the earliest influences on their formation, their adolescent and later frustrations generated the common desire in them for change and the catalyst in their drive for power. It was this loose disparity incidentally that helped the emergence of Nasser, the most disciplined and desirous of power among them, as the undisputed leader of the group and eventually the sole ruler of Egypt.

> Vague nationalist ideas and resentments of colonialism constituted the principal motive for the officers' action. Details of objectives, of means and ends, were disparate in their minds, and their vision of the future hazy and unclear . . .
>
> The Free Officers appeared as the champions of change and reform, because their social condition, their class was different from that of established authority—the *ancien régime*. 25

One of the factors that enabled the Free Officers to seize control of the armed forces so easily was the fact that senior officers in command till then did not constitute a military élite wholly identified with the political régime. They were part of the governing élite or directorate, but not necessarily of the ruling class. It was therefore unlikely they would defend the latter wholeheartedly. Nor did the Wafd, the landed plutocracy and official class, or the new élite of financiers, entrepreneurs and industrialists control the armed forces. Rather the overwhelming majority of officers were of lower, petit bourgeois backgrounds similar to that of Nasser and his fellow conspirators. Significantly too, none of these came from working-class or peasant-farmer backgrounds, or for that matter from official religious families. Coptic officers constituted a miniscule proportion of the corps, so that among the Free Officers there was reportedly only one. After 1936, that is, there was a "proletarianisation" of the officer corps with the influx of mainly children of lower-class Muslim families, the same class of families from which were also recruited the followers of the Ikhwan and Young Egypt. But these represented at the same time a generation of aspiring youth that had benefited from the rapid expansion of secondary education in Egypt.

For a long time the officer corps was controlled by the monarch and fairly isolated from the rest of society and its political upheavals. If anything, it performed the ultimate task in maintaining public order and security against dissident, demonstrating civilians. It was the régime's shield against disorder and rebellion—and revolution. To this extent the officer corps was not, by any standard, a vanguard élite in radical Egyptian politics. That is perhaps the reason why when a cabal within the officer corps seized power in July 1952 it did so alone, without the participation or assistance of any civilian organisations that were equally opposed to the *ancien régime* and possibly better organised. Rather the Free Officers relied on secrecy with a view to a sudden *coup* at a propitious time when the public at large would be so thoroughly alienated from their rulers as to eagerly embrace their new soldier saviours. Above all, with the firm seizure of the army, the largest state institution, the conspirators would be able to impose their will on the rest of society.

Notes

1. *Rose el-Youssef*, Vol.50, No.2428, 3rd March 1975. Among the air force officers were Wagih Abaza, Hasan 'Izzat, Ahmad Suudi, Hasan Ibrahim and Abdel Latif Boghdadi, most of them members of Young Egypt.
2. See Anwar al-Sadat, *Asrār al-thawra al-misriyya* (Cairo, 1965), especially pp.45–130.
3. Ahmad Hamrush, *Qissat thawrat 23 yulio* (Beirut, 1974), pp.96–103.

4. Ibid., p.97.
5. Sadat, *Asrār al-thawra al-misriyya*, pp.75–101. Cf. Muhammad Subeih, *Batal la nansāhu, Aziz al-Masri wa 'asruhu* (Beirut, 1971), pp.119–291.
6. In 1953 he was appointed Director of the Liberation Province.
7. Sadat, *Asrār al-thawra al-misriyya*. For further details of these activities see Hamrush, *Qissat thawrat 23 yulio*, pp.100ff. For instance, Pilot Officer Muhammad Radwan, who managed to reach the German lines and went to Germany, was arrested by the Allies in Berlin in 1945, tried and sentenced to a fifteen-year prison term and a £2,000 fine. He was released after 1952 and employed in the Department of Public Affairs, Armed Forces.
8. See Muhammad Husein Heikal, *Mudhakkirāt fi al-siyāsa al-misriyya* (*Memoirs about Egyptian politics*) (Cairo, 1953), Vol.2, pp.227–46; Muhammad al-Tāb'i, *Min asrār al-sāsa wa al-siyāsa al-misriyya, misr mā qabl al-thawra* (*Secrets of Egyptian politicians and politics: Egypt before the revolution*) (Cairo, n.d.), pp.178–310. See also Gabriel Warburg, "Lampson's ultimatum to Faruq, 4 February 1942", *Middle Eastern Studies*, Vol.11, No.1, pp.24–32; and Muhammad Anis, *Arba' fibrāyer fi tarikh misr al-siyāsi* (Beirut, 1972).
9. For an Egyptian interpretation (mainly leftist) of events and developments in this period, see Anouar Abdel Malek, *Egypt, military society* (New York, 1968); Shuhdi Atiyya al-Shafei, *Tatawwur al-haraka al-wataniyya al-misriyya* (*Evolution of the Egyptian national movement*) (Cairo, 1956); Tariq al-Bishri, "'Ām 1946 fi al-tarikh al-misri" ("The year 1946 in Egyptian history"), *al-Talī'a*, Cairo, February 1966, pp.50–88; and his *The political movement in Egypt 1945–1952* (Cairo, 1972), pp.75–178; Abdel Moneim al-Ghazali, "Mauqif 21 febrāyir 1946 min al-tarikh", ("The events of 21 February 1946 in history"), *al-Talī'a*, Cairo, February 1966, pp.51–100; Muhammad Hasan Ahmad, *Al-ikhwān al-muslimin fi al-mīzān* (*The Muslim Brethren in the balance*) (Cairo, n.d.), especially pp.84–8; Ahmad Farid Ali, *Kifāḥ al-shabāb was ẓuhūr Jamal Abd al-Nasir* (*The struggle of youth and the emergence of Nasser*) (Cairo, 1963); Abd al-'Azīm Ramadān, *Tatawwur al-haraka al-wataniyya fi misr* (*The evolution of the national movement in Egypt*) (Cairo, 1968); and a dramatisation of these events in Ahmad Hussein, *Wahtaraqat al-qāhira* (Cairo, 1968).
10. See Sadat, *Asrār al-thawra*, pp.65–6, and 186ff. See also *al-Musawwar*, Cairo, No.2529, 30 March 1973, pp.8–10.
11. Sadat, *Asrār al-thawra*, p.62.
12. Ibid., pp.216–50. See also Kamil al-Sharif, *Al-ikhwān al-muslimūn fi harb filastīn* (*The Muslim Brethren in the Palestine War*), 3rd printing (Beirut, 1969). Second printing appeared under the title *Qitāl al-fidā'iyyin fi harb filastīn 1948* (*The fight of the guerrillas in the Palestine War 1948*).
13. Sadat, *Asrār al-thawra*, p.45.
14. Masri urged Sadat that young army officers must act against the régime and its British masters. "There is no salvation." he advised Sadat, "except in a military *coup d'état*". Sadat, *Asrār al-thawra*, p.62. Tariq al-Bishri in his *The Political Movement in Egypt*, p.461, opined: "Aziz Ali al-Masri appeared to the younger generation of officers as a military reformer and old-style rebel who believed in German militarism and its technical superiority. His great hatred for the British appealed to them. He also represented for them the experience of the revolutionary soldier who, in his youth, had founded secret political organizations [of Arab Officers in the Ottoman army], and who believed in political action by soldiers." On Aziz Masri, see PRO FO 371/19076 and 21936. See also Majid Khadduri, "Aziz Ali al-Masri and

the Arab Nationalist Movement", *Middle Eastern Affairs*, No.4, pp.140–63 (St Antony's Papers No.17), London, 1965. See also Ahmad Hussein, *Īmānī* (Cairo, 1936), *passim*, Salah al-Din al-Sabbagh, *Fursan al-'uruba (Knights of Arabism)* (Baghdad, 1956), and Subeih, *Batal la nansāhu.*

15. Hamrush, *Qissat thawrat 23 yulio*, p.246.
16. See footnote 1.
17. Sadat, *Asrār al-thawra*, pp.250–66. Cf. Hasan Ibrahim in Hamrush, "Shuhud Yulio", in *Rose el-Youssef*, April 1977, and Hamrush, *Qissat thawrat 23 yulio*. Kamal al-Din Rifaat in his memoirs, *Harb al-tahrir al-wataniyya, mudhakkirat Kamal al-Din Rifaat*, edited by Mustafa Tibah (Cairo, 1968), pp.35–61, claims the first tract or handbill bearing the Free Officers imprimatur appeared early in 1946. The discrepancy between his account and that of the others cited arises probably from the activities of Mustafa Sidqi's group, which co-operated with the Muslim Brethren and other radical groups in the student-workers' demonstrations of February-March 1946. See Tariq al-Bishri, "'Âm 1946 fi al-tarikh al-misri".
18. It is reported that Osman Nuri, a Free Officer in Intelligence, kept the conspirators informed. See Hamrush, *Qissat thawrat 23 yulio*, Vol.1, p.149. Another officer was Abdel Muneim al-Naggar, who later was appointed Ambassador to Paris and Baghdad and subsequently Governor of Daqahliyya province.
19. Ibid., pp.161–3.
20. Ibid., p.165.
21. Ibid., p.147.
22. Ibid., pp.182–8. See also Nāsir al-Din al-Nashāshibi, *Al-hibr aswad . . . aswad* (Paris, 1976), *passim*.
23. See Miles Copeland, *The Game of Nations* (London, 1969), pp.47–60.
24. Hamrush, *Qissat thawrat 23 yulio*, pp.182–8, accepts the proposition that the Free Officer conspirators had established contacts with US Intelligence representatives just before the *coup*. As a member of HADETU, Hamrush in his book naturally gives prominence to the links between the leaders of the conspiracy and the American CIA. Equally naturally, he gives greater weight to the contribution of Marxist officers in the political maturation of the army conspiracy, especially after 1949. Thus he claims that through Khalid Mohieddin and Yusuf Siddiq they were largely responsible for the drafting of the "Six Principles of the Revolution", and the wider radicalisation of the officer corps and army ranks. More significantly and correctly, he emphasises the great appeal Nazi propaganda had before and during the war for some of these officers.
25. Hamrush, *Qissat thawrat 23 julio*, p.212.

CHAPTER 6

Nasser and the Army Conspiracy

When Nasser became involved in the army conspiracy he capitalised on an epochal crisis in Egypt; the kind of crisis in the history of nations which is characterised by the blatant cynicism of politicians, the disparity between an imposed order on one hand and the manner of existence and aspirations of a new generation on the other. The crisis had, moreover, the makings of a decisive one, because of the conjunction of objective and subjective conditions which usually herald a radical shift in men's lives. The end of the war, for one, had produced a new balance of forces throughout the world: decolonisation was seen as inevitable: the economic and political face of the Middle East region itself was changing. The three aspects of the Egyptian crisis comprised the long-term consequences of the 4 February 1942 Palace Incident, the impact of the political *malaise* of the forties, and the defeat in the Palestine War.

The return of the Wafd to power in January 1950, with its need to placate the electorate by responding to the more pressing social and economic problems of the day as well as to the demands of a critical new generation within the party, had inaugurated a period of unprecedented freedom in political life. Expression was literally unfettered; newspaper debates drowned the country. Consequently, there was a marked increase in the political activity of new and older groups on the right and the left—Young Egypt now turned socialist, the Brethren and the Marxists—culminating in the burning of Cairo on Black Saturday, 26 January 1952.

In this tense and uncertain atmosphere, a military conspiracy which rejected rash, quixotic acts of violence stood a good chance of maturing. By its nature it had to be a limited movement within the confines of the officer corps. It had to remain circumspect since its detection could have cost the conspirators their lives as it nearly

did.[1] Also, in a climate of free political debate, it was relatively
safe for officers to establish a close relationship with the newest
articulators of opposition to the *status quo* of old politicians and the
monarchy in the press and elsewhere.

There were, from time to time, proposals by some officers to
assassinate several prominent politicians and senior army officers,
and to engage in sabotage against British installations and personnel.
These were, it is reported, consistently rejected by Nasser in favour
of less dramatic political action and the methodical strengthening
of the movement within the army.[2] It is probable that Nasser
rejected violence because, until 1950-1, there was no solidly
organised officer movement which he exclusively controlled.

Until 1949, Nasser had been determined to keep his own role in
the conspiracy secret. "He insisted", Sadat writes, "that Amer
represent him in all dealings of the movement with other officers."[3]
More significant was Nasser's insistence on an independent army
organisation, free of any deals with outside groups. He resisted the
Brethren's recruitment campaign in the officer corps which was
conducted by Major Mahmud Labib. Instead he satisfied himself
with having Abdel Moneim Abdel Rauf of the army movement as
the chief liaison with the Brethren.

Nasser's concern, however, was allegedly to "educate" the army
officers in the importance of sound political organisation, and to
overcome the isolation of their movement from other radical,
similarly motivated groups in Egypt. With the massive street
demonstrations after February 1946, the opportunity arose to
collaborate with student and worker groups and radical organisations of the right and left. The Palestine War led to the renewal of
the links between the army officer movement and the Brethren.
Later, the Canal Zone anti-British operations of the Brethren, the
Wafd Vanguard and Young Egypt guerrilla groups further
strengthened these links, without subjecting the officer movement to
their political control. The long-term aim, Sadat writes, remained
"to overthrow the monarchy in Egypt".[4]

The deterioration of the political situation in the country in the
period 1950-2 was so marked that the régime was under attack from
all opposition quarters, especially the Muslim Brethren and Young
Egypt, now re-formed as the Egyptian Socialist Party. The social
pattern of the country was one of sharp contrasts. There were a few
inordinately rich and millions of destitute land-hungry peasants,

many of whom by then had come to live stacked upon each other in the city in idleness. There was a corrupt court and a drunkard for a king, surrounded by grasping native and foreign courtiers. There were some 200,000 privileged foreigners in business, commerce and financial enterprises. Against these was pitted the new élite of Egyptian entrepreneurs and a growing number of university graduates who aspired to a greater slice of the economic cake. There were foreign troops on Egyptian soil—the British garrison in the Suez Canal area. Finally, the Arab countries in the Fertile Crescent were in turmoil after the post-Palestine War upheavals. In short, the conditions associated with rebellion, if not revolution, were propitious: rapid change, a demographic explosion and the movement of masses of people from the country to the towns, all of them suffering the hardships of economic privation. All of this was grist to the conspirators' mill.

The army conspirators exploited all their links and connections both within the establishment, now tottering under massive attack, and the several organisations of the fragmented opposition forces. The technique paid off, largely because Nasser insisted on confining membership in the army movement of officers. He distrusted the Brethren because of their earlier co-operation in 1946 with the Ismail Sidqi government in purging the Communists, as well as for their known, vast connections with pro-Palace and other party politicians.

In an atmosphere in which Ahmed Hussein of Young Egypt called openly for the overthrow of the régime by force,[5] the officers could probe the areas of weakness and weigh the options open to them. They were well briefed on all other opposition groups, especially the Brethren, without giving away their own intentions. After all, many of the Free Officers themselves had become politically active for the first time against the régime and the British through these civilian organisations.

What emerges from the preceding narrative about the various radical groups and their links with army officers of the same persuasion over a period of ten to fifteen years is the perceptiveness of Nasser in deciding sometime in 1949 on a different—and original —strategy in the pursuit of power. The spate of political assassinations and bombings of public places and British installations of the previous five years in which Sadat and other officers were involved had led nowhere. Most of the thunder and agitation was being generated by the Muslim Brethren. Nasser, instead, chose to construct quietly a small clandestine organisation within the officer corps, using tactically all of his and his fellow-officers' links with known extremist groups, including the Marxists who began to stir again after 1945.

Many of the army officers linked to these groups became known to Nasser and his closest associates during the Palestine War and the anti-British operations in the Canal Zone. Nasser's own postings as an instructor to several army courses—military academy, infantry school, Army Administration School, Staff College—provided him with further opportunities to recruit new members to the officers' conspiracy.[6] He sought to forge new links with an emerging group on the left of the Egyptian establishment, namely, the Wafdist Vanguard (*al-Tali'a al-Wafdiyya*), whose most prominent personality was Ahmad Abul Fath,[7] whom Nasser had first met in 1946 or 1949. Among the Marxists, he cultivated the lawyer Ahmad Fuad, member of HADETU, through the mediation of the Marxist Free Officer Khalid Mohieddin (member of Iskra) and Yusuf Siddiq, member of HADETU.[8] The journalist Ibrahim Talaat of the Wafdist Vanguard's *al-Gumhur al-Masri* also featured prominently in the period 1950–2. Talaat was an old leading member of Young Egypt; his sister was married to the Communist Ahmad Fuad. Nasser used all of them for the attainment of his ends. They were especially helpful in liaising with the Wafdist hierarchy.

By 1949 Nasser realised that neither his old Young Egypt Society nor the Brethren could really attain power. Whereas the Brethren had spent themselves in the Canal Zone, the Palestine War and in a war of attrition against government security forces (their Supreme Guide, Banna, was assassinated in February 1949), Young Egypt was utterly dependent on the personality of one man, Ahmad Hussein; its old political supporters, Ali Maher, Saleh Harb and Aziz al-Masri, were no longer the powerful figures in Egyptian politics they were in the thirties or during the war. Nasser, therefore, decided to organise an independent attack by officers opposed to the *status quo* from within the citadel. Furthermore, he assessed correctly the shifting forces within the surrounding Arab region, America's desire to press Britain to leave Egypt and the Middle East, and the significance of the Cold War between East and West just signalled by a series of crises and confrontations over Greece, Turkey, Iran, Czechoslovakia, Berlin and Korea. According to his confidant, Muhammad Heikal, the affront to Egyptian pride and dignity inflicted by the 4 February Palace Incident, together with the influence of the Brethren and proliferating Marxist groups, "were the historical condition that formed Nasser's destiny, that made him the symbol of lost dignity and hopes unfulfilled."[9]

This is not to say that by 1949 or 1952 Nasser's vision of a new Egypt no longer derived from a source common to most of these groups. It was still very much the one he first acquired from his early association with Young Egypt and the broad radical nationalist perception of the thirties—in fact from his hazy "class" consciousness. What was different was his conspiratorial style, his conception of power and its uses, his decision to take exclusive power in the name of an army movement free of any arrangements with parallel civilian organisations and their followers within the army. In this respect he was like Lenin in grasping the crucial importance of a tight organisational apparatus.

Several fortuitous factors gave him great leeway in his planning. His more activist fellow-officers, who had collaborated with extremist groups, sooner or later ran foul of the authorities. Sadat had been jailed in 1942, subsequently interned in a concentration camp, from where he escaped in 1944. In 1947, his involvement in a number of bombing incidents and assassinations in Cairo led him back to prison.[10] Others, like Boghdadi, Abdel Moneim Abdel Rauf, Khalid Mohieddin, the Salem brothers, Rashad Mehanna and Kamal el-Din Hussein were in some way or another linked to political movements. Equally important, perhaps, is the fact that Nasser recognised the ineffectiveness of General Aziz al-Masri as a man of the past. This could explain his reluctance to meet him until early 1950.[11]

There has been much dispute among the Free Officers and associated revolutionary groups like the Brethren about the sequence of events leading to the *coup* of July 1952. The exact origins and evolution of the army conspiracy, or conspiracies, which culminated in the July 1952 *coup* and the eventual rise of Nasser to power in Egypt will remain obscure for some time yet. All comment about them will remain the subject of controversy and disagreement, especially when there are so many different versions regarding Nasser's role in the conspiracy. Thus, the Muslim Brethren have claimed the greatest credit in the making of Nasser, the revolutionary ruler of Egypt. Young Egypt and the Wafdist Vanguard have made similar claims. HADETU claim they made the greatest contribution to Nasser's political education and social consciousness. There will

always be those who will contend that Nasser was barely involved
in the conspiracy before 1950–1, and that he only exploited it, or
rushed to pluck the fruit of their efforts when it was ripe—a sort of
"usurper of the unfinished revolution". Writing in the sixties, Sadat,
for example, probably had no choice but to assign to his then master,
Nasser, most of the credit for the organisational success of the
officer conspiracy, at least after the war. Be that as it may, it was
Nasser, in the final analysis, who acceded to power, to the post of
Rayyes, Chief of the Egyptians.

There is, however, a disparity between Nasser's own story of the
Free Officer conspiracy and that of Okasha. In his *Philosophy of the
Revolution*, Nasser wrote:

> I remember one day, upon the [UN] decision to partition
> Palestine in September 1947 [note: the UN Partition Resolution
> was voted upon in November] the Free Officers met and
> agreed to assist the Palestine resistance. Next day I went and
> knocked on the door of the home of el-Haj Amin al-Husseini,
> Mufti of Palestine.

That Nasser met with the Mufti in 1947 is reported by others too.
Okasha, who was not a member of the Free Officer executive in
1950–2, and probably did not know of the pre-Palestine War
organisation, wrote: "The Palestine War expedition came to an end
with its benefits and evils . . . The expeditionary force returned home
and the idea of the Free Officers grew."[12] Most informants are
agreed, however, that the underground leaflets by the Free Officers
as of November 1949 were written and edited by Nasser and Hamdi
Obeid, and reproduced and distributed by Khalid Mohieddin.[13]

Immediately after the Palestine War, those disaffected officers who
were not otherwise active in various radical organisations decided to
assassinate the country's political leaders, beginning with Nahhas
Pasha, whose home they bombed that year. Nasser, at variance with
other reports, must have at least acquiesced in, if not approved of,
this decision, otherwise he would not have taken part in the attempt
on the life of General Sirry Amer less than three years later.

Before he died, Salah Salem asserted that the executive committee
of the Free Officers was first formed in November 1949. Its members
were: Nasser, Sadat, Amer, Salah and Gamal Salem, Boghdadi,
Khalid Mohieddin, Hasan Ibrahim, Abdel Moneim Abdel Rauf.
Zakariyya Mohieddin, Hussein Shafei, Yusuf Siddiq and Abdel

Moneim Amin joined it later. This group, after the *coup* in 1952, constituted the Resolution Command Council.

Sadat's writings, however, suggest that the first resistance cell in the army was formed by Zakariyya Mohieddin and himself in Manqabad in 1938, and that the anti-British, anti-Establishment resistance movement in the officer corps went through three stages. First, in 1940–2, officers mainly reacted to the state of Anglo–Egyptian relations in the context of the war. They were angered when the pro-Axis Ali Maher government was dismissed in June 1940, and, along with it, their hero, General Aziz al-Masri. The following year they were exercised over British objections to the stationing of Egyptian army units in Mersa Matruh and demands that they either be disarmed or withdrawn. Sadat, Wagih Abaza, Hasan Izzat, Ahmad Suudi and Abdel Latif Boghdadi (the last four air force officers), all of them members either of Young Egypt or the Brethren, decided to act. They considered impeding the British withdrawal from the Western Desert by sabotaging communications. But the British military authorities intervened by securing a purge and extensive transfer of Egyptian officers. Again in February 1942, after the Palace Incident, they thought of organising protest demonstrations in the Officers' Club. More important, they decided that the political system headed by the King must be destroyed.[14]

Reminiscing about the anti-British activities of this group of officers during the War, Abdel Latif Boghdadi wrote in 1953:[15]

When the Germans were close to Egypt, I, Ahmad Suudi, Hasan Izzat, Muhammad Wagih Abaza (all of us in the Air Force) and First Lieutenant Anwar Sadat thought it our duty to do something against the British. We formed a secret organization in the Air Force to disrupt and impede the British withdrawal from the Western Desert by sabotaging their lines of communication and supply . . . We solicited subscriptions and contributions from other officers and sympathetic civilians to buy tools and explosives . . . Eventually, Suudi escaped and was killed. Sadat and Izzat were arrested and cashiered.

The second stage, 1945–8, many Free Officers have referred to as the Propaganda Stage. They proceeded with the construction of a secret organisation within the officer corps and the recruitment of members at a time when Young Egypt and the Brethren had increased their terrorist activities. The years 1949–52 constituted the third stage, during which an executive committee was formed. One must nevertheless note that for six years, from 1944 to 1949, the underground activities of army officers were confined to Sadat and a few radical officers working in collaboration with civilian groups of bombers and assassins.

The Free Officer conspiracy must also be seen in the context of deteriorating Anglo–Egyptian relations from the time of the Sidqi–Bevin talks in 1946 to the unilateral abrogation of the 1936 Treaty by the Wafd government in October 1951. The most serious political dispute in 1950, for example, was over the withdrawal of British forces from the Canal. By then, the Egyptian army had been defeated in Palestine, the Cold War had turned hot in Korea, inter-Arab politics had experienced the disorienting impact of a series of military *coups* in Syria, and Arab régimes were immersed in a round of mutual recriminations. The emergence of the state of Israel had brought the United States, a superpower, into a more direct involvement in the region, while the Cold War and the problems of Britain in the Middle East prompted the Western powers to seek new regional defence arrangements.

But the Wafd had become corrupt. It intensified its campaign against the British in Egypt largely in order to divert public attention from its sagging popularity. Whereas the Egyptian priority was to secure the British evacuation of the Canal, agreement was complicated by the demand for unity with the Sudan. HM Embassy first tried to reach agreement with the Wafd's Foreign Minister, Muhammad Salah-eddin, "a person of little consequence with no high standing in the Wafd party, who could only drift with what he took to be the tide of opinion."[16]

Meanwhile, press exposés of the arms scandals, implicating the King and his courtiers, exacerbated the domestic crisis. There was mounting hostility to the Wafd from all radical groups in the country. At the same time, the alienation of its traditional recruits, the "middle classes", was complete. Pressed from all quarters, the Wafd in August 1951 let the mob loose to agitate freely against the Anglo–Egyptian Treaty. When in October 1951 it abrogated it unilaterally by decree, it also rejected the Allied proposals for a Middle East Defence Organization (MEDO) that would have replaced the Anglo–Egyptian defence arrangements over the Canal. As Sir Thomas Rapp of the Middle East Office wrote,

"Desultory negotiations on evacuation and the Sudan dragged on until August when they finally ended in deadlock. In retrospect . . .

the early part of 1951 in Egypt was to appear as the calm before the storm."[17]

Amidst the withdrawal of Egyptian labour from British Canal bases and the sabotage of installations the Middle East Office dispersed. Its Political Division withdrew to Fayid, while its Development Division moved to Beirut. The Egyptian army made token defence preparations along the desert road to Cairo. But they were clearly not a serious military deterrent to any action the British might have taken. In the meantime, that inveterate intriguer, General Masri, contacted the British to offer his solution to the Anglo–Egyptian dispute:

> we should contrive to make him Prime Minister in place of Nahas Pasha, and we would then settle the question of the future of our forces by their permanent transfer to the opposite bank of the Canal. He contended that with his authority such a solution could be made acceptable to nationalist feeling.[18]

One can only assume that General Masri was counting on his links with the radical groups of the right and with officers in the Egyptian army to support him in his bid for power. His, however, was a fanciful gesture.

At the end of 1951, Egypt was "a terribly unhappy country". In Cairo, there was "something of a police state atmosphere everywhere and a lack of confidence and a feeling of *malaise* . . ." wrote the otherwise undependable Owen Tweedy in his copious and, on the whole, dull diary.[19] But this uneasy, tense atmosphere had been in the making ever since the assassination of Prime Minister Ahmad Maher in February 1945 by one Muhammad al-Issawi Awadallah, one-time member of Young Egypt and later of the National party. A year later, in January 1946, Amin Osman Pasha, "blue eyed boy of the [British] Embassy", was assassinated.[20] An earlier, unsuccessful attempt on his life was part of the terror campaign against the Wafd and its collaborators. Young Egypt and other terrorist groups, no doubt encouraged—and subverted—by the Palace, had threatened death to all the "traitors".

More important for the army conspiracy was the clash between British troops and Auxiliary Police in Ismailiyya, the so-called Buluk Nizam incident, in January 1952, that led to the burning of Cairo—Black Saturday. It completely alienated the army from the government, the Wafd and the King. In a letter to her son, the wife of

Thomas Russel Pasha, Commandant of the Cairo Police, wrote,[21] "The situation now appears to depend largely on how loyal the Egyptian Army is. A large part is said to be anti-King." At the same time, the King contemplated a *coup* of his own, with the prospect of Ali Maher as Prime Minister, whose clients from Young Egypt had participated so actively in the burning of Cairo on 26 January.

Curious and intriguing in this connection is Sadat's report that in 1951-2, Nasser asked Captain Gamal al-Qadi to approach his uncle, Abdel Latif Mahmud Pasha, a Wafdist Minister, with a view to "reaching an understanding with him on the kind of assistance the Wafd believes our military organization can offer in restraining the King in his attacks on the Constitution."[22] Nasser also pressed another Free Officer, the Muslim Brother Colonel Rashad Mehanna, to approach his relative, Fuad Serag el-Din Pasha, Secretary-General of the Wafd party, with a similar suggestion. Mehanna refused, but another Free Officer, Lieutenant-Colonel Ahmad Anouar, who later became Commandant of the Military Police and was subsequently employed in Nasser's Presidential office, offered to make the approach.[23]

If Sadat's report is accurate, it suggests that as late as 1952, perhaps immediately after Black Saturday, Nasser had not yet decided on a *coup*, but was still considering an "alliance" of sorts with the Wafd against the monarchy. This of course may have been merely a tactical consideration and temporary expedient.

United States policy was another complicating factor in the crisis of 1949-52. The US Ambassador in Cairo, Jefferson Caffery, an Irish-American, seemed to harbour anti-British sentiments, and to encourage the Egyptians in their implacable anti-British course. American policy appeared to many British observers not simply hostile to Britain, but also contradictory if not in fact schizophrenic. Seeking to extend their influence in the Middle East in response to the quickening Cold War, Americans considered the British presence in Egypt as colonial and morally indefensible. At the same time, they expected Britain to remain the bulwark of Western defence in the region.[24] Ali Sabri (later Prime Minister under Nasser) of Egyptian Military Intelligence for instance liaised with the US Military Attaché in Cairo. He was able to ascertain the Americans' benevolent neutrality, if not actual support, towards the July 1952 *coup d'état.*[25]

Equally propitious circumstances for the conspiracy were the troubles in rural Egypt in 1951-2. There were serious peasant uprisings against major landowners such as Badrawi Ashur, brother-in-law of Fuad Serag el-Din, as well as in the estates of Prince Muhammad Ali and Prince Yusuf Kamal. To what extent the social structures in the country were in transition, as Lacouture avers, and to what extent these disturbances were a manifestation of a crisis of state power is an arguable matter. That the masses of peasants, provincial and urban petite bourgeoisie appeared disinherited there is no doubt. But their suffering is measured in centuries, if not millennia.

Writing in 1970, Jean Lacouture remarked generally that the conspiring young officers shared one desire, to transform Egypt. To what, they did not quite know. Nor exactly how to do it. His triple "pyramid of alienation" is a vivid description of their feelings: alienation from foreign occupation, hence the desire to rid Egypt of it; alienation from the economic system, hence the desire to change it in such a way as to attain "social justice", and alienation from the ruling class, hence its elimination between 1952 and 1954.[26] The mixture of motives nevertheless remained odd: a tradition of fervent romantic nationalism, dating from the 1919 revolt, mixed with agrarian conservatism, vague notions of social reform, and political cynicism. The imprint of thirty years of Egyptian national experience was one of the priority of the *national* cause over the other problems of the religious community and the economy. Young Egypt, the National party and the Muslim Brethren had all left their unmistakable imprint on them, and especially on Nasser.

Yet in the final analysis, amidst all these groups and their activities, the advantages of an executive committee for the Free Officer movement in the critical two-year period, 1950-2, were secured by the single-minded concentration and organisational ability of Nasser. His direction of more systematic propaganda and an efficient "intelligence service" enabled the Free Officers to exploit more effectively the power vacuum created in the country gradually since 1946 and precipitously after the burning of Cairo in 1952. Meanwhile, his own experience during that time must have alerted him to the ease with which he could usurp power. The ease with which the conspiracy succeeded in overthrowing the *ancien régime* was crucial to further developments. It dazzled Egyptians, high and low; and the lesson was not lost on Nasser, for it confirmed his visceral

view of Egypt's political soul and historical continuity; Egypt cannot
do without a king for long.

Notes

1. Subeih reports that General Haidar Pasha, Army Chief of Staff, had ordered
   the arrest of the members of the Free Officer Executive on 10 July 1952. But
   as he informed his adjutant, no other than Major Salah Salem of his intention, the Free Officers were immediately alerted. See Muhammad Subeih,
   Batal la nansāhu, Aziz al-Masri wa 'asruhu (Beirut, 1971), p.436.
2. Reports about these are to be found in the works already cited by Sadat,
   Subeih, Hamrush, and Nasser's own tract.
3. Anwar al-Sadat, *Asrar al-thawra, al-misriyya* (Cairo, 1965), p.188.
4. Ibid., p.216.
5. See some of his articles and editorials of that period reproduced in *Qadiyyat
   al-tahrid* (Cairo, 1957).
6. See Gamal Abdel Nasser, *Palestine War Memoirs* in Muhammad Subeih,
   Ayyām wa ayyām (Cairo, 1966).
7. Editor of *al-Misri*, Abdul Fath was to prove an invaluable informer to the
   conspirators during the Officers' Club election crisis in 1951–2. He also
   warned them of the government's plans to arrest all the Free Officers on
   20 July 1952, thereby precipitating the *coup*. Earlier that year Nasser, Kamal
   al-Din Rifaat and Hasan Tuhami, all of them Free Officers, ambushed the
   car of the army chief-of-staff, General Husein Sirry Amer, with machine-gun
   fire outside his house.
8. According to Tariq al-Bishri, *The political movement in Egypt 1945–1952*
   (Cairo, 1972), pp.416–74, Khalid Mohieddin joined the Communist movement during the war, and Yusuf Siddiq after the Palestine War.
9. Muhammad Heikal, *Nasser: The Cairo Documents* (London, New English
   Library, 1972), p.18.
10. See *al-Musawwar*, Cairo, 23 July 1953, and Sadat, *Asrār al-thawra*, pp.197–
    220.
11. Reported by Kamal el-Din Rifaat in a private interview, London, 1972.
12. Sarwat Okasha, "Al-khitta allati nuffidhat fi 23 yulio" ("The plan that was
    executed on 23 July"), *Al-Tahrīr*, Cairo, No.23, 29 July 1952.
13. See ibid. and Saniyya Quraa, *Haris al-majd, Jamal Abd al-Nassir, (Guardian
    of Glory, Gamal Abdel Nasser)* (Cairo, 1969). See also Ahmad Hamrush,
    Qissat thawrat 23 julio (Beirut, 1974).
14. See Sadat, *Asrār al-thawra*, pp.66–72 and pp.185–6.
15. Quoted in M.F. al-Wakil, editor, *Hādhihi al-thawra (This revolution)* (Cairo,
    1953), pp.188–9.
16. Sir Thomas Rapp, Private Papers, St Antony's College, Oxford, p.373.
    Sir Thomas served as a consul in Egypt in 1925. He returned to Egypt in
    1950 as a member of the new Middle East Office set up by Foreign Secretary
    Ernest Bevin after 1945 to fill the gap left by the dismantling of the extensive
    wartime organisation.
17. Ibid., p.395.
18. Ibid., pp.408–9.
19. St Antony's College, Oxford, Book II, pp.26ff.
20. An expression used oddly by Thomas Russell Pasha, Cairo Police Comman-
    dant, in a letter dated 5 March 1945 in connection with the assassination of
    Prime Minister Ahmad Maher. Private Papers, St Antony's College, Oxford.

21. Letter dated January 1952. Ibid.
22. Sadat, *Asrār al-thawra*, pp.268–9.
23. Fathi Radwan claimed in *Rose el-Youssef*, No.2463, Cairo, 25 August 1975, that the first contacts between the Free Officers and the Wafd were made in 1950 by Wing Commander Wagih Abaza via his relative Fikri Abaza, editor of the weekly magazine *al-Musawwar*.
24. Sir Thomas Rapp, Private Papers, pp.402, 410.
25. See Sadat, *Asrār al-thawra*; Hamrush, *Qissat thawrat 23 yulio*, and Miles Copeland, *The Game of Nations* (London, 1969).
26. Jean Lacouture, *Nasser* (Paris, 1971), especially p.137, and Tariq al-Bishri, *Al-Haraka al-siyasiyya fi misr*, 1945–1952 (Cairo, 1972).

CHAPTER 7

Consolidation of Power:
The Elimination of Rivals

The account of the *coup d'état* on 23 July 1952 has been told several times. So far here we have emphasised its origins and antecedents, as well as the political conditions in which it succeeded, with some reference to Nasser's own behaviour. The next phase after the assumption of power was its consolidation. Our interest here too lies in Nasser's behaviour—and personality. We make two assumptions in this connection. First, Nasser, from the start, aimed at the exclusive control of the revolution by the Free Officers.[1] Second, he sought to ensure, from the outset, his own control over the new Free Officer establishment as an essential step toward his ultimate control over the Egyptian state.

Commenting on the intention of the Free Officers upon their assumption of power, Sir Anthony Nutting, writing in 1971–2, remarked:

At this point in time Nasser and his Free Officers had no intention whatever of governing Egypt themselves. For one thing, they had neither experience nor qualifications for the task, having spent their adult years exclusively in the armed forces. For another, as Nasser freely and frequently admitted, they had no political programme other than the broad aims outlined in their six-point manifesto, from which revolutionary policy was subsequently evolved on a pragmatic day-to-day basis. Indeed, throughout the years of preparation for the revolution they had kept themselves as a body aloof from all political associations. True, many of them, including Nasser himself for a brief while, had had individual ties with the Muslim

126

Brotherhood and a few more were connected with the Communist party.[2]

It is not clear whether Sir Anthony Nutting reached his conclusion strictly on the basis of his own observation and judgement, or whether he accepted the subsequent statements of Nasser and his associates. Although it is a perfectly reasonable conclusion for an outsider to reach, it is more likely, as was argued in the preceding chapters, that first, Nasser intended the Free Officers to lead and control a revolution, and second, that he and several of his Free Officer colleagues did not simply have individual ties with other radical organisations, but were members of them at one time or another. Some of the revolutionary policy of the Nasser régime did indeed evolve as a reaction or response to a combination of internal and external conditions and events. But the initial declarations of policy and several of the earliest reform measures of the Free Officers were not simply pulled out of their military hats; they had long been suggested and promoted by the radical groups to which several Free Officers belonged. Furthermore, lack of experience or qualifications did not inhibit army officers, say, in Syria or Iraq, from taking power by force. Inexperience or lack of qualification are perhaps causes of failure to use power properly or to retain it; they do not preclude army officers from assuming it.

The consolidation of power took place on at least two levels over the period 1952–4. The first issue was the total control of the armed forces by the régime; the second entailed the neutralisation and eventual destruction of other existing loci of political power—the monarchy, political parties, senior officials, land-owning, financial, industrial and commercial members of the old ruling class. A necessary corollary of this twin objective was the control of education, the media, professional syndicates, trade unions, the rural structures in the countryside, the religious institutions and orders, the administration and bureaucracy, eventually, the whole society. Most important is the fact that the consolidation of the new régime's power on the two main levels occurred largely as a result of Nasser's relentless drive for personal power. Without this, many of the events and patterns of relations between members of the new élite, or between individual officers and Nasser himself, cannot be explained satisfactorily.

Sir Anthony Nutting obviously based his conclusion in part on Nasser's subsequent explanation that, after the burning of Cairo on

26 January 1952, he (presumably, the Free Officer Executive Committee) considered mounting a *coup* in order to restore Nahhas to power. But the Free Officers were implicated in the bombing of Nahhas Pasha's residence some time before that, and the machine-gun ambush of General Sirri Amer's car. The discussion of Egyptian materials considered here and the testimony of Nasser's associates suggest that the Free Officers were satisfied with the appointment of Ali Maher as Prime Minister after those tragic and cataclysmic events in January. Equally, in July 1952, Ali Maher as the Prime Minister of a civilian Cabinet was acceptable to the Free Officers, not simply because he had been anti-British in 1939–40, but more fundamentally because he was the kind of "strong man", an Atatürkist Egyptian politician, and because he had consistently supported the radical organisations of the 1930s towards which the Free Officers gravitated in their youth.[3]

In August 1952 the Free Officers were still proclaiming their willingness to co-operate with the political parties. In presenting their movement as a popular revolution they emphasised its link in a chain or series of national revolts going back to 1798.[4] July 1952 was described as the culmination of the national struggle that began with Omar Makram against the French:

> The revolution of 23rd July is the fulfilment of the aspirations
> of the Egyptian people in the modern age to govern itself . . .
> from the day Omar Makram led the popular movement for the
> appointment of Muhammad Ali as governor of Egypt . . . the
> day Orabi demanded a constitution . . . the day in 1919 when
> Saad Zaghlul demanded independence from the British.[5]

The fact remained that the Free Officers had grabbed power by force. Their ostensible leader was a relatively unknown major-general, and the members of the RCC obscure young officers. To be sure, a new generation of Egyptians had come to power. But to what end, no one was certain. There were others about who claimed an equal if not prior right to lead a revolt against the *ancien régime*, and they were prepared to question—even challenge—the army's usurpation of that right. A struggle for power was inevitable.

The Egyptian left has accused the Free Officers in general and Nasser in particular of being counter-revolutionary, and having pre-empted the real revolution. What was clear from the outset was that the soldiers sought to control the machinery of the state to the exclusion of all other interested groups in the country. The elimination of rivals became a precondition of all other measures. Soon the extraction of unquestioning obedience from Egyptians high and low became the preferred policy of the Free Officers, and the solicitation of alternative views on the likely course of the revolution was abandoned.

The Struggle for Power

The easy success of the *coup* came as a surprise to its perpetrators. It was a success beyond their expectations. By 4 a.m. on 23 July 1952 the Free Officers found themselves in control of the armed forces. The reaction of the population to their first communiqué, broadcast at 7.30 a.m., was friendly, in some cases demonstrably so. In a sense, they were not quite sure what the next step would be. With King Faruq and his floundering government in Alexandria, the Wafd and the Ikhwan with a multitude of followers on the loose, the fate of the army movement remained in the balance. The politicians, for their part, did not know exactly who these officers, or what their objectives, were. A frantic game of probing to find out ensued.

The soldiers realised that the monarch had to be challenged first. As the sovereign, his swift removal would take the wind out of the sails of his supporters. One difficulty, however, arose because the conspirators themselves did not agree among themselves over what to do with the King. There were those among them, like Gamal Salem and Zakariyya Mohieddin, who pressed for his execution. The majority, however, counselled his deposition and exile, for they were not yet prepared for the abolition of the monarchy. The officers were unanimous, though, about purging the court of undesirable courtiers and Palace officials. The main political point they seemed to want to make was that they, the revolutionary officers, represented the will of the people. And in this intention to assume sovereignty lay the seeds of the inevitable abolition of the monarchic system a year later. In more practical terms, the quick recruitment of a large number of officers loyal to the junta into key posts in the emerging administration of the new régime supplied an irresistible momentum to the RCC's eventual assumption of power. It represented a sort of multiplying effect mechanism for the creation of a new ruling class, a new power élite and political directorate.

The soldiers received the willing collaboration of leading jurists such as Suleiman Hafez and Abdel Razeq al-Sanhuri in the first days of their régime. These were bitterly opposed to the Wafd party and wished its destruction, and consequently they eagerly provided the expertise the soldiers needed in the delicate promulgation of their earliest decrees and thus lent a legal authoritativeness to their acts of power. Such legal expertise was invaluable in the forced abdication of the King and his exile. Meanwhile, the public was kept in the dark regarding many of these measures, in order to avoid any disturbances or opposition.

Equally invaluable was the assistance of these jurists in the question of a Regency Council to act for the new infant King Ahmed Fuad II, by glossing over—in fact, ignoring—constitutional requirements and parliamentary precedures. A rapid series of "dismantling" decrees—the abolition of titles, the reduction of perks and privileges for Ministers and officials, such as the use of official cars, etc.— impressed a gaping public. Yet none of these palliatives obviated the inevitable struggle for power between the RCC and the civilian forces, and within the RCC and the officer corps themselves.

They invited Ali Maher to form a government. He was useful for creating the impression that the military prepared for the reinstatement of a healthier constitutional order, but he remained powerless to govern. Moreover, his known autocratic tendencies pushed him into a series of manoeuvres which further weakened the civilian forces and hastened his own clash with the soldiers. Meanwhile, the junta expanded its executive membership on 15 August 1952 from 9 to 15, a measure pressed by Nasser. This meant a wider representation and recruitment of adherents from the armed forces. More harmful to the chances of a return to civil government was the RCC's extensive appointment of ever larger numbers of "loyal" officers as "commissars" in government departments, economic and other institutions (*mandub al-qiyada*). "Dual rule", one of effective power wielded by the RCC and of formal authority resting in a civilian Cabinet, held sway temporarily.

Abdel Nasser knew instinctively that the revolution would pass through a transition period during which many errors would be committed and purges conducted. He did not wish that his colleagues absorb the knocks of this early phase. He decided therefore that they should assume the less prominent functions of "Secretary General" to the various civilian Cabinet ministers in order to learn from them the secrets of governing and administration which differed radically from the ordering of military affairs. The administrative knowledge of most of the officers, including members of the RCC, was almost non-existent. Nasser therefore did not wish them to take over completely before they had acquired adequate training.[6]

From this arrangement emerged the function of "Representative of the RCC" in all areas of state administration, and the inevitable clash between civilian Ministers and their military overseers.

Maher objected to the appointment of officers to civilian posts as constituting a burden on public funds. He opposed the agrarian reform law as drafted by Suleiman Hafez and the Marxists Rashed Barawi and Ahmad Fuad. He thought 500, not 200, *feddans* ought to be the limit of ownership. He disagreed with the RCC over the holding of elections. On the whole, Ali viewed the discomfiture of the political parties, particularly the Wafd, and the presumed inexperience of the soldiers as the ideal combination of a political vacuum which he could fill. But the army's arrest of two dozen politicians in early September without consulting him or his government emphasised his impotence. Barely 46 days after forming a government, Maher resigned. On 7 September Naguib assumed the premiership of an otherwise civilian Cabinet. He was the first soldier since Orabi to become Prime Minister of Egypt. Two days later he proclaimed the Agrarian Reform Law.

In retrospect, one may view Ali Maher as an effective temporary instrument in the army's consolidation of power immediately after the *coup*. Through him the junta was able to project the vague intention of a return to constitutional parliamentary government. At the same time, Ali's antipathy to the political parties contributed to the overall weakening of their power and thus neutralised their role. However, Ali and the junta could not co-operate seriously because Ali was, despite his maverick political record, essentially a man of the old political world, and one who belonged to the rich land-owning bourgeoisie. He and his colleagues stood to lose a great deal as a result of the Agrarian Reform Law, whereas the soldiers did not. It was therefore natural that as an alternative to agrarian reform Ali proposed fiscal measures, chief among them graduated taxation, as a way of gradual social and economic reform.

The junta nevertheless got much political mileage out of these early measures. Very shortly after grabbing power they managed to abolish several millennia-old institutions, exploit the fragmented

civilian forces and dazzle the multitudes with their dramatic—even
if some were practically meaningless—reform measures. The RCC
clearly gained in strength while its adversaries weakened. Purges and
exposés of corruption were good publicity and heralded a real clash
between the saviours and the exploiters. Naguib's popularity soared
as the junta promised a better tomorrow. A society comprising
65 per cent peasants enthusiastically welcomed the relatively mild
agrarian reform law, thus giving the Free Officer movement a great
deal of public goodwill in their purported programme of social
change. The soldiers, that is, had struck a heavy blow against the
land-owning élite and the economic base of its power, and the
masses approved.

Thus galvanised, the RCC's push toward greater power was
inevitable. An open clash with all organised political groups began
with the so-called purification campaign. Since the officers were not
dependent upon the support of a political party as such, their attack
on these organisations was not unexpected or problematic. Yet, for
at least six months after July 1952, the junta deliberately gave the
impression abroad that they were working for the restoration of
constitutional government. In the meantime, they postponed action
pending "purification". Corruption and revolutionary tribunals were
quickly set up. These implied that a return to constitutional government required first a purification of the country's political forces.

What constituted a purified political world was to be decided by
the junta. The officers in power, that is, alone would decide at will
whether other political groups could exist or not, especially when
the Parties Reorganisation Law of 9 September 1952 subjected
parties to army control under the Ministry of Interior. Arrests of
several leading politicians accompanied the promulgation of this
law, so that the determination of the soldiers, undefined as their
objectives may have been at that time, to assume greater power
became clear. At the same time, these measures had the devastating
effect of discrediting all politicians. The parties, in other words, were
dissolved and their reconstitution was made wholly dependent on
the army's approval. Nahhas, for example, resigned the leadership
of the Wafd in the face of the junta's steamroller tactics. Nahhas is
reported to have told his colleague, Ibrahim Farag Messiha, a one-
time Wafdist Foreign Minister, "The Army is a steamroller. Nothing
will stop it short of a public fiercely attached to democratic principles
and the constitution."

The role of the purge was wider and far reaching, involving the peremptory dismissal of state and other officials for political reasons, the denial of their pension rights and other compensation for service, the trial of leading personalities for "agrarian reform crimes" by military courts, and the free play of defamation without legal recourse.

Once the constitution had been abolished in December 1952, it was very difficult to restore, and elections were inevitably postponed until after an agreement with Britain over evacuation had been concluded. The students and the press, especially the Wafdist press, opposed and demonstrated against the junta's anti-constitutional course throughout the autumn, and a committee of fifty members under Ali Maher's chairmanship to draft a new constitution was appointed in January 1953. It simply faded away. Yet a few days later, the junta confiscated property and other assets of political parties, declared severe measures against a vaguely defined category of citizens: all of those who "obstruct the aims of the army movement and endanger the national interest". A decree making the Commander-in-Chief's acts supreme (i.e. sovereign) and unaccountable in effect gave the junta absolute power, which was very soon "legitimated" in a three-year transition period with a provisional eleven-article constitution. All of these measures were accompanied by further arrests of political party members, Communists and others "connected with foreign powers".

Although one may consider such measures extreme in countering student opposition and the criticism in the press, they reflected a significant shift in the junta's approach to power: that of autocracy. Three years later, in 1956, another shift occurred towards personal autocracy. Nevertheless, during the transition period, 1953–6, the RCC combined a series of popular measures with executive acts calculated to bring recalcitrants to heel. Inevitably, fear became the dominant feeling among all other political elements in the country, and soon these were reduced to silence.

On the mass level, the army's publicity campaign throughout the country, headed by the popular, benign General Naguib, affected a fusion between the "popular will" and the junta. It purported the foundation of a mass-based popular movement. The Liberation Rally, formed on 23 January 1953, supervised by officers without prior political experience, kept the political community amorphous and at the same time under firm army control. As a new political force the Rally could claim to be free of the taint of the old political parties and therefore had no need to share power with them.

The eleven-article Provisional Constitution of 10 February 1953, basically a reaffirmation of the so-called Six Principles of the Revolution, preceded the further destruction of the old order. The corruption and revolution tribunals sat between May and September. They tried and discredited scores of leading politicians and their cohorts. In a few months (March 1954) the parties were smashed and their leaders rendered ineffective.

Meanwhile, Nasser, as Minister of Interior and Secretary-General of the Liberation Rally, "explained" the junta's position regarding political groups: "they were not opposed to parties as such, only to their corrupt leaders. Thus the Liberation Rally was designed not as a party, but as an instrument for the reorganization of popular forces."[7] As part of this reorganisation, the army was ready to abolish the monarchy and proclaim a republic by June 1953.

The Extermination of Allies

When the Free Officers took power, they released most political prisoners from the *ancien régime* under a general amnesty between July and October 1952. But they inaugurated their own rounds of political arrests very soon in September 1952 and again early the following year. With the King and political parties out of the way, the gradual control of the media and the masses via the Liberation Rally, opposition to the junta could now come only from the officer corps itself, minor groups such as the Communists, and the massive Ikhwan movement.

The industrial strife in the Misr Textile Company factories in Kafr el Dawar in August 1952, resulting in clashes with the police, casualties, arrests, convictions and executions, caused a division between members of the RCC. Khaled Mohieddin and Yusuf Siddiq, on the left, objected to the harsh measures against the workers. The security services, controlled by Nasser and his friends, proceeded to neutralise the left in general by driving them out of the media, banning their older publications, arresting leading officers associated with them and forcing the resignation of others, as for example Yusuf Siddiq from the RCC. The wave of arrests, lasting from April to June 1953, culminated in a trial of Communists in July, so that by the end of the year all Communist organisations had been destroyed or driven underground.

Coping with the powerful Muslim Brethren, however, was a more difficult task. The long-standing close relations between them and the Free Officers before the *coup* seemed to continue after it. Yet the clash between them erupted in the early days of the régime over the inclusion of Muslim Brother Ministers in the first civilian Cabinets, over the Regency, the amnesty of previously convicted Muslim Brother assassins and the Brethren's insistence that the Free Officers follow their general policy. Soon tension increased over the Brethren's approaches to General Naguib and their efforts to infiltrate the army and police, especially after Abdel Moneim Abdel Rauf and Rashad Mehanna had been ousted from the highest councils of the Free Officers' régime.

For about two years the RCC and the Brethren coexisted—even co-operated—because they needed each other. The RCC found the Brethren convenient allies in the period of its struggle against the monarchy, the old political parties and the left. The Brethren, on their part, hoped eventually to control the army movement through their officer members and sympathisers. At the end of 1953, apart from the Free Officers in the army, the Ikhwan represented the only organised movement left intact in the country, commanding a large following and constituting an alternative to army rule.

The explosion came after university student demonstrations in January 1954 during a memorial service for the "Canal Martyrs". Clashes with the police resulted in casualties, and Ikhwan members openly used firearms. The RCC ordered the dissolution of the Brethren on the grounds that they opposed agrarian reform, infiltrated the officer corps and the police with a view to subverting them, maintained a secret paramilitary organisation and contacts with Britain, and blatantly tried to impose their guardianship over the Free Officer régime. The Supreme Guide and members of his Supreme Council were arrested along with some 500 other members of the organisation.

Nasser and the RCC did not proceed with this drastic, dangerous measure until they had succeeded in splitting the Brethren's hierarchy.[8] At the same time, they hoped to soften the blow by soliciting the Brethren's vast following with pious visits to the tomb of their founder and first Supreme Guide, Hassan el Banna; in short, by reassuring the rank and file that the army was not opposed to their movement as such, only to the mischief of its current leaders.[9]

Whereas the Free Officer junta emerged victorious from their clash with the leaders of the *ancien régime*, the Communists and the Muslim Brethren, their firm control of the officer corps in the armed forces at the beginning of 1954 was not yet assured. The internal struggle for power which soon raged within it in February–March 1954 was not only the fiercest and most dangerous the régime experienced, but from its outcome emerged Nasser, "the autocrat of all Egyptians".

Barely six months after the *coup*, officers in uniform were arrested on orders of the RCC. Senior officers had been purged or neutralised during the first 48 hours of the *coup*. Yet in their first three months in power the junta found it necessary to dismiss 500 officers of all grades. The less dangerous—or less harmful—of the senior officers were quickly appointed to civilian posts, ranging from Ministerial sinecures to diplomatic missions abroad. The fate of Colonel Rashad Mehanna of the Regency Council in the early days of the régime was an indication of a trend and pattern. When as a Muslim Brother member of the organisation "Youth of Muhammad" he tried to exploit his Regency position, the RCC dismissed and arrested him. When artillery officers proposed that members of the RCC should be elected, many of them were arrested or cashiered in January 1953 on a charge of plotting to assassinate the sitting members of the Council. Arrest and torture of brother officers date from this time.[10]

Some Council members, particularly Naguib, objected to these measures, thus causing further rifts among its members. The excuse of the Nasser-led faction was that there was a danger of a counter-*coup*. By mid-1953 one may therefore assume that the Free Officer movement as a wider organisation of officers in the armed forces had ceased to exist separately from the RCC and the immediate cliques of its members. The RCC itself became the movement, refusing to share power with, or be accountable for, its actions to a wider constituency of officers.

With the Communist Yusuf Siddiq out of the country,[11] the only effective opposition to the repressive measures of the Council came from the remaining Communist on it, Khaled Mohieddin. He objected to the increasing number of political prisoners, the imposition of army control over trade and labour unions. He was pressed to sever his links with the left, and at the same time was accused of fomenting mutiny in the armour corps. The gathering storm within the army, however, can best be considered from the perspective of Nasser's behaviour and his ultimate triumph, that is, his transformation from a *primus inter pares* in the RCC to its unchallenged chief.

Notes

1. Until 1954, the military regime rarely referred to the "revolution" (*thawra*) but to the "army movement" (*harakat al-jaysh*).
2. Sir Anthony Nutting, *Nasser* (London, 1972), p.38.
3. See Muhammad Auda, *Mīlād thawra* (*Birth of a revolution*) (*Cairo*, 1974); Muhammad Subeih, *Ayyām wa ayyām* (Cairo, 1966) and Ahmad Hamrush, *Qissat thawrat 23 yulio* (Beirut, 1974), Vol.1 esp. pp.224–30.
4. See, for example, Hasan Marei and Amin Mustafa Afifi Abdullah, *Thawrat shaab* (*A people's revolution*) (Cairo, 1954).
5. Nasser in *The Philosophy of the Revolution* (Washington, 1955).
6. Fathi Radwan in *Rose el-Youssef*, Cairo, No.2462, 18 August 1975. Radwan points to the fact that Naguib's Cabinet included seven members of the National party, five members of the reformist intellectual organisation known as The Pioneers (*Ruwwād*) founded by Ahmad Hasanein Pasha (Abdel Jalil al-Emary, Abbas Ammar, William Selim Hanna, Fuad Galal, and Abdel Raziq Sidqi), and one independent engineer, Murad Fahmi.
7. *Collected Speeches*. This view was first expressed in a speech at Mansura on 9 April 1953. See *Hādhihi al-thawra*, pp.197–9.
8. See P. J. Vatikiotis, *The Egyptian Army in Politics* (Bloomington, 1961 and Greenwich, Conn,. 1975), pp.71–96; and Hamrush, *Qissat thawrat 23 yulio*, esp. on Sheikh Hasan al-Baquri, pp. 239–45 and 300–10.
9. On the relations between the soldiers and the Muslim Brethren, see Hamrush, but see also the controversial recent article by the young Egyptian historian Abdel 'Azīm Ramadan in the Cairo weekly *Sabāh el-khair*, No.1056, 1 April 1976.
10. See Hamrush, *Qissat thawrat 23 yulio*, pp.307–23.
11. Siddiq was dismissed from the RCC early in 1953 and exiled abroad. He returned secretly to Egypt, but was arrested in 1954 and imprisoned until 1956.

CHAPTER 8

Nasser Triumphant

Purging and Purification

The proclamation of the Republic on 18 June 1953 marks the turning-point in the intention of the soldiers to assume permanent power, and the transformation of the RCC from a revolutionary directorate to a government. It also provided the proper arena for the resolution of the power struggle between Nasser and Naguib which was largely determined by the critical matter of the control of the armed forces.

Naguib became President of the Republic in addition to being Prime Minister and chairman of the RCC. But he relinquished the post of Commander-in-Chief of the armed forces and War Minister. At the insistence of Nasser, and over the opposition of Naguib and other RCC members, Abdel Hakim Amer was promoted from major to major-general and appointed commander of the armed forces. Amer was Nasser's close friend; his foremost task now was to impose the RCC's firm control over the armed forces and prevent further trouble by dissidents. To this extent, his appointment to the top military post the day after Naguib became President of the Republic seemed to check and balance the two major protagonists for power, Nasser and Naguib, in the RCC.[1]

With the task of controlling the army assigned to Amer, Nasser could concentrate on strengthening the role of the RCC and the new Cabinet; and, in turn, his own position within both. As Vice-Premier and Minister of the Interior, he controlled the internal security services. Salah Salem, an anti-Naguibist, took charge of the crucial National Guidance (Propaganda) ministry, while Boghdadi went over to the war ministry. In October 1953, Gamal, brother of Salah, Salem took charge of the Ministry of Communications, and Zakariyya Mohieddin replaced Nasser at Interior. The Cabinet in which RCC members served for the first time was clearly stacked against Naguib, while Nasser's friend Amer, with the beaverish assistance of his *chef de cabinet*, Captain Shams Badran—a future, ill-fated war Minister—purged and reorganised the officer corps to Nasser's specifications and advantage. All of these developments marked the beginning of Nasser's serious attempt to construct his own power base within the RCC and the officer corps at large. The repeated clashes in the RCC with Naguib, Khaled Mohieddin and others over policy regarding parties, political prisoners and officer arrests, the alarming hostile reaction of students and the press to certain measures all suggested to him the need to prepare for a power struggle.

By February 1954, on the heels of the Brethren disturbances over the "Canal Martyrs", the army movement was plagued by internal divisions, foremost among these being the split between Naguib and the pro-Nasser members of the RCC. The prisons and internment centres were full. Naguib expressed his displeasure at the Amer-Badran army policy of transfers, dismissals and assignment of officers to civilian posts. He objected to the death sentences passed on party leaders, including the proposed house arrest of 75-year-old Nahhas Pasha, and refused to approve them. A few months before that he had protested against the arrest and torture of artillery officers and the execution of at least one among them by refusing to approve the sentence of the military court. He deplored his humiliating treatment by RCC colleagues such as Gamal Salem and Zakariyya Mohieddin, and the manipulation of the media against him.

On 23 February Naguib felt he could not carry on as RCC chairman and President; he submitted his resignation in writing to Kamal el-Din Hussein, secretary of the RCC. Nasser took over as Prime Minister and proceeded to accuse Naguib of demanding dictatorial powers. The next day Naguib's telephone was disconnected, his personal bodyguard was disarmed and replaced by new troops under the command of Muhsin Abul Nur (many years later Secretary of the ASU). Naguib was placed under house arrest and the office of the President of the Republic was declared vacant pending the return to constitutional government.

Trouble broke out immediately in the army. Armour corps officers, loyal to Khaled Mohieddin—the only RCC member besides Naguib opposed to the repressive measures of the Council—reacted violently. Sarwat Okasha, another armour Free Officer, resigned as editor of the junta's new magazine *al-Tahrir* after a quarrel with

Salah Salem, the responsible Minister. He was replaced by Sadat and packed off as military attaché to the Paris embassy.[2] The armour corps held a meeting in their mess, attended by yet another Free Officer of the corps, Hussein Shafei. They ordered the RCC to return Naguib to office.

When Nasser confronted them during the night of 23 February, he was faced with a deluge of opposition to the RCC from line officers. Whether intimidated or acting on the principle that discretion is the better part of valour, Nasser returned to his RCC colleagues and suggested the formation of a new government under Khaled that would quickly lead the country back to constitutional life. For good measure, he regaled his colleagues with the dramatic sound of tanks in the background during his acrimonious meeting with the armour corps officers in their mess that night. He impressed his colleagues further with the rebellious officers' disapproval of their own conduct at the top. Cleverly, perhaps, Nasser at the same time teased his RCC colleagues by urging them to resign and leave it all—the revolution and the country—to Khaled and Naguib. After all, he seemed to suggest, the country wanted Naguib, and a handful of officers constituting the RCC could not hope to stem the tide. Naguib was brought back to the premiership on 28 February.

The prospect of retreat under the pressure of popular demand for a return to constitutional government led by an "alliance" between Naguib and the left was too much for several members of the RCC. Conservatives among them, like Kamal el-Din Hussein, Boghdadi and the Salem brothers, warned Khaled not to turn the country over to the Communists.

In the early hours of the morning of 25 February Nasser accompanied Khaled to the armour corps officers' mess to inform them of the decision to dissolve the RCC, reinstate Naguib as President of the Republic with Khaled as the head of a three-month transition government which would hold elections for a constituent assembly while RCC members returned to their army units. Amidst wild applause Khaled seemed to have triumphed—if only temporarily.

After going to inform Naguib at his home of the decision, Khaled returned to the corps' headquarters, only to find that junior officers, loyal to Nasser and other RCC members, had rejected the RCC decision and threatened to use force. Some even tried to attack Khaled personally, but were prevented from doing so by Salah Salem and Amer. Among the leaders of these dissidents were Captain Kamal el-Din Rifaat and Hasan Tuhami (both soon thereafter became close associates of Nasser, eventually attaining Ministerial rank), Lieutenant-Colonel Ahmad Anwar, Commandant of the Military Police, Major Magdi Hasanein (director of the Liberation Province) and Wing-Commander Wagih Abaza of Young Egypt fame. In fact they were all of the right, ex-members of Young Egypt or the extremist National party and artillery officers in the main who had brought up and trained their guns on the armour corps headquarters. Several armour corps officers were arrested. Kamal Rifaat went off and arrested Naguib in his home, and held him prisoner in the Almaza Artillery mess. Salah Nasr, the nortorious Chief of Intelligence in the sixties, who was then CO of Naguib's personal guard, facilitated the arrest. Only the direct intervention of Amer secured Naguib's release several hours later.

The Free Officers had torn themselves apart. Officers in other military districts, including Alexandria, opposed Naguib's resignation. Demonstrations raged in Cairo and Khartoum, an indication perhaps of Naguib's popularity. But popularity in the streets was not of the essence in deciding that particular struggle for power. By now Khaled found himself opposed by the anti-Communists in the RCC, who commanded a vast following among infantry and artillery officers. His position was precarious. Some RCC members urged his arrest, others suggested his exile abroad. Nasser, though, reminded his colleagues that the real problem was not Khaled but Naguib. If the latter were reinstated, so should Khaled be too.

The situation became dangerous when a military court chaired by Gamal Salem tried arrested armour corps officers. General Amer, the Commander-in-Chief, was warned that if the trials proceeded the armour corps would use tanks to blast his GHQ. Meanwhile, street demonstrations continued, with demonstrators shouting slogans such as, "To prison with Salah, to prison with Gamal. No revolution without Naguib." There were serious clashes with the police. Naguib returned to his offices on 27 February amidst continuing demonstrations and demanded a clarification of the powers of the presidency. Nasser remained Prime Minister. The next day huge demonstrations in Abdin Square resulted in scores of casualties and mass arrests. Within three days of this incident leaders of the Ikhwan and the founder-leader of Young Egypt, Ahmad Hussein, Wafdists and Communists were arrested. The universities were closed down. Naguib now demanded the release of political prisoners.

Meeting without Naguib, who was on a 24-hour visit to the Sudan, and without Khaled who, on the advice of his cousin Zakariyya, had gone to Wadi Natrun, the RCC recognised the importance of avoiding a head-on collision with Naguib when his popularity appeared overwhelming. Instead they agreed on a policy of reconciliation which they announced in the famous 5 March 1954 resolutions. These provided for a constituent assembly to be elected by a referendum in July that would debate and promulgate a new constitution, and act as a parliament in the interim. Press censorship and martial law were to be lifted and political parties allowed on the basis of the new constitution. They also promised to release all political prisoners.

The effect of the 5 March resolutions was echoed in a virulent press campaign in favour of a return to parliamentary life. In the meantime Nasser relinquished all powers to Naguib as President and Prime Minister. In a press conference, he aired the idea of a socialist republican party under Naguib through which the soldiers would contest the projected elections. Privately, he used Amer in the army and Ibrahim Tahawi in the Liberation Rally to strengthen his position against Naguib with a variety of groups, including remnants of the old political parties.

Relations between Naguib and Khaled on one side and Nasser and the rest of the RCC on the other remained strained and tense. Naguib perhaps assumed his popularity with the general public would attract the support of the old political forces to him in the forthcoming elections. Nasser, however, depended on his grip over the armed forces via Amer, the rapidly expanding security services, the equally tightly controlled media, the trade unions and youth organisations under the Liberation Rally, and the supervision of National Guidance Minister Salah Salem and Interior Minister Zakatiyya Mohieddin.

Civil disturbances in the period from 19 March exacerbated the situation. Some RCC members now demanded tough measures to maintain public order. On 25 March the RCC met with all its members present, including Naguib and Khaled. Boghdadi proposed a firm decision in the choice between the retraction of the 5 March resolutions and the blanket removal of all restrictions on political activity. The latter course was chosen with two very important decisions: the RCC could not reconstitute itself into a party; instead it would disband on 24 July 1954 when a constituent assembly would be elected directly. The RCC were saying in effect that the army movement would come to an end on that date.

The effect of these decisions on the officer corps was immediate and devastating. They argued that the RCC was relinquishing power and responsibility precipitously, a move which to them indicated a plot to help the return of the old politicians and the left to power. Such a gloss on events attracted the sympathy of the Ikhwan, who were also opposed to the return of "democratic political life".

On 27 March the country exploded in vast demonstrations. Lorries carrying workers from the industrial suburbs of Cairo, peasants from upper Egypt and masses of Liberation Rally youth converged on the capital, screaming "no parties and no parliament; do not abdicate, Gamal; no partisanship and no elections". With the connivance of the chief of Military Police and the chief of the CID, the mob attacked the members of the Council of State—the highest judicial body in the land—who were in session to consider the repressive measures of the RCC. [3]

After three days of turmoil the army was in the streets maintaining order. Salah Salem announced a series of decrees indefinitely postponing the resolutions of 5 and 25 March. Instead it opted to remain in power at least until after the conclusion of an evacuation agreement with Britain. Naguib was ousted from the premiership and the RCC. The junta retained him in office as President of the Republic in order to placate public sentiment.

A fierce campaign against all those "liberal" critics' groups around the *Misri* Wafdist newspaper of the Abul Fath brothers, *Rose el-Youssef*, the weekly magazine, and others was conducted by the army-controlled media. Their editors were arrested and tried. A series of tough measures was passed against corruption, for the purification of the press and discipline in the universities. So was a law to protect the revolution promulgated, and another for the better selection of local and municipal council officials. Professional syndicates and associations were dissolved, including the Press Union Council on the charge that its members received funds from secret foreign sources. A decree on 14 April announced that no one was to hold public office who had held one between February 1946 and July 1952. This meant practically everyone of the old political world. On 17 April Nasser became Prime Minister, bringing into his Cabinet eight other RCC members. Khaled disappeared in Alexandria and resigned. Nasser offered him the only option open to him, namely, to leave the country as a member of a delegation from the newly created National Council for Production.

Soon a *coup* plotted by armour corps officers led to wide arrests and purges, the trial and sentencing of several among the officers in June. In the meantime, the Muslim Brother, Abdel Moneim Abdel Rauf, had been arrested along with five or six others. At the end of May over 250 Communists were arrested, tried and sentenced to prison terms in July. The leader of the old palace Iron Guard, Captain Mustafa Kamal Sidqi, together with members of his National Democratic Front, were also purged out of the army. The initialling of the Anglo–Egyptian agreement on 27 July was accompanied by mass arrests of Muslim Brethren officers and NCOs, especially since the Brethren were opposed to the provisions of the agreement. This led to serious clashes between the Brethren's secret paramilitary organisation and the security forces. Their student leader, Hasan Doh, preached popular resistance to the army movement from the pulpit of the Friday prayers.

The end of the Muslim Brethren came in Alexandria on 26 October, seven days after the signing of the Anglo–Egyptian agreement. Nasser was addressing an audience of 10,000 workers from the Liberation Province when he was shot at by Mahmud Abdel Latif, a worker from Embaba in Cairo and a member of the Brethren's Secret Organization. "O men", shouted Gamal,

> let everyone remain in his place . . . my life is yours, my blood a sacrifice to Egypt. I speak to you with God's help after the mischievous tried to kill me. Gamal Abdel Nasser's life is your property; I have lived for you, and will do so until I die, striving for your sake. [4]

The fateful nine shots fired by Abdel Latif not only enabled Nasser to suppress his last formidable opponents, the Ikhwan, they also transformed the feelings of the masses towards the rising despot. From that day on, whenever he ventured among them he was mobbed by militant enthusiasts, by crowds that seemed literally possessed. Two years later, the Suez affair begot Nasserism.

That same night of 26 October there were so many arrests of Muslim Brethren that at the internment centres they were, it is alleged, given cards to fill in their names and addresses. In November a special People's Court, presided over by Gamal Salem, with Anwar Sadat and Hussein Shafei as members, tried over 800 prisoners. The military courts tried another 250. Six Brethren were executed, among them such prominent members of the Supreme Council as Abdel Qader Odeh, Muhammad Farghali, Hindawi

Duweir and Ibrahim el Tayyeb. Naguib, who had circulated his views on the Anglo–Egyptian agreement in a private memorandum to the RCC which the Muslim Brethren printed and distributed without his knowledge or approval, was relieved of his remaining duties as President of the Republic in mid-November and placed under house arrest.

By the end of November, two years and four months after the *coup*, the chosen figure-head and father-figure of the young Free Officer movement was out, political parties had been abolished and their leaders put in prison, opposition liberal newspapers were closed, the most important Islamic religio-political mass movement in the twentieth century forced to go underground, attempted counter-*coups* by officers put down, professional syndicates, trade unions and student organisations truncated, emasculated or suppressed.

It is clear that General Naguib's resignation in February 1954, following his disagreement with RCC members over matters of policy and the allocation of authority, had serious repercussions among the public which were disconcerting to the junta. But the public aspect reaction to Naguib's resignation was not the decisive element. The junta was alarmed, rather, at the division among officers' ranks over this issue. Muslim Brethren sympathisers, upper-class and Communist army officers rallied to restore Naguib to office. The story was circulated at the time that armour corps officers, commanded by Major Khaled Mohieddin, led an armed demonstration in favour of Naguib, and that Nasser had to "talk himself" out of this difficulty in Abbasieh Barracks.

This incident was the first serious indication that the ranks of the RCC and the army movement were divided. It also underlined the necessity of a more complete, systematic purge of these ranks. Nasser, the effective leader of the RCC, had realised this necessity earlier when the RCC removed Colonel Rashad Mehanna from the Regency Council in October 1952.

At the same time, the incident encouraged disaffected political groups to intensify their courting of Naguib. Before making Naguib Prime Minister again, however, the junta appointed Nasser military governor of Egypt, a measure intended to obstruct the possible alignment of Naguib with the civilian political forces. It also permitted the RCC to institute sweeping purges in the armed forces.

Publicly, though, Nasser employed ingenious tactics to disarm his enemies. By 5 March 1954 he feigned a *rapprochement* with political groups, when the RCC announced its decision to restore parliamentary forms beginning with a constituent assembly to be elected in June of that year. To confuse its enemies further, the junta ordered the release of certain political prisoners, especially members of the Muslim Brethren who had been arrested earlier in the year. The question which remained unresolved and which eluded the rejoicing political parties was whether the adherents of the Free Officers in the army and the RCC would permit the voluntary self-liquidation of their movement as the announcement of 5 March proposed.

Wafdists, socialists, Communists, Muslim Brethren and other journalists were lured by the RCC's relaxation of repression measures to align themselves with Naguib. Meanwhile, the originally secret network of the Free Officers set out to work independently, under Nasser's guidance, to counteract a possible return to power of old political groups. The Liberation Rally, controlled by its secretary-general Nasser and Free Officers loyal to him, was able to organise students and trade unions into mass demonstrations against the proposed return of constitutional life. The demonstrations of 25–27 March in Cairo and Alexandria and the general strike of public transport workers were manifestations of the total control and regimentation achieved by the Liberation Rally as an arm of the RCC élite generally, and Nasser personally. More important was the protest of junior Free Officers against the proposed relinquishing of authority by the junta in July 1954 and their virtual threat to assassinate those RCC members in favour of this change. This was perhaps a clear expression of loyalty to Nasser's leadership of the army movement and implied a mandate to the RCC to eradicate all opposition to it. On 28 March the RCC announced the indefinite postponement of the proposed June elections for a constituent assembly, and ousted Naguib from the premiership and the RCC.

Naguib versus Nasser

The clash between Naguib and Nasser was inevitable, if on no other count than that of the difference in age and generation. Despite Naguib's relatively illustrious military service record and his consistently sympathetic attitude towards young officers and their concerns under the monarchy, he was still by temperament and experience—perhaps even preference—closer to the liberal elements of the old order than to his younger radical colleagues in 1952. As an invited outsider, the putative leader of a young officer's successful *coup*, he had been lent the official role of authority without the power to go with it. He was conveniently old enough for the public to take the *coup*'s perpetrators seriously, and at the same time committed enough to the need for a clean-up of the Egyptian political world to accept the risk involved in the usurpation of state power by force. Once, however, the RCC imposed their control over the army and proceeded to use it in order to extend their control over the state, Naguib's options were limited.

Unavoidably, though, as the first public face of the triumphant but obscure Free Officer movement, he attracted the sympathy and support of large sections of the public. As the rebel soldiers proceeded to methodically demolish the old order, Naguib understandably entertained the ambition to lead the Egyptians back to a better democratic government. But if he did so, he was building on sand, for the real power lay in the army which, within a year, was firmly under the control of Nasser and his RCC supporters. Nevertheless, Naguib almost succeeded, for when the clash occurred he had acquired formidable popular support as well as that of the armour corps at least. The real leaders of the *coup*, the élite of the Free Officers, found themselves in February–March 1954 under massive popular attack, and were forced to retreat between 28 February and 25 March. The retreat, as it turned out, was a tactical manoeuvre which had the effect of isolating Naguib from the movement's crucial constituency—the army and the RCC. The "defender of democracy" was sedulously exposed as the ally and preferred candidate of the corrupt old political forces, the fanatical Muslim Brethren and the godless Communists.

The tactics against Naguib were orchestrated by Nasser. [5] Utilising his friend Amer in the army, he out-manoeuvred Khaled and his dissident officer supporters. Through Ibrahim al-Tahawi and Abdullah Tuaima of the Liberation Rally and an alleged £4,000 bribe paid to al-Sawi Ahmad al-Sawi, leader of the General Transport Workers, he stage-managed the thunderous demonstrations of 26 to 29 March against the 25 March resolutions for a return to parliamentary government. [6] Nasser, in short, was not prepared to see several years of effort and careful preparation for a take-over of state power blown away in favour of Naguib. From the beginning he cautiously projected his leadership by the occasional public outburst against the British and imperialism. There was a power vacuum in the country and if anyone was to fill it, it would be himself, not Naguib.[7]

The February–March 1954 struggle for power is important to the extent that it also outlined the style of Nasser's subsequent long rule.[8] It further shaped his perceptions and approach to power. It identified his enemies and traced the bases of his future strength— the army and the various administrative structures of the state— especially once he had divorced power and authority from the wealthier groups in society. The weightier, more credible threats to his drive for power had been tamed, neutralised or eliminated: the British, the radical right and left, the formal political parties, Naguib and the officer corps. From a *de facto* chairman of the RCC, vice-premier, Minister of the Interior and secretary-general of the Liberation Rally in 1953, Nasser at the end of 1954 was Prime Minister, and a year and a half later President of the Republic. The political fortunes of his associates on the RCC now depended entirely upon his own favour, and the vast state bureaucracy—the governing machine—was supervised by officers loyal to him or his subordinates. The purged officer corps now saw its increasingly privileged position and prosperity dependent upon the survival of the régime with Nasser at its head. The small working force in the trade unions hoped for an industrially oriented régime to better their lot, and the peasants, sweetened by agrarian reform, hoped for more of the same. As the emerging new élite, the officer corps was no longer interested in intrigue or counter-*coup* plots.

Thus the quiet, retiring, awkward and shy *bikbashi* became the *caudillo* of Egypt in 1954, in whom the terrifying power of the state, whether under a Pharaoh, Mamluk *amir*, Sultan, Khedive or king, was now concentrated.

Nasser's Pursuit of Power

The distinction, however, must be made between the early swift measures of the Free Officer movement to consolidate its power and assume control of the state on one hand, and Nasser's own tactics and manoeuvres to achieve domination on the other. Throughout his political life Nasser was concerned to ensure his own primacy; the process of eliminating his rivals began in 1952 with the expulsion of Abdel Moneim Abdel Rauf and Rashad Mehanna and ended in 1969 with the dismissal of Ali Sabri. Here we shall be concerned to illustrate Nasser's behaviour in his pursuit of supreme personal power.

By June 1953, when a republic was proclaimed, the old political forces in the country had been more or less neutralised. Disagreement and rivalry arose, however, among the revolutionary officers, and for the next year or so Nasser's attention was fully turned to this matter. At this time, the main threat to his primacy came from the benign-looking, pipe-smoking, affable General Naguib, whom the young conspirators had chosen as their "leader".

Commenting twenty years later on Naguib's putative memoirs, President Sadat expatiated on the general's role in the 1952 *coup*. He asserted that the general was not a party to the conspiracy. What really happened, according to Sadat, was that at 3 a.m. on 23 July, Prime Minister Naguib Hilali and his Minister of Interior, Murtada al-Maraghi, rang General Naguib ordering him to suppress the rebels. Naguib rang Nasser to find out what was happening and Nasser invited him to join them (the conspirators) at Army GHQ. When Naguib got there, Nasser made him "chief" of the officer movement on the spot. On 17 August, Nasser recommended to his RCC colleagues they make Naguib, who incidentally was Abdel Hakim Amer's commanding officer, chairman of the Council. As for the conflict in February–March 1954 between Nasser and Naguib, Sadat reports that it arose over Naguib's intention to establish a Presidential Council into which he wanted to bring representatives of the Muslim Brethren and other political parties.[9]

Nasser managed to depict Naguib as the enemy of the Revolution, allied to the discredited old politicians and the feared Ikhwan. His advantages in the conflict were overwhelming. As secretary-general of the Liberation Rally, he could manipulate the masses at will, had access to a new panoply of propaganda and, through his officer appointees, could stir the trade unions. As Minister of the Interior at the same time, he controlled the security services. Above all, he could rally the officer corps against the restoration of civilian rule by reminding them of their prospects in power. The chief weakness of his position, on the other hand, lay in the fact that within a year Naguib had become identified in the minds of the people as their defender against corruption. His popularity posed a serious threat to Nasser and many other Free Officers.

Both the Ikhwan and the left saw in Naguib their possible ticket to power against the autocracy of the Nasser-led officers, a majority of the RCC members. Both groups, however, tried to use Naguib. He thus caused a real split in public opinion and within the officer corps. In short, the man the officers hand-picked as their affable, docile leader was now in a position to challenge the RCC's authority and to force the army to return to their barracks. The demonstrations in February–March 1954 demanded precisely that, as well as the restoration of political parties and the constitution. The right and the left joined forces behind Naguib; RCC member Khaled Mohieddin led the armour corps in support of Naguib. The RCC was dissolved. But Nasser's supporters in the Liberation Rally and trade unions organised counter-demonstrations. Heikal has called this a Nasser manoeuvre, and so did Kamal el-Din Hussein and others: [10] "You want Naguib, you can have him; you want political parties back, you can have them." But before proceeding with this tactic, Nasser was confident the army was in his hands. [11]

Through agrarian reform, the dissolution of political parties, the abolition of the monarchy, the various corruption, revolutionary and military court tribunals, Nasser eliminated the threat against his power from the old political establishment. In his successful contest with Naguib he weakened the Ikhwan preparatory to their dissolution and proscription. With his swift, severe reaction to the labour troubles in Kafr el-Dawar a month after the *coup*, he served notice on the left that he would not countenance their agitation. Meanwhile, the agreement he signed with Britain over the Sudan in February 1953 and over evacuation in July and October 1954 left him free, as Prime Minister, to concentrate his attention on the internal consolidation of power. The new Ministry of Guidance, first under Salah Salem, and later under the old radical nationalist Fathi Radwan, supplied him with the requisite propaganda means.

Luck too helped in the form of an eventful and momentous twenty-month period between February 1955 and October 1956, from the Israeli raid on Gaza, the Baghdad Pact, the Bandung Conference and the Soviet arms deal to the nationalisation of the Suez Canal and the Suez War. All of these events gave him a new regional and international source of influence, popularity and power which none of his rivals and adversaries could withstand. In 1954 he enjoyed a popular image as a skilled in-fighter, a tough but realistic diplomatic negotiator and the ruthless executioner of assassins among the Ikhwan and godless Communists against the people. His tract, *Philosophy of the Revolution*, was then published just in time to install the hero firmly in the imagination at least, if not the mind, of the public.

Notes

1. Yet Nasser did not quite trust Amer completely. It has been alleged that he maintained direct links with junior officers in Amer's office, such as Salah Nasr, who succeeded Ali Sabri as Director of General Intelligence in 1957, Ahmad Anwar of the Military Police and Hamdi Ashur. See Ahmad Hamrush, "Shuhud yulio", *Rose el-Youssef*, Cairo, 4, 18 and 25 April 1977. Here it may be noted that in 1966 Nasser arrested several members of Amer's private office, such as Ali Shafiq, on the charge of smuggling.
2. The junta had created the publishing group *Dār al-Tahrīr*, which published the newspaper *al-Gumhuriyya* and the magazine *al-Tahrīr*. Several officers-turned-journalist were assigned to work in this establishment. But the connection between them and Intelligence was always a close one. Nasser used the group for his own propaganda purposes, especially during his power struggle with Naguib. Thus when Naguib complained to Nasser in November 1954 about the press campaign against him, Nasser promised to have it stopped. He had Naguib arrested instead. See Nasīr al-Din al-Nashāshibi, *Al-hibr aswad . . . aswad* (Paris, 1976), pp.83, 128–70.
3. See Hamrush in *Rose el-Youssef*, April 1977, and *Qissat thawrat 23 yulio* (Beirut, 1974), pp.323–83. See also Abdel Latif Boghdadi, *Mudhakkirat* (*Memoirs*) (Cairo, 1977).
4. Reported in *al-Ahram*, 27 October 1954.
5. For example, Captain Hussein Arafa, of the Military Police at that time, has since claimed that, on orders from Nasser, he supervised the printing and distribution of propaganda leaflets and tracts impugning Naguib's character, behaviour in office and political connections. See Hamrush, *Rose el-Youssef*, April 1977. At the same time, he was ordered by Nasser to infiltrate Communist groups that at that time supported Naguib.
6. See Gohar, *Al-sāmitūn yatakallamūn* (Cairo, 1975).
7. See his early speeches and statements on a variety of occasions throughout the country as reported in *Hādhihi al-thawra*, especially those of September–December 1952 and February–April 1953.
8. For Naguib's version of that power struggle, see *Memorie, 1919–1973*, translated by Clelia Sarnella Cerqua (Florence, 1976).
9. *Al-Sayyād*, Beirut, Vol.30, No. 1511, 20 August – 6 September 1973.
10. Fuad Mattar, *Bisarāha 'an Abd al-Nasir* (*Frankly speaking about Nasser*) (Beirut, 1975), p.44. See also pp.41–5. See also Kamal el-Din Hussein, "Qissat thuwwar 23 yulio", *al-Musawwar*, Cairo, 19 and 29 December 1975, 2, 9, 16 and 23 January 1976.
11. Some have described the Nasser–Naguib struggle for power as a contest of wills. See Sami Gohar, *Al-sāmitūn yatakallamūn.*

PART III

Ruler of Egypt

To find pleasure in power is to be corrupted by it—there are
many examples.
Forgive! We are human; we cannot help doing wrong—
Euripides, *Hippolytus*.

The principles of a free constitution are irrevocably lost
when the legislative power is dominated by the executive.—
Gibbon, *The History of the Decline and Fall of the Roman
Empire*.

Whatever positions he held in the Free Officer régime before April
1954, Nasser was the effective ruler of Egypt for eighteen years,
from the moment the military *coup* he led succeeded on 23 July 1952
to his sudden death on 28 September 1970. He enjoyed a Machiavellian *fortuna*, but he also possessed *virtù* in the sense of political
dexterity and charisma. Since heroes are not born, only constructed,
he had the necessary qualities and opportunity, for he appeared at
the right coincidence of events and convergence of conditions the
Egyptians needed for their hero-making. Above all, he had the will
to power that removed all obstacles before it, and that was behind
such epochal events as the abolition of the monarchy, the smashing
of the old political forces, the nationalisation of the Suez Canal,
the building of the Aswan High Dam, and the inauguration of a
strident anti-Western Arab policy in the Middle East. In short,
Nasser seized the opportunities presented by a historical turn in the
affairs of Egypt at mid-century.

He was a strong, capable ruler, who always managed to overcome the obstacles that faced him and emerge from difficulties
without losing the confidence of the masses. He suffered two
terrible set-backs in his long rule, the first was the dissolution
of the union between Egypt and Syria . . . the second was when
Israel smashed Egypt's military power in a few hours.[1]

If this is a fair overall assessment of Nasser as ruler of Egypt, the question arises, how did he attain and maintain this position? The first part of the question was dealt with in the earlier chapters of this study. Attention here will be focused on its second part.

The answer lies partly in Nasser's control and use of the basic structures of state power: the army, the security services and the administration. But it also lies in part in his social and economic policies, and his communication with the masses—his use of the spoken word. The political and security arrangements Nasser devised were crucial to his retention of control over the state and its main instrument, the government. His economic and social policies, with their gyrations, were in response not merely to the needs of the country, but also clearly related to the requirements of his personal rule. Finally, his frequent communication with the people was, in the absence of voluntary and intermediate political institutions, essential to his legitimacy.

By 1962, ten years after the *coup*, Nasser had transformed Egyptian nationalism from a relatively liberal to an authoritarian populist movement, characterised by the cult of the chief, the prince, who is acclaimed by the nation through plebiscite. With this kind of mandate, also within the first ten years of his leadership, Nasser set out to industrialise Egypt in an autocratic way, and rule her by decree. The aim was, on the face of it, legitimate, but the means were arbitrary. To what extent Nasser's arbitrary approach to these major national issues was also tyrannical is another matter. The fact remains that what he could not achieve by consent or agreement, he did so by fiat, sheer strength of will and repression. Opposition to his schemes for the salvation of the nation was not simply illegal, it was sinful. It was this atmosphere which constituted the psychological basis of Nasser's relation, as *El Rayyes*, the Chief, with the mass of Egyptians. Having convinced them of the necessity of his schemes for the regeneration of a betrayed, humiliated nation, Nasser extracted their acquiescence to the supremacy of his personal rule.

There were in Egypt perhaps all the conditions needed for the emergence of Nasser, or the Nasser-type populist, charismatic autocrat. Exaggerated expectations of independence since 1923 remained unfulfilled. The population explosion caused the mass migration of peasants to the cities, without adequate industrial or other economic development to absorb them. Glaring contrasts of wealth and poverty became even sharper, thanks to mass communications media and the beginnings of a post-war consumer economy. The radicalisation of certain strata in society during a period of cultural disorientation, economic dislocation and political frustration undermined national unity and culminated in the collapse of a ruling dynasty and its political order. Meanwhile, other reasons led to the withdrawal of a foreign power from the country. The spread of secondary education, the rise of industry, commercial and financial enterprise, a world war accompanied by rapid technological change and having an inflationary effect generated a sense of insecurity among the inchoate masses of the aspiring, formally educated youth. Together with post-war notions of integrative nationalism at a time of decolonisation and the retreat of Europe from Asia and Africa, the needs of Egyptian society were such as to create a mood highly receptive to the radical exhortations and salvationist promises of a new, young native ruler.

The attraction of a saviour implies the unquestioning acceptance of his command and direction. It also implies a beginning which cannot allow previous political structures to survive; these must be destroyed in order to make way for new ones—or none. So also must men of experience and independent judgement be prepared to accept the directives of a new ruler who, in the historical context of the crisis, comes close to being a demiurge; otherwise they must be neutralised or liquidated.

With these broad considerations in mind, Nasser's political and security arrangements for his rule may be viewed from the perspective of his approach to power, his exploitation of modern nationalism, his handling of economic and social policy, and his mastery of modern mass propaganda methods as a mob orator.

Note

1. Ahmad Hussein, *Kayfa 'araftu Abdel Nasser was 'ishtu ayyāma hukmihi* (Beirut, 1973), p.144.

CHAPTER 9

The Political and Security Apparatus

Nasser knew what he did not want, but not quite what he wanted.—Heikal in Fuad Mattar, *Bisaraha 'an Abdel Nasser.*

The revolution abolished the difference between the state and the government . . . With the deification of the State the three powers of government—the executive, legislative and judicial, even the fourth power, that of the press—were fused. They became the four arms of the Leader in whom was the will of the State.—Louis Awad, *Aqni'at al-Nasiriyya al-sab'a.*

Control of the Army

It took the new régime of soldiers just under three years to abolish all political parties and eliminate all overt opposition to their rule. Before proceeding to the creation of vehicles of mass support, Nasser in particular was anxious to impose his control over the more crucial structures of the state, namely the army, the bureaucracy and the security services. He seemed to favour a bureaucratic kind of despotism over a military one. The state of Egyptian society and its economy decreed this preference.

Through the control of these structures, Nasser could extend his control over lesser institutions—trade unions, education, the media and the press, professional syndicates, youth organisations, religious and economic institutions—and the population at large. Although he perceived the durability of popular support for his plans, Nasser did not wish his power to depend on it. He correctly gauged Egypt's traditional stratification, capped by a highly centralised bureaucracy that always served as the instrument of the ruler; in fact, it was always entirely dependent upon the ruler. Complemented by an efficient police, or security, system, it could be devastatingly effective.

Nasser did not have to create either of these two state structures and instruments of control. A bureaucratic hierarchy was of millennial vintage. An internal security system—the dreaded political police—had been fully developed in the turbulent years from 1946 to 1952, during the hunting of Communists, Muslim Brethren terrorists and other subversives.[1] What he had to do was to strengthen them and bend them to his purposes.

With the dissolution and proscription of the Ikhwan, the elimination of General Naguib and the virtual suppression of all organised party opposition, the RCC emerged, at the end of 1954, as the undisputed ruling élite—the political directorate—of Egypt. The pattern followed by Nasser in consolidating his hold over the political and administrative structures of the state is revealing. Besides key ministries controlled by RCC members, he had to ensure the loyalty, or at least guard against the defection, of the civilian administrative cadres. By December 1954 he was able to appoint trusted army officers in key bureaucratic offices to supervise the work of civilian departments. Despite the use of civilian economic and other experts in Cabinet posts (Finance, Economy, Commerce, Industry, Justice, Foreign Affairs and Agriculture), he was able, by the appointment of committees and commissions directly responsible to him, for the co-ordination of policy, to impose effective control over all the activities of the state.

Within the RCC and the lesser ranks of the Free Officers, personal loyalty to Nasser soon became the condition for political survival. Those who initially harboured independent political views were either relegated to unimportant sinecures or dismissed. Colonels Ahmad Shawqi and Lutfi Wakid of Infantry, for example, were ejected early on for their leftist tendencies. Khaled Mohieddin paid the price for his defection during the Nasser–Naguib rift and for his Communist leanings with exile to Europe. Muslim Brother Abdel Rauf was expelled from the Free Officers' executive. Colonel Rashad Mehanna, who tried to use his position on the Regency Council to bid for power in alliance with Muslim Brethren leaders and with the aid of artillery and armour officers was dismissed from the council in October 1952. When a rival group of officers sought to elect him president of the Officers' Club in December 1952, he was cashiered from the army, placed under house arrest, and his fellow-conspirators were tried by military tribunal.

The army then as the foremost base of Nasser's power received his earliest attention. It remained the central constituency and primary source of his régime's legitimacy, because it was viewed from the start as the protector of the Free Officer revolution.

A common characteristic of the armies of Arab countries is that they were originally formed by outsiders as internal security forces. Yet in some of them, in the Fertile Crescent and Egypt for instance, there had been a nucleus of officers antedating this formation. In Iraq and Syria, for example, there were ex-Ottoman Army officers, many of whom had also served in Sherif Hussein's Arab Revolt. In Egypt there were those from the pre-British occupation army of the Muhammad Ali dynasty.

After independence, the general tendency was for the social reality of these countries to impose its pattern on their armies: kinship and sectarian links among officers developed or were forged. But not in Egypt. There the officer corps after 1936 seemed to go its own way. Instead, when political activity among officers became common, it followed the pattern of graduating groups from the military academy. Fellow-cadets became the basis of cliques and factions in the officer corps, so that when the RCC came to govern Egypt, each member tended to bring in his own "friends", thus expanding his clique. There was a multiplication effect in this respect as the state under the Free Officer régime took over an even greater number of institutions and national activities. The absence of sectarian links, however, reduced the chances of a chain of *coups* and counter-*coups*.

The combination of early purges and his defeat of Naguib in effect put Nasser on the road to controlling the armed forces. Without Field Marshal Abdel Hakim Amer, however, he might not have succeeded. The importance of their relationship was brought home on more than one occasion, as for example when differences between the two men arose over the secession of Syria from the UAR in 1961, during the Yemen War in 1963–4 and the Six Day War in 1967.[2] In fact, it was after 1961 that Nasser allowed the growth of an elaborate apparatus in his private office, the secret security services and, after 1964 or 1966, a secret "vanguard organisation" in the ASU. Nasser intended both of these personal agencies to counter rival power cliques that might form around Amer in the armed forces, as well as in the political organisation that was formally launched within the framework of the National Charter after 1962. It was also during these years that Nasser broke with erstwhile close colleagues and his decline set in. It was the period of the "centres of power", privileged cliques and "hidden governments", which were first exposed guardedly in 1966–8 and then glaringly in May 1971.[3]

Nasser did not perceive the role of the army in society strictly as a military institution, but as a bureaucratic system that could administer sanctions, and as an old boys' network that could dispense patronage. He denied it the chance of developing a corporate military professional ethos. The need for wider conscription of university graduates after 1960 into direct commissions became an additional source of his control over the army. Nor was Nasser interested in the army as the instrument of a militaristic régime. Rather he considered it one for the militarisation of politics; that is, an instrument for the control of the non-military institutions of society.[4]

With his central role as Nasser's surrogate in controlling the armed forces, Amer had a free hand in discharging his task. He appointed to command and other key posts officers loyal to him who, in turn, appointed to lesser positions under their command officers loyal to them. Soon,

> the security of the nation in the view of these officers became confined to the task of placing other officers under surveillance by using police methods in order to discover their views on events. This information they reported to their masters . . . The surveillance was in addition to the usual activities of Military Intelligence and other state security services . . . Thus officers found themselves living in an obscure, strange atmosphere. Opportunity came to those who joined one of the cliques.[5]

Amer's control of the armed forces virtually from 1953 to 1967 may have served Nasser's political and security purposes admirably, but it proved disastrous for the country's defence. Beside his meagre professional preparation and experience for the top military post, Amer's 15-year-long command eroded the quality of the Egyptian officer corps. He was essentially a "political commissar" in whose hands were concentrated all military affairs. Thus from the very beginning in 1952–4, in order to secure wide army support for the 1952 *coup*, Amer allowed the emergence of new officer cabals directly loyal to him, whose members later came to exert great influence and wield immense power in the affairs of the state. The convention was established quite early on concerning conduct and policy within the military institution of loyalty to the *Mushir*, the Field Marshal and, through him, the *Rayyes*, Nasser. Merit, expertise or competence became secondary considerations. These new officer cliques incidentally increased their influence during the Yemen War and the Ikhwan conspiracy crisis of 1965–6.

It was absolutely essential for Nasser's political arrangements to render the officer corps *coup*-proof. For this purpose he had to assign his most loyal friend the crucial task of watchdog. Amer was not known for his keenness as a soldier or a disciplinarian. But he possessed an easy-going extrovert personality necessary for the job. Louis Awad, writing in 1975, thought the Amer–Nasser relationship over the army had at least one salutary effect:

> Nasser's régime needed the military and political guarding of the army, especially internally, so that what Nasser did to Faruq would not happen to Nasser himself. Amer served Nasser to this end most faithfully. But he also served Egypt well since he spared her the evil of repeated military *coups* and counter-*coups*.[6]

Nasser's manipulation of the army through Amer for political survival may be illustrated from the Suez War in 1956 and the Six Day War in 1967. The rout of the Egyptian forces in Sinai was due in part to the lack of adequate preparation first, and the frivolous, off-hand dismissal by Nasser and his advisers of the possibility of a British military response to the nationalisation of the Canal second. Recently, some of his old colleagues alleged that when the Anglo–French landing occurred in Port Said, it came as such a shock to Nasser that he collapsed.[7] But when United States opposition brought the Anglo–French military campaign to a halt,

> Egyptian propaganda media grabbed this golden opportunity to transform the rout in Sinai into a strategic withdrawal planned in advance, and to portray a few hours' resistance before Port Said fell as a great act. They then proceeded to compare acts of Egyptian resistance to the resistance movements in Russia and Europe during the Second World War. This way, the truth was buried, reality was ignored and the real causes of the defeat suffered by the Egyptian armed forces covered up.[8]

The quality, morale and performance of the Egyptian armed forces deteriorated further under this arrangement in the Yemen War, 1962–7. Whatever other strategic considerations were involved, the Egyptian military involvement in the Yemen in 1962 was linked to the break-up of the UAR the previous year. Egyptian leadership in Arab affairs had suffered a serious defeat; an initiative was needed to restore confidence in Egypt and her capabilities, or more precisely, in Nasser as an Arab leader. It is now known that the Egyptian decision to intervene in the Yemen was partly based on misleading claims by Yemeni political exiles living in Egypt.[9] Headed by Dr Abdel Rahman al-Baydani, these misled the Egyptians about the strength of the opposition inside Yemen and the presumed death of the Imam during the Sallal-led *coup* in September 1962. Soon, Egyptian troops operating in the Yemen found themselves ill-prepared, as a regular army, to fight tribal guerrillas. Casualties were high, equipment ill-suited and cumbersome.

The military involvement in the Yemen had certain deleterious effects on the armed forces and, by extension, the country. Leaving aside the five-year drain on manpower and resources (approximately £E4,000 million, or one million pounds for each of the 4,000 villages in Egypt), the free skies available to the air force against the Imam's guerrillas and the police type of operation on the ground bred a degree of self-deception and complacency in the Egyptian command. There were extraordinary field promotions of officers without adequate qualifications or training.

The social ill-effects on the officer corps, however, were the worst of all. Extraordinary privileges for those serving in the Yemen led to pressure from volunteers using nepotism and patronage. Vast profits from a rampant black market in imported luxury goods accrued to those officers who could transport them back to Egypt at government expense and free of customs duties. Favourable treatment regarding housing and services for these veterans compounded the corruption and became a national scandal.

One difficulty which arose during the Yemen War related to the need to expand the officer corps. By 1964, there was a critical shortage of trained officers, to some degree the result of that war. Ever since 1936, when the army was expanded, the military academy had been unable to train an adequate number of officers. Nor could the need be met from conscripted university graduates and reserve officers. In the late 1950s training missions to the Soviet Union further reduced the ranks of qualified officers available for troop command. So did the Yemen War. Meanwhile, the opening of a War College (the Nasser Academy) in the early sixties siphoned off yet further numbers of officers. A sizeable expansion and a completely reorganised command structure were therefore necessary in the mid-sixties.

At this point the fortunes of the military institution, Amer and, by extension, President Nasser, were limited to the convolutions of an army establishment that was controlled by a system of "political officer" cliques. A key personality in all of this was Shams Badran. Born in 1929, he graduated from military academy in 1948, along with Shaarawi Gumaa (Minister of Interior after 1965) and Sami Sharaf (Secretary, later Minister, to the President). In the fifties, Amer appointed Badran director of his private office in charge of officers' affairs, that is, personnel and administration. He was then a mere captain. In this capacity, Badran however controlled postings and the composition of training missions abroad. More important still, he supervised the overall work of military intelligence.

Badran developed a close personal relationship with the Field Marshal over the years. He was promoted from captain to brigadier without further training or qualifications. When suddenly in the autumn of 1966 he was appointed Minister of War, he was the first officer in many years to occupy that post. Until then, Amer, as commander-in-chief and first vice-president of the Republic, represented the interests of the armed forces in the government. The appointment came at the end of vast transfers and new appointments in army commands earlier in the summer over which Badran had virtually exclusive control. These were based on the formula "loyalty before merit", that is, considerations other than professional competence governed appointments to senior posts in the armed forces. By then too, Badran's power in the state was extensive and within the armed forces practically unlimited. He used peripheral and complementary organisations formed, for instance, during the Suez crisis—the National Guard, the Youth Organisation—to provide jobs, literally salaried sinecures with privileges, for incompetent officers.

What helped Shams Badran in succeeding to establish his power and influence is the fact that he was one of a group working with the Field Marshal. Most of the members of this group were notorious for opportunism and corruption, whereas he alone among them exhibited determination and reasonableness, and enjoyed a better reputation.[10]

Badran's role, however, and the declining reputation of his inner circle attracted Nasser's attention and evoked the resentment and distrust of the public. By 1966, too, relations between Nasser and his close friend Amer, which began to deteriorate during the Syrian secession crisis five years earlier, had worsened. Nasser suspected Badran of being the apprentice to the sorcerer Amer, and consequently felt threatened. The relationship collapsed and Badran fell from favour and office as a direct result of the Six Day War.[11] In the meantime, however, neglect and incompetence had become the hallmarks of the Egyptian military establishment under this cosy arrangement.

Internal Security

If in order to render the army *coup*-proof and insulate it from wider political activity the price in terms of military preparedness and defence was too high, the price paid by the public for Nasser's other security arrangements was equally high. A veritable pyramid of intelligence and security services, at times complementary and at others competitive, was constructed over the years. The labyrinthine complexity and venality of these services were exposed for the first time in August 1967 and February 1968. Closely related to these were the intricate, sultanic "special services" performed by the Office of the President and the secret vanguard organisations in the ASU.

With the exception of Amer and Muhammad Hasanein Heikal, close friends and collaborators of Nasser, the key people in this pyramid before 1970 were Ali Sabri, Zakariyya Mohieddin, Shams Badran, Sharawi Gumaa, Sami Sharaf, Amin Huweidi and Salah Nasr. All of them at one time or another were intimately connected with the administration of the intelligence and security agencies— the Mukhabarat.

The army indeed was the earliest, first base of Nasser's power. "My parliament", he is reported to have said to General Robertson during the negotiations over the Suez Canal base, "is the army. Do you think the army led a revolution simply in order to make me ruler? . . . The army rather expects me to achieve the aims for which it launched the revolution."[12] Later, Nasser frequently paid tribute to the role of the officer corps in the revolution, as for instance in his address to the newly elected National Assembly on 23 July 1957 and again in his famous Port Said Victory speech on 23 December 1957.

By the end of 1954, however, he had created alternative bases for his power by the establishment of a powerful secret security service, the re-organisation and expansion of the even more intricate state administrative machine controlled by his appointees. Moreover, by 1967, periodic purges had paralysed the army, while the secret services and the bureaucracy had come under the control of a secret vanguard organisation, whose members had been hand-picked by Nasser and his lieutenants. Thus the Mukhabarat was pitted against the army; the secret vanguard political machine of his personal office against the ASU. "Abdel Nasser was secretive by nature and temperament," Hussein Dhu'l Fiqar Sabri, Director-General of the Foreign Affairs Ministry under Nasser and brother of Ali Sabri, wrote in July 1975, "therefore he governed by secret means and institutions."[13]

Some of the most powerful figures in the Nasser régime, whether in the Cabinet, the ASU or the Presidential Office, were in one way or another part of the vast security network and intelligence services. Zakariyya Mohieddin was Minister of Interior for nearly a decade and Prime Minister in 1965–6. Ali Sabri, from air force intelligence, was Nasser's *chef de cabinet* in 1954–7, Chief of Intelligence until 1956, and later Prime Minister and Secretary of the ASU Executive Committee until 1969. His reputed leftist leanings were, one suspects, a contrivance of Nasser's in order to check his powerful, puritanical and efficient Interior Minister, Zakariyya Mohieddin. It also balanced his articulate and engaging confidant and mouth-piece, Muhammad Hasanein Heikal, who disliked Sabri. Sharawi Gumaa, Minister of Interior in the last years of the régime, and Sami Sharaf, Minister of Presidential Affairs and long-time counsellor to the President, were also key figures in these services. They acquired even greater influence in 1968 after the sacking of General Intelligence Chief Salah Nasr, and when the rift between Ali Sabri and Zakariyya Mohieddin, on one hand, and the President on the other, widened. All of these men and several others eventually formed their own cliques. The Mukhabarat mushroomed in personnel, and acquired a vested interest in the operation of a secret, or "hidden government", because

their main task—and source of livelihood—comprised in

suggesting to their chief, Nasser, the existence of conspiracies against him, and that they were protecting him from them . . . Nevertheless, Nasser's grip on Mukhabarat was powerful. They could do nothing without his approval.[14]

Actually the overt public and secret political arrangements were an extension of Nasser's personality, his perception of power and his belief in what constituted the national interest. According to Hussein Dhu'l Fiqar Sabri,

His intuitive, instinctive characteristics which helped him prepare the 1952 *coup* were reinforced. Political arrangements for state power were made as if they were a vital extension of his personality. Their members were from the élite of those he trusted, although he never quite trusted any of these institutions. His evaluation of lieutenants was predatory to the extent that it was qualified by constant suspicion . . . These lieutenants were under constant testing, always fearing a sudden fall from favour . . . After his fantastic success over Suez, he increased his dependence on covert political arrangements, using its multifarious apparatuses, but never himself directly. This was the reason why he came to rely even more heavily on "trusties". Yet he continued to direct them himself, exploiting them for his own purposes while at the same time giving the impression publicly that he knew nothing of their operations.[15]

Nasser's Political Style

Nasser governed Egypt with the same methods he used to organise the conspiracy of Free Officers before the 1952 *coup*. Hussein Sabri in fact goes on to suggest a fundamental insecurity about Nasser in explaining his obsession with secrecy. "His rule of government was that of the man who is not secure unless he acts through a secret apparatus," he wrote. "In fact so secret that its basis was the underground cell, whose many strings he controlled without one knowing of the existence of the other . . ." One can therefore assume that all the so-called "centres of power" in the country were commanded and directed by Nasser, in spite of his indirect use of them. Moreover, despite the creation of such ostensibly political organisations for the public's participation in the country's political life as the Liberation Rally (1953–6), the National Union (1957–61), the ASU and the

National Assembly (1962–), and amidst all the plots and counter-plots throughout eighteen years of rule, Nasser never trusted any of them, whether progressive or conservative. Instead, he preferred to appeal to a popular base for his political power—and supremacy. He consistently refused to establish any public political body unless this was prepared to offer him absolute, unquestioning loyalty.

In short, in the political arrangements Nasser made for his rule, he avoided the definition or clear demarcation of responsibilities and the foundation of a system of public accountability for his power. This remained "unlimited" and unaccountable. Writing in 1975, Louis Awad argued that it is difficult for Nasser's contemporaries to judge his régime, because when even the use of public funds is not accountable to elected public bodies, it is difficult to secure answers to questions of fact about, say, the public sector of the economy.[16]

That Nasser led Egyptians in making an enormous leap from the past is not doubted. He abolished the monarchy and *ancien régime* and smashed the power of a land-based élite; he negotiated an end to the British presence in the country. But he hardly eliminated exploitation; he merely replaced that of the old ruling class with that of a new class. "Raise your head, brother . . ." he screamed. "But who dared raise his head to say what was on his mind?"[17] However, in the first two years, Nasser could comfortably argue, as he did on 20 June 1953, when outlining the reasons for the pro-clamation of the republic, that the army *coup* was directed against a "rotten system, headed by a foreign dynasty, propped up by a foreign power and feudalism". The measures taken immediately were therefore necessary: "Faruq's deposition and expulsion, the smashing of feudalism, and the ending of the British occupation." This quick response of the Free Officers to the "popular will", according to Nasser, placed within less than a year "a native Egyptian at the head of the Egyptian State".

Nasser's political arrangements may be traced from his earliest utterances, which heralded the creation of organisations like the Liberation Rally, the National Union and the ASU. So can the outline of his economic and social policies. With the inauguration of the Liberation Rally on 6 February 1953 and after huge popular ceremonies, Nasser, as its secretary-general, was already exposing himself to public view more frequently. His tour of the provinces, alongside Naguib, and his own speeches promoting the Rally's slogan, "unity, order, work", foreshadowed his later actions. The

Rally, according to Nasser, was not like the old political parties, because "Egypt has become the property of the governed, not as it was that of the governors". "I assure you," he said, "we shall not rest over any social oppression and national humiliation. Nor will we surrender after today to any political tyranny or foreign occupation."[18]

His vision of political arrangements for the country is also discernible in his public statements concerning the abolition of the monarchy, the establishment of a republic and the launching of the Liberation Rally. The monarchical régime, he declared, destroyed itself once the worm of corruption and treachery ate into its throne. "It is the foremost cause of the British occupation that lasted for 70 years," he argued. It had allied itself with colonialist power and caused the enslavement, impoverishment and backwardness of the Egyptian people.

> The past cannot be retrieved . . . because it was one of political tyranny, social oppression, the greedy pursuit of wealth and influence. The Liberation Rally is not a political party, and it is not conceived as such in order to provide privileges and gain for its members, or to satisfy their desire for power. The reason for its formation is the desire to organize the powers of the people, and to build a society on a new healthy foundation. The Liberation Rally is the school in which the people will learn the true meaning of elections.[19]

Clearly, then, Nasser did not envisage the creation of a political party. Instead he sought—and preferred—an amorphous "popular" mass organisation to be controlled by the Free Officer movement in the army and ultimately by himself. He covered it up by a new political myth which he projected in his various promises to the Egyptians. Now they were to forgo political institutions in favour of a policy aiming at the defence of "Egypt's dignity". Thus in his 26 July 1956 nationalisation speech in Alexandria, he communicated his new myth with his report of US Envoy George Allen's mission, during which the latter threatened Nasser with dire consequences if he nationalised the Canal. He handed Nasser a letter from Secretary of State Dulles, the contents of which "were wounding to Egypt's dignity . . . The era when Egypt's policy was formulated abroad", Nasser shouted, "is over. So is the epoch when a simple threat could topple governments in Cairo."

This new style of "you and I together" disposed of the need for elaborate institutional arrangements, until politically Nasser could say to the Egyptian people, "I am you," in a sort of mystical fusion. In 1975 Louis Awad explained the meaning of a "united leadership" under Nasser as the "eighteen year long monologue".[20] By 1 November 1956 he could assure the people, "whenever Washington speaks, I shall tell them, 'Perish in your fury.' Death is preferable to humiliation." (By then of course, the arms deal with the Soviet Union was over a year old.) This way, even in the absence of any elected political institutions to which he could have been account-able, Nasser—and the Egyptians—could claim, "He derives his power and authority from his fellow-citizens; from the people that governs itself."[21]

After Nasser's first election as President in June 1956, and the adoption of a new constitution, the Liberation Rally was supplanted by a National Union within whose framework a National Assembly was to be elected. But the Suez episode had already shown the Liberation Rally to be superfluous. Nor were political institutions necessary when the myth of class harmony in society had by 1959 become one of Nasser's political weapons. "There are no class differences any more. We are blessed with freedom and independ-ence; there are no agents of foreign powers or traitors among us."[22]

But what can one make of all the institutional arrangements which began with the Liberation Rally and ended with the ASU? Or of the famous National Charter of 1962 that was intended to be the ideological basis of the new revolutionary socialist Egyptian state? How far did these various attempts to provide the legitimate basis for a new political order succeed?

In surveying Nasser's repeated attempts at constructing a public political base for his régime, from the Liberation Rally in 1953 to the ASU in 1962–4, his provisional or permanent constitutions in 1953, 1956 and 1965, one observes that he managed to abolish the difference between state and government, between these two and himself. Instead of separating the powers of government, he fused them; instead of separating religion and state, he re-integrated them. Egyptian nationalism that surfaced in 1919 was sacrificed in favour of a wider Arab national identity for Egypt. Natural rights and civil liberties under the law, the right to association and free speech were all diluted or abolished in favour of transforming society by a revolutionary process. As Louis Awad drily remarked, "the law under the Nasser régime went on holiday;" and the measure of political acts was no longer an "objective criterion" but the "personal decrees and decisions of the ruler . . . The deification of the State led to the fusion of all state powers."[23]

In practice, Nasser at the head of an army *coup d'état* shared power with a civilian "front" government only briefly, from August to September 1952. His struggle for power against Naguib for the next eighteen months occurred under conditions favouring his victory. Early on, by February 1953, the autocratic collegial rule of the RCC under a provisional constitution for a three-year transition period established military (i.e. RCC) control over Ministers in government, and all other state structures, including the Liberation Rally. As Nasser himself described it, this was a period "of demolition and liquidation" of old forces. Once he became Prime Minister in April 1954, decision-making was centralised in and monopolised by the soldiers in the RCC and, after 1956, in Nasser himself.

The new institutional framework eliminated temporary "dual rule". The soldiers no longer needed to share power with others. Politics as an activity for the pursuit of security and advantage was denied to all groups, except the new political directorate of soldiers. It was instead now confined to a campaign by the soldiers to mobilise mass approval for the decisions they took, and to form tight security arrangements against opposition to their rule. The Liberation Rally and the National Union were no more than palliatives for a superficial public participation in political life, decreed by the new autocrats, once external fetters and domestic threats to their supremacy had been eliminated.

It was inevitable that elections after the emergence of Nasser as sole ruler in 1956 should be straightforward plebiscites. Legislative assemblies such as the new National Assembly of 1957 were no more than gatherings of carefully selected deputies to approve government decisions. They met at the pleasure and on the sufferance of the Chief. Nor was there a need any longer for the semblance of collegial decisions by the original cabal of officers. The RCC was characteristically disbanded after the referendum in 1956. Its most prominent members easily made the transition to "state politics" so long as they were prepared to recognise Nasser's supremacy. They came to share in the benefits of power, but not in power itself. In any case, Nasser began to construct a civilian makeweight to them in his governments. By 1969, only two of the original RCC members were still holding high state office, namely, Anwar Sadat and

Hussein Shafei. The rest had either resigned, been dismissed or demoted.

Constitutional developments after 1956 amounted really to minor adjustments. On 5 March 1958, for instance, a new provisional constitution was announced five weeks after the union with Syria in order to extend the prevailing Egyptian political system to Syria. In September 1962, four months after Nasser's presentation of his National Charter, there was a perfunctory recognition of new conditions and the need for new social and economic policies. In addition to the Cabinet, there was now formed a twelve-member Presidential Council responsible for national policy. It supervised the work of the Cabinet which administered the policy. But these were basically technical amendments. They did not affect the fundamental political arrangements of Nasser's régime.[24]

After the secession of Syria from the union on 28 September 1961, some of these technical amendments were necessary. More pressing, though, was the need for an overall political reorganisation, which explains in part the drafting of the National Charter. The new Constitution of March 1964, on the eve of Nasser's election to a second term as President, was vaunted as constituting a qualitative change from previous political arrangements. But all it really allowed was for the National Assembly elected under its provisions to censure the government or one of its Ministers. The President, however, as in all previous constitutional arrangements of the régime, could still dissolve the Assembly. Built into all these gyrations in political organisation and changes of government was always Nasser's unchallenged control, since the objective remained the prevention of any opposition to his rule.

Interesting among Nasser's series of governmental reorganisations were those that came after 1965. Domestic trouble with the Ikhwan, a further deterioration in relations with the United States and the latter's eventual stopping of wheat shipments to Egypt were all reflected in them. The resulting economic crisis required a government of technicians to help weather the storm and guide Nasser through the difficulties. Thus Zakariyya Mohieddin was dismissed and a Cabinet of experts was formed. Similarly, after the June 1967 War, the Abdel Hakim Amer affair and the extensive purging of the officer corps, Nasser on 19 June assumed the premiership himself. At the same time he continued to exercise total control over foreign policy as he did ever since Bandung in 1955. Foreign Minister

Mahmud Fawzi was no more than a diplomatically experienced adviser and assistant.

Whatever the extent of his weakened personal rule after June 1967, Nasser persisted in maintaining it by manipulation of, if not real change in, the political order, proving for the next three years that there could be no real opposition to him possible. The corollary of this, however, was the intensification of a power struggle among the cliques at the top of the pyramid, that is, those closer to him. But this struggle was primarily a contest for favours from the Chief, for influence and advantage not always related to the public interest.

Generally, then, Nasser throughout his career made the kind of political arrangements which allowed for a pyramidal structure of power with himself as the supreme unchallengeable authority at the summit. There was little room for political competition among lesser groups. What there was of it was among top "courtiers" and senior members of the state administration, including the security apparatus. As for the various political organisations, the Liberation Rally, the National Union and the ASU, they all failed as institutions of political renovation. New cadres or élites could not emerge unless these were recruited by one or another clique at the top of the power structure.

Notes

1. Russell Pasha had retired as Commandant of the Cairo Police. On this period, see Tariq al-Bishri, *Al-Haraka al-siyāsiyya fi misr* (Cairo, 1972).
2. Hussein Arafa has claimed that the first Nasser–Amer rift occurred over the nationalisation of the Suez Canal in 1956, when Nasser failed to inform Amer, his Armed Forces Commander, well in advance of his intention to nationalise the Canal. See Ahmad Hamrush, "Shuhud yulio", *Rose el-Youssef*, Cairo, 4, 18 and 25 April 1977.
3. See the newspaper reports of the Shams Badran (Minister of Defence) and air force officer trials in 1968 in *al-Anwar* and *al-Nahar* of Beirut. See also the relevations of Ahmad Kamil, briefly Director of General Intelligence in 1970–1, in the Ali Sabri, Salah Nasr, Sami Sharaf and Shaarawi Gumaa trials in 1971, in Beirut's *al-Nahar* and Cairo's *al-Ahram*. See also Fuad Mattar, *Ayna asbaha Abd al-Nāsir fi jumhūriyyat al-Sādāt (What happened to Nasser in the republic of Sadat)* (Beirut, 1972), who reproduces Ahmad Kamil's testimony on pp.93–155, and P. J. Vatikiotis, "Egypt's Politics of Conspiracy", *Survey*, Vol.18, No.2, Spring 1972, pp.83–99.
4. See P. J. Vatikiotis, "Some political consequences of the 1952 revolution in Egypt", in P. M. Holt (ed.), *Political and Social Change in Modern Egypt* (London, 1968), pp.362–87, and H. Dekmekjian, *Egypt under Nasser* (Albany, New York, 1971).
5. Salah al-Din al-Hadidi, *Shāhid 'alā harb 67 (Witness to the 67 War)* (Cairo, 1974), pp.81–2.

6. Louis Awad, *Aqni'at al-nāsiriyya al-sabaa* (*The seven masks of Nasserism*) (Beirut, 1975), p.127.
7. Sami Gohar, *Al-sāmitun yatakallamūn* (Cairo, 1975).
8. Hadidi, *Shahid 'ala harb 67*, p.45.
9. Hamrush, *Rose el-Youssef*, April 1977. It has since been reported that in an aside to King Faisal at Jedda in 1965, Nasser pointed to Sadat and said, "He brought us into this," and "We want an end to the affair." See Nāsir al-Din al-Nashashibi, *Al-hibr aswad . . . aswad* (Paris, 1976). Hasan Ibrahim, however, stated in 1977 that everyone in the Presidential Council meeting concurred in the decision to intervene in the Yemen. See Hamrush, *Rose el-Youssef*, April 1977.
10. Hadidi, *Shāhid 'alā harb 67*, p.29.
11. See Mahmud al-Gayar (private secretary to Nasser), "Rajulān qatalā al-Mushir Amer" ("Two men who killed Amer"), *Rose el-Youssef*, No.2482, Cairo, 5 January 1976.
12. Abdel Qadir al-Bindari and Najib Ilyas Barsum, *Thawrat al-hurriyya* (Cairo, 1961), p.91.
13. Hussein Sabri, *Rose el-Youssef*, Cairo, No. 2459, 18 July 1975.
14. Ahmad Hussein, *Kayfa 'araftu Abdel Nasser was 'ishtu ayyama huknihi* (Beirut, 1973), pp.81–2.
15. Hussein, *Kayfa 'araftu*.
16. Hussein, *Kayfa 'araftu*.
17. Hussein Sabri, *Rose el-Youssef*, 18 July 1975.
18. Quoted in *Hadhihi al-thawra*, p.172.
19. Ibid., pp.291–2.
20. *Hadhihi al-thawra*, p.129.
21. Ibid., pp.24–6.
22. Speech in Syria on 28 February 1959. See *Khutab al-ra'īs . . . fi'l-'Īd al-awwal lil-jumhuriyya al-arabiyya al-muttahida* (*The President's speeches on the first anniversary of the UAR*), Cairo, Kutub Siyasiyya series, No.99.
23. *Khutab al-ra'īs*, p.113.
24. The rifts between Nasser and his colleagues, such as Amer, Kamal el-Din Hussein and others continued. See the statements and allegations by some of these in Sami Gohar, *Al-sāmitūn yarakallamūn* (Cairo, 1975).

CHAPTER 10

Nasser and the State

The New Political Order

The defence of the soldiers' revolution—and soon Nasser's personal rule—was linked to a change of régime. But the new political organisations like the Liberation Rally were not intended to broaden the movement's popular base. Nasser was more interested in creating a vehicle through which he could forestall political agitation by rival groups such as the Wafd and the Ikhwan. Thus on 23 February 1953 he warned those who thought the army *coup* aimed merely at overthrowing the monarchy:

> This aim is a minor objective compared to the wider aims of our revolution. The latter seeks to change the political system for the benefit of the people. It is therefore necessary to defend the revolution against those who try to deter it from its course and prevent it from attaining its ultimate goals. [1]

Once they had dissolved all the old political parties the military régime could use their new political organisations as pens to marshall the populace. That the purpose of the Liberation Rally, for example, was one of regimentation was asserted by Major Salah Salem—the bluntest member of the RCC—when on 11 April 1953 he told an audience at Mit Ghamr, "We did not come to you for votes, because we do not aspire to rule or to become members of parliament. We came to seek your co-operation and unity." [2] This policy enabled the military régime to clear trade unions, student organisations and professional associations of antagonistic elements. The pattern became clear when Nasser formed his first Cabinet in April 1954. The key Ministry of Social Affairs and Labour, for instance, went to a member of the Free Officer inner circle, Kamal el-Din Hussein. He systematically purged all trade unions and labour organisations of opposition elements. He performed the same task among student

174

organisations after he became Minister of Education in June 1956.

The tediously elaborate structures of the National Union after 1956[3] and the ASU after 1962 attest to the complex arrangements for Nasser's control. These organisations may be considered to have been schemes that facilitated his guidance of a public autocratically governed by him. At the same time, they checked those who might otherwise have conspired against his régime. Integration—the elimination of factionalism—was the purpose of the exercise. Needless to say, factionalism was inevitable, but only within the confines of Nasser's power cliques.

The Communists, for example, had been neutralised by 1964. Their bedraggled remnants who emerged from concentration camps and prisons were absorbed in the bureaucracy, the media and the press. The combination of state repression and Soviet support for the Nasser régime left the Communists no alternative but to survive as best they could on Nasser's terms. A proliferation of magazines and journals during those years and an expanded *Ahram* establishment headed by Nasser's confidant, Heikal, dispersed them in their editorial and administrative posts.[4] Nasser's régime could now speak with several voices, ranging from the right to the left. Coexistence between the Communists and Nasser did not however preclude the occasional reminder type of arrest of both rightists and leftists, as in fact occurred in 1966.

The Ikhwan, on the other hand, though at bay, exploded again in the summer of 1965. They constituted enough of a serious danger for Nasser to arrest several thousands of them, and to try to execute their leading ideologue, Sayyid Qotb. Nevertheless they remained a dangerous source of sedition in the armed forces.

A certain amount of superficial debate, confrontation and opposition was allowed periodically in the National Assembly, the ASU and the media. But this confined its targets mainly to the sins of a top-heavy bureaucracy. It hardly questioned Nasser's own conduct in office, or sought to limit his power and render it publicly accountable. Nor did it contemplate putting up alternatives to his régime.

The Communists and Ikhwan were periodically fought by the coercion of a repressive security and intelligence service. The prospect of the only credible opposition to the Nasser régime lay in the armed forces. Paradoxically—perhaps naturally—this was not forthcoming so long as the army remained the régime's only genuine constituency and main source of support precisely because of the privileges it—and particularly the military ruling caste controlling it—came to enjoy under the régime.

The answer to the question, "Did Nasser reshape Egypt's political structure?" cannot therefore be unequivocally answered in the affirmative or negative. That he overthrew an earlier governing élite and political class which controlled the state is not in doubt. That he even partly affected that structure by his introduction of a centrally planned and controlled economy and a mass political organisation is also true. Through agrarian reform, nationalisation and industrialisation he affected a choice for the transformation of Egyptian society and its economy, and permitted the emergence of a substitute governing élite and ruling class.

On the other hand, there is no evidence of Nasser favouring a wider public participation in the formulation of policy, the making of decisions, or the questioning of either; that is, calling the régime to account. He did of course shift the balance of power in favour of those groups in society that worked for him, for the retention of his power and personal rule—the so-called "new classes". These, however, came mainly from his relatively reliable constituency, the army. But he failed to create cadres for a new political order, that could also exercise initiative in public policy, in spite of repeated attempts to do so and to mobilise independent support from the masses. Instead, he occasionally had to inoculate their inertia and total dependence with a dose of his charismatic and imperious leadership. In short, he chose, in the end, to take over an existing state structure, abolish its as yet inexperienced institutional underpinnings for limitation and accountability, and fashion it to his own purposes.

Consequently all efforts to organise political institutions for the régime were partly frustrated by his privileged lieutenants on whom he had to rely for his personal rule. The "scientific socialism" of the 1962 Charter did not mean in practice the further secularisation of society and public endeavour. The Islamic dimension to Egypt's choices in the public domain persisted.[5] Arab socialism stubbornly rejected class notions regarding Egyptian or Arab society in the name of national unity and in order to retain control over any change. The conditions for the army's supremacy in politics remained national unity, a sort of integrative ideology, and an avoidance of pluralistic voluntarism.

If Egypt's political revolution at mid-century consisted essentially of her emancipation from foreign rule, national unity was the minimum ideological requirement. Later, though, the social and economic revolution under the autocracy of a charismatic leader required the exclusion of Egyptians—except for the new privileged military class—from all meaningful political activity. Group interest and other differences could not be allowed to express themselves. The revolution had been decreed from the top, above this rigid, regimented heap of national unity. Hence it could not easily succeed.

The Trauma of June 1967

The most serious threat to Nasser's position came from his friend and closest colleague, Field Marshal Abdel Hakim Amer on 11 June 1967, the day after Nasser had gone back on his resignation from the presidency. Amer, it is reported, resented Nasser's attempt to lay the blame for the defeat of Egyptian arms in the June War on him, and sought to make a show of force if only to restore his position and prestige, not in order to oust Nasser. Typically, other officers and state officials implicated in the affair were close to Amer, or had worked in his office: Salah Nasr, Abbas Radwan, Shams Badran, the commanders of the "Saiqa" Parachute Commando Regiment (Galal al-Hureidi) and of the Inshass Air Base (Tahsin Zaki). Badran, for his part, tried to gather military academy graduates of his 1948 class to aid the conspiracy.[6]

Within six months of weathering this most dangerous challenge to his position, Nasser had reorganised the High Command of the armed forces by making himself Commander-in-Chief, appointing General Muhammad Fawzi Minister of War and creating a National Security Council over which he presided. He assumed control over all military promotions to the rank of colonel or higher. He announced a new Cabinet on 20 March 1968 in which only Hussein Shafei of the old RCC members remained as Vice-President and Minister of Waqfs. Ali Sabri was made Secretary of the ASU. Members of a new cabal organised within the ASU were also prominent among the new Ministers. Zakariyya Mohieddin resigned as Vice-President.

For the next ten days, Heikal in his *Ahram* leaders prepared the way for Nasser's famous Manifesto of 30 March, "Mandate for Change". He wrote of the need for a new generation to take over from the old bureaucrats in the centre of power and their civilian followers. He complained that the most powerful army clique was in Mukhabarat. Its villainy had deadened society; its members had been overtaken by events and could no longer seriously lead the revolution. It was time for a change. Proposals for strengthening civil liberties flowed from Heikal's pen. The Thanks to the immense popular support expressed for the President in the demonstrations of 9–10 June 1967, Heikal mused, "we were able to liquidate the centres of power that had grown up in the régime."[7]

Nasser now introduced elections for membership to the ASU Higher Executive Committee, relinquishing his prerogative of appointing members. In early October eight members had been elected, three of whom were well-known Free Officers: Ali Sabri, Anwar Sadat and Hussein Shafei. The Central Committee, however, was formed of 148 members in addition to Nasser, after a referendum on the 30 March Manifesto in May. A concerted propaganda campaign led by Nasser assisted by Heikal in the *Ahram* throughout this period referred to the four revolutions, 1945–52, 1952–6, 1961–2, and the new one of 9–10 June 1967. The demonstrations in Nasser's favour were now considered to constitute a popular revolution, to which Nasser responded with a reorganisation of the régime, based on the wider involvement of the new generation and greater civil liberty.

Further developments in this direction, however, were so complex and cumbersome that it was hardly fair to expect public enthusiasm for the intricate, multi-stage process of elections. A temporary committee to supervise the elections was announced on 22 May, over whose deliberations Nasser presided from an elevated dais. The four stages of elections for some 7,500 committees and units of the ASU at various levels were set for 25 June and 4, 6 and 8 July.

All this furious activity was accompanied by the usual slogans, posing and empty gesturing. Thus on 4 June 1968 the armed forces declared 5 June a day of mourning. A new National Defence Force militia was launched yet again. More meaningful, presumably, was the organisation of a National Defence Council in November 1968.

Meanwhile a worse eruption of student troubles occurred in Alexandria and Mansura in early November. There were severe clashes between demonstrating students and security forces resulting in several deaths and scores of injuries. Leaflets prepared by students setting out their grievances were distributed. Later in the month there were more dangerous developments. Teachers' colleges and religious institutes demonstrated against regulations of the Ministry of Education, and the troubles spread to secondary and vocational training schools. The three days 23–25 November saw the worst period of the disturbances centred in the Engineering Faculty of Alexandria University. Soon the trouble spread to Cairo University. Charges against *agents provocateurs*, including a certain Muhammad Mahmud el-Haddad, who was branded an Israeli spy, were announced by the government. There were wide arrests in October and November, and the meeting of an extraordinary National Congress on 27 November to deal with the grave situation.

Heikal in the meantime continued to criticise the old ASU leadership in his newspaper, whereas Nasser prepared for the selection of nominees to stand in the National Assembly elections on 9 January 1969. Talk of an "open society" and fortification of the home front against the Israeli menace continued while Nasser proceeded to strengthen his parallel secret organisation to the National Assembly. A special secret organisation in the ASU was formed for various parts of Cairo at least, as for example the one for Kasr el Nil headed by Minister of Information Muhammad Faiq. The problem of restless, troublesome students continued to plague the régime on and off for a few more months.

Nasser's Response to Crisis

Nasser's rule and political style are best illustrated in the occasions when he has had to make certain perfunctory political concessions to the public. A quick recapitulation of his attempts to construct a national political base suggests that their motivation arose from a reaction to other difficulties, some economic, others political. Thus the implementation of the provisions of the 1956 constitution were delayed by the Suez crisis. In May 1957, he appointed an executive committee consisting of trusted colleagues—Abdel Hakim Amer, Zakariyya Mohieddin (Minister of Interior) and Abdel Latif Boghdadi (Minister of Economic Planning)—to screen some 2,500 candidates for election to the 350-seat proposed National Assembly the following July under the National Union. Half of the candidates were rejected as unsuitable or unacceptable.

Even though the features of the new political arrangement included compulsory voting and suffrage for women, candidates still needed to find a £E50 deposit and had to be literate. In any case, nomination in the final analysis was a gift in the hands of the supreme autocrat. The National Assembly, which held its opening session on 22 July 1957, was therefore hand-picked and tightly controlled by Nasser. Except for minor criticisms of routine bureaucratic problems, it met mainly to approve government (that is, Nasser's) decisions.

Its one attempt to force an investigation of the Liberation Province, or the suspect activities of its director (Magdi Hasanein, a Free Officer) was resented by Nasser, and he sought to influence the proceedings of the Assembly. [8] All the same, the National Union's secretary-general, Anwar Sadat, declared in November 1957 that its aim was the "creation of a socialist, democratic, co-operative society free of all political, social and economic exploitation".

The life of the Assembly elected under the National Union scheme was, however, short. In March 1958, it was dissolved when Syria united with Egypt to form the United Arab Republic (UAR). The details of the new arrangements for the National Union should not detain us here. Suffice it to note that they were such as to facilitate the extension of Cairo's, or Nasser's, control over Syria too. [9] This development in itself was one of the main reasons for the dissension in 1959 between the leaders of the Syrian Baath party that had originally pressed for union with Egypt and Nasser. It led to the resignation of Salah el Din al-Bitar from the UAR government, and accelerated the collapse of the Baath's civilian leadership and the Syrian military's control of the party.

The Syrian Secession

The 1962 National Charter and the ASU, the political organisation it provided for, were in a way a direct consequence of the Syrian secession in September 1961. With the loss of the other partner, Syria, in the union, a major shake-up of administration and political arrangements was inevitable. In fact, the Syrian affair caused the first serious rift between Nasser and some of his closest associates, members of the original Free Officer conspiracy, particularly Field Marshal Amer, who had served as Egyptian pro-consul and special envoy of the President in Damascus. Possibly his gauleiter role in Syria partly accounted for Syrian disillusionment, resentment and ultimate secession. Moreover, elements that surfaced as prominent forces in the Damascus secession *coup* were considered by Nasser as representing the old notables, financial and commercial interests in Syria. These of course—as much as those in Egypt—had reacted sharply to Nasser's socialist decrees of July 1961 which, among other things, further reduced the limit of land ownership from 200 to 100 *feddans*. More unacceptable was the fact that Nasser prepared and announced them without prior consultation with or discussion in the National Assembly.

It was logical therefore for Nasser, in reacting to the Syrian secession—in fact, the rejection of his rule—to further tighten his control over the economy with yet another series of socialist decrees later that autumn (October). These paved the way and supplied the momentum for his National Charter the following May which, on paper at least, expressed his decision to travel down the road of socialism. But this too was an overspill of his resentment, feeling of insecurity and suspicion in the face of events in Damascus. He realised Egyptians questioned the hasty—nay, instant—union with Syria some four years earlier and could not afford a loss of prestige. A drastic reorganisation of political arrangements was necessary with security as the foremost consideration.

The six weeks of debates over the National Charter in the National Congress of Popular Forces were perhaps the only ones of their kind throughout the life of the Nasser régime. They indicated the persistence of pockets of criticism and laid bare widespread feelings of frustration and discontent. Nasser, however, never intended the openness of these debates to set the tone and style of any future political deliberative bodies. He cleverly allowed everyone to let off steam after the Syrian adventure. In doing so he had a clearer idea of public opinion trends, the mood of the country and more significantly who or what groups were more likely to prove troublesome. The Congress all the same approved the Charter unanimously by acclamation. In the end, it too was an occasion of "applause democracy" at its best.

The statutes for the ASU were announced in October, providing for some 7,500 units on all national and local levels, with over four million members. As in the case of the 1956 constitution, the implementation of the Charter had to be delayed because of the eventually abortive Tripartite Talks for Arab Unity with Syria and Iraq in the spring of 1963.[10] Elections for a new Assembly to meet on 23 July 1963 had to be postponed to November. Candidates to the 360 seats (350 elected, 10 appointed by the President), had to be over 30 years old and literate. Now, however, 50 per cent of them had to be workers and peasant farmers, a change from the earlier arrangements. Although the definition of a peasant and a worker was made clearer, it was difficult to see how the majority of these, who were illiterate, could qualify.

Typical of Nasser's balancing act was the lifting of martial law when a provisional constitution was announced on 22 July 1963, the day before the new Assembly met. But on the following day he introduced emergency powers that allowed him the retention of overall control whatever happened under the new political arrangements. He also reorganised the government, abolishing the old Presidential Council of 1961 and replacing it with the appointment of seven Vice-Presidents, of which Amer was made the first. Ali Sabri was appointed Prime Minister and the newly elected Assembly duly proceeded to nominate Nasser to another six-year term for the presidency. The plebiscite held in March 1965 gave Nasser 99.999 per cent of the vote. Some might assume that the near unanimous election of Nasser was an indication of public approval for the new changes he had introduced into the country's political arrangements. More accurate, however, is the inference that very little had changed to shake his total control. Nasser rather weathered the lingering post-secession crisis and came out of it more or less unscathed. None of the specific grievances had really been dealt with.

The Economic Crisis 1965–6

Greater difficulties, though, soon arose with the economic crisis of 1965–6. The strains of an over-ambitious first five-year plan (1960–5) were just beginning to be felt.[11] Deteriorating relations with other Arab states—Saudi Arabia especially—and the United States did not help matters. The drain in men and resources in the Yemen war stalemate was an added complication. One of the most disastrous results was the further control of the state's daily affairs by the "new class" of influential army and intelligence people. Neither the elaborate though creaking ASU organisation nor the apathetic Assembly was effective in checking the drift towards greater crisis.

In these circumstances clandestine opposition forces among the Ikhwan and the Communists began to stir, despite the latter's forced accommodation with the régime one or two years previously. In the countryside, a state bureaucracy, inflated after agrarian reform in order to run the agricultural co-operative schemes, the ASU and other organisations, had turned into local power groups pitted against a lingering galaxy of local provincial notables, officials, village headmen and still influential families. Within the top echelons of the régime itself rival cliques of soldiers and power groups competed for advantage. Nasser's new Prime Minister, Zakariyya Mohieddin, desperately tried to cope with the economic crisis, featuring inflation and shortages of basic essential commodities. In desperation he opened the floodgate of emigration, and thousands of professionally trained Egyptians left for Canada and other parts, causing a serious drain on the country's skilled human resources.

Suddenly, in August 1965, a large number of Ikhwan were arrested on charges of conspiring to assassinate Nasser and senior Ministers. Among those arrested were leading members of the society, including Sayyid Qotb. Several Communists, allegedly pro-Chinese, were also arrested. The following spring, in April 1966, there were more arrests of so-called feudalists following bloody incidents in the countryside.

Within a year of the political reorganisation, Nasser was faced with an economic and political crisis. Neither agrarian reform with its corollary scheme of co-operatives nor the ASU and new Assembly had produced the desired effect. Instead, power cliques persisted both in Cairo and the provinces, bent on the pursuit of their interests. The vast political reorganisation that created the ASU and its ancillary institutions failed to erode the power of the régime's "new class".

Again, characteristically, although Nasser in the National Assembly attacked "these centres of power", his instinct was not to transform the Assembly into a serious legislative body. Instead, he quietly created his own special secret organisation within it and the ASU, consisting mainly of hand-picked ex-officers and civilians. These were to act as a makeweight to the competing rival power cliques and eventually constitute the new Nasser equivalent of the old Free Officer cabal in the army.

Nasser's putative hope back in 1962 to inspire a new political consciousness among the masses and promote the cadres of new leadership from a younger generation—as for example from the co-operatives, trade unions, provincial and local government—through his elaborate ASU remained unfulfilled. But perhaps this was never really his intention, since his actions and policy remained at variance with his proclaimed intention. The ASU remained ineffective because it was fettered. The dearth of new cadres was due to Nasser's continued muzzling of the only group of Egyptians who could have provided them: the educated, articulate élites. Building "socialism without socialists" was just as zany as building "democracy without democrats". When the cultural gap between the educated urban élite and the traditional rural society of the Egyptian masses is taken into account, the obstacle to political development becomes insurmountable. The new network of vested interests defeated any possible effects of Nasser's new political arrangements.

It was with this political and economic shambles that Egypt went to war in June 1967. Some of it was the result of domestic and foreign pressures. Much of it, however, was due to Nasser's singular approach to power, and his reactive behaviour that was always motivated by the desire to retain absolute control over affairs. He was not prepared to take any risks.

It was not enough for Nasser in his stirring speech of 24 September 1962 to inveigh against reactionaries, the "Israeli cancer" and against class divisions in a "true democracy". Nor was it enough for him to assert the "necessity and inevitability of socialism" or the "socialist solution" for Egypt. Similarly, in his opening speech to the newly elected Assembly on 26 March 1964, the same themes of anti-imperialism and anti-Zionism were no proof of his favourite contrasting slogan, "How we were and what we have become."

Although a reaction to the Syrian secession, the "socialist solution" outlined in Nasser's National Charter may have been more than a simple tactic. Yet the Charter as a whole "encompassed specific stands and reactions of the President", particularly against those who opposed him in the UAR (1958–61). Soon the popular institution—the ASU, the National Congress and Assembly—held too many meetings (1964–6), but did precious little practical work. "Speakers in them", wrote Hussein Sabri, "competed in praising the revolution. Extended criticism or the suggestion of investigating specific cases of power abuse in public institutions were slapped down as libellous and conspiratorial behaviour."[12] In any case, Nasser had decreed the notorious Law 119 of 1964 as part of the emergency powers the moment he announced the provisional constitution and lifted martial law. Under this statute, state prosecution agencies were relieved of limited remand in investigating cases of alleged crimes against the national interest or security. It was not rescinded until 1972.

Another obstacle to the development of these political institutions was Nasser's own temperament and behaviour as head of state and government. It is reported that when Nasser was still only a Minister in the government, he was on the whole tolerant, kind in his dealings with colleagues, a patient and good listener in joint RCC-Cabinet meetings. He rarely spoke for or against any particular issue. But this was exactly the opposite of his behaviour once he became Prime

Minister, and later President, with all affairs concentrated in his hands.

> The Council of Ministers under his chairmanship became an audience. Nasser was the only speaker; Ministers listened dutifully and took down notes, received instructions. If one of them wished to comment or speak he had to ask his permission. But Nasser was human . . . and could lose his temper if a Minister touched upon a sensitive issue. . . . He shook his legs nervously in anger—or delight. [13]

After the terrible tribulations of 1967–8, however, Nasser, according to another witness, reverted occasionally to being a good listener, even seeking advice and delegating some authority. Nevertheless, his man, Amin Huweidi of Intelligence, was still the liaison between the Ministers and the presidency. [14]

After the June War

After the June War, however, Nasser's approach to his mass constituency was solicitous. He affected a keen awareness of widespread criticism of the régime. He promised to end the privileges of certain influential groups and grant greater freedom to the citizens. He even made a friendly gesture to his old feudalist enemies by ordering the desequestration of some of their assets. He released several Muslim Brothers from detention. He overhauled the intelligence services—but did not reduce their strength or importance.

The student riots and workers' demonstrations of February and November 1968, however, came as an unexpected blow to Nasser's recovery from the 1967 débâcle. In magnitude and ferocity they were the first since 1954, indeed since 1952. The immediate pretext for the February disturbances was the angry public reaction to the light sentences passed on the Commander of the air force, General Sidqi Mahmud, and other senior officers for their failure in the June War. Considering the workers' demonstrations, however, the cause of the upheaval must be sought in the deteriorating economic and political situation. A common popular complaint in those days was, "We accept the régime did not do much for us, but being a military one, it could at least have given a good account of itself in the war against Israel." Students in particular were protesting against police interference in the university, government control of student unions and generally ruthless state repression. They were also venting their frustration against the régime's network of privilege. "Heikal, Heikal, you servant, you forger of dreams," they chanted.

Nasser quickly sought to dissociate himself from his discredited minions: the power cliques in the army and intelligence services. In fact, he had been already alluding to these "centres of power" in his speeches of the previous year.[15] He also shed most of his old Free Officer colleagues; he fired Zakariyya as Prime Minister. Only Hussein Shafei, Anwar Sadat and Ali Sabri of the old guard remained as Vice-President, Speaker of the Assembly and secretary of the ASU respectively. He brought in civilians, mainly academics, lawyers, economists and engineers in to his Cabinet. But this did not mean civilians were now at the centre of power; they were only executors of his will and policy.

The year from February 1968 to January 1969 was a critical one for Nasser. In trying to weather the storm of domestic unrest he promised Egyptians a new political deal—the 30 March Manifesto and a newly elected Assembly (9 January 1969). The more sophisticated and experienced among the Egyptians did not believe him. He himself never quite intended to allow them greater political freedom. His illness meanwhile—diabetes, arteriosclerosis and other cardiovascular ailments—compelled him to go to Russia in the summer of 1968 for a few weeks of treatment and rest cure. It compounded the difficulties perhaps when it was publicly announced as a bad case of the flu. Soon after his return came the second round of student troubles in the autumn of 1968, only this time better organised and more violent. The Ikhwan and Communists were involved, and the demonstrations engulfed most of the major centres in the country— Alexandria, Mansura, Cairo and Asiut.

Nasser had to respond to what looked like serious political unrest. He was without most of his old guard Free Officer colleagues. His civilian appointees were ineffective in the face of the real instruments of power, the army and the secret security services. He was a physically debilitated man, not his old energetic rabble-rousing self. His options were really two: either to proceed with a serious liberalisation of his régime, allowing the partial satisfaction of the articulate public's demand on one hand, or to embark upon a further tightening-up of his personal control over the state on the other. The first option would have meant the erosion of his personal power. But it also entailed the added risk of triggering off adverse reaction from the "centres of power" in the army and intelligence services who would have felt menaced.

In the end he chose the second option. It had the added advantage of keeping the "centres of power"—which were anyway a natural outgrowth of his régime and political style—intact. He therefore reacted to the crisis with tough measures against dissidents, put on spy and conspiracy trials of seven Egyptians accused of planning to assassinate him and senior Ministers back in May 1968, and tightened internal security generally.

Within a few months Nasser indulged in his usual balancing act. The government crisis in the autumn of 1969 when he dismissed Ali Sabri as secretary of the ASU was its overt manifestation. It was also a reverberation of his attempt to depoliticise the armed forces' command by getting rid of the last remnants of the late Field Marshal Amer's power clique. At the end of the year Nasser was President, Prime Minister, president of the National Congress of the ASU and chairman of its Higher Executive Committee. He controlled, that is, policy-making, the minor legislative functions of the Assembly and the executive powers of government in the Cabinet.

The years from 1966 to 1968 then were the most critical in Nasser's rule. Whatever power factions crystallised around Ali Sabri in the ASU, whatever the dangers of the alleged Ikhwan plot or the conspiracy of officers loyal to Amer in 1967, or the bolder opposition of land-owning families highlighted by the tragic incident in Kamshish in 1966,[16] they were all proof of opposition to Nasser. Civilian and military pockets of resistance began to stir and by the mid-sixties there was a reaction to his personal rule.

Nasser's Concept of Government

Heikal explained the crisis by arguing that centres of power arose only after Nasser was forced to curb his responsibilities because of his illness, and delegate many tasks of state to his deputies. Moreover, he had to deal with the reconstruction of the armed forces after the June War and strengthen relations with the Soviet Union, the main supplier of Egyptian arms. At the same time, though, he argued that Nasser did not need any political party base in order to govern or achieve his aims. The use of the media, he asserted, was superior for Nasser's purposes to any party as a means of reaching the masses, "Because he was constantly before the masses, talking to them face to face . . . or through radio and television."[17]

Another Egyptian defined Nasser's political organisation problem thus: "After eleven years of mass support for the revolution, what was needed was the organization of this support, the creation of the communication lines between the base and this popular mass support."[18]

Heikal, though, conceded the régime needed a political organisation, but Nasser believed the mobilisation of the people could best be sought through national achievements—the Aswan High Dam, factories—and that it would be more effective than through a political party. The millions who benefited from the Dam and factories would be automatically partisans of Nasser anyway. But Heikal soon lapsed into moments of rationality and candour: "the age of a popular leader is not the age of political parties." More cryptic is Heikal's feeble excuse of Nasser's secret political organisation: "The revolution was still open to attack in Egypt and the Arab World . . . The secret organisation was a guarantee for the revolution's survival."[19] Nasser thought his secret organisation could revive a moribund ASU by breathing into it a spirit of national unity and at the same time prevent the rise of factions within it.

Like many others, Heikal too claims that back in 1952 it had never occurred to Nasser that he would govern. Developments, however, soon imposed rulership on him. The abolition of the monarchy in effect placed sovereignty in the RCC. Other measures to consolidate the power of the new soldier rulers all required legislation by decree to found a new authority. Opposition from the Ikhwan is perhaps what convinced Nasser to seek a political organisation. But Heikal's suggestion that at first Nasser depended on the unorganised masses is ludicrous.[20]

Heikal also subscribed to another widely held theory that Nasser was against the King but not against political parties; that he even invited the Wafd to take over power because he believed it represented the majority of Egyptians, on condition they implemented agrarian reform. This theory however does not hold up under closer scrutiny. Nasser failed to create his own party, let alone allow other so-called revolutionary parties to organise. He was a hegemonist of power. Why, for instance, dissolve all parties except the Ikhwan, against whom there was clear evidence of wishing to undermine his power? The left made its disastrous bid for power in Kafr el Dawar back in August 1952. The fact remains that Nasser could not countenance parties because he would not permit any alternative to his rule. In order to dominate he had to destroy all available alternative centres of leadership.

There might therefore be another explanation. As a result of the power struggle in February–April 1954, Nasser identified his enemies as being the Ikhwan, the Communists, the old political parties and those small sections in society that were economically and financially better-off. The appeal of the Ikhwan to the masses he tried to dilute if not altogether eliminate with an Islamic Congress which he launched in November 1954. Later he reorganised the Azhar University and its affiliated institutions with the Azhar Law of June 1961, hoping to control it better by "modernising" it. He also paid his respects to Islamic sentiment by recognising the Islamic sources of Egypt's Arab socialism, especially in the National Charter of 1962.[21] The thunder of the Communists at this point was stolen, Nasser believed, by the adoption of "scientific socialism", planning and social-economic reform. As for the old political parties and the more affluent groups in society, Nasser thought he could simply separate political power from wealth through agrarian reform, expropriation and nationalisation, a ceiling on incomes and stiffer taxation. But he only enabled new power cliques in his régime to acquire wealth through influence.

By 1956, Nasser was on the way to rendering the army the main source for the recruitment of a new élite which he, from time to time and as the need arose, tried to counter with his own populism—the projection of Nasserism. Before personalising all of these changes as charismatic leader, he methodically concentrated power in his own hands from June 1953 to June 1956; from chairman of the RCC, Vice-Premier, Minister of Interior and secretary-general of the Liberation Rally (while Intelligence was headed by Zakariyya Mohieddin and the armed forces by Abdel Hakim Amer) he became the President of a "republic" elected by 99.9 per cent of the voters in a plebiscite.

Actually the concentration of power in his own hands was a fact by November 1954, after he had six Muslim Brothers hanged, several hundreds more arrested and brutally treated, scores of army officers purged and Naguib ousted from every state office. At the beginning of 1955 Nasser dominated the government and the state. In the meantime, the RCC was purged of extreme leftists and extreme rightists. As for the state administration, the bureaucracy, it came to be supervised by his officer nominees. So was the army and the new state political organisation, the Liberation Rally.

Having removed the most serious threat to his own position, Nasser was now ready to venture abroad into the arena of Arab leadership, tangling with Nuri el Said of Iraq over the Western-sponsored Baghdad Pact, and generally attacking the continued Western presence in the Middle East. Hussein Arafa claims Nasser asked him towards the end of 1954 to put certain feelers out regarding the possibility of securing arms from the Soviet Union. Arafa contacted Muhammad Kamil al-Bindari, a one-time Minister and Egyptian representative in Moscow and then president of the Egyptian Council of Peace.[22] He also proceeded to erect the ostensibly legal-constitutional framework for his personal leadership: the 1956 constitution and provision for a National Union to elect members to a new National Assembly. Above all, using the media, the press and the National Guidance Ministry he began seriously to project his charismatic leadership to a captive, adulating audience.[23]

Thus Nasser's successful projection of the image of imperialism's challenger in the Middle East and champion of national independence movements in Bandung was reflected in the rapturous procession upon his return to Cairo on 22 April 1955. His theme of national self-respect and dignity was further strengthened by the arms deal with the Soviet Union announced in September 1955. It reflected not only his defiance of the West as the ultimate expression of Egyptian independence, but also suggested to the simple minds of his swarming audiences the emancipation from a reliance upon the West in the struggle against Israel, a struggle that was terrifyingly brought home to Egyptians earlier in February of that year when the Israelis raided Gaza. An Egyptian was to write later (1973) that with this, "we came to be ruled on a military basis, without limits or rules."[24] "Soon", he added, "one man's word put a man in jail; another from the same man released him."[25] Suez did the rest. "Nasser's success in turning the Suez defeat into a political victory and the union with Syria turned his head until he imagined that the history of Egypt began with him and he forgot all about the past."[26]

Nasser the Populist

Nasser in short was for a government for the people but not by the people. He saw himself as a plebeian autocratic reformer, a benevolent despot, who insisted on monopolising the initiative for change. His distrust and outright rejection of political parties, for example, was enunciated clearly on at least two occasions. Addressing the opening session of the new National Assembly on 23 July 1957, he said:

There was between you and us a party system which divided the nation. Principles were not the basis of differences. Rather it was selfish pursuit of power and riches—the very livelihood of our people. All this had to go . . . so that we could once again meet together . . . The abolition of parties was a battle on the road to independence.[27]

Again, in his famous Port Said "Victory" Speech on 23 December 1957, Nasser justified the National Union as a means of facing the challenge of the powers after Suez, and for rendering the government a true expression of popular will. He rejected the idea of a political party, even a single-party organisation, because "the party, by the very meaning of the term, represents only a part of the people, and the single party accordingly means the monopolisation of political action by a section of the people."[28]

Nasser's rejection of parties was complemented by a constant appeal to his special relationship with the masses. Upon his re-election to a second term as President of the Republic after the promulgation of the 1964 constitution, he declared, "I feel unlimited gratitude to the masses of our great struggling nation, hoping each day to satisfy them; something that is beyond my capacity to do because I possess nothing beside my work and life." Or again after the events of June 1967,

I did not consider for a moment that the demonstrations of our people . . . on the evening of June 9 were a tribute to me personally. Rather I saw them as a determination to carry on the struggle. I have said often this people has given me more than I ever dreamt at any time.[29]

Later that summer, faced with the Amer–Badran conspiracy, student disorder and other upheavals the following winter, Nasser lashed out against the centres of power and secret organisations of *his* régime, attacked the privileged "new class", including the three-year-old ASU and solemnly declared, "I am with the people." After dealing with the Amer affair he told the people how he protected them against a greedy power clique in the army, whereas three years before that he had told the new National Assembly on 25 March 1964, "We must at all costs prevent the emergence of a new class, that believes privilege is their due inheritance from the old ruling class." And he always combined his warnings against the danger of seditious counter-revolution at home with admonitions against foreign attempts to topple the revolution in Egypt ever since 1965.[30]

Nasser's difficulties with erstwhile colleagues and the exposure of his corrupt state machine led him to mount a frantic campaign to mobilise his "street constituency" against all power groups within the state. He revived a favourite theme of old, that of independence and national liberation, reminding his audiences that outsiders continued to wish to undermine Egypt's independence, especially during the period of transition to a socialist order. "We are independent today in spite of all of them . . . But they will not let us remain independent," he told the ASU Congress in Asiut on 8 March 1965. The greatest protection against these diabolical machinations of outsiders was still national unity, "the unity of the power of all the people that has replaced the alliance between feudalism and capitalism." Egypt's independence moreover was in the mainstream of national liberation movements against imperialism and colonialism throughout Asia and Africa.

Cleverly, after the 1967 War, Nasser resumed his populist tone regarding his dependence on the people in continuing the struggle against Israel. "We want", he said, "a popular resistance: some people who are armed, some with daggers and knives, others with mere clubs and sticks.[31] But he also had to reassure his "street constituency" that the very close relationship with the Soviet Union after 1967 did not compromise Egyptian independence. "We secured arms from the Soviet Union in 1955," he conceded. "But the Soviet Union did not impose any conditions or make any demands on our conduct of policy that can possibly now or later insult our national pride."[32]

Although Nasser's populist tirades may have temporarily swayed the populace, some of his former RCC colleagues who had fallen from power bitterly denounced him as a dictator, not a populist. Kamal el-Din Hussein wrote to Field Marshal Amer from prison on 24 October 1965: "I regret the revolution has been transformed into one of terror. No person is certain of his fate once he utters a free opinion in order to satisfy his conscience and perform his patriotic duty."[33] As for Nasser himself, Kamal el-Din reminded Amer, "Did I not warn you once that if he insists on his own deification it is useless to collaborate with him?"[34]

One must consider such criticism with scepticism, for it is *post hoc* and partly the result of bitter resentment. None the less, Kamal el-Din Hussein's references to specific instances of Nasser's direct interference in order to obstruct the proceedings and work of the first National Assembly in 1957–8 are serious and borne out by similar evidence from other sources. It is a charge also levelled at Nasser by Abdel Latif Boghdadi, president of that first Assembly. As for Nasser's screening of nominees for election to that Assembly, Hussein describes the process as "the beginning of the phoney democracy", involving Nasser's extensive use of his and his wife's relatives to man several agencies of his political network. As one-time Education Minister, Hussein is equally critical of Nasser's interference in educational policy, an interference intended to placate the masses.

The context of Hussein's criticism, however, is important. He had initially attacked Nasser and Amer—the régime, that is—after disagreements over the socialist decrees of 1961–3, the Yemen War in 1964 and the clash between the régime and the Ikhwan in 1965. In his criticism he intended to show that Nasser had not only gone beyond the limits of proper behaviour for a Muslim but also reneged on his own values, principles and earlier commitments. Addressing Amer further in his letter, Hussein continued,

> You cannot deny, nor can Gamal Abdel Nasser deny, our common national Islamic orientation ever since we met each other . . . You know very well we all swore on the Holy Book and the Revolver in a dark room in the Salibiya quarter together with . . .[35]

This is an allusion to the earliest orientation of the group that later became the nucleus of the Free Officer movement.

Heikal denies Nasser was a dictator, because the latter governs strictly as he wills, ignoring the wishes and interests of the masses. Nasser, on the contrary, did not govern in this way. According to Heikal, Nasser in fact "expressed the popular will", as for example when he abolished the monarchy, nationalised the Suez Canal and expelled the British from Egypt. But did he also reflect the popular will when he sent Egyptian troops to the Yemen, or when he united Egypt with Syria? Heikal concedes that at that "stage of development" there was no popular participation in the making of public policy; that Egypt under Nasser was a "democracy by consent" not by "participation"—a charming distinction.[36] The fact remains that even after 1967, Nasser came to rely more and more on secret organisations staffed by his own men in order to govern the country and maintain his personal rule.

After 1967 Nasser was head of state, chief of government, boss of the ASU and Commander-in-Chief of the armed forces. There was hardly room left for a collective leadership of old comrades. However, the pre-1967 abrasive, aggressive style of confrontation with all and sundry was gone. It was replaced by one of moderation and a convenient truce with all. Palestine after 1967, for example, was no longer a "sacred duty", only an Egyptian political question. Egypt instead became the supreme duty.

In his remarks to delegations that came to congratulate him on the nationalisation of the Canal on 28 July 1956,[37] and in an interview with the *Daily Herald*, he responded to the charge of being a dictator as follows:

> I don't know, you must judge. Foreign papers say I am a dictator, a Pharaoh. But a dictator is one who governs his country in spite of its people. It is up to you to find out if this is so in my case.[38]

He also told a reporter from *Life* magazine on 14 July 1959 that foreigners called him "Hitler of the Nile" and "Arab imperialist" because they believed he opened the door to Communism in the Middle East. And he defiantly declared, "I stand accused of being a fanatic Arab nationalist."

Nasser's Control of the State

The state under Nasser was not the creature or the instrument of a party, an ideological movement or class. Rather the reverse was the case. The state, controlled by Nasser and a group of subordinate lieutenants—the composition of which changed from time to time to suit the autocrat's purposes—gave birth by decree to movements, ideologies, parties and even new "classes". The primary function of institutions was one of mobilising the masses to adhere to the policies of a political directorate, controlled and manipulated by a supreme autocrat in order to impose the semblance of national unity. Even when it became necessary to transform the economy through an expanded public sector implementing the state's plan for accelerated economic growth via industrialisation after 1956, the extensive development of a state-controlled economy undermined any changes in favour of a socialist transformation of society.

The "socialist solution" enunciated in the Charter of 1962, involving systematic planning, the tighter control of national and foreign capital investment and a broadening of public participation, was more of a necessity of power for the régime than a genuine ideological commitment to socialism. Even in 1970 it had hardly affected the masses of poorer Egyptians. Its benefits, such as they were, accrued to a privileged minority, comprising about 780,000 independent workers and medium owner-farmers in the countryside, who make up no more than 10 to 15 per cent of the rural population, and lower- and middle-class salaried employees and professionals in the cities. The rate of national savings was so low as to hardly offer any prospects of public participation in state enterprises. Foreign capital—particularly Western capital—was hardly anxious to invest massively in adverse or uncertain conditions. On the whole then, the famous nationalisation laws of July–October 1961, 1963 and 1964 were, again like those of 1956–7, more political than economic in their effect. They were also the expression of a feeling, after the break-up of the UAR in September 1961, that the so-called upper bourgeoisie who had shared power with the army until then should no longer do so. The socialist decrees specifically aimed at dismantling their power, and reaffirming the primacy of the military cadres in the new political class. It is noteworthy in this connection that on 10 September 1961, only eighteen days before the secession of Syria from the union, a new Military College of Science and Technology was opened, where officers were to be trained for technical and managerial posts.

The state control of the economy was further tightened by the creation of a wider, more intricate network of administrative structures, commissions, organisations and boards. Their staffs were recruited more and more from the new bureaucratic-technocratic cadres and the officer corps.[39]

Throughout Nasser's political career the emphasis was on tight organisation controlled by the state rather than on the development of even limited deliberative institutions for the definition of national goals or the formulation of public policy.[40] There was no serious attempt to decentralise and diffuse power. Rather the basic formula remained unaltered: that of a traditional centralism coupled to the dynamic leadership of a charismatic ruler. The most that Nasser conceded after 1961 was to wrap his personal concentration of power with a disposable cloak of eclectic ideology, comprising a mixture of Egyptian nationalism, socialism and Arabism. The most that was diversified periodically were the functions of state agencies and individuals within a framework of centralised power. This was obvious in the period beginning with the National Charter in 1962 and ending with the defeat of June 1967.

The "Egyptian Spring" of liberalisation in 1962—another one was occasioned in 1968—and the series of governmental reorganisations between 1961 and 1968 did not amount to a democratic prelude. Rather they remained tactical moves by Nasser, who allowed his detractors the fleeting luxury of criticism. Thus on 14 May 1965, he told the ASU, "the era of revolutionary administrative measures is past;" that the time had come for political reorganisation. But by this Nasser did not contemplate the creation of opposition groups within the ASU or the Assembly. He wished instead to assuage the effects of his concentration of power by an act of controllable paper decentralisation. The difficulty was that his power and that of the state structure serving it were not derived from a party or ideological movement. It was therefore difficult to construct a new political organisation that would control state power structures when he in fact dominated them.

An additional constraint was the fact that after 9 June 1967, Nasser was no longer the "incontestable leader" of the revolution. Before 1956, he and his Free Officer colleagues were against the *status quo*. They had grabbed power in order to change it. They had transferred authority from the King and other political institutions of the country to themselves. They had deprived those who led these institutions of their economic and financial power. Possibly after 1954 there were alternative courses open, but the Suez episode in 1956 precluded all of them except the one of Nasser's personal hegemony. It highlighted his ambition and perhaps vision, and supplied the momentum for his personal rule for another decade. The break came in 1966–7. The combination of domestic difficulties and the June War, together with his advanced illness, slowed down this momentum. The collapse of the military command in 1967 was arguably the main cause.

After 1967 therefore Nasser paid the price of his not encouraging the emergence of intermediate arrangements between himself and the people. Upon defeat, the dilution of his charisma was inevitable. The people asked, "Who made you Chief? Gamal, you are asleep; wake up, Gamal." "Use your army against Dayan, not against us." These were some of the slogans of protest in 1968. The people wanted, and he himself realised the time had come, to supplement his leadership with institutions. Yet this was the one thing Nasser was unable—and unwilling—to do, for he was at his best when manipulating the masses in the great populist tradition of the charismatic leader. His rule had become so personal that he was no longer fit to modernise society in the sense of creating more solid institutions of authority, allowing the people a free choice, or ameliorating their economic plight.

As radical leaders of a nationalist movement, Nasser and his Free Officer colleagues transformed the movement itself into an organisational weapon. They claimed it provided them with the basic institutional apparatus for political modernisation and economic development. If the ASU, say, is considered to be the political embodiment of that apparatus, its designation as a state political organisation soon rendered it into an administrative structure, so that its existence did not imply a real shift from a reliance on force for rule to a reliance on institutions. Nor did it introduce a significant change in the overall patterns of political life in the country. As a mass organisation it deceptively papered over the persistent structural political cracks.

The moral basis upon which the Free Officers—and Nasser after 1954—claimed to govern Egypt was that of revolution. This implied a commitment to transform society radically. The Nasser régime succeeded in neutralising the political élite of an older social-economic order. But it appears to have done little more than that. A multi-layered amalgam of an older and a new society tended to coexist. Soon the new was superimposed on the old. Mass political organisation remained a malleable and nebulous "revolutionary" concept. It enabled the new ruler to ignore the need for "first principles", or rules and institutions to embody them.

For a long while, foreign students of Egypt considered the Nasser régime a revolutionary "mobilising" type of polity. This suited their peculiarly Western typology of régimes which tended to exaggerate differences between régimes by paying too much attention to the ideological tone of their leaders' pronouncements, but hardly any attention to their structural bases. Westerners became prisoners of their own conceptual schemes and categories, from which they made unreasonable inferences that did not stand up to close scrutiny. To the ASU, for example, which they identified as a mass party organisation, they attributed by inference certain functions without closely examining the extent of the institutionalisation of its structure.

Today modern governments everywhere have achieved a near-monopoly of force. Yet political power in the more developed states is normally based on the overall social structure rather than this monopoly of force. This plainly was not the case in Nasser's Egypt. In fact even the developed states have recently experienced serious challenges to their monopoly of force, if violent social unrest and other types of conflict are any indication.

Nasser, then, did not produce a political organisation, only a system of state power and a machine for communicating slogans to the people that was not limited by law. He in fact was the source of law and used, as long as it was possible, the populism of the charismatic leader to maintain the semblance of national unity. As such, he united the people only in his person, and shunted aside all other élites in society by not permitting any intermediate institutions to rise between his personal state power and the masses. He blurred national with social and economic objectives on the grounds that there could be no class divisions in Egypt, only national solidarity. His assumption of total responsibility rendered most people irresponsible.[41] Consequently, he could not construct a new or different polity. Giving Egyptians a sense of identity and dignity was not the same as turning them into responsible citizens. Thus while for over a decade, between 1956 and 1967, Nasser projected the image of the idolised charismatic leader who concentrated all state power in his hands, he had to depend on the Behemoth of a monstrous bureaucracy and a terrifying security service for the running of his state and the maintenance of his personal rule.

If the failure of the Bonaparte adventure in Egypt with its resultant chaos in Cairo spawned Muhammad Ali the Great in 1805, the failure of the *ancien régime* to deal with pressing problems, its cutting of all links with a protecting foreign power and the dreadful burning of Cairo by the destitute mob in January 1952 gave birth to Nasser.

Notes

1. *Hādhihi al-thawra*, p.143.
2. Ibid., p.209.
3. On the National Union, see Anwar al-Sadat, *Maana al-ittihād al-qawmi* (*The meaning of the National Union*), a pamphlet (Cairo, 1957).
4. See the series of articles by Professor Fuad Zakariyya in *Rose el-Youssef*, 14 and 21 April 1975.
5. See Fauzi Najjar, "Islam and Socialism in the United Arab Republic", *Journal of Contemporary History*, Vol. 3, July 1968, pp.183–99; Malcolm H.

Kerr, "The Emergence of a socialist ideology in Egypt", *Middle East Journal*, Vol.16, No.2, Spring 1962, pp.127–44. See also Muhammad Ibrahim Hamza, *Ishtirākiyyat al-islam wa al-ishtirākiyya al-gharbiyya* (*The socialism of Islam and Western socialism*) (Cairo, 1961). For a general discussion of the role of Islam in Egyptian policy under Nasser and further references to Egyptian sources, see P. J. Vatikiotis, "Islam and the Foreign policy of Egypt" in J. Harris Proctor (ed.), *Islam and International Relations* (London, 1965), pp.120–57.

6. See the text of charges against the conspirators and their "confessions" in *al-Ahram*, 13 September 1967. On the arrest and suicide of Amer, see *al-Ahram*, 16 September 1967. See also, al-Nahar's *al-Kitāb al-sanawi* (*Year-book*), 1967, pp.218–20. Details of these events remain confused and obscure. Recent statements about them by those involved must be treated with caution. See, however, Sami Gohar, *Al-sāmitūn yatakallamūn* (Cairo, 1975); Mahmud al-Gayār, "Rajulān qatalā al-Mushir Amer", *Rose el-Youssef*, No.2482, Cairo, 5 January 1976; and Ahmad Hamrush, "Shuhud yulio", *Rose el-Youssef*, Cairo, April 1977.

7. In *al-Ahram*, 31 March 1968.

8. See the allegations by Abdel Latif Boghdadi, at that time President of the Assembly, in Sami Gohar, *Al-sāmitūn yatakallamūn*.

9. See Patrick Seale, *The Struggle for Syria* (London, 1965).

10. See Riad Taha (ed.), *Mahādir jalsāt mubāhathāt al-wahda* (*Minutes of the 1963 unity talks*) (Cairo, 1963), and Malcolm Kerr, *The Arab Cold War: Gamal 'Abd al-Nasir and his rivals, 1958–1970* (London, 1977).

11. For a more or less official statement on the first Five Year Plan, see Ali Sabri, *Sanawāt al-tahawwul al-ishtirāki* (*The years of socialist transformation*) (Cairo, n.d.), an evaluation of the first Five Year Plan. On the problems of planning in Egypt, see the more technical B. Hansen and G. Marzouk, *Development and economic policy in the UAR* (Amsterdam, 1965), and the more general survey by Patrick K. O'Brien, *The Revolution in Egypt's Economic System* (London, 1966).

12. Hussein Sabri, *Rose el-Youssef*, 18 July 1975.

13. Fathi Radwan, reminiscing about the Nasser régime, in *Rose el-Youssef* No. 2464, Cairo, 1 September 1975.

14. Dr Abdul Wahhab al-Burullusi, one-time Minister of Health (1968), in *Rose el-Youssef*, No.2468, Cairo, 29 September 1975.

15. As well as those of 23 July and 23 November 1967 after the Six Day War.

16. Where an official of the Co-operatives Administration was murdered.

17. Fuad Mattar, *Bisarāha 'an Abd al-Nasir* (Beirut, 1975), p.112.

18. *Mahādir jalsāt mubāhathat al-wahda* (Cairo, 1963), p.80.

19. Fuad Mattar, *Bisarāha*, p.114.

20. Ibid., pp.40ff.

21. See *The Charter* (Draft), English Text, 21 May 1962, published by the Information Department, Cairo.

22. Hamrush, "Shuhud yulio", *Rose el-Youssef*, April 1977.

23. The press was nationalised in May 1960. Before that, as soon as the Free Officers came to power, they launched their own press organs under the general management of the Tahrir Publishing Organization, which published the newspaper *al-Gumhuriyya* and the magazine *al-Tahrir*.

24. Ahmad Hussein, *Kayfa 'araftu Abdel Nasser was 'ishtu ayyāma hukmihi* (Beirut, 1973), p.49.

25. Ibid., p.51.

26. Ibid., p.67.

27. Also quoted in *Al-Mawsū'a al-nāsiriyya* (*The Nasser encyclopedia*) (Beirut, 1973), p.112.

28. See his objections to the formation of a single party in the verbatim report of his discussions with the committee to consider the formation of the ASU in *al-Tali'a*, Cairo, Vol.1, No.1, January 1965, pp.9–26.

29. Anniversary of the Revolution Speech, 23 July 1967.

30. See interview with *Le Monde*, 18 February 1970, reproduced in *Ahādīth al-Ra'is Jamal Abd al-Nasir lil sihāfa al-ajnabiyya* (*Nasser's interviews with the foreign press*) *1968–1970* (Cairo, n.d.), pp.107–12, esp. p.109.

31. Anniversary Speech, 23 July 1967.

32. Second Session, General National Congress, 28 March 1969.

33. Quoted in Sami Gohar, *Al-sāmitūn yatakallamūn* (Cairo, 1975), p.79.

34. Ibid., p.81.

35. Ibid., pp.97–8.

36. Fuad Mattar, *Bisarāha*, pp.95–6.

37. Quoted in *Khutab al-ra'is Jamal Abd al-Nasir* (*Speeches of President Nasser*), Ikhtarna Lak Series (Cairo, n.d.), pp.1371–7.

38. Ibid., pp.1428–9. Needless to say, asking citizens of a repressive régime if they find their ruler popular or acceptable is a meaningless question.

39. See *al-Mawsū'a al-nasiriyya*, pp.129–43.

40. See the Charter debates in the spring and summer 1962. The Congress of Popular Forces in 1943–4, and Nasser's speeches of 12 November 1964 and 25 February 1966, all reported in *al-Ahram*.

41. This is the thrust of Louis Awad's *Aqni'at al-nāsiriyya al-sabaa* (Beirut, 1975).

CHAPTER 11

Nasser's Economic and Social Policy

Other reasons aside, overpopulation in Egypt has been the result of the successful development of the country's agriculture for a century and a half. Muhammad Ali, Khedive Ismail and the British all worked for the development of agricultural production. Traditional basin was abandoned in favour of perennial irrigation with the building of barrages, irrigation canals and drains and a dam at Aswan (1902). Moreover, the relatively successful attempt by a new generation of Western-educated and technically trained Egyptians after 1850 to use modern technology for the economic development of their country has been an added accomplishment. These developed further the requisite infrastructure of transport, irrigation, power, education and other ancillary services for a more intensive and profitable agriculture.

After independence in 1923 and as part of the momentum of the national independence movement, a modicum of industrial and commercial development occurred under the leadership of the Bank Misr group of enterprises, especially in textiles, the processing of foodstuffs, beverages, sugar, alcohol and transport. With protective tariff policies since the Depression in 1930, even greater strides were made. The Second World War further encouraged an import substitution consumer goods industry. A certain amount of capital accumulation had also occurred during the war. A relatively good public works, power, transport and education infrastructure existed in 1945. More important, Egypt disposed of a relatively experienced political and administrative cadre, even a rising, though small, native financial and entrepreneurial class.

Egypt's prospect for industrialisation at mid-twentieth century therefore appeared fair because she enjoyed relatively favourable conditions for an industrial transformation. Socially, she was blessed with a fairly homogeneous population, free of the sharp sectarian and ethnic divisions to be found elsewhere in the Middle East. Moreover, after the war and particularly after 1954, she received huge amounts of foreign aid.

It is not our purpose here to examine in detail the Egyptian economy before or after 1952. There are several studies which do that.[1] What interests us here is the way in which the Free Officer régime and Nasser in particular dealt with the overall economic and social problems of the country. In order to arrive at only a general assessment of their record, it is necessary to briefly consider some of the following matters: the nature of Egypt's economic problem at mid-century; the kind of economy she enjoyed on the eve of the military *coup* in 1952, and what options were open to the new military rulers and Nasser in particular in dealing with pressing economic and social problems; the major decisions they took and policies they adopted in coping with them; whether these were justified and sensible. Clearly, we cannot, and do not, propose to deal with these matters in detail. What we hope to do is to relate a general enquiry into them to Nasser's rule.

The context, however, is important. Egypt's population at mid-century was poor and unhealthy. Its average real income and consumption were very low. Income was very unequally distributed. In 1955 for instance 55 per cent of national income was received by 20 per cent of the population. Life expectancy for males at birth was only 35 to 36 years. Although after the Second World War production and real income rose and the terms of trade improved, the population increased at the rate of 2.5 per cent per annum. After the brief Korean War cotton export boom, the country experienced adverse trade balances; output and income dropped to pre-1914 levels. When the soldiers grabbed power national production barely kept pace with the increase in population which, with a declining death rate, led to a population explosion. Economic progress in the circumstances appeared difficult if not unlikely without a drastic transformation of the economy in terms of investment and production both in agriculture and industry.

The constraints presented by economic conditions on the Free Officer plans to transform Egyptian society were indeed great. Agriculture was the dominant sector of the economy, contributing one-third of national production and employing two-thirds of the labour force. Already by the Great War it had been transformed from a traditional subsistence sector into a highly commercialised enterprise that managed somehow to feed a population which had increased four-fold in the nineteenth century. Yet between 1914 and 1952 the gains achieved by the expansion of the cultivable and cropped areas were in part negated by a high rate of population increase, so that cropped land per population head steadily decreased. Cotton, a highly developed, commercialised cash export crop in the mid-fifties still earned 80 per cent of Egypt's foreign exchange. On the whole, it was clear that Egyptian agriculture at mid-century had reached a point of diminishing returns.

Improvements to be sure were possible, particularly in two areas. One was the tenurial arrangements which were inefficient. For example, 50 per cent of cultivators were tenant farmers on short leases, with no security and paying high cash rents, so that their indebtedness was perennial. Over 70 per cent of farms were small, under five *feddans* (feddan = 1.03 acres). Ownership of land, the other area, was unequal. Both of these features in Egyptian agriculture could be and were reformed. Yet even with reform beyond improving efficiency and redistribution, there remained little scope for expanding agriculture further. The rapid growth of population outstripped the feasible rate of adding to the cultivable area of the country. The logical conclusion was to diversify the economy by creating new opportunities for production and employment outside agriculture, namely, in industry.

The *ancien régime* had come to this conclusion, and a five-year plan was drawn up in 1947. But this aimed mainly at improving infrastructure and public services. Nor was an industrial sector non-existent before 1952.[2] Between 1930 and 1950 nascent Egyptian industry was dominated by the manufacture of consumer goods. Protected by high tariffs and a world war these replaced certain foreign consumer goods in mass demand: foodstuffs, sugar, alcohol, cigarettes, salt, flour, textiles, furniture, shoes, cement and other building materials. The number of people employed in industry doubled. Yet in 1952 industry still made only a small contribution to national output (15 per cent), and employment (about one-tenth of the labour force). Moreover, most manufacturing activity was dominated by large corporate enterprises of the Bank Misr Group, the Abboud Enterprises and a few foreign-owned holding groups. There were also many very small-scale owner-operated family enterprises, or ones employing very few hands. Then the meagre 10 per cent overall ratio of savings to national income made the financing of industrial projects difficult. A higher preference remained for land and building investment. There was also a shortage of technical and managerial skills outside the resident foreign communities. The bulk of the labour force was uneducated, unskilled and unhealthy. On the whole, then, the economy on the eve of the military *coup* was, in terms of a production to population ratio, stagnant.

The question therefore facing the new military régime was one of how to develop the economy in terms of plain growth, in agriculture first in order to help feed the people, and in industry second in order to employ more of them. There was not much room for expansion in agriculture, although efficiency could be improved. Opportunities for production and employment therefore had to be created outside the agricultural sector. The Free Officers' subsequent decision, in 1956–7, to industrialise rapidly on a large scale seemed the only alternative. But the difficulty lay in how to do that. They were faced with the vexing problems of investment and capital formation in a rather poor country, the lack of skills, the cost of raw materials and the availability of foreign exchange. Nasser, incidentally, proceeded with his plan for the transformation of the economy more gradually than is often assumed. Because of his political style and his insistence on total control he did it in an autocratic manner. Nevertheless, he was assisted in his task by a respectable history of state regulation of the economy, state investment in infrastructure projects and state interference via legislation in the social aspects of economic activity.

Egypt never had a thorough-going *laissez-faire* economic system. Under Muhammad Ali in the nineteenth century the economy was centrally directed and controlled—in fact monopolised—by the Viceroy. Even though from 1860 to 1952 a free market economy prevailed, it was always subject to state interference, regulation and control. The state, moreover, always retained responsibility for the irrigation system with its vast periphery of public works so important to the predominantly agricultural economy of the country. After the Great War the government showed some concern with the planning of the agricultural economy in trying to protect it against the vagaries of nature and the fluctuations of an international commodity market. With greater education and experience, Egyptian governments and political leaders in general showed greater concern with rural poverty, conditions of employment in agriculture and industry, and the regulation of food stocks and prices. Thus an Agricultural Credit Bank was founded in 1931 to provide cheaper credit for farmers. Voluntary co-operatives were already in existence and widespread. A scheme to build Combined Rural Centres offering expert agricultural advice, health and social services was launched by the new Ministry of Social Affairs in the 1940s. There was also concern with labour legislation during and after the Second World War governing conditions of industrial employment in particular. Thus the Trade Union Act of 1942 recognised collective bargaining by trade unions.

Government interference in the economy generally increased, prompted mainly by welfare considerations. Regulation of trade and commerce expanded apace. The state contribution to capital formation, especially in improving infrastructure, increased. The launching of an Industrial Bank in 1949 indicated that the Egyptian authorities already recognised the need for economic growth in industry if they were to create alternative opportunities for production and employment outside agriculture. Greater government regulation of the economy and hints of central planning suggested that even the *ancien régime* at mid-century believed it was the task of government to accelerate economic growth by a greater and more direct participation of the state in production. The idea of an expanded public sector was, that is, already accepted in principle.

Agrarian Reform

The same preoccupation with a protracted struggle over sovereignty with Britain and involvement in inter-Arab politics which plagued the *ancien régime* also acted as a constraint on the new Free Officer régime in its first two years in power. First there was the struggle for power among them, Nasser versus Naguib. At the same time they were taken up by negotiations for the British evacuation of the Suez Canal zone. They were hardly in a position to concern themselves with the long-term reform of the economy. Instead, their economic policies were effectively a continuation of measures already initiated by their predecessors in power.[3] Thus public investment continued to be directed mainly into infrastructure in order to promote further private enterprise and attract foreign capital.

The exception was agrarian reform.[4] The speed with which the Free Officers decreed and implemented land reform was due firstly to their commitment since the 1930s to redistribute land to landless peasants and work towards a more equitable distribution of income.[5] But it was due even more to their immediate political need to destroy the economic power of the land-based élite, consisting of big landowners who were the members as well as the mainstay of the old

ruling class. Irrespective of its technical and other economic merits
or drawbacks the Agrarian Reform Law of September 1952 was
possibly the singular achievement of the Nasser-led officer régime,
whose social effects are yet to become completely clear. It was,
needless to say, mainly a negative political act directed more against
the destruction of the old ruling class and less at the resolution of
Egypt's agricultural problems. Its tangible effects on rural society
have not been too great, although one could make a case for the
panoply of new institutions—co-operatives, credit facilities, expert
services—that arose from the reform.

Large estates which accounted for over one million *feddans*
owned by 2,000 people disappeared, thus reducing slightly the degree
of inequality in land ownership. Conversely, the average size of small
holdings increased slightly. The total area of medium-sized holdings
(3–5 *feddans*) also increased. The measure did not redistribute land
to all the nearly three million rural families in the country—there
was not that much land to redistribute—but it did benefit some half
a million families.

The Agrarian Reform Authority set up to implement the reform
measures concentrated on the requisition and distribution of land,
and the further organisation of co-operatives. Having redistributed
over 800,000 *feddans* by 1970 and requisitioned nearly 185,000
feddans for the public domain, the Authority grew into a vast
bureaucratic institution. Its supervision of co-operatives was
impressive, albeit bureaucratically cumbersome. Beneficiaries of
agrarian reform were compelled to join a co-operative in which the
Authority's representative organised production and the marketing
of crops. The co-operatives, in turn, became the suppliers of credit,
fertilisers and seeds.

Owner-farmers undoubtedly benefited from the new arrangements.
They received technical advice and assistance in improving the
productivity of their land. Co-operatives generally provided better
and cheaper credit, inputs and organisation. Agricultural credit
through the Agricultural Bank increased nearly eightfold by 1970,
and it was provided on better terms than when these new lending
institutions did not exist, and their function was performed by
private institutions or individual money-lenders at high interest rates.
For several years running (e.g. 1960–7) such credit was available free
of interest. Normally, the interest ran on an average at 4–5 per cent.

Generally, then, agrarian reform allowed the government to
assume the functions of the old landlord, and to implement the

distribution of land and improve productivity. But it also gave the state the monopoly of the wherewithal for agricultural production via the co-operatives. It also allowed it to use co-operatives as agencies of taxation, since these controlled all inputs—technology, credit, seed, fertiliser, etc.—and the marketing of produce, especially cotton.

Agrarian reform did change the traditional pattern of agriculture in the sense that it broke down the old neat division between the state and farmer. But it had little impact on the mass of Egyptian peasants. It benefited mainly a small group of peasant farmers. Compared, however, to other sectors of the economy, the agricultural sector experienced the most extensive redistribution of income. Thus the reform fixed maximum rents on land and laid down regulations for leaseholds and share-cropping in tenant farming. Another source of benefit was state expenditure on rural social services, which went up by 70 per cent in fifteen years. But the centre-piece of these services, the Combined Rural Centres, on balance, left much to be desired. Of over 800 projected, only about 350 had been constructed by 1970.

On the whole, then, agrarian reform was not extensive. To be sure, it dispossessed the big, very rich landowners, but it left intact the class of medium owners who constitute the basic structure of the community in the Egyptian provinces and the countryside. Their power in other words was retained, especially when agrarian reform was not aimed against private property. To this extent the social and political structures in the countryside were barely affected.[6] Moreover, the vast majority of rural families remained unaffected by the reform. Most of them remained what they always were—simply landless.

Even though agriculture's share in GNP declined from 40 per cent in 1952 to under 30 per cent in 1964, due to rapid expansion in the industrial, construction and public services sectors of the economy, it was still, in 1964, the major sector in the Egyptian economy, employing over 55 per cent of the labour force and claiming the major share in the composition of national exports. Yet the *per capita* income in agriculture continued to be far below that in the other sectors.

Agrarian reform, however, accelerated the application of technology to agricultural production. It also helped the shift from a cash to a production nexus, especially when loans were advanced against the security of crops instead of land, as was the case before

1952. Robert Mahro, who argued in his book, *The Egyptian Economy, 1952–1972*, that agrarian reform "sought limited improvements in the distribution of wealth, and benefited the upper section of the lower-income group", and that it should be seen as "a set of complementary measures and its impact assessed over a long period of years," nevertheless concluded that "the land reform laws reflect an awareness of the main aspects of the agricultural problem— distribution of landownership, disparity of incomes and unsatisfactory tenancy agreements . . ."[7] on the part of the Nasser régime. Institutions, he believes, replaced landlords, and that he adjudges a good thing. Galal Amin, on the other hand, emphasises the persistent neglect of agriculture and the growing inequality, or gap, between rural and urban incomes in Egypt.[8]

In the mid-1960s Nasser defined the socialist society in Egypt as one of sufficiency and justice for all that would eradicate the differences between classes. Yet the agrarian reform of 1952 and its several subsequent emendations from 1958 to 1969, including its extension to cover charitable endowment (*waqf*) lands, the confiscation of royal estates in 1953 and the ceiling on individual holdings down to 50 *feddans* did not apparently affect the relations between classes in rural Egypt. It only inflated the group of smallholders and substituted the relations of power and authority with a state bureaucracy for those of tenants with landlords. The new institutions of Combined Rural Units, co-operatives and other services were really an extension of the state bureaucracy. It also tended to create a new "caste" that was infused into the state's new economic and social structures between 1952 and 1964, when the state became the main entrepreneur. Nasser, in turn, controlled the whole edifice, for by then he had destroyed the land-owning élite, decimated the small commercial "bourgeoisie" and firmly established an unrivalled—almost militarised—public sector in the state economy.

It should be noted, for instance, that agrarian reform was not successful in properly implementing new tenancy and rent regulations, or in observing minimum wages for migrant agricultural and other landless peasant labour. To be sure, overall agrarian policies redistributed income from owners to tenant farmers and some categories of wage-earners. But whereas the land-owning farmer had a high propensity to save, the tenant farmer and wage-earner did not. Their high propensity was to consume.

Despite agrarian reform, agricultural output by 1963 was not growing fast enough, leading to food shortages and inflation. The difficulty was overcome for a few years by a large measure of dependence on wheat shipments and related aid from the United States. In this way, the diversion of valuable foreign exchange from industry—then the régime's highest priority—was temporarily averted.

However one assesses the economic significance and impact of agrarian reform, its political importance for Nasser and his régime is not in doubt. When its economic results proved meagre, given rapid population growth on a limited area of land, it became imperative to create opportunities for production and employment outside the agricultural sector. Massive industrial development as the only means of rapid economic growth became the policy of the régime. A singular attempt to buttress both further agricultural production and industrialisation was the construction of the Aswan High Dam. It represents a remarkable achievement in irrigation, control of water supply for land reclamation and intensified land utilisation. It also represents an attempt to adjust traditional patterns of land use and water allocation. Its other main benefit was seen to be the supply of cheap power for industry. There were to be also corollary benefits in flood control, navigation and fishing.

The Aswan High Dam

The High Dam[9] was the culmination of a long process in the development of the Egyptian irrigation system and the rational allocation of Nile waters. Successive nationalist groups were committed to the realisation of this massive, monumental project. The Free Officers completed it over a period of a decade. It came about as a result of a political decision by Nasser to live up to the nationalist commitment of his generation. The Dam thus became a major expression of national independence—Nasser's favoured slogan of "dignity and self-respect"—especially after his nationalisation of the Suez Canal had expressed his defiance of foreign power.

In addition to the problem of financing the construction of the High Dam and the complex technical difficulties involved, the project presented serious ecological constraints. The introduction of perennial irrigation in all of Upper Egypt meant the wider spread of the dreaded disease, bilharzia. The creation of an artificial lake—Lake Nasser—entailed potential climatic changes, such as rainfall and evaporation leading to salinity. It was also expected to affect the Delta-Mediterranean region to the north some 750 miles downstream. The soil moreover would be deprived of nutrients from the diminishing and eventual absence of silt deposits; there would be sea erosion. There was also the gigantic human problem of moving and relocating a whole population, the Nubians.

The régime weighed these disadvantages against the Dam's anticipated benefits. Thus the cultivable area would be increased by 1.2 million *feddans*, a target incidentally never achieved. A change in crop patterns would yield a net increase in agricultural output, and production generally would benefit from flood control. Above all, the new push for industrialisation would be helped by the availability of a new, relatively cheap, source of electric power (10,000 million kWh per annum, even though in 1970 only 7,000 million kWh were consumed). In fact, even today not all the Dam's turbines are operating. The slowing down of industrial development and production due to lack of capital and other difficulties renders the power generated by the Dam unusable. However, were industrial production to grow to its desired maximum, the country would require at least twice if not three times the power the Dam as it now stands could generate. Nor was the by-product of a fisheries industry as easy to develop since it required huge investments in cold storage facilities and transport.

Theoretically at least, the wider social implications of the High Dam were equally attractive to the régime. The dream of electricity in 4,000 villages would produce a new pattern of life in rural Egypt for the first time in its history. So far, however, Egypt has been unable to exploit all the potential benefits of the Dam. The magnitude of ancillary capital investment required for all its complex facets to be brought to bear on the Egyptian economy and society has been beyond the régime's capacity, whether under Nasser or his successor.

The sense of achievement and national pride in having constructed this massive edifice is not doubted. Unfortunately, perhaps, its final completion in 1967–70 coincided with a period when war and its difficult aftermath had put a damper on Egypt's economic development, especially industrial growth. There have been those who argue that the Aswan High Dam is no more than a monument to Nasser's autocracy and megalomania; that it is economically a white elephant and ecologically a potential disaster; and that above all it pawned Egypt's resources and economy to the Soviet Union. The truth of the matter is that the effects of such a structure in all its complexity cannot be gauged except over a long period of time, say, a generation or two. What is important is that generations of Egyptians have in one way or another adumbrated its desirability. It was Nasser who fulfilled this nationalist aspiration. His autocratic approach helped; so did his willingness to enter into an economically—and ultimately politically—disadvantageous relationship with a superpower, the Soviet Union, in order to achieve it. But he may have introduced into his country the long-gestating basis for a change in economic and social patterns if the Aswan High Dam is viewed as a fantastic national technological-industrial base.

The Expansion of the Public Sector

Practically every student of the Egyptian economy under the Nasser régime agrees that there has been continuity as well as a break in the country's economic history after 1952. The continuity was most marked in the first four years, 1952–6; the break occurred gradually first after 1956, and more abruptly after 1961, when the so-called socialist solution of centrally directed comprehensive planning was adopted. The constraints on Nasser's policy of rapid economic growth and the transformation of Egyptian society remained great indeed. Besides the availability of capital, skills and other requisites of rapid economic growth, he was also faced with the dilemma of rapid growth versus consumption, a greatly inflated bureaucracy to cope with a vastly expanded public sector, and the crippling expense of an aggressive Arab and foreign policy, entailing two wars with Israel within a decade and a civil war in the Yemen in between.

Nasser made the break with the past to the extent that he moved the Egyptian economy from a free private enterprise to a massively state-controlled and centrally planned one in less than fifteen years. One could argue he reverted to the Muhammad Ali model of the early nineteenth century. The element of continuity in this process lay in the fact that some government intervention, as indicated earlier, was always exercised by the state before 1952. Moreover, both Egyptianisation and diversification had been major economic aspirations of the Egyptian national movement since the 1920s. What Nasser really accomplished was the nationalisation and comprehensive planning of the economy with greater vigour, determination and, some would argue, ruthless abandon.

The nationalisation of the Suez Canal in 1956 constituted the turning-point. Its corollary of the expropriation or nationalisation of British, French and other foreign commercial enterprises and assets in the country laid the foundation of the new public sector of the Egyptian economy. The establishment of a Permanent Council for the Development of National Production and its successor, the Economic Organisation in 1956–7, marked Nasser's intention to embark upon a radical, aggressive national economic policy.

Nasser used political pretexts for the further expansion of the public sector. After the 1956–7 seizure of foreign assets and nationalisation of foreign concerns, including the Suez Canal and the banks, he used the Congo crisis of 1960–1 to nationalise Belgian concerns in Egypt and sequestrate the assets of Belgian nationals. Similarly he utilised domestic and inter-Arab crises in 1960–3 to take over Egyptian enterprises headed by the Bank Misr and Abboud groups. The socialist decrees of those years reflected the momentum of the state's involvement in the economy.

Before 1952, public, i.e. state, ownership of the means of production was confined to irrigation and part of the transport infrastructure, particularly railroads, petroleum refining and public domain agriculture. Ten years later it was extended to all financial institutions, public utilities, transport (excluding taxi-cabs), industrial concerns, insurance, department stores, large hotels, the media and the press, export–import trade and the marketing of major agricultural crops. Within a decade the régime eliminated both foreign economic activity and the major native independent centres of economic enterprise in the country. Sequestrations of the property and other assets of individual Egyptians followed after the Syrian secession in October–November 1961. A series of decrees in 1964 completed the state's take-over of the economy.

Both agrarian reform and massive nationalisation, whatever their economic consequences, were safe political measures, since they affected only a small group of Egyptians, namely, the rich landowners, financiers and monopolists in commerce and industry. These people were associated with the *ancien régime;* by 1962–4, they were branded as opportunistic reactionaries who wished to undermine the Nasser-led revolution and its new socialist state. They were accused of disloyalty and of having links with imperialist powers and their agents.

The central question concerning Nasser's expansion of the public sectors is whether he genuinely aimed at the establishment of a socialist system or at simple statist hegemony. Ali Sabri, a key figure in those years of the drive for a centrally planned economy, characterised the first Five Year Plan (1960–5) as the "years of socialist transformation".[10] He argued that before 1960 the régime operated on the bare original Six Principles of the Revolution. The basis of the public sector was laid as of 1956, beginning with the nationalisation of the Suez Canal, the seizure of foreign holdings, corporation and banking institutions. "The state was able", in this way, to "own an economic base" for comprehensive planning, for growth and development and the doubling of the national income. The nationalisation of the essential means of production, effected further by the 1961–4 socialist decrees, together with the Aswan High Dam project, became the expression of the determination to introduce comprehensive change.

According to Ali Sabri, the first stage of the "socialist revolution" was accomplished when the soldiers overthrew the old political order. The second stage consisted of setting up a "socialist society" by transferring the means of production to state ownership. However, because Nasser did this autocratically through a vast new military-bureaucratic establishment, these means of production never came under public control, or scrutiny. So that with comprehensive planning and rapid industrialisation came the immense inflation of government expenditure on services rather than on capital goods production. For a long time, moreover, control over the economy was exercised mainly by the apparatus of the military establishment. Sabri himself conceded when he was Prime Minister in 1966 that the first Five Year Plan was more than fully implemented in public services, which effectively required a vastly expanded bureaucracy, whereas in production it fell far short of the mark. As a result public indebtedness rose rapidly. Thus by 1967 there were over 1.5 million public officials, a 2,000-million dollar public debt and a 25 per cent share for the military of the annual state budget.

Before the first Five Year Plan Egypt's population was over 25.5 million. At the end of it it had grown to over 29.5 million. National income stood at under £E1,300 million in 1959/60. By 1965 it had risen to over £E1,750 million, so that *per capita* income rose by only £E10, from £E50 to £E60. But consumption, especially by the lower classes, rose sharply. Industrial output registered a 50 per cent increase, but over a third of this was in services, a very high proportion of the total.

Problems with balance of payments deficits, imbalances in the execution of various projects in the Plan, bureaucratic centralism and over-manning presented added difficulties for the projected transformation. The infrastructure for a rapid growth of the public sector was generally poor. Roads were inadequate, imported raw materials often difficult to secure or afford, factories opened before power to work them was available. Lack of managerial skills was papered over by the recruitment of personnel from other government departments and army officers. All these problems aside, many critics of the Plan have argued that it was no more than a blueprint for state investment. Even then capital goods were neglected. In the process, the nationalisations required to create the public sector resulted in higher public consumption, an inflated and cumbersome bureaucracy and reduced savings.

Nasser's economic policy gave the state the leading role in industry, and in this way, he effected some changes in its structure. Whereas before 1952 it was mainly concerned with consumer goods, after 1952 Nasser enabled it to move into the production of inter-mediate goods and consumer durables, as well as some heavy industrial production such as iron and steel, and electricity. More-over, he achieved new forms of government intervention in the whole economy. However, although by the early sixties the growth of industrial output reached 12 per cent, after that it declined to less than half of that rate. Despite its growth, industry managed to absorb only a small proportion of the increased labour force. At the same time, it acquired a vast administrative superstructure with new problems.

It is more likely that Nasser's economic policy in both agriculture and industry, as expressed in the socialist decrees of 1961–4 and his National Charter of 1962 were aimed at improving the prospects of rural and urban lower classes, specifically the so-called petite bourgeoisie. That a small group of these attained a slightly higher standard of living and a measure of social mobility cannot be denied. But he did this by expropriating and nationalising the sources of upper-class wealth, bringing them into state ownership. The restructuring of agricultural ownership and production, and of the public sector were both aimed at the redistribution of national income. Similarly, fiscal measures in the form of new direct taxation on incomes, ceilings on salaries, regulation of dividend payments, new work legislation and insurance were all aimed at this particular constituency.

Political reasons after 1956 therefore prompted Nasser to move away from an earlier economic policy. By 1960 capital formation became primarily a state function or responsibility. The state assumed nearly exclusive responsibility for investment along with its commitment to comprehensive planning. The new slogan of a "socialist democratic co-operative society" was to be given further strength and more substance in the 1962 National Charter. The ambiguity regarding the private sector, or even a mixed economy, was abandoned in favour of a state capitalist scheme. P. K. O'Brien described the situation in the mid-sixties as follows: "By the end of 1964 almost all large companies throughout every field of economic activity had been nationalized, and the public sector consisted then of enterprises both controlled and owned by the state."[11] Private enterprise now came to play a minor role.

Although experts estimated twenty years for the execution of the Plan which aimed at doubling national income, Nasser insisted on ten. The difficulty was that its financing depended on savings, foreign loans and grants. The government could hardly expect to finance the Plan from private or national savings or from direct taxation in a poor country like Egypt. Thus Nasser's economic policy, in the final analysis, was the result of political considerations, that is, his political priorities. It partly failed because despite the state's control of the economy, much of its comprehensive planning and execution depended on too many external factors, such as foreign loans and other aid. Meanwhile the rate of investment by the state far exceeded that of savings, requiring the government to borrow heavily from abroad and eventually facing serious balance of payments difficulties and therefore forcing it to slow down its investment programme.

Equally unrealistic was the Charter's promise both to raise living standards and attain social justice. A spate of social legislation to regulate wages, working hours and conditions, health and social insurance measures hardly affected the majority of workers in agriculture and non-corporate sections of trade and industry. In fact the last category in the private sector still employed two and a half times as many workers as the public sector. Consequently a privileged group in the public sector became the beneficiaries of these measures. Their impact on the overall redistribution of income, for example, was negligible. In fact the nationalisation and sequestration of private property in 1960–4 affected a very tiny class of people who owned a disproportionate share of national wealth.[12] This was particularly true of land ownership and ownership of corporate enterprises stock. Furthermore, the charges of exploitation remained even in relative terms somewhat meaningless when the output of the average Egyptian worker remained very low and his wages in contrast to those of workers in other countries equally abysmally low.

The immediate concern of Nasser therefore was the control, not necessarily the ownership and distribution, of wealth. He extended government control over the whole economy first gradually and after 1961 rather abruptly, so that the demise of private enterprise was the culmination of this process. Nasser mistrusted the old bourgeoisie and, given the economic needs of the country, was anxious to channel private investment into state-approved directions. To some extent the areas he pushed forward—agrarian reform, the Aswan High Dam, nationalisation—reflected his earlier political preferences, deriving in the first instance from Young Egypt's hazy notions of a social revolution. To this extent he had to make the state the prime mover of a new industrial revolution or trans-formation. Other political developments from Suez to the Syrian secession and the Yemen war helped to harden his anti-capitalist or private enterprise attitude in favour of a command state economy. This, however, was not even remotely socialist, but a directed, centrally controlled, or étatiste, economic policy.

The matter of control was perfected under Nasser, but the economy's performance could not be ordered so easily. Economic-ally, perhaps, the policy might have worked. But it failed politically. It was not efficient because the quality of men in government and the public sector was generally low; education and training remained poor, and several foreign policy episodes, including war, marred it. Much of its potential efficiency, say, in production, was equally impeded by excessive government regulation and pricing policies.

Nasser, however, had no choice but to go for rapid economic growth. Given the rapid growth of population and the limited area of land available for further agricultural expansion, it was imperative to create new opportunities for production and employment outside agriculture. Industrialisation was the obvious answer. It did not prove successful because after 1957 the bias was for capital-intensive development which ignored the vast cheap labour available in the country. As a result, employment opportunities in the countryside were not exploited, and there was no spread of rural industries. Instead of maximally utilising the country's abundant and cheapest resource, labour, the régime opted for an indiscriminate use of expensive modern technology. At the same time much of the revenue from nationalised assets was used to finance increased military and other state expenditure. A part of it was transferred to higher incomes for state bureaucrats and managers, as well as to finance the perks for Nasser's crucial military constituency. Throughout this exercise there was no control by any popular elected public body.

The beneficiaries of Nasser's economic policy in the long run were the small group of skilled and semi-skilled labour in large-scale industry and commerce, the urban salaried class and middle peasants in the countryside, as well as the growing numbers of "communicators" in the media, press, information and propaganda services. In implementing his economic policy, however, Nasser was denied the supreme fiscal measure of direct taxation in raising revenue with which to finance social and other services. In short, in 1962 he promised a welfare state more or less without a prayer of being able to finance it because, in a formally decreed socialist Egypt, social welfare could not be financed by direct taxation. In a scheme where taxation began at £E1,000 per annum net income, it was difficult to find many Egyptians who made that much money in a year. Consequently, social welfare measures remained confined to civil servants, employees of public corporations and the larger private enterprises. Thus, of a seven million total labour force in 1966, only 1.5 million were covered by some kind of social security.

To be sure, investment in industry increased greatly and economic growth of about 3–7 per cent per annum did occur over a period of a decade (1956–66). These were accomplishments of the Nasser régime. In his speech to the Congress of Popular Forces on 24 September 1962, Nasser asserted "the necessity of the socialist solution" for Egypt's economic problems. Two years later he tried to justify his new economic policies to the National Assembly by reminding them that until 1952 power in the country was in the hands of sixteen rich families, a condition corrected by his July 1961 decrees. One hundred Egyptian and foreign families, Nasser asserted, held the equivalent of £E1,000 million of the country's wealth. In order to attain sufficiency and justice, his régime had introduced agrarian reform, embarked upon the construction of the Aswan High Dam and vast reforms in education and other public services. The war was one against imperialism and backwardness, he declared. Listing major problems facing the country in agriculture, industry, health, housing and prices, he conceded the existence of serious difficulties with the bureaucracy, inflation and domestic production. But he also justified the concentration of powers in his hands "in order to take decisive action." A year later, in his Labour Day Speech on 1 May 1965, he admitted of difficulties faced in the administration of the public sector, emphasising the importance of resolving economic problems, and in particular the achievement of a higher rate of saving.

It would appear then that by the mid-sixties Nasser's economic policy of rapid economic growth via industrialisation had run into serious difficulties. His determination, as formulated in the National Charter, to raise both consumption and investment at the same time could not be carried through. Much of the investment and resultant growth depended heavily on foreign borrowing and aid, creating difficulties with the balance of payments. In the meantime while investment in industry rose, expenditure on services rocketed. Most of the manufacturing still consisted of consumer goods and only a small proportion of labour was engaged in it. With hardly any private or government savings to fall back on, by 1966 the government was forced to cut down the rate of investment and adopt a deflationary policy.

Political considerations and factors prompted the régime to allocate a greater proportion of investment to services, including housing, price stabilisation, wages and salaries, and less to agriculture or industry. Similarly, political factors guided the development and expansion of the educational system. Between 1952 and 1970 the number of pupils in primary and preparatory schools tripled, in secondary schools it almost doubled, in secondary technical schools it increased eightfold, and in universities it rose by nearly five times. Unfortunately, this rapid expansion, especially at the secondary and university levels, created new problems of overcrowding and unemployment. Enrolment in primary schools never exceeded 60–65 per cent of all eligible children. Teacher training lagged behind. Classrooms became intolerably and counterproductively overcrowded. Physical disabilities, such as the lack of classroom space and the absence of post-schooling and adult educational programmes in the countryside, helped keep the rate of illiteracy at 75 per cent. After 1962, the policy of entitling every university graduate to a job in either the government administration or the public sector of the economy led to the inflation of the bureaucracy and an additional burden on the national exchequer. The government tried after 1965 to limit the number of university places as well as channel entrants more into scientific and applied technology courses. Basically, though, the hope of absorbing many more school-leavers in manufacturing was never realised. In the meantime, the quality and standard of middle and higher education dropped sharply.[13]

In health and housing, too, Nasser tried to deal with the problems. He introduced a programme of health services reform, coupled to one of birth control and family planning. Expenditure in these fields rose, but the uneven distribution of doctors and hospital beds in the country, together with the widespread incidence of parasitic diseases and high infant mortality rates rendered these efforts inadequate. In the countryside especially the lack of adequate social security and old pension schemes forced the *fellah* to depend for his future security on a large family. The continued unequal distribution of wealth in the country further prevented him from responding to family planning schemes. In the absence of alternative social security arrangements, the *fellah* remained unimpressed by these schemes.

The erection of subsidised, cheap popular housing estates did benefit many of the industrial and lower-paid government employees in urban areas. It also helped clear one or two of the Cairo area slums. An equal investment was made by the régime in housing for the public sector employees and other government officials, such as managers and army officers. The problem of rural housing, however, remained unattended to. With Nasser's deflationary policy after 1964–5, investment in such public projects naturally dropped.

Expansion in all these directions suffered from an inability to sustain it. But it was also undermined by its poor quality, deriving in part from Nasser's rigid control. Thus political control over education at all levels was paralleled by similar dictation over all cultural organisations and activities, including the nationalised media and the press. Arts boards, the press and broadcasting, national educational commissions and research organisations were all brought under strict central control and directed by carefully selected, loyal Nasser appointees. All came under strict government control when Nasser appointed trusted though not necessarily competent ex-officers. Such control grew when educational and cultural programmes were reorganised between 1956 and 1964, a period of so-called ideological reconstruction.

Similar rigid political control over labour legislation and the organisation of trade unions prevailed. Thus in April 1959 trade unions were reorganised under Anwar Salama, a Nasserist leader of the Petroleum Workers' Union. Strikes remained illegal, but the minimum daily wage was raised to £E0.250, a measure that was not enforced before 1961. New insurance schemes for industrial workers were introduced and other social security arrangements. After 1961 profit-sharing schemes for workers and employees came into force. As most of these measures applied to or were implemented in the public sector, workers in it acquired a relatively privileged status *vis-à-vis* the masses of workers outside it. Concentrations of industrial workers grew up around the new industrial centres in Aswan, Zagazig and Fayyum in addition to older ones in Shubra al Kheima, Helwan and Mehalla el Kubra.

Yet instead of the expected growth of industrial production, Nasser's economic policy led to excessive growth in services. Employment policy was aimed mainly at absorbing the formally educated into the tertiary sector of the economy, the service sector. In fact there was an alarming growth of services independently of the rest of the economy. A mark of continuing massive poverty was the fact that in 1968 direct taxes still yielded only a third of the revenue accruing from indirect taxation. Continuing high pressure of population and lingering unemployment gave a parasitical aura to the whole economy.

Nasser, however, was an integrationist and hegemonist, and not only in economic matters. Thus he integrated all the judiciaries in Egypt, abolishing the religious (Sharia) courts in 1955/6. He completed the integration of the educational system by reorganising the Azhar in June 1961 as a modern university teaching both religious and secular subjects.[14]

The Consequences of Nasser's Economic Planning

On the face of it, Nasser's achievement has been the very creation of a public sector. Whether it worked or not under his rule is in a sense irrelevant. It has not been dismantled as yet, and the day may come when conditions are propitious for it to be fully utilised and better run. To this extent it constitutes a permanent feature in Egypt's future economic development. What may be additionally required is a different political economy. That of Nasser's, characterised as it was by a very autocratic state corporatist tendency, may be replaced by one of a ruthless socialist plan. But there are those who contend that neither of these seems politically and socially feasible in Egypt, and that a more rational use of the public sector in a mixed economy is the answer.

Apart from the massive infusion of foreign capital that the further growth and development of the Egyptian economy will require, a politically less monolithic social and educational policy is just as necessary. Although Nasser expanded education on all levels and "organised" national cultural activity, his priority for political conformity and control undermined their quality, and in the long run eroded their productive potential. Neither education nor the trade unions nor any of the other professional and cultural syndicates and associations could claim an independent status under Nasser. Their bureaucratisation impeded their otherwise important role. Their total political control from the centre stifled them completely. As Galal Amin put it,

> new factors associated with revolutions tended to make . . . bureaucracies even more inefficient and wasteful. In revolutionary regimes political considerations gain supremacy over those of efficiency. The politically loyal is thus preferred to the able but politically passive, while highly paid but fictitious jobs are created simply to accommodate a political figure removed from power but too dangerous to turn into an enemy. Even nationalization could be used against any economic reasoning to punish a political opponent.[15]

Some of the wider social consequences of Nasser's economic policy were appalling. It was not only the new employment opportunities of developing industry that attracted growing numbers of people to the city. It was also the neglect and deterioration of conditions in the countryside. Soon rapid urbanisation was dissociated from the growth of manufacturing, having further detrimental effects on economic development. The latter cannot be divorced from the determination of upper-income groups and the state for rapid capital accumulation via savings. The new governing élite under Nasser did not exhibit any such propensities. On the contrary, both they and the state were more inclined to consume, the former for selfish reasons, the latter for political ones. Corruption in the conduct of economic affairs and venality in public life are universal human failings. In the rigidly controlled command state economy of Nasser's Egypt these reached alarming proportions. A public sector run largely by a cumbersome bureaucracy and hampered by a miasma of regulations, licensing requirements and other politically determined controls inevitably led to the attempt by many to bypass or escape them. "Middle men and contract" millionaires quickly appeared to milk the public sector and bypass state regulations.

Comprehensive planning of the economy was probably, on strict economic grounds, premature for Egypt. But Nasser adopted it basically for political reasons, chief among them his wish to further safeguard his control over the state. Consequently it led to serious imbalances, such as greater consumption with all its attendant ills, rather than capital goods production and industrial development.

The twin aims of national independence and modernisation entailing economic and social transformation were to be attained by a formidable state apparatus and a new economic technocracy. The first, not uncharacteristically for Egypt, was recruited from the lower and middle strata of society—the secondary school and university graduates and army officers—that is, the aspiring young. The second was recruited from those educated further abroad in Europe, the United States and the Soviet Union. Yet both of these groups in the state machine were dominated by the military, the new ruling class, and eventually, the new "state capitalist" class. Moreover, the new technocracy was placed astride an old bureaucratic pyramid, contributing to the further over-centralisation of state functions and activities. Consequently, policy decisions were taken at the very top of the power pyramid and implemented by these subservient groups of the state machine. There was barely any initiative at levels below the top.

Muhammad Ali the Great at the beginning of the nineteenth century never claimed he wished to create a modern society, only a modern and powerful state. *Etatisme*—state capitalism—was his preferred economic approach and instrument, a common enough phenomenon in Egyptian history since private ownership was a relatively recent—later nineteenth-century—development. Moreover, under the Mamluks as much as under the Pharaohs, military men played an active and long role in the country's economy. Muhammad Ali used his new modern army and emerging native administration, both trained and fashioned by foreigners in his employ, to carry out his ambitious agricultural and monopolistic industrial schemes. In the process he nurtured a new privileged class of both native Egyptians and resident foreigners. The latter in particular ran the commercial and financial aspects of that economy.

Nasser, on the other hand, was not satisfied with his control of the machinery of state and government; he took total political power and, in mid-twentieth century, pre-empted all ideological alternatives. He also aspired to transform Egyptian society. To that end he adopted socialism in the sixties but would not countenance the presence of socialists in the country, or the creation of the institutions needed for its development and functioning. In fact, he sought to establish order and discipline so as to impose "social peace" and national solidarity". To that end he adopted something like a corporatist order.[16] But this policy also led to new forms of exploitation by an oppressive military-bureaucratic élite whose members soon carved out new fiefdoms of interest, privilege and profit. Very soon there was hardly any ideological or political cohesion between them, only a fierce rivalry and competition in a haphazard pursuit of advantage and survival. Ultimately, even Nasser's apparent corporatist political experiment degenerated into an agglomeration of avaricious cliques within his new political élite. This permanent ambivalence on his part together with his charismatic autocracy inevitably gave rise to a new economically privileged class in the country.

It is therefore difficult to assert that Nasser made a clean break with the past. Muhammad Ali's experiment collapsed after his death precisely because he monopolised it and otherwise stunted the growth of modern political institutions in the country. He left no political groups loyal to his experiment who would defend and maintain it; only a strange grandson, Abbas Pasha, on the throne, who proceeded to dismantle most of his grandfather's work. Nasser's monopolistic approach too has caused his experiment to suffer partially the same fate, even though the objective constraints on its further development in the 1970s were not wholly of his own making. Surely, though, his style and obsessive preoccupation with the security of his paramount position contributed to at least a less efficient, less competent and more venal handling of economic and social affairs than might otherwise have been the case.

Nasser's socialism in fact was characterised by a pervasive bureaucracy that was needed to implement a massive system of controls. In the end it succeeded in restricting initiative and impeding growth. In the context of a political despotism the privileged cadre of this bureaucracy and state security apparatus acquired all the trappings of profligate capitalism, namely, luxury, waste and cynicism.

Notes

1. Charles Issawi, *Egypt in Revolution* (London, 1963, 1965); Patrick K. O'Brien, *The Revolution in Egypt's Economic System* (London, 1966); Robert Mabro, *The Egyptian Economy, 1952–72* (London, 1972); Galal Amin, *The Modernization of Poverty, A Study in the political economy of growth in nine Arab countries, 1945–1970* (Leiden, 1974); and the incisive analysis of the Nasser régime by John Waterbury, "Egypt: The wages of dependency" in A. L. Udovitch (ed.), *The Middle East: Oil, Conflict and Hope* (Lexington, Mass., 1976), pp.291–351.

2. On economic developments in the inter-war period, see Robert L. Tignor, "The Egyptian Revolution of 1919: new directions in the Egyptian economy" in Elie Kedourie (ed.), *The Middle Eastern economy, studies in economics and economic history* (London, 1976), pp.41–67, and Marius Deeb, "Bank Misr and the emergence of the local bourgeoisie in Egypt", in ibid., pp.69–86.

3. See P. J. Vatikiotis (ed.), *Egypt since the revolution* (London, 1968), pp.7–83.

4. On agrarian reform generally, see Sayed Marei, *Agrarian Reform in Egypt* (Cairo, 1957), and Saad Gadallah, *Land Reform in relation to social development in Egypt* (Columbia, Missouri, 1962), and Gabriel S. Saab, *The Egyptian Agrarian Reform* (London, 1966).

5. Such programmes of national economic and social reform were publicised by Young Egypt, and later the Vanguard of the Wafd party.

6. Cf., however, Iliya F. Harik, *The political mobilization of peasants*, a study of an Egyptian community (Bloomington, Ind., 1974), and James B. Mayfield *Rural Politics in Nasser's Egypt: a quest for legitimacy* (Austin, Texas, 1971).

7. Mabro, *The Egyptian Economy*, pp.82, 73, 66.

8. Amin, *The Modernization of Poverty*, pp.86–107.

9. On the Aswan High Dam, see Tom Little, *High Dam at Aswan* (London, 1965). See also Mabro, *The Egyptian Economy*, pp.83–106.

10. Ali Sabri, *Sanawāt al-tahawwul al-ishrirāki* (Cairo, n.d.).

11. Sabri, *Sanawāt al-tahawwul al-ishtirāki*, p.135.

12. See Mahmud Murad, *Man kāna yahkum misr?* (*Who used to govern Egypt?*) (Cairo, 1975).

13. See Louis Awad, *Al-jāmi 'a wa al-mujtama'*, (Cairo, n.d.) and Amin, *The Modernization of Poverty*, pp.61–71.

14. See Nadav Safran, "The Abolition of the Shar'i Courts in Egypt, I and II", *The Muslim World*, Vol.48, No.1, January 1958, pp.20–8 and 125–35.

15. Safran, "The abolition of the Shar'i Courts", p.44.

16. On corporatism, see Philippe Schmitter, "Still the century of Corporatism", *The Review of Politics*, Vol.36, No.1, January 1974, pp.85–132.

CHAPTER 12

The Lure of Arab Nationalism

The Roots of Nasser's Arab Nationalism

It is futile to try to establish whether or not Nasser believed in a political doctrine of Arab nationalism. The early influences of radical political movements in the mid-1930s disposed him personally towards a more Islamic-Arab emphasis on Egypt's role in the Middle East. So also did his experience of the Palestine War in 1948–9. In the final analysis, though, Nasser's Arab nationalism was more of a deliberate choice of state policy that promoted Egypt's leadership of the Arab world than an abstract ideological preference. He believed that an Arab region free of foreign power influence would allow Egypt a leading role in its affairs and destiny—and at the expense of other Arab contenders. Where he differed from previous Egyptian rulers was that he was less circumscribed than they were in involving his country in Arab affairs.

It is not so much the formulation of the so-called "Arab Circle" of Egypt's role and destiny in his *Philosophy of the Revolution* that is significant. More important is his vision of its instrumentality and how close Egypt, under his rule, came to using it successfully for her own ends. A combination of circumstances permitted Nasser to make Egypt's cause, whether in the conflict with Israel as of 1955, or the dispute with Nuri el-Said of Iraq over the Baghdad Pact in 1955–8, or the Suez War against Britain and France in 1956, the cause of all the Arabs.

Heikal wrote that before the Palestine War Nasser was strictly an Egyptian nationalist. His Arab national consciousness developed gradually after the 1947 UN resolution for the partition of Palestine, and his subsequent involvement in the training of Palestinian and Muslim Brethren volunteers to fight in Palestine followed. He also suggested that Nasser was so affected by the plight of the Palestinian Arabs in 1948 that he asked the Free Officers to disband in order to devote all their energies to the Palestine cause.[1] The real reason, though, may have been the fact that the King's agents had practically uncovered the officers' conspiracy. At the same time Nasser was conscious of the importance of Syria to Egypt's security and the dangers presented by Israel in control of Palestine. In military college he must have studied the Allenby campaign of 1917–18. He may even have been convinced that "the foremost arena of the struggle against imperialism is the Arab Middle East".

A more plausible proposition is that Nasser's Arabism was a modern extension of Muhammad Ali's and Ibrahim Pasha's "Arab" policies in the nineteenth century and those of Kings Fuad and Faruq in the twentieth, all of which were prompted by the realities of the Egyptian situation. Muhammad Ali and his son Ibrahim used force and conquest to carve out an "Arab" empire in the first half of the nineteenth century. But in the end they were prevented from doing so by a concert of European powers. Kings Fuad and Faruq dabbled in a convoluted, dubious Arab–Islamic diplomacy. Nasser, however, used propaganda and subversion and, when he tried war in the Yemen, his Arab policy collapsed. Moreover, in mid-twentieth century, his Arabism had to have a populist thrust and an anti-imperialist chauvinist tone, and eventually a "socialist" twist. The Baath movement in the cause of Arab unity, for example, was gaining momentum in the Fertile Crescent at a time when Western power was retreating and Western influence receding from the region. No Egyptian ruler of the day could have ignored the trend, or failed to exploit it. Nasser's intention to do just that was perhaps made public as early as May 1953 when President Naguib inaugurated the Voice of the Arabs radio programme in Cairo.

A cynical explanation of Nasser's Arabism was given by his one-time friend and later critic Ahmad Abul Fath who, in 1962, wrote that Nasser did not respect the Arabs, but on the contrary believed in their impotence. He appreciated, however, the instrumentalism of the potential possessed by them—petroleum, money and popula-tion—in the pursuit of his aims and ambition.[2] Incidentally, even during the acrimonious and abortive Tripartite Talks on Arab Unity in the spring of 1963 with Iraq and Syria, Nasser's vision was strategically and politically one of the extension of Egyptian influence in the region:

> With the inclusion of Iraq in a union of Egypt and Syria the unified state would secure the oil wells and pipelines in the

east to the Suez Canal . . . from Asia to Africa. The Iraqi army would be brought up to Israel's borders. Its possibilities would be greater than those of France, commanding a population of fifty million.[3]

Like his predecessors, Nasser appreciated the danger of allowing the Fertile Crescent to fall under the domination of a rival Arab power, e.g. Iraq or Saudi Arabia. His sense of Egyptian history suggested to him that that Arab region was always a sort of eastern defence line for Egypt. Throughout the centuries its control by hostile forces constituted a threat to Egypt. So much for Nasser's practical, strategic perception of the utility of Arab nationalism as an Egyptian policy. But he was also convinced that only Egypt could fill the role of Arab leadership by virtue of her experience, social and cultural achievements, her human resources and skills.

Nasser's personal disposition and apparently genuine sympathy with the Arab cause, however, were the other dimensions of his policy of Arabism. "I recall," he reminisced in 1954,

as far as I am concerned that the stirrings of an Arab conscious-ness crept into my thinking when I was a secondary school pupil. I used to go on general strike on November 2nd of each year in protest against the Balfour Declaration.[4]

He told Desmond Stewart the same story in an interview on 1 April 1957, when he claimed that he was "converted" to Arab nationalism while a secondary school pupil.[5] As a member of the Young Egypt Society, Nasser was influenced by Ahmad Hussein's propaganda for and involvement in Arab questions of the day, especially that of Palestine in 1936 and later in 1947–8.

As early as 1935 Ahmad Hussein called for an alliance between the Arab states in order to break Egypt's isolation. In 1936, the visits of Is'af bey Nashashibi, Sheikh Muhammad Ali al-Tahir and the Palestinian rebel 'Izz al-Din al-Qassam made a great impression on Young Egypt members, and Nasser was one of them. The 1939 Round Table London Conference over the Palestine Question to which Egypt was invited also had its impact. Ahmad Hussein, for instance, claimed that the Conference was an admission by Britain and a recognition by Egypt and other Arab states that the Palestine question was an Arab problem.[6] He attaches to the pro-Axis anti-British military *coup* of Rashid Ali el Geylani in Baghdad in 1940 a similar significance, if not equal importance, for its effect on the consciousness of Egyptian youth over the "Arab cause".[7] And he reminds his readers that in 1947–8, Young Egypt had formed the "Mustafa al-Wakil Battalion" to fight the Jews in Palestine under the command of the Egyptian army officer Abd al-Aziz Hamdi.[8]

Aware of the widespread suspicion that Egypt was "the least Arab of the Arab states", Nasser never passed up an opportunity to protest Egypt's Arabism. Addressing an ASU Congress in Asiut on 8 March 1965, he declared in the colloquial: "Our fatherland is not only Egypt . . . Egypt's Arabism is not a matter of policy or tactics; it is one of destiny, being and life." This contrasts sharply with his statements during the Suez crisis in 1956. Arabism or Arab nationalism hardly featured in his addresses to Egyptians. But Nasser had begun to use it as a means of rallying Arab support outside Egypt and in projecting a new Arab leader's image abroad, until he became the symbol of the Arab presence, dignity and reputation in the world. In return—and gratitude?—the Arabs helped create the Nasser myth. "Port Said", he told his Egyptian and Arab audiences on 9 November 1956, "was a sacrifice in the national cause of Egypt and that of Arabism." "Arab nationalism", he told his interviewer from the Cairo weekly *Akher Sa'a* (5 December 1956) "has become the ideology of a whole region." But in a statement to the *New York Times* on 18 October 1956, he emphasised the strategic and political importance of Arab nationalism and unity to Egypt: "Egypt must not live isolated from the rest of the Arabs, because once we are isolated, we shall be defeated separately."

The perception Nasser had of a truncated Arab nation, of a unity that could be were it not for the "divisive imperialists", was one commonly held by the average Arab since the First World War. It was also one common to all radical national youth movements since the 1930s.[9] Addressing the National Assembly in January 1965, he said,

Imperialism has divided the Arab countries. It has dismembered the Arab nation after World War I, using Zionism and later Israel . . . The defeat in 1948 was due to our lack of independent power. We were under the domination of Imperialism. How could we fight Israel in Palestine when it was set up by Britain and America and at the same time obtained weapons from them . . . Britain and America gave Israel weapons, but none to us. This is what really happened.

But by the mid-sixties, though in retreat and disarray, Nasser still assured the Egyptians that Arab unity and the Arab revolution were inevitable. By then the combination of the polarity in the Arab region between revolutionary and reactionary régimes had added an Arab ideological gulf, as well as an Arab socialist crust, to radical nationalist movements.

> It immediately became clear to us that Egypt, like the rest of the constituent parts of the Arab nation, would not be able to safeguard her security except when grouped with her sister countries in Arabism, in a strong union . . . Arab nationalism for us acquired the characteristic of both a political doctrine and a strategic necessity.[10]

Nasser's dual perception of Arab nationalism, consisting of a sentiment of solidarity with other Muslim Arabs on one hand and a practical political-strategic instrument of Egyptian policy on the other, characterised his view of Arab politics. The central role of Egypt in both perceptions he expressed not only in his tract, *The Philosophy of the Revolution*, but repeatedly to the outside world. Thus he explained in an interview with *Look* magazine on 14 June 1957,

> I do not think of myself as a leader of the Arab world. But the Arab peoples feel that what we do in Egypt reflects their collective hopes and aspirations. This is what I meant by an Arab role in my book *The Philosophy of the Revolution*.

Nor was the historic Islamic element lacking in Nasser's perception, for he was always keen to portray imperialists as the modern successors to the Crusaders. He projected the myth of past Arab unity that repelled aggressors, as in the time of the Crusaders, without realising that the latter were not defeated by Arab leaders of a united Arab nation. Nevertheless, the Kurdish Saladin model was always in the forefront of his projection of potential Arab power. Saladin was, of course, a ruler of Egypt.

The Purpose of Nasser's Arab Nationalism

It is in Nasser's and the Free Officers' actual Arab policy from the mid-fifties to the mid-sixties that their adoption of Arab nationalism as a state, even revolutionary myth, can be assessed. It is irrelevant to argue how much of this adoption was deliberate on their part, or was forced upon them by the pressure of events in their own country and the Middle East, let alone how much of it was a conscious ideological preference. The fact remains that the course of Egypt's Arabism can be traced in her rulers' responses to developments in the region and the needs of their policy as they perceived them. Thus until the resolution of the Anglo-Egyptian dispute over evacuation there was hardly a departure from traditional Egyptian policy. Nasser and the Free Officers did not feel the need to assume a pan-Arab posture or to solicit wider Arab support. They merely hoped that with the retreat of Britain from their country, they could entertain a greater and more active role in search of influence in the Arab world. Hence the early creation of the Voice of the Arabs radio programme. Until then the régime was, on the whole, content to cultivate an Islamic theme, linking nationalism to religion in recognition of the importance of Muslim communities in Asia and Africa. The new Islamic Congress, founded in November 1954, under the chairmanship of Anwar Sadat, with its several publications, scholarship programmes, religious institution facilities and medical and other social welfare activities abroad, reflected the Free Officers' view of a possible wider Egyptian role.

There are those who have interpreted Nasser's adoption of Arabism as an Egyptian anti-Western policy as early as 1954–5. Thus Ahmad Abul Fath argued in 1962 that until then Nasser and the Free Officers were in favour of a pro-Western policy in order to attract massive financial aid. The implicit assumption here is that when they came to power in 1952, the Free Officers, including Nasser, had no ambitions beyond governing Egypt, and that only a year or two later did Nasser begin to realise the great potential of an Arab role for Egypt. That realisation demanded an anti-Western policy in the region, even though Nasser's ousting of Naguib had elicited a temporary Arab campaign against him, to which he had to respond. When after the Evacuation Agreement with Britain, the Western alliance, led by the United States, sought to introduce collective security pacts in the region, culminating in the controversial Baghdad Pact of January 1955, Nasser reacted violently. Abul Fath asserts that Nasser's hostility was due to his deep resentment at being humiliated by the West. For it seemed to him the West was anchoring its Middle Eastern policy in Nuri el-Said and the Hashemite rulers of Iraq, his rivals for Arab leadership. Salah Salem's tour of the Arab states that winter was intended to drum up support for Egypt.[11] Similarly, Heikal has averred that, until the

Suez crisis, Nasser was preoccupied with domestic policy. The Arab dimension to his policy was added after the Baghdad Pact.[12]

The growing economic crisis at home[13] further justified the violent campaign against Iraq, and a personal contest between Nasser and Nuri dominated inter-Arab relations for the next three years. Its practical consequences paid temporary dividends for Egypt. Iraq's rivals, Syria and Saudi Arabia, moved closer to Egypt. In view of the Israeli raid on Gaza in February 1955, the alliance with Syria in March 1955 was seen at the time as a diplomatic *coup* for Nasser.

The tense situation and Nasser's exhilaration over the prospects of Third World leadership in Bandung in April 1955 propelled him towards a dramatic pursuit of new avenues to security. Foremost among these was the solicitation of arms from the Soviet Union, ostensibly as a reaction to the West's refusal to supply Egypt with arms on conditions acceptable to Nasser. The secret military mission to Moscow that year included the Communist lawyer, Ahmad Fuad (member of HADETU), who was later to feature prominently in the drafting of the so-called Socialist Laws in 1961. The announcement in September 1955 of the Soviet Arms Deal had an immediate and electrifying propaganda effect on the rest of the Arabs. It catapulted Nasser to a position of prominence among the Arab heads of state long before Suez was to secure him at least the temporary adulation of the Arab masses. Even his enemies among the Arab rulers had to momentarily salute his defiance of the West. Or as Abul Fath put it succinctly, the arms purchase agreement with the Soviet Union in the hands of Nasser was "une baguette magique capable de modifier tous les sentiments et de renverser totalement la situation."[14] Even Nasser himself was surprised at the Arab reaction, and is reported to have told Heikal, "I did not expect all this commotion over a purchase of arms."[15]

A reconstruction of events in fact suggests that Nasser reached the conclusion at the end of 1954 that an aggressive Egyptian role in Arab affairs required a fundamental realignment of forces in the region. He recognised that a continued relationship with the Western powers would automatically circumscribe his Arab policy, especially if he joined new Western regional security pacts. He also realised that a dominant Egyptian role in Arab affairs presupposed the building up of a sizeable military force. Consequently, he was duly disturbed at developments in late 1954 and early 1955 regarding Western security arrangements in Turkey and Iraq. At the same time, the Soviet Union was no less exercised over these developments in the context of the Cold War. By January 1955 Nasser's and the Soviet Union's interests in opposing Western policy seemed to converge. This suggested to Nasser the possibility of challenging Western arrangements with Soviet support, while the Soviet Union saw its chance to break up the strategic-political monopoly of the West in the region. The preliminary contacts and negotiations for Soviet arms to Egypt date from these early days in 1955, and Nasser's public statement in September 1955 was only a belated announcement of an already ongoing arrangement.

Egypt's challenge of the West's arms supply monopoly in the Middle East, the Egyptian–Iraqi clash over the Baghdad Pact, Nasser's propaganda campaign against other Arab rulers over his Voice of the Arabs radio and his subversive activities against the régimes of Jordan, Iraq, Lebanon and Libya were manifestations of his decision to follow a new radical policy, one of greater involvement in Arab affairs. Thus subversive operations in Jordan date from this period, helped by Syrian and Saudi money. They became most intense in 1956–7. Similar action in Lebanon and Libya was directed by the military attachés in Egypt's embassies in those two countries.[16]

Equally advantageous for his Arab image was Nasser's drawn-out haggling with Dulles and the West over the financing of the Aswan High Dam project, culminating in the nationalisation of the Suez Canal and the Suez War. It was a golden opportunity, a circumstance for real grandeur among the lesser Arab state leaders, most of them still tied to a relationship with one foreign power or another. It was also a veritable turn-about for the régime, from a relatively traditional pro-Western orientation and circumspect approach to the Arab world in the hope of attracting Western largesse to a combination of a "neutralist" Third World stance and an aggressive anti-Western policy in the Arab Middle East as a prelude to a more active involvement in Arab affairs. The alliance with the West forged in the Anglo–Egyptian Evacuation Agreement of 1954 evaporated in the smoke of the Suez War.

By 1956, Nasser's motivation and choice became clear. In order to strengthen his position at home he had to abandon an Egypt-first oriented policy in favour of a more strident Arab-oriented one. In order to ensure his supremacy among Arab rulers, he had to link his policy of Arabism to the struggle against imperialism and its remaining Arab clients, foremost among them Iraq. Needless to say, the Russians in 1954–5 clearly grasped Nasser's motivation, as well as his political and economic needs at home, and decided to hitch their more aggressive Middle Eastern policy on to Nasser's pursuit of his regional ambitions. They were equally concerned over the West's sponsorship of regional security arrangements in the Middle East.

A combination of circumstances and coincidence of events pushed Nasser towards Arabism and the adoption of Arab nationalism and unity both as a means and an end simultaneously. The heady concatenation of events—the Evacuation Agreement with Britain, the defiance of the West as reflected in the Soviet Arms Deal and Bandung—encouraged him to carve out a role for Egypt in the region. His rejection by the West when it adopted his rivals in the Fertile Crescent infuriated him. The first series of events increased his popularity with the Arabs. The Western response to them generated wider Arab sympathy for his defiance of it. Nasser seized the opportunity. After proclaiming the new constitution, he told a rally in Republic Square, Cairo, on 16 January 1956: "They tried to deceive us. What do you want with the Arabs, they said. But we shall not be deceived . . . We shall establish our membership in the Arab being." It was the first Egyptian constitution to declare Egypt an Arab state.

Obsessed with "positive neutralism" after Bandung as a means of greater manoeuvre in his dealings with the great powers, Nasser began to emphasise the Arab nationalist theme in his policy. In Syria and Jordan, meanwhile, his natural, though as it turned out temporary, allies, the Baathists, were gaining political momentum and some power. Their cry of Arab unity before all else was to serve Nasser's purposes well for a few years. When he nationalised the Suez Canal in July 1956, the reverberation of his act had a seismic effect throughout the Arab countries, especially in Syria and Jordan, but soon also in Lebanon and Iraq. While the schizophrenic Americans saved him and his régime from certain collapse in November 1956, they proceeded two months later to mount a political-diplomatic offensive to contain him and his new arms suppliers, the Russians, centred on Iraq, Jordan, Saudi Arabia, Lebanon and even Syria. This was the still-born, or at least abortive, Eisenhower Doctrine. By then, however, it was too late to stop the Nasser-led march of Arabism, for he had transformed the "Arab world into a sea, a jungle of slogans and blood . . . Nasser fanned it with his exhortations against reactionaries and the enemies of the people who wished to impede his march."[17] He had made Arab unity "the dream of the masses, not only the hope of leaders and the elite."[18]

Nasser's amazing fortune comes through in these early years of the search for an Arab role too. The conclusion of an evacuation agreement with Britain was possible only because he compromised over the Sudan and the retention of a British base on the Canal under whatever guise. The British retreat from their overseas possessions, dominions, colonies and bases was already in full swing several years before that. Similarly the nationalisation of the Canal and Nasser's subsequent survival of an Anglo-French military attempt to overthrow his régime were due equally to changing conditions in the balance of world power. To this extent Nasser did not expel the British from Egypt; rather the British were forced to leave Egypt during Nasser's rule. He thus happened to be about at the right historical juncture. But it allowed him to effect a fusion between his and Egypt's destiny and that of the rest of the Arabs, and to transform Egypt from the traditionally least Arab state to the leader of a new revolutionary Arab nationalist movement aiming at Arab unity. In fact, one Arab commentator asserted that Nasser forced the Egyptians to become Arabs politically, especially over the Palestine Question.[19] "We shall all defend our freedom and Arabism," he screamed in his 26 July 1956 Suez nationalisation speech, "and work until the Arab nation extends from the Atlantic Ocean to the Arab Gulf." He went on to identify the imperialists' "destruction of Palestine" as an attack on Arab nationalism, because "they know we have a nationalism that unites us from the Atlantic to the Gulf. They have to contend with this force for the first time in history."

Abortive Involvement in the Fertile Crescent and the Yemen

Egypt's involvement in Arab affairs and her identification with an Arab nationalist trend reached a peak with the union between her and Syria in 1958, and the subsequent collapse of the Hashemite régime in Iraq. The civil war in Lebanon in the same year and the military *coup* in the Sudan were seen at the time as further evidence of Nasser's Arab nationalist bandwagon. What helped the bandwagon's momentum in part was the belief by many other Arabs that Nasser could solve the Palestine problem. It was an involvement, however, that differed from the later one in the Yemen in the early 1960s. The former was directed at the liberation of Arab countries from their links with imperialism and their deliverance from imperialist agents who ruled over them. The latter was more of an internecine Arab struggle between Nasser-led forces of "revolutionary Arab nationalism" on one side against those of Arab reactionaries on the other.

Heikal has suggested that Nasser admired Baathi ideas regarding the unity of the Arab nation. The Baath for its part believed in 1957–8 that it had found a hero who could express and transform them into political reality. This hero was Nasser.[20] At the same time, Nasser for his part was seeking to strengthen his position *vis-à-vis* his Iraqi rivals and Syria, he believed, could serve that purpose well. How far he also believed a union with Syria could provide him with the basis for a "nutcracker" strategy against Israel is a matter for conjecture. At least his public utterances throughout 1958, the year of union, emphasised the theme of Arab nationalism and unity, which he linked to the defence against imperialism and his campaign against Iraq and the Baghdad Pact. "Today we live in an age of Arab unity", he told his audience on 25 February 1958. Two days later, he singled out Jordanian and Iraqi political figures —Samir Rifai, Fadhil Jamali and others—as imperialist agents, who "are more dangerous than imperialism itself".

> I pity the prime minister of Iraq who said the Syrian people cheer but have no power, and say to him, I see the Iraqi people in shackles, facing fire and steel . . . I say to Murjan, we do not depend on Britain and America or Russia or any other state, but on God and the people [2 March 1958].

Nasser repeated the same attack in a speech to the Syrian armed forces ten days later, after having charged the Saudis with an attempt to bribe Colonel Abdel Hamid Serraj (chief of Syrian Intelligence) to sabotage the United Arab Republic. "Arabism not Pharaonism is our political ideology," he asserted in a rally at Evacuation Square in Damascus on 9 March 1958.

The alacrity with which Nasser agreed to the precipitate union with Syria in February 1958 was prompted by his desire to neutralise Iraq and Jordan. Thus the Egyptian anti-Iraqi and anti-Jordanian propaganda campaign began very soon after the union. Nasser called their leaders "traitors who cannot last forever . . . There is no place for foreign domination, no place for colonialism and its agents, there are no spheres of influence," he announced before going off to Moscow in April 1958. The inter-Arab struggle had now become one between the "forces of liberation" led by Nasser and the "agents of imperialism". Nasser was certain of the inevitable fate of his enemies. At a popular rally in Alexandria on 24 June 1960 he referred to a similar fate that befell their predecessors, such as King Abdullah and Nuri el Said, "running in the streets wearing women's clothes in order to hide and escape. But there is no escape."

In the summer of 1958 it was difficult not to believe that Nasser's Arab policy and Egypt's brand of Arab nationalism were close to a historic triumph. The Hashemite régime in Iraq had been overthrown by a military *coup*; Lebanon was in the throes of a civil war in which one side, the Muslim community, sympathised with the UAR and looked to it for support. Whatever the extent of Syrian and Egyptian involvement in the Lebanese conflict may have been, Nasser actively lent his moral and financial support to the so-called Arab nationalist elements in it, as well as to those in Iraq. Jordan and Lebanon sought and received Anglo-American military protection, and Iraq entered a phase of turbulent political instability, culminating in an Egyptian-sponsored and -financed abortive *coup* in Mosul in February–March 1959.

Within less than a year Nasser's aggressive Arab nationalist policy ran into serious difficulties. Saudi–Jordanian opposition to it stiffened. The Iraqi upheavals resulted in a blood bath, from which emerged a closed, brutal régime that eventually passed through a series of *coups* and counter-*coups*, without any advantages for Egypt. Disagreements between Nasser and the Baathists in Syria produced a dicey internal security situation. Subversion of the UAR from within and without became a distinct possibility. At the same time, the deteriorating relations between Nasser and the Russians over the issue of Arab Communists in Egypt and Syria further weakened Egypt's Arab policy and reduced her options.[21] Soon Egypt's involvement in the Congo and her ambitions for an African policy led her to overextend her capabilities.

All the same, between 1957 and 1960 Nasser managed to arouse Arab nationalist hopes for unity like no other leader in the region before him or since. He had at his command two weapons that no Arab leader before him possessed, an elaborate propaganda machine and a terrifying intelligence network. Propaganda and subversion became Egypt's stock-in-trade for the attainment of Arab leadership. The one sought control of the "Arab streets", the other of governments or the machinery of state in the Arab countries.

Both of them were used effectively, perhaps too effectively, until the denouement and opposition became inevitable. What there is no doubt about is the fact that Nasser won a popularity among the Arab masses which no other Arab ruler or leader could match. No Arab state, during his period, escaped his attention and/or intervention. They all became targets, at one time or another, of attack by the Voice of the Arabs radio.

Iraq under Brigadier Kassem did not end the Cairo-Baghdad rivalry. In fact, by the autumn of 1959 Nasser's Arab nationalist policy was in disarray and retreat. His troubles with the Baath forced him to impose more direct control over the Northern Region (Syria) of the UAR by the appointment of Field Marshal Amer as his pro-consul and gauleiter in Damascus. Nasser's troubles with Moscow were compensated by the resumption of US aid to Egypt and his *rapprochement* with some other Western countries, West Germany and the United Kingdom. Nevertheless, 1960–1 spelled the end of militant Nasserite Arabism for a while. With the secession of Syria from the union in September 1961, Egypt under Nasser was never again to play as predominant a role in the affairs of the Fertile Crescent at least. The Tripartite Arab Unity talks between Iraq, Syria and Egypt in the spring of 1963 were lengthy, acrimonious and unproductive. Their value consisted in laying bare the differences between Nasser and Egypt on one hand, the Iraqi and Syrian Baath parties on the other.[22] They also revealed Nasser's more realistic approach to Arab politics, his instrumental view of Arab nationalism and his disregard for other Arab politicians. Arab nationalism was now to be used for his own ends, inaugurating a prolonged feud with the Saudis, especially over the Yemen.[23]

By then Nasser had also lost interest in the fractious Fertile Crescent, which always bewildered the Egyptians anyway. In 1963 he was already deeply involved in the Yemen, and somewhat more active in North Africa. Arab nationalism in his view was no longer simply a movement to liberate the Arab countries from imperialist domination. After all, there were revolutionary army officers in power in Baghdad. Even secessionist Syria was governed by a revolutionary Arab nationalist party, the Baath. Lebanon had reverted to its old delicate and precarious communal balancing act in a post-civil war period of reconciliation and reconstruction. Egypt, however, had in the meantime further radicalised its revolutionary aims by adopting socialism alongside Arabism in its state policy as proclaimed in the 1962 National Charter. Her attention was now directed to planned rapid economic growth and a more ideologically based political organisation in a push to eliminate the last vestiges of so-called reaction. The Yemen venture was viewed by the Nasserite élite at least in this light and from this perspective. As the senior revolutionary Arab régime, they argued, Egypt sought to support a revolution in Sanaa that had just overthrown a medieval régime, and to protect it from the machinations of an equally reactionary monarchy in Saudi Arabia. The centre of Egypt's radical Arab nationalist policy had shifted to south Arabia. The old polarity of Arab nationalism struggling against colonialism and its agents in the Arab world was now replaced by a new polarity of Arab revolutionaries struggling against Arab reactionaries for the leadership of the Arab world.

Hasan Ibrahim, an original member of the RCC, stated in 1975 that Nasser did not at first wish to get involved in the Yemen. On the strength of what turned out to be misleading information, he and the rest of the Presidential Council (created after the break-up of the UAR), agreed to support Sallal's *coup* in the Yemen, though initially only "morally and symbolically".[24] Once they became involved however,

> Nasser felt his leadership of the Arab nation would be undermined if he were to withhold further support for the Yemeni revolution. Moreover, he felt his self-respect and dignity were also at stake, especially since he considered the contest in the Yemen to be one between Faisal of Saudi Arabia and himself. Thus he ordered the deployment of a whole army corps in the Yemen.[25]

Heikal too reported in 1973 that Nasser was opposed to intervention in the Yemen, "because he was one of the few Egyptians who had been there before and therefore knew that the country was backward and lacked any economic or political bases for revolution". But Heikal went on to explain that Nasser decided to intervene because he was facing several difficulties at the time. He was being attacked by other Arabs, especially the Syrians, after their secession from the UAR. He was in trouble with the Soviet Union over Iraq and Communists at home. Moreover, he believed that the failure of the Sallal insurrection against the Imam's forces would amount to a political victory for his Saudi opponents. There was also, one suspects, the intrusion of Nasser's perception of an American-led conspiracy against radical régimes in the region, using their Saudi clients in the Peninsula. How far the long-term economic considera-tion of access to a rich oil-producing Arab area entered into Nasser's calculations is a matter of conjecture. The economic needs of a country like Egypt with its frightfully poor ratio of resources to population render such calculations sensible. And so the Egyptian intervention in the Yemen, which began with a few advisers and a battalion of troops, escalated by 1964 to a massive operation deploying some three divisions with armour, artillery and air support, in all between 50,000 and 70,000 men.

Heikal deplored the administrative involvement of Egypt in Sanaa that required such a long stay and made Egyptians prisoners of local circumstances, including the weakness of the Sallal régime. But he claimed one great advantage resulting from Egyptian inter-vention; it opened the Yemen to modernisation, and further radicalised south Arabia, leading to the independence of South Yemen. On the other hand the proximity of Egyptian military force to Arabian oil wells provoked a Western attack on Nasser and Nasserism leading up to the June War of 1967.[26]

Nasser's North African Ventures

Nasser's mixture of Arab nationalism and revolution appealed to the Arabs in North Africa. Tunisians and Algerians sought the support of Egypt in their struggle for independence from France. For a decade (1955–65) relations between Egypt and the Algerians were close. The political arrangements of the Algerian revolution under the FLN (National Liberation Front) were made basically in Cairo and Tunis. The Algerian provisional government formed in September 1958 received the early support of Egypt.

The Arab–Muslim factor aside, in practice, the interests of Nasserite Egypt and Algeria's war of independence against France happened to coincide. Encouraged by closer ties with the Soviet Union, Nasser had just embarked upon a varied policy that included union with Syria, support for Black Africa and "positive neutralism". Having survived the Suez War, he had intensified his efforts to undermine the remaining presence of his enemies—Britain and France—in the Arab world.

Upon the independence of Algeria in 1962, however, what remained of this close relationship between Egypt and Algeria was the personal tie between Nasser and Ben Bella. Despite efforts by the Egyptians to attain a leading position in the agricultural, technical and educational development programmes of Algeria, the Algerians preferred massive financial and technical aid from France. Thus the Nasser–Ben Bella personal friendship and revolutionary camaraderie were of little consequence for Egyptian policy in North Africa. When Boumedienne ousted Ben Bella from power in June 1965, relations between Egypt and Algeria deteriorated and remained cool until the 1967 Arab–Israel war.

After independence, in fact, every one of the North African states —Algeria, Morocco, Tunisia—reconsidered their relations with the Egyptian leader. President Bourguiba of Tunisia became an inveterate, though erratic, critic of Nasser. He did not trust Nasser's motives in leading an Arab nationalist revolution or his manipulation and domination of the Arab League. He also rejected Nasser's intransigent policy regarding Palestine. Bourguiba equally denounced Gamal's policies in the Yemen and south Arabia. He severed his country's relations with Egypt in 1958 and again in 1966.

Morocco too had good reasons to remain cool towards Nasserite Egypt. In the border dispute with Algeria in October 1963, Egypt sided with the Algerians, and King Hassan II suspected Nasser of promoting the subversive activities in Morocco of the opposition leader Mehdi ben Barka. Only after 1965, when Nasser's radical Arab leadership was in decline and he had to accept a more peaceful coexistence between himself and other Arab régimes did Morocco's relations with Egypt improve.

Thus in the Maghreb too Nasser experienced the same opposition to his push for Arab leadership that he did in the Arab East. The tenacity of newly independent Arab states in North Africa in following their own development and policy equalled that of those in the east.

Libya, on the other hand, was to play a part in Nasser's last attempt at an Arab initiative. Unlike the Maghreb states, it has had a closer relationship with neighbouring Egypt. The Italian invasion in 1911 evoked the natural Islamic sympathy of Egyptians. After the Italian occupation political refugees from Cyrenaica, including the Senussi leader, resided in Egypt. About 4,000 Cyrenaicans received military training in Egypt during the Second World War.

Egypt's interest in Libya this century was a significant factor in Nasser's policy. An early indication of that interest was the dispute between Egypt and Italy over the Jaghbub Oasis on their border in 1924–5. Immediately after the last war, in 1945–7, Egyptian governments expressed keen concern over the disposition of Libya by the victorious allies. They argued that Libya was an Arab country, that Egypt should act as trustee over its territory pending independence, and if independence was not achieved, the country ought to be united with theirs.

Even though during the Suez War Libya declared its solidarity with Egypt and the Arab cause against Israel, Nasser condemned it for permitting Western military bases on its territory. Relations between the two countries thus deteriorated in 1957, when the Libyans suspected Egyptian agents of subversive activities,[27] and concluded an accord with newly independent Tunisia, not a friend of Nasserite Egypt.

During the first decade of its independence (1951–61), Libya too, like Tunisia and other weak Arab states, remained wary of its Egyptian neighbours. Relations with Egypt remained cool.[28] By that time, however, sparsely populated Libya had struck it rich with oil, and consequently attracted the keen interest and closer attention of Egypt as well as other Arab states. Nasser put greater pressure on Libya to rid itself of foreign bases. Quite likely, he also stepped up the activities of Egyptian agents in that country, for in 1962, the Libyan government found it necessary to purge the small officer corps of its new army, members of which had come under Nasserite influences. Nevertheless Nasser's policy of propaganda, diplomatic pressure and plain subversion produced some tangible results in Libya.

In 1964 the Libyan government requested Britain and the United States to negotiate the evacuation of their respective military bases in the country. In 1965 it contributed £15 million to the useless United Arab Military Command, cancelled a British missiles contract and nationalised banks and certain other foreign enterprises. When the Arab–Israel crisis broke out in 1966–7, a government statement underlined Libyan pride in its Arab nationhood and its willingness to face the challenge of Zionism and fight for the liberation of Palestine. During the Six Day War, it declared a state of war with Israel, allowed token North African forces despatched to support Egypt to pass through its territory, and stopped pumping oil to the West. It offered financial assistance to Egypt, Jordan and the Palestine guerrillas of about £30 million a year. In 1969, before the *coup* of Colonel Qadhafi, it negotiated with Cairo an agreement favourable to Egypt over the recruitment and employment of Egyptian teachers in Libya.

Closer relations between Egypt and Libya developed under the régime of Colonel Qadhafi. A deep Egyptian involvement was reflected in the fact that Egyptian experts, paid for by Egypt, helped organise and maintain the new Libyan military régime's internal secret security service. When Nasser walked out of the Rabat Summit conference in December 1969, in which rich Arab states refused to increase their financial subvention of Egypt, he went directly to Tripoli. There, after only three days of talks, he signed an agreement with Libya and the Sudan to co-ordinate military, economic and political action against Israel. An economic unity agreement signed in April 1970 between the three countries covered work and residence privileges in all of them by their respective nationals, and was clearly to Egypt's advantage. Libya came to provide work for nearly 100,000 Egyptian teachers, administrators, nurses, doctors, technicians and military instructors. It also undertook to bear part of the cost for the construction of a Suez–Alexandria pipeline (SUMED). When, however, Nasser accepted the Rogers peace plan in July 1970, relations between the two countries became strained, and Qadhafi proceeded to improve his relations with Algeria.

Nasser's quick adoption of his fiery rebel protégé, Colonel Qadhafi of Libya, was prompted by very practical reasons. He saw —as did his successor—in his Libyan policy a way of recapturing the initiative in the struggle for Arab leadership, and considered Libya a rich source of financial support and arms supplies necessary for Egypt's conflict with Israel. Therefore he proceeded to use Qadhafi for that purpose. He also realised the long-term economic and strategic value of such a rich, underpopulated and geographically contiguous country to his own country's future development.

The Economic Case for Nasser's Pan-Arabism

There has been some controversy over the effect of Nasser's Arab policy on Egyptian identity. This has ranged from accusations that Nasser abolished the name of the country, thus creating a serious identity problem for the Egyptians, to the argument by militant Arab nationalists that there is no contradiction between an Arab political identity and seven thousand years of Egyptian history. The conservative Muslims comfortably fell back on the Islamic roots of

Arab nationalism, whether under Nasser or any other leader. Cairo, after all, does not only house the headquarters of the Arab League. It is also the seat of the venerable Azhar with its university and several affiliated religious institutions. The left tried to give an ideological force to Arab nationalism. It viewed it simultaneously as a liberation movement against imperialism and a movement for economic and social reform leading to socialism and political democracy.[29]

A good case can be made for the deliberate choice by Egypt, under Nasser or any other ruler, of an Arab nationalist policy on the basis of her economic and strategic needs, without the necessary conversion of its rulers or people to a "political ideology" of Arab nationalism. Egypt is the most populous state in the Arab Middle East: an estimated 37 million in 1977 and a projected 55 to 60 million in 2000. Or as one American economist recently put it, "Egypt trembles on the edge of a Malthusian disaster, which may be speeded up by the ecological disaster of the Aswan Dam."[30] She is hopelessly dependent on the importation of food to feed her burgeoning population. Consequently, her balance of payments is, more often than not, adverse, forcing her to borrow money heavily. A series of wars with Israel has compounded the difficulty by adding a staggering military bill estimated at over £1,500 million on top of other expenditure.

The Free Officer régime and Nasser, especially since 1957, sought a way out of this difficulty in the rapid industrialisation of their country. However, lacking natural resources, particularly sources of energy in abundant quantities, capital for investment and all the required skills, they had to resort to outside help. And all this added to the country's external indebtedness. For many years the Soviet Union supplied much of the finance for industrial and infrastructure projects—the Aswan High Dam, steel and aluminium plants—while the United States and other Western countries supplied the grains and cereals needed to feed the population. Even were the Egyptians to succeed in the industrialisation of their country, they would have to maximise their exports in order to offset their vast import bill for capital goods, raw materials and food. The most natural outlets or markets for Egyptian exports of goods, skills and labour from Egypt's excess population are the Arab countries.

Egypt's economic problems then are of such magnitude that all her rulers, including Nasser, could well conclude they could be dealt with only in a regional context. Her highly developed agriculture has perhaps reached its absolute limits, i.e. a point of diminishing returns, in feeding the Egyptians. Egypt's need therefore to industrialise in order to survive makes the resources and potential markets of other Arab countries very attractive indeed. Under-developed, oil-rich states could become the recipients of Egyptian manufactured goods as well as labour. A greater development of agriculture in the Fertile Crescent, North Africa and the Sudan for instance could help feed the teeming Egyptian masses more cheaply, perhaps, and more conveniently.

In these conditions a regional Arab policy is not only an economic imperative for Egypt. It is also a political necessity if she is to avoid a total dependence on outside powers, whether East or West. It also has the possible advantage of attracting capital investment into Egypt from rich Arab sources, especially when Egypt's capital needs are, and will remain till the end of the century, massive.

Nasser was haunted—and, one hopes, daunted—by the dismal economic prospects of his country. He was also aware of the fact that without Arab markets Egyptian industry would not succeed. Thus on purely economic grounds Nasser's adoption of an Arab nationalist policy made eminent sense. What was disastrous about it was his approach and style in the pursuit of that policy. This provoked the opposition of the richest Arab states and the indiffer-ence of many others. Instead of Arab economic co-operation, not to mention integration, there was minimal trade between them. In the end, it also forced Nasser into total dependence on the Soviet Union.

The fact remains that whether under Nasser or another ruler, Egypt in 1952–70, more than ever before, had no choice, if only for economic reasons, but to become involved in Arab affairs. Notions of self-sufficiency were mere fantasy and anachronistic. The only alternative has been a politically onerous dependence on a foreign power. It is the nature and extent of the involvement, however, on which Nasser's personality and approach to power had a devastating effect. In fact, not only did his Arab policy collapse in the mid-sixties, but he personally became disillusioned with the Arabs and no more so than in the last few months of his life.

Most revealing of this disillusionment were his meetings with heads of Arab states in Cairo in September 1970 to deal with the crisis in Jordan over the Palestinian guerrillas. By then he had become militarily more dependent on the Soviets,[31] and had agreed to explore once again American peace initiatives.[32] Above all, his country was broke. "Are we prepared to fight in Jordan?" he asked his colleagues rhetorically in their Cairo meeting on 24 September 1970. "Frankly, no," he answered.

> If Israel entered Lebanon we shall not be able to dislodge her. I say this for the historical record . . . Our South Yemeni brethren can say we have grown old and they are young. But we have learnt caution after 1967, and after the Yemenis dragged us into their affairs in 1962, and the Syrians into war in 1967. That is why I said yesterday I am not prepared to send troops to Jordan.[33]

He had grown tired of the Palestinians, particularly their leaders. He equally resented the revolutionary rhetoric of the Iraqis, South Yemenis and the Libyans. His revulsion was complete:

> This morning [Thursday, 24 September 1970] I called together Abu Iyad and his lot. I asked them what it is they want [in Jordan]. Did they want to claim that the Jordan army has surrendered so that they can compose songs about it? In the People's Republic of South Yemen they say that Algeria's stand is good because Algeria issued a statement . . . The Yemenis have given us a headache. What can they do in this case? What are their capabilities?[34]

Addressing all his assembled Arab colleagues, he further said in desperation,

> You issue statements, but we have to fight. If you want to liberate, then get in line in front of us. We don't want auctions. If you wish to speak, do so with proper calculation. I have 650,000 troops and in December I shall have 750,000. What has Iraq done? It has reduced its military budget . . . He who is anxious to fight against King Hussein is free to do so.[35]

Finally, responding to Qadhafi's demand that the Arab states intervene in Jordan on the side of the Palestinian guerrillas, Nasser said scornfully,

> The Syrians intervened without careful consideration of all the factors and had to withdraw . . . I cannot move a single

soldier. He who has brigades let him deploy them . . . We went
to war in 1967 for the sake of Syria not Egypt. We suffered
19,500 casualties. We cannot afford to gamble again and make
it possible for Israel to cross the Canal.[36]

It could be said that Nasser, like most Egyptians, felt most
comfortable in his insularity that derived from the geography,
history and culture of his country. But he also felt insecure about
Egypt's isolation from the rest of the Arab world. Independence for
Muhammad Ali in 1805–49 from the Sultan in Istanbul and the
great European powers required of him an aggressive regional
policy. It ranged from Arabia in the East to the Fertile Crescent
and Greece in the Eastern Mediterranean. The same problem,
nay dilemma, faced Nasser 150 years later. Only the conditions had
changed: a far more intractable and parlous economic situation at
home, an array of independent Arab states in the region and a
complex international setting. Muhammad Ali conquered the
provinces of his weakened master, the Ottoman Sultan and Caliph
of Islam. Nasser tried to cajole, subvert or unite the weak but none
the less independent Arab states. He may well have believed in the
underlying unity of the Arab nation and the need for a strong man
like himself to bring it about. But he also sensed, if not fully realised,
that the success of his country's development could well depend on
his success in leading this disparate collection of Arab states.

His final disappointment and revulsion with Arabism was due to
a combination of factors. Military defeat in 1967 robbed him of the
capability to pursue a revolutionary Arab policy. He was forced to
lower his sights from seeking Arab unity to settling for Arab
solidarity with some benefits to Egypt paid for by his erstwhile
Arab enemies. His régime at home had degenerated into one of
cliques competing for influence, gain and power, thus partly undermining the economic programmes so vital to his country's development and survival. Most harmful of all to his pride—and talent
perhaps—was the rejection of his leadership by the other Arab
states.

Nasser's disillusionment with the Arabs in 1967 turned into
bitterness, leading him to lash out at everyone and to destroy his
colleagues in the process. His one concern seemed to be that of
remaining in power. The disappointment, however, was mutual.
Charles Helou, one-time President of Lebanon, is reported to have
said, "Nasser was a prisoner of his dreams and ambitions. But his

ability was short of the dreams and hopes of the Arabs in him . . . Thus when in 1965 [at the Arab Summit] he informed gathered heads of Arab states he had no specific plan to recover Palestine, they turned against him."[37]

Notes

1. Fuad Mattar, *Bisarāha 'an Abd al-Nasir* (Beirut, 1975), pp.98–9.
2. Ahmad Abul Fath, *L'Affaire Nasser* (Paris, 1962), pp.239ff.
3. Riad Taha (ed.), *Mahādir jalsāt mubahathat al-wahda* (Cairo, 1963), p.244.
4. Nasser, *Philosophy of the Revolution* (Washington, 1955).
5. Reproduced in Ikhtarna Lak Series No.8, pp.1575–84.
6. Ahmad Hussein, *Nisf qarn maa al-'urūba wa qadiyyat filastin* (Beirut, 1971), pp.67–8.
7. Ibid., pp.55–75.
8. Ibid., p.122; see also *Wahtaraqat al-Qahira* (Cairo, 1968), *passim*, and *al-Duktur Khalid* (Doctor Khaled) (Cairo, 1964).
9. See Chapters 1, 2 and 3 above.
10. Interview with Desmond Stewart, April 1957, Ikhtarna Lak Series No.8, pp.1575–84. For selected recent interpretations of Nasser's Arab policy, see Peter Mansfield, *Nasser* (London, 1969); Jean Lacouture, *Nasser* (Paris, 1971); Dino Frescobaldi, *Nasser* (Milan, 1970); Robert Stephens, *Nasser, A political biography* (London, 1971); A. I. Dawisha, *Egypt in the Arab world* (London, 1976).
11. Fath, *L'Affaire Nasser*, pp.239–40. See also Nasir ali Din al-Nashāshibi, *Al-hibr aswad . . . aswad* (Paris, 1976), pp.99–111.
12. Mattar, *Bisarāha*, p.135.
13. On economic difficulties in the early days of the régime, see P. K. O'Brien, *The Revolution in Egypt's Economic System* (London, 1966), and Robert Mabro, *The Egyptian Economy* (London, 1972).
14. Fath, *L'Affaire Nasser*, p.245.
15. Ibid.
16. See Uri Ra'anan, *The USSR Arms the Third World: Case Studies in Soviet Foreign Policy* (London, 1968), pp.13–85. See also the memoirs of Anthony Eden, *Full Circle* (London, 1960), pp.341–53.
17. Ahmad Hussein, *Kayfa 'araftu Abdel Nasser was 'ishtu ayyāma hukmihi* (Beirut, 1973), p.140.
18. Ibid., p.141.
19. Nashashibi, *Al-hibr aswad . . . aswad*, pp.71–87.
20. Mattar, *Bisarāha*, pp.137–8.
21. Thus his famous Port Said anti-Communist speech on 23 December 1958 was the signal for the arrest of all known pro-Communist officers. The following March (1959), the security services arrested scores of civilian leftists in one fell swoop.
22. See Taha, *Mahādir jalsāt mubāhathāt al-wahda;* Malcolm Kerr, *The Arab Cold War: Gamal 'Abd al-Nasir and his rivals, 1958–1970* (London, 1971) Munif al-Razzaz, *al-Tajriba al-murra (The bitter experience)* (Beirut, 1967); General Abdel Karim Zahr al-Din, *Mudhakkirat (Memoirs)* (Beirut, 1968).
23. Nashashibi, *Al-hibr aswad . . . aswad*, pp.176–88.
24. Sami Gohar, *Al-sāmitūn yatakallamūn* (Cairo, 1975), p.59.
25. Abdel Latif Boghdadi in ibid., p.61.
26. Mattar, *Bisarāha*, pp.152–4.
27. The Libyan authorities, for example, closed the Egyptian Club in Tripoli.

28. See P. J. Vatikiotis, "East-West Arab Relations" in A. J. Cottrell and J. D. Theberge (eds.), *The Western Mediterranean: its political, economic and strategic importance* (New York, 1974), pp.14–34.

29. See Ismail Sabri Abdullah, "Gamal Abd al-Nasir wa al-qawmiyya al-arabiyya" ("Nasser and Arab nationalism"), *al-Tali'a*, Vol.6 (Cairo, November 1970), pp.63–8.

30. Kenneth Boulding, "The International system in the Eighties: Models of international peace" in Gabriel Sheffer (ed.), *Dynamics of a Conflict, a re-examination of the Arab-Israel conflict* (New Jersey, 1975), p.17.

31. SAM missiles were already in place, manned by Soviet crews, and Soviet pilots were, as of the spring of that year, flying reconnaissance and defence missions over Egypt.

32. He had already accepted the American Rogers Plan and a cease-fire on the Canal.

33. Musa Sabri, *Wathā'iq harb Oktobar* (*Documents of the October War*) (Cairo, 1975), pp.166, 169.

34. Ibid., p. 170.

35. Ibid., p.171.

36. Ibid., p.185.

37. Nashashibi, *Al-hibr aswad . . . aswad*, p.204.

CHAPTER 13

The Challenge of Israel

Like most Egyptians, Nasser before 1955 exhibited a certain ambivalence towards Israel and the Arab-Israel conflict. Neither in his *Philosophy of the Revolution* nor in his *Palestine War Memoirs* is there a clear indication or unequivocal statement of his feelings towards that state. That his experience in the Palestine War strengthened his determination to overthrow the old order in Egypt is not doubted. The Palestine question, however, remained at least until September 1954 peripheral to his purely Egyptian preoccupations. The interest he and his colleagues showed in the series of *coups* in Syria in 1949 suggests they considered the débâcle in Palestine a point of departure for their, by now, seditious plans at home.[1] Kamal el-Din Hussein's report of Colonel Ahmad Abdel Aziz's dying words in battle, "the real battle is in Egypt," to Nasser and his comrades was taken to heart.

The evidence from his own published statements suggests that Nasser in those days perceived both Zionism and Israel as "progressive" elements in contrast to the "rotten" Arab régimes in the Middle East, especially if his reported conversations with the Israeli officer, Yeruham Cohen, are to be taken seriously. Some outside powers, the UK and the USA for example, considered Nasser and his régime in its early days as being "moderate" over the Arab–Israel conflict, and believed Nasser capable of reaching an accommodation.[2]

This benign public image of Nasser and the Free Officer régime in its early stages with regard to Israel was in part inferred from their own attacks on the King and *ancien régime* for committing the unprepared and ill-equipped Egyptian army to the Palestine battle in 1948. Yet Egypt has been involved in every Arab–Israel war since that time. Nasser's attitude to Israel evolved with his Arab policy, or his struggle for Arab leadership, and his adoption of an anti-Western policy at home and in the Middle East region as a whole.

Zionism and Israel soon became the agents and forward outposts of imperialism, deadly threats to the Arab nation, and alien intruders to be expunged from the Arab heartland.

> The danger of Israel is its existence as it now stands, with all it represents. The first thing it represents—as history and experience have proved—is that it cannot survive without imperialism. It stands for imperialism. It serves imperialism and its objectives of domination and exploitation . . . It follows that the triumph of freedom and peace in liquidating imperialism cannot occur without affecting Israel's existence . . . It is one and the same battle.[3]

Nasser's earlier ambivalence toward Israel must also be viewed in the context of his rebellion against a world which he perceived as hostile and evil. His rebellion, incidentally, cannot be explained in purely ideological or economic, i.e. class, terms.[4] It is overladen with Nasser's cumulative sense of the violence done by an alien civilisation, one represented by British power in his view, to Islam generally, Egypt specifically and the wider Arab–Islamic community peripherally. "The Crusades", he could proclaim, "marked the beginning of the dark ages in our land;" or otherwise assert, "There is no doubt the Arab Circle is the most important and has the closest link with us."[5]

As a rebel, Nasser sensed the emergence of new and different conditions and forces affecting both the balance of world power and the relations of the Middle Eastern countries. He could still "analyse" and "explain" to his constituencies the impact of the clash of these forces on their environment. At that stage therefore—when Nasser was not yet a self-proclaimed revolutionary, projecting an Arab nationalist or Arab socialist ideology—he did not pass the death sentence on Israel. Rather he speculated on what this new state was, represented or could become:

> It has been clear that imperialism is the most prominent force in this region. Even Israel herself is not more than a product and manifestation of imperialism. Had not Palestine fallen under a British mandate, Zionism could not have found the needed assistance to realize its idea of a National Home in Palestine. It would have remained a madman's fantasy, with no hope of ever materializing.

Until 1954, therefore, Israel for Nasser was not an entity he perceived as having its own independent existence, momentum and dynamic. It was no more than a satellite in the firmament of the real threat to the Arabs—imperialism. To combat imperialism inevitably entailed fighting Israel, until fighting Israel replaced the struggle against imperialism.

At that early stage also Nasser did not share the Palestinian or eastern Arab unrealistic "all or nothing" approach to the confrontation with Israel. Later, when Israel came to constitute for him both a major issue and an intractable problem of his radical Arab policy (1957–67), the idea of a "permanent struggle" took shape. On 24 June 1960 he defined the permanent struggle as follows: "It is our sacred duty to recover land taken from us by force." On 24 September 1962 he referred to the "cancer in the Arab region that is Israel." Even earlier, on 20 June 1960, he declared, "We shall never waive the rights of the Palestinian people . . . their honour is part of the honour of the Arab nation." Nasser reverted to the idiom of his old political mentors, among them Ahmad Hussein, who some years before that had asked rhetorically,

> We believe in peace. But how can we be at peace when the foreigner has rejected it and insisted on expelling one group of our nation from their home; inserted barbed wire into our sides and throats in the form of this awful state, the state of Israel . . . We must therefore be alert and prepared . . . in a permanent state of struggle in order to expel the aggressors from our country . . . There can be no peace in the Arab East until the aggressors first evacuate our territory.[6]

In fact, back in 1948 most Egyptians viewed the fight of the Jews for independence in Palestine as one of armed gangs. One government Minister, for example, stated that in their view Israel was not a legitimate state upon which Egypt could declare war. Rather they viewed it as a collection of armed gangs which were terrorising the population. On this basis they ordered a few units of the Egyptian army to move in and suppress these gangs.

Once, though, Nasser had committed himself to his oft-proclaimed three revolutions, a national revolution, a social revolution and an Arab revolution, he could not avoid promoting the idea of the "permanent struggle" against Israel. In the meantime, he had to forgo—and postpone—the utilisation of any immediate

creative capacity of his new régime for a social revolution in the
cause of a future totality of Arab liberation. After 1956 at least his
speeches were obsessed by the theme of how Britain handed over
Palestine to Zionism, how it armed the Zionists; how the United
States aided Zionism and Israel, enabling "world Jewry and
Zionism to conquer a beloved part in the heart of the Arab fatherland, so as to be the tip of imperialism's bayonet inside the Arab
nation, a source of danger and terror." The collusion between
imperialism and Israel, Nasser always reminded his audiences, was
clear.

> But it is impossible for Israel to triumph over us, the Arab
> people, in any case . . . therefore, we can never relinquish the
> rights of the Palestinian people, because, as I said in the past,
> the honour of the Palestine people is the honour of the Arab
> nation . . . We always view the imperialist countries as partners
> in the tragedy that has befallen a part of the Arab nation, the
> people of Palestine . . . Our sacred duty is to regain possession
> of the conquered land. [7]

Even in his 26 July 1956 Suez Canal nationalisation speech, Nasser
emphasised how "Imperialism attempts to undermine and weaken
Arabism by the creation of Israel."

Contrary to a widely held notion, there was nothing particularly
irrational about Nasser's hostility to Israel after 1954 and 1956. The
bitterness of a lost war in 1948–9 and the sentiment of Islamic
solidarity aside, there were practical considerations of policy in
Nasser's refusal to end his country's or the other Arabs' confrontation with Israel. For himself and his country there were several.
The conduct of an aggressive Arab policy required the adoption of
the Palestinian cause and the leadership of the struggle against
Israel. The Israeli view of Nasser's Egypt as the most important
state in their struggle for acceptance and survival in the region
further encouraged Nasser in his new posture. Even the great
powers' implicit recognition of Nasserite Egypt as the local power
that might conceivably maintain order and stability in the region
seemed to approve of Nasser's posture, or at least the considerations
that lay behind it.

It was only at the end of 1954 that Nasser authorised Palestinian
refugees in Gaza to organise commando raids across the border with
Israel. This was the result of a decision to unleash a virulent

campaign against Western interests in the region in connection with an Egyptian policy of greater involvement in Arab affairs. The policy was decided upon once the agreement with Britain to evacuate the Suez Canal base had been concluded. It is incidentally in this context that the arms deal with the Soviet Union announced in September 1955 ought to be viewed, and not simply as a reaction to the denial of arms to Egypt by the West, as well as Nasser's attack on the Baghdad Pact, and his subsequent propaganda and subversion campaigns in Jordan and Lebanon.[8] The commando raids provoked the massive retaliatory Israeli raid on Gaza in February 1955. The Soviet arms deal in September 1955 raised not only Nasser's expectations of eventual victory over Israel, but also those of other Arabs. Together with the Suez episode the following year, Nasser's new militancy in the conflict with Israel was firmly established in the eyes of the Arabs and the rest of the world. The 1956 Suez War, which brought in its wake a United Nations Emergency Force (UNEF), on the Egypt–Israel border, allowed Nasser a decade of militancy without, however, the risk of another military clash.

To what extent the Arab expectation of Nasser's militant anti-Israel posture dragged Egypt into the 1967 war disaster has been a matter of great controversy and debate. After all, neither in 1956 nor in 1967 did Egypt directly attack Israel. Rather the roots of Egyptian involvement lay in Nasser's strident Arab policy of the decade separating the two wars. His policy of "no war, no peace" during those ten years paid off relatively well in terms of some economic and social progress at home. It was made possible, however, by the interposition of UNEF and his supremacy in Arab councils until 1963 at least. After that it became difficult for Nasser to maintain his Arab leadership while at the same time conduct a war in the Yemen and ward off the attacks of his Arab rivals in Saudi Arabia, Syria and North Africa. The new militancy of the Palestinians under Shuqeiri and his successors moreover placed further constraints on his ability to manipulate the Arab front against Israel without risking any concrete action. Attacked from practically every Arab quarter and criticised by a new constellation of conservative Islamic states led by Saudi Arabia, Nasser in 1966 was in danger of completely losing the initiative in Arab affairs.

Yet none of these specific events or developments caused a sudden change in Nasser's attitude to Israel. His view of that country was transformed during the decade between the Suez and Six Day wars. He came to see Israel more and more as a serious threat to Egypt's projected economic and political role in the region. He no longer exhibited the same ambivalence about it as he did before 1955. Rather his belief in the artificiality and non-organic intrusiveness of the Jewish state became firmer. As his Arab position improved between 1956 and 1960 and as his relationship with the Soviet Union became closer, Nasser felt that he could one day defeat Israel. He considered Israel a transient phenomenon in the Middle East that would not withstand the sheer force of Arab numbers, or the fact that the time factor worked in favour of the Arabs.

> Today, we are building up our strength and I say that time is on our side and that the manpower of the Arabs can attain superiority over the arms given by the West to Israel . . . The cause of the Palestinians does not permit any bargains or retreat . . . With the passage of time we will win the Palestine cause, because we are right and have the manpower. And I say one day the Arabs will recruit two to three million men in order to liberate Palestine and restore the rights of the Palestinian people regardless of how many arms Israel receives from the West.[9]

All these considerations, together with the need to retain Arab leadership, made Nasser more willing to risk an open confrontation with Israel in 1966–7. Considering his hurt pride as a result of developments in the Arab world in 1961–3 and his declining prestige in 1964–6, his sense of honour and dignity was more acute than ever, adding the required irrational element in his response to events.

There were those who considered Nasser in 1957–67 a pacifist in the Arab–Israel conflict. But that impression was the result of circumstances, such as the presence of UNEF on the ground, Egyptian economic domestic needs and Nasser's Arab policy. There was, however, no moral acceptance of Israel. On the contrary, Nasser, though more realistic in his assessment of Israel than other Arabs, seemed to subscribe to a wider emotional Arab monolithic concept of the Middle East, from the Atlantic to the Gulf. To this extent he also came to share in the more chauvinist Arab version of the region's history as having begun with the Arabs and Islam. In fact it can be said that during that decade his charismatic leadership and temporarily successful Arab policy joined with his earlier sense of humiliation, shame and revenge to harden him in his hostile attitude to Israel. Moreover Arab adulation, together with growing Soviet support, supplied the illusion of the ability to avenge the losses of the past and raised his, as well as the other Arabs', expectations of victory. One Palestinian Arab journalist confessed that in Nasser he had found "a god", in the sense of an Arab leader who would finally enable him to return to his native land.[10]

It is therefore plausible to view the four years from 1963 to 1967 as the road to the abyss of the Six Day War. Extremist Arab régimes in Damascus, the strident anti-Israel rhetoric of Iraq, the new militancy of the Palestinians and the treacherous shoals of Arab summit meetings in 1964–5 over the Yemen stalemate all contributed to Nasser's precipitate actions in 1966–7 against Israel. He actually deplored and derided Arab bravado over Israel when on 20 January 1965 he warned:

> The Arab countries should not talk together and then each wait for the other to enter the battle against Israel, and let the other down as happened in 1948. If we did that again and we were defeated for a second time, it would be impossible for the Arabs to raise their heads again.

His brinkmanship in May 1967 over the Tiran Straits, Sharm el-Sheikh and the expulsion of UNEF were manifestations of his heightened militancy in the face of mounting Arab accusations of his inaction and in response to his declining Arab leadership.

That Nasser in May 1967 may not have intended to go to war against Israel is of course possible. In any case, this rather indeterminate question has been discussed widely. It is also irrelevant whether or not the Soviets misled him about Israeli intentions in Syria. Equally peripheral is the controversy regarding the difference of views between Nasser and his military advisers over the matter of a first strike against Israel during that fateful month. What is important is the possibility that by 25 May Nasser moved from a reluctance to go to war to a belief that if war came he could win it. Otherwise, it is very difficult to explain his confident, strident—even belligerent—public statements between that date and the outbreak of hostilities. He was perhaps misled into such confident complacency because he was encouraged in his brinkmanship by the seeming success of his diplomatic initiative that month. Furthermore, all these diplomatic moves constituted militant acts in the eyes of the Arabs, even though in themselves they may have appeared at the time as no more than rash or impetuous gestures. The previous November (1966) he had improved his Arab position *vis-à-vis* his conservative Islamic rivals, Saudi Arabia and Jordan, by concluding a military alliance with Syria. On the following 30 May, his erstwhile bitter enemy, King Hussein of Jordan, embraced him over the signing of a Jordanian–Egyptian military pact. Nasser on 1 June 1967 was thus back at the centre of the Arab stage, defying Israel in the name of all the Arabs, and once again commanding the attention of the world. These were all reinforcing and reassuring factors in his push to extract maximum benefit from his defiance.

The available evidence[11] suggests that in mid-May 1967 Nasser made three basic assumptions in his decision to confront Israel. He believed he could depend on the Soviet Union to support him and so offset or counter American backing of Israel. He could in turn depend on the United States to restrain Israel, for by then he was convinced Israel would not dare act without American approval. Finally, his armed forces had been extensively reorganised in 1964, and trained and well equipped by the Russians. In his numerous statements and press interviews that month he made it clear his armed forces were the strongest in the region, and that if Israel wanted war, he welcomed it. Thus at the moment when Nasser had committed himself to certain acts which the Israelis considered belligerent and provocative, Nasser also miscalculated the reaction of his enemy. By then he too had come to believe the myth that Israel was no more than the "vanguard of imperialism" in the Middle East, and therefore incapable of an independent response to his challenge. It is even certain that the lapse of five days between the Nasser–Hussein military alliance and Israeli action had convinced Nasser that he had got away with his brinkmanship without war.

The crushing defeat of Egyptian armed forces in Sinai in the Six Day War constituted a defeat of Nasserism in the Arab world. It was followed by a rapid decline of radical Arabism identified with Nasser, without, however, a destruction of the Nasser régime in Egypt, or the erosion of the Arabs' moral rejection of Israel. This rejection in any case did not arise from any Israeli policy or behaviour, but from the fact that it existed as a *Jewish* state amidst what the Arabs considered to be their own exclusive environment or milieu, the "Arab region". The belief in the transience of the enemy, that is, was not abandoned by the Arabs. As for the Egyptians, defeat galvanised them into a frenetic support of their vanquished President, because now their own land, not that of the Arab nation, was under enemy occupation. The Egyptians too did not abandon their belief in Israel's transience, because now they believed they could prepare to undo the new post-1967 territorial *status quo*, that is liberate Sinai, with international approval, since it was Egyptian, not Arab or Palestinian, territory that was involved. The confrontation was now transformed into one between Egypt the aggrieved party and Israel the aggressor state.

"No war, no peace, no recognition", became the post-1967 formula and basis of Egyptian and Arab policy at the Khartum Summit. Nasser had to opt for this kind of policy—or non-policy— on two counts: in order to satisfy his new Arab financial backers, and in order to respond to a revived Egyptian patriotic demand for the eventual recapture of the Sinai. Interestingly enough, it occurred when Nasser's own commitment to, as well as involvement in, Arab affairs had been perforce reduced. Soon, though, the resumption of a static war of attrition across the Suez Canal forced him on to the path of greater militancy. Only this time (after 1968) it was a militancy more closely related to Egyptian state interests as he perceived them.

At home, on the positive side, the defeat of 1967 accelerated the liquidation of the Yemen war, crushed the elements of sedition in the army, and restored Nasser's complete domination of Egyptian affairs. The only new element in the confrontation with Israel was Nasser's willingness to consider a settlement in Sinai on the basis of UN Resolution 242, but not to negotiate a peace treaty.

All the same, the "no war, no peace, no recognition" of Israel stand could not be adhered to for very long. New constraints on Nasser's policy emerged from domestic troubles, demands for military revenge among certain elements within the Egyptian officer corps, and the rising militancy of the Palestinian resistance move-ment. Still Nasser stood firm in his rejection of a "people's war" against Israel. But by the end of 1968 Israeli air attacks inside Egypt increased, causing public resentment. The popularity of the Palestinians was rising. Nasser had no choice but to declare a war of attrition in March 1969. At the same time the only way he could react to demands for a negotiated settlement was to refuse direct negotiations with Israel. But the Israelis stepped up their deep penetration air attacks against Egypt. Nasser suspected complicity between the superpowers and once again turned to the Arabs for help. In the Summit at Rabat in December 1969 he put his case before them, but elicited meagre response from the assembled heads of states. He walked out in disgust. When on 22 January 1970 the Israeli air force raided Shadwan in Egypt, Nasser secretly paid an urgent visit to Moscow, where he demanded a complete SAM3 missile air defence system, and threatened the Kremlin leaders: "Unless you help me, I shall resign." By the spring, Egypt's air space was being guarded not only by Soviet missile batteries and their Russian crews but by Soviet aircraft flown by Russian pilots.

It was clear in the summer of 1970 that the Arabs were not prepared to assist Nasser in his Sinai predicament—in fact, many seemed to revel in his difficulty—and the Israelis were not moving towards an accommodation. When, therefore, the United States came forward with its so-called Rogers Plan for a cease-fire and an end to the war of attrition on the Canal, Nasser was ready to accept it. In April 1970 he appointed Muhammad Heikal Minister of Information to prepare public opinion for this radical departure in policy. In June he paid his last visit to Moscow. On 23 July 1970, he declared Egypt's formal acceptance of the Rogers Plan as it now had the approval of his patron superpower.

Nevertheless, throughout the post-1967 period Nasser remained as ambivalent about an accommodation with Israel as ever. He realised that coming to terms with Israel could have meant relinquishing Arab leadership. For the same reasons he persisted in his rejection of a separate Egyptian settlement with Israel.[12] He identified the one and only reason for the severance of diplomatic relations with the United States as the latter's continued support of Israel. In fact, he continued to perceive the United States as a power that wished to subjugate Egypt; hence its unconditional support of Israel. Ever since 1965, he argued, "Their strategy has been to overthrow all progressive Arab governments . . . And they use Israel as their instrument in the execution of this policy. As for the British, they have become satellites of America."[13] He repeated the same view to Sulzberger and Reston of the *New York Times*.[14] In other words, Nasser continued to see America as being synonymous with Israel, and her policy therefore a threat to Egypt. "Israel is America's forward base in Western Asia," he told an Indian reporter.[15] He never relinquished his belief that Israel was expansionist.[16] Thus in his view, "There are no hawks and doves in Israel.

Rather Israel represents for us two things: the expulsion of the Palestinian people from their land, and *a permanent threat to the Arab nation.*"[17] For these reasons, even when Nasser had decided to accept the Rogers Plan he still clearly refused to contemplate the prospect of recognising Israel, unless it first evacuated occupied Arab territories and solved the problem of the Palestinians.[18] In May 1970, he went so far as to formulate his rejection of a Jewish state in Palestine: "We reject that state's occupation of our lands. And we reject its insistence on denying the legitimate rights of the Palestinian people in their country."[19]

Even though he was compelled to accept a cease-fire on the Canal, Nasser continued to state publicly, "We are all aware that Israel does not want peace,"[20] because he argued, "War is inherent in the construction of Israel itself. It is part of its plans and policy."[21] Whether he was actually as fanatic or as extreme over Israel as other Arabs is immaterial and irrelevant. What is important is the fact that to the very end of his life he at least publicly expressed an uncompromising attitude to that state. "Arab Jerusalem must remain Arab. Otherwise there will be no peace."[22] "It is impossible for an Arab, be he Christian or Muslim, to forgo Jerusalem."[23] So that even after the defeat in 1967 he saw no contradiction between Arab nationalism and Egyptian interest. He thus continued to reject proffered formulae for an Israeli withdrawal from Sinai only. Rather he insisted on linking it with a withdrawal from other occupied Arab territories in Golan and the West Bank, as well as the satisfaction of "the legitimate rights of the Palestinians".

It was perhaps natural for a charismatic Arab leader of Nasser's standing not to abandon altogether his view of the conflict with Israel even after a crushing military defeat. However, the evidence on balance suggests that Nasser himself was convinced of the prospect of victory in the long term. Emotionally he shared the overwhelming Arab rejection of Israel in the Middle East, for he subscribed to the concept of a historically predominant Arab ethos and rule in the region (i.e. that the Middle East had no history before the Arabs and Islam). At the same time, Egyptian state interest and policy in the region decreed an anti-Israel position.

If the moral rejection of Israel is considered irrational, an Egyptian policy of confrontation with it could well have been based on a cool consideration of interest. After all, Egypt and Israel are, so far, the only two potentially credible industrial regional powers. Ideally, they could together lead the region in development given their human resources, industrial capabilities and military strength. On the other hand, the competition between them for the leadership of the region's development could be fierce. Nasser was keenly aware of this implicit—and latent—competition, and feared its outcome. That is the real significance of his repeated assertions that Egypt cannot turn away from events or affairs in the Arab world, or that Egypt cannot develop in isolation from it. "Our enemy is Israel," he stated bluntly on 20 January 1965. "Progress to us is death for Israel," he told his audience in Minia on 9 March 1965.

A more cynical explanation of Nasser's preference for a "no war, no peace" condition as regards Israel may have been his desire to retain a tight grip over Egyptian affairs in the face of a permanent external threat. It also helped him postpone the tackling of numerous domestic economic and social problems. At the same time, it permitted him an initiative in Arab affairs he would not otherwise have had, especially after 1965. And this was no original departure from the general—if nominal—policy of his predecessors in the *ancien régime*. Had he lived after 1970, he may have been led by circumstances into adopting exactly the policy of his successor. There is no doubt that even as he accepted the Rogers Plan, Nasser was preparing for another war. The SAM missile air defence system, the massive re-arming and resupply of the Egyptian armed forces were all under way before he died. In fact, he too was beginning to view the conflict with Israel as basically one of territory and control over the core Middle East rather than one of just Arabs against Jews or Palestinian Arabs against Israelis.

Notes

1. Fuad Mattar, *Bisarāha 'an Abd al-Nasir* (Beirut, 1975), pp.98–9.
2. See Miles Copeland, *The Game of Nations* (London, 1969).
3. Opening statement to the National Assembly, Cairo, 24 March 1964.
4. Ahmad Hamrush, incidentally, in his *Qissat; thawrat 23 yulio* (Beirut, 1974), tries to explain the 1952 *coup* in Marxist class terms. Heikal, on the other hand, who was close to Nasser, offers a more straightforward explanation of Nasser's rebelliousness: "He was always a rebel, a characteristic which stemmed almost certainly from his reaction to the stern traditionalist views of his father who, as a post office clerk in Upper Egypt [*sic:* in fact, in Lower Egypt], was a junior member of the Egyptian bureaucracy." See Muhammad Heikal, *Nasser: The Cairo Documents* (New York, 1973), p.19 (London, New English Library, 1972, p.30).
5. Nasser, *Philosophy of the Revolution* (Washington, 1955).
6. Ahmad Hussein, *Al-ishtirakiyya allati nad'ū ilayha* (Cairo, 1951), p.28.
7. Speech to Popular Congress, Alexandria, 24 June 1960.

8. See Uri Ra'anan, *The USSR Arms the Third World* (London, 1969), pp. 1–174, and Nāsir al-Din al-Nashashibi, *Al-hibr aswad . . . aswad* (Paris, 1976).

9. May Day Rally speech, Cairo 1965.

10. Nashashibi, *Al-hibra aswad . . . aswad*, pp.71–87.

11. See Salah al-Din al-Hadidi, *Shadid 'ala harb 67* (Cairo, 1974); Salah āl-Din al-Munajjid, *A'midat al-nakba* (*The pillars of disaster*) (Beirut, 1968); Walter Laqueur, *The Road to War: The Origin of the Arab–Israel Conflict* (London, 1968).

12. Interview with Clifton Daniel of the *New York Times*, April 1969, reproduced in *Nasser's interviews with the foreign press 1968–70* (Cairo, n.d.), pp.41–57.

13. Interview with correspondent of *Le Monde*, February 1970, ibid., p.109.

14. In March 1969 and February 1970 respectively. See ibid., pp.31–8 and 93–103.

15. Ibid., pp.116–117.

16. Ibid., pp.25–7, 43.

17. Ibid., p.71.

18. Ibid., p.48, 101–2.

19. Interview with Charles Foltz of *US News and World Report*, May 1970, ibid., p.127.

20. Ibid., p.151.

21. Ibid., p.118.

22. Ibid., p.75.

23. Ibid., p.128.

PART IV

El Rayyes

CHAPTER 14

Nasser, Chief of the Egyptians

Nasser enjoyed greater power and adulation than any ruler of Egypt before him . . . even the pharaohs.—Tawfiq al-Hakim, *Watha'iq fi tariq 'awdat al-wa'i.*

What was so attractive about Nasser for the Egyptians was the fact that he was so different from the "Westernised" rulers they had known since 1923, yet so thoroughly native—and traditional. His charisma lay in his ability to excite their emotions. His explosive career was a constant source of amazement, admiration, disbelief, apprehension and fear, love and hatred. *Gamal ma byitraga'sh,* "Gamal does not retreat," became the common cry after Suez. "We are independent despite their [the *imperialists'*] opposition and plotting," Nasser would remind his adulating crowds. He was Robin Hood, Sindbad, Saladin, *ftewwa* and pharaoh all rolled into one. The monument to his pharaonic political descent was to be the High Dam at Aswan. The human debris, victims of his terrifying police state, was to be the evidence of his prowess as a *ftewwa*.

Nasser's contempt for the imperialists was equalled by his utter contempt for politicians, bourgeois semi-Westernised intellectuals, salon pseudo-aristocrats and his own colleagues. His disregard of political institutions was Alcibiadic. [1] His mandate, he always claimed, was from the people; he only reflected their will. He expressed shallow notions of democracy, authority and power: "The sole basis of authority in the developing countries is the masses." [2] "Alone, I cannot do anything," he asserted upon his re-election as President in March 1964. Even after the 1967 war and the disturbances among workers and students in 1968, [3] Nasser could claim in his famous speech of 30 March 1968 that he had been given a fresh "mandate for change".

His utterances about socialism, economic development and social change were muddled, ideologically indeterminate, banal. Nevertheless, they were accepted as being in favour of the little people and against the big bullies and their foreign friends.[4] The ideas themselves were not, however, of the essence. More important was the fact that his manner of speech, idiom and the values he expressed were of the native variety and at a popular level.

Until 1952, the two main groups which expressed their ideas and publicised their programmes in radical nationalist and traditional terms were Young Egypt and the Muslim Brethren. The latter especially were successful in attracting a mass following on any reckoning. They appealed to the vast majority of Egyptians unaffected by Europe, and addressed them in a familiar, attractive Islamic idiom. But they also appealed to those who had had a brush with the West and rejected it. Nasser's appeal was in that tradition and idiom. Whereas all his other fellow-conspirators among the officers soon came to cavort with the politically defunct *haute bourgeoisie*, Nasser never did so. What was politically essential to his career and monopoly of power was that the miserable myriads of Egypt had found a spokesman—and an idol. The idol to be worshipped had arrived but as some of Nasser's own colleagues have described his career: "He was a good starter, but a lousy finisher."

Highlighted here is the contrast between the fantastic expectations Nasser aroused in the Egyptians and his failure to fulfil them. Despite the failure, he remained a leader of miraculous capacity for political recovery, akin to Egypt's cult of resurrection. Joseph Horne in an appreciation of Nasser on BBC Radio Four on 25 March 1971 suggested that "Egypt must be one of the most intensely conservative countries in the world—conservative, hidebound, lacking initiative, in a way that would make the Monday Club look like a collection of urban guerrillas."

This leaden, stubborn immobility of Egyptian society was a source of great frustration to Nasser, its proclaimed liberator and saviour, who for eighteen years was forced to deal with the most pressing issues of national survival. But even a society chained to its deep-rooted shackles of conservative indifference can readily admire the evictor of monarchs, fat politicians and foreign masters; the dextrous manoeuvrer in the crisis of February–March 1954 and power juggler; the realistic negotiator of July–October 1954;[5] the demolisher of the violent Muslim Brethren and the torturer of the

godless Communists. Above all, Nasser's youthful nationalist
enthusiasm appealed to that society's waiting and watchful, long-
suffering but inert romanticism, mixed with mystical, magical and
ritual practices. He was like something out of a national spiritualist
seance, a *zār*.[6]

Nasser furthermore did not live in palaces; he only worked in
them. Like the vast majority of his fellow-Egyptians he did not read
highbrow literature—native or foreign. He took no real interest in
the arts, even though he mobilised, that is bureaucratised, art and
its practitioners. He confined his reading to newspapers and
magazines; he ate *ful, ta'miyya* and *mulokhiyya*.[7] When he wished
to be entertained he watched Hollywood films, or one of those
endless, tear-jerking sagas of unrequited Arab love, for hours on
end. Um Kulthum met practically all his musical needs. His only
concession to alien indulgences and pastimes consisted of smoking
American cigarettes and playing tennis. He had the cunning and
suspicious nimbleness of the *baladi*, the native as distinguished
from the "Westernised", but he retained the *baladi*'s cultural
shallowness and banality, as well as his conservative social preferences.

An Ismail Sidqi in the early thirties may have, albeit autocratically, introduced the most radical changes in the institutions
of state and government in recent Egyptian history. But he did so
on the basis of a rational assessment of Egypt's condition and needs.
Moreover, his response to these was related to his understanding of
the ends of government. Yet by education, upbringing and temperament, Sidqi was both intellectually and emotionally too far removed
from the level of the *baladi* and petit bourgeois.[8]

Zaghlul and Nahhas too, despite their apparent populism and
genuine popularity, were by education, experience and prolonged
political apprenticeship equally alien to the raw, visceral founder,
which Nasser was, of a "new class" and "native court". Although
adulated by the masses, Zaghlul died in 1927 a mere "leader of the
1919 revolt" and "father of the independent Egyptian nation".
But Nasser died a pharaoh, a god-king, the worshipped idol of the
nation. While in power he had created a new military-bureaucratic
"class", the political directorate and governing apparatus—*al-gihaz*
—of his régime, which he controlled absolutely. Egypt under him
once again acquired a hydraulic master, a *rayyes*, of the great
'izba, or farm, which is Egypt. And, as Captain Adolphous Slade
put it captiously though brilliantly in describing the new bureaucracy

in Turkey in 1867, the state became, for this new class, the Estate.[9]
Nasser, perhaps unwittingly, imposed the greatest and widest
servility on the country in its modern history: Egyptians became
farafir, or figaros,[10] and the law of survival was expressed in the
formula of the jungle, "I am Sultan, the Lion . . . Law of Being."[11]
Yet whatever his achievements and failures, Nasser satisfied for
eighteen years the Egyptians' thirst for that mystical feeling of
resurrection and fulfilled their anticipation of The Idol.

Nasser's charisma may well have anaesthetised the Egyptians. The
fact remains that his autocracy founded little that is politically
lasting, even though it may have provided the outlines of social and
economic change in the future. What was perhaps important for
the average Egyptian was the fact that *'Antar*, the legendary Arab
hero and Abu Zeid el-Hilali, hero of Egyptian folklore, were back.
History as projected by Nasser became for the Egyptians a romance.
If they were worried, for instance, about the problem of Islam
versus modernism, Nasser Islamised modernity rather than get
stuck in the quagmire of his predecessors who tried to modernise
Islam. Primitive, pseudo-democratic notions like *ijmā'* (the consensus of the community), *shura* (consultation) were resurrected
when the teachers of religion, already servants of the ruler for a
hundred years or more, reinforced his power.

Nasser carried the Egyptian's long-sought dignity and self-respect
against the evil spirits of an inimical world on his sleeve, where all
his brothers and sisters could see it and him battling their enemies.
The evacuation, Suez, the UAR, the High Dam, all of these were
like a *zār* which lifted the heavy burdens of misery and powerlessness
from their stooping shoulders and washed away the *'ār*, or shame,
of centuries of oppression and domination. Nasser himself, the
righteous shepherd, came to constitute and represent the very
escape from reality so common in a society riveted to an inhuman
chore of existence. What is most interesting about him is that he
was able to retain his mass appeal while openly pursuing a total
concentration of personal power. To be sure, his amazing ability
at vilification, his blistering invective against his enemies expressed
what the crowds were unable to express themselves as well for so
long.

It is unfair to describe Nasser as a typical Arab demagogue, or a
simple modern mass leader. He was more than that, because he was
a thoroughly native Egyptian sultan, of extraordinary, albeit un-

creative (sterile?) political cleverness. Very intelligent and shrewd, he did rather well within the political-historical context of a tragic Egyptian dilemma at mid-century. It is his shallowness which defeated him in the end. The shallowness derived from the formative-psychological basis of his national movement which lay deep in his background and experience of poor native crowds, the Young Egypt's populist, authoritarian, irrational and primitive national socialism, and the Muslim Brotherhood's earthy, visceral Islamic idiom.

On the other hand, it must be noted that it is not so difficult to become a messiah of *futuwwat*, or Robin Hoods, with an elemental notion of justice, arrogance and cupidity, and a quick and powerful mind which is undisciplined, or devoid of cultural depth. The justice of the *futuwwat* is primitive because it is sought by the club, the *nabbut*. But it is in the final analysis purposeless beyond leading the community in instant, spasmodic rebellion against oppression. In such circumstances, "It was dangerous to trust the sincerity of Augustus: to seem to distrust it was still more dangerous."[12]

For eighteen years Nasser perfected a technique of control, but produced no system of power. He deliberately kept his top group of lieutenants fluid, formless. His essential cynicism was fed by his exaltation in power, his scorn of institutions and contempt for politicians. Perhaps he could afford it, because he was able to convince the vast majority of Egyptians that he had transported their country from one age to another. To the other Arabs he gave Nasserism, which simply meant an aspiration to change and a weightier Arab presence in the world. The excitement of the trans-formation—real or imagined—the illusion of the promised better tomorrow was the essence of his magic appeal and the foundation of his legitimacy. Actually, he was the Chief with no clearly identifiable legitimacy. So long as he lived he seemed to possess it. Only death relieved him of it. In these circumstances, his actions were acceptable regardless of their consequences. Even defeat became victory in the emotionalism, sentimentalism and mass hysteria of the worshippers, whether revealed over his resignation from office or upon his death. "There is no God but Allah, and Nasser is the beloved of Allah," became the funeral chant.

Perhaps Nasser's singular obsession was to found an Egypt without foreign occupiers. This was the millennial fate of the country which haunted him. Thus for a decade Egypt worshipped the hero who came to resurrect her, the native son who would guarantee continuity in a new life. In exchange for a dream—some would say, baseless and chimeric—as well as the promise of self-respect, Egyptians abandoned all their gains of recent vintage. When he was gone, they remained, on balance, the losers on most counts. They discovered what Englishmen had discovered over 320 years before, or in the words of John Buchan, "A republic cannot be made merely by decapitating a monarchy."[13]

Nasser has been described as a man of crisis, a creature of emergencies, who died feeling his way, groping for something beyond the grasp of his limited intellect and experience. This would explain the fact that he did not leave a political legacy or code of principles behind him. But Tawfiq al-Hakim has been wrong for forty years; Egypt's consciousness may be thousands of years old, but a "mover" is not all she needs.[14] Ibn Khaldun at least seemed to think that protest movements and revolutions would be rare in Egypt. So far, however, it has had to have hydraulic masters, the occasional historical figure referred to as *rayyes*; Muhammad Ali the Great with his Barrages, the British Agents and Consul-Generals with their Aswan Dam (1902), and Nasser with his High Dam.

In common parlance, the flattering epithets for Nasser were *al-wahsh* (the beast), *ftewwa* (tough guy), *al-sa'idi* (Saidi, or Upper Egyptian), *far'on* (Pharaoh) and *Kafur* (the Mamluk tyrant). These folksy metaphors were not idle utterances. Rather they are symbolic of the fact that the ruler represented the reality of Egypt as perceived by the masses of Egyptians, the requirements of her existential condition. It is therefore difficult to argue that Nasser's behaviour was a deviation from Egyptian political tradition, or even in terms of his own historical "generation". As a *ma'bud*, an idol, Nasser "arose from the people: he did not descend from heaven", in the words of Hakim.

Nasser became fused with Egypt. In his speeches, he rarely said, "I know" or "I think" (only "I decided, I chose"): he always said, "We all know . . . who our enemies are." According to Heikal, "he became part of our history." He caught Egypt at a time when he and his generation were thoroughly alienated from their rulers and their country's foreign associations. So was the whole country. "Lift up your heads, the days of oppression are over," he shrieked in October 1954: "if they kill me, there are thousands of other Gamals." By 1957, the days of new oppression had begun in the name of Egypt's eternal theme song, "Death and Resurrection, Resurrection and Death."

Notes

1. See Ahmad Abul Fath, *L'Affaire Nasser* (Paris, 1962) and Muhammad Heikal in Fuad Mattar, *Bisarāha 'an Abd al-Nasir* (Beirut, 1975). This is also the impression one gets from the deliberations between Nasser and the Committee on the organisation of the ASU cited above, as well as from his discussions with representatives of the Iraqi and Syrian Baath parties over the project of unity between the three countries in the spring of 1963 as presented in Riad Taha (ed.), *Mahadir jalsat mubahathat al-wihda* (Cairo, 1963). Nāsir al-Din al-Nashashibi, *Al-hibr aswad. . . aswad* (Paris, 1976), after making allowances for his exaggerated reports and personal disappointment in Nasser, leaves the reader with the same impression.
2. From his address to the ASU Congress in Asiut, 8 March 1965.
3. See Muhammad Jalal Kishk, *Mādha yurīdu al-talaba al-misriyyin (What do the Egyptian Students want?)* (Cairo, 1969).
4. See his speeches to the National Assembly in 1964 and Popular Congress in 1965.
5. What most Egyptians overlooked were the detailed provisions of the agreement which were in effect the same as those which no Egyptian political party before 1952 dared accept.
6. The common practice of a spiritualist seance, where the spirits are recalled and consulted on various matters. See Ahmad Amin, *Qāmūs al-'ādāt wa al-taqālid wa al-ta'ābir al-misriyya (Dictionary of Egyptian customs, traditional practices and expressions)* (Cairo, 1953), p.217. See also E. W. Lane, *The manners and customs of the modern Egyptians*, first published 1836 (London, 1954).
7. Local staple diet: the first two from the native bean; the third is a green grown in Egypt and used in a variety of soups.
8. A perusal of the Alexandria Municipality Archives to which Sidqi was appointed Secretary in 1908, the *procès verbaux* of his Cabinet meetings in 1930–3, his electoral speeches, his brilliant Committee on Trade and Industry Report, 1977, and his diary which he kept on exile in Malta, and other relevant sources provide adequate evidence to support this view. See Muna Abul Fadl, *The Ismail Sidqi Regime*, unpublished Ph.D. thesis, University of London, 1975.
9. See his *Turkey and the Crimean War* (London, 1867).
10. Taken from the famous play *al-Farāfīr* by Yusuf Idris (Cairo, 1963). Dr. Louis Awad renders *al-farafir* as "figaros".
11. Taken from the allegorical piece by Yusuf Idris in the *Ahram*, Cairo, November 1972. Idris was reporting on the killing of circus performer and lion-tamer Muhammad el-Helou, by his leading lion, "Sultan".
12. Gibbon, *The History of the Decline and Fall of the Roman Empire* (Philadelphia, 1845) (Rev. H. A. Milman (ed.)), Vol.I, p.111.
13. *Oliver Cromwell* (London, 1934), p.249.
14. See his *'Awdat al-wa'ī* (Beirut, 1974). Quotations here from the original typescript of the book which the author gifted to this writer in January 1973. The typescript is dated July 1972.

CHAPTER 15

The Rhetoric of Revolution

> He moved the masses in most parts of the Arab nation by
> speech and broadcast . . . He toppled the Baghdad Pact by
> words broadcast over the air. He undermined the British
> colonial presence in South Arabia with the broadcast word
> too, not through partisan political leaders who travelled
> from Egypt to South Arabia in order to move the masses.—
> Muhammad Heikal, *Frankly Speaking About Abdel Nasser.*

Like the popular Egyptian singer, the late Um Kulthum, whose
songs often lasted for two hours, Nasser's speeches too were often
long, repetitive—and effective. They sent his audiences into wildly
rapturous demonstrations of enjoyment, approval and applause.
Only Mustafa Kamil, the fiery Egyptian nationalist leader some
fifty years before him, could sway the crowds with his speeches the
same way Nasser could in a popular rally. Like Ahmad Hussein
before him, Nasser too had to discover his oratorical powers, for at
first he was an awkward speaker, shy and hesitant. For a while, he
used the neo-classical language of the newspapers and radio, reading
from a prepared text from which he did not depart. Heikal reports
that Nasser preferred written texts when indisposed or when
addressing the National Assembly, especially if this involved
reference to statistics, or some major announcement of policy as in
the famous 23 July anniversary speeches.[1]

It was perhaps on 26 October 1954, when Abdel Latif fired those
badly aimed—though fateful—nine shots that Nasser discovered he
could harangue his mass audiences extemporaneously. Gradually,
he developed an oratorical style of his own which combined neo-
classical Arabic with Egyptian colloquial—the language of the man
in the street, the peasant in the fields, as well as that of the chatty
confidence of the family gathering. He perfected it further during
the Suez crisis in 1956 and the union with Syria in 1958–61. By
1958, he could communicate not only with his constituency at

home, but also with his wider Arab audiences in the Middle East and North Africa—in fact, everywhere. It could be argued that the mainstay of his Arab policy was the impact of its powerful rhetoric. To this extent Nasser was perhaps the most successful communicator with the Arab masses in modern times, the most accomplished user of the spoken word.

The New Era of Egypt

One of Nasser's earliest speeches was to the students at Cairo University on 15 November 1952. In it he associated himself with the contribution of students generally to the national struggle and emphasised the similarity of their aims with those of the Free Officer movement. He reminded them how when he was a student he had participated in the struggle for independence: how he shared their dreams and aspirations since he too had clashed with the security forces of the *ancien régime* and suffered physical injury. Then he went on to assert, "Here at the university, in this place, grew this revolution, which aims at defeating colonialism and its collaborators, and at achieving complete independence." The aims of the army movement, he claimed, were the same: "It seeks to liberate the fatherland, and to restore constitutional life. All we desire is to secure full freedom for the people, a freedom that no one can tamper with." [2] There was in this, one of Nasser's earliest speeches, a tone of peaceful diffidence and a clear attempt to convince the students that he and his fellow-officers who had grabbed power the previous July were from the same background and shared common aspirations with them.

In one of his earliest public statements, a press interview on 29 December 1952, Nasser projected the grim determination of the Free Officers to finally rid the country of the British military presence. "We are prepared to be reasonable," he said sweetly, "but the English have been promising us over the past seventy years that they will evacuate the Suez Canal zone. They have not yet done so. Egypt today can no longer tolerate excessive procrastination and temporizing." [3] At the same time, he signalled the Egyptian public, for the majority of whom the new régime of the soldiers remained an unknown new master, that the Free Officers were different from the old politicians who had made similar promises in the past but were never able to fulfil them. The new soldier rulers, he asserted, can very easily revert to their original profession of warriors in order to fight against the British in the event the latter reneged on their undertaking. After all, the soldiers were of the people, and had been themselves involved in anti-British activities in the recent past.

> If the government of the new order, after all the efforts that have been exerted, felt that we cannot rid our country of the British occupation, rest assured that the leaders of the revolution will withdraw from the responsibility of rule in order to lead the people in a war against the English. It will not be a conventional but a guerrilla war: hand grenades will be lobbed in the dark of the night, and English soldiers will be murdered in the streets. Guerrilla operations will spread so quickly that the English will realise they are paying a very high price for their occupation of our country. At worst, our struggle will be like that of Samson in the Bible: we shall bring down the temple over our heads in order to break the heads of our enemies amidst us. [4]

Note the threat of destruction against the enemy, the promise of an apocalyptic end to any stubborn British policy, the fusion of a Free Officer policy with already common popular operations against the British in the country since 1946 at least. Yet Nasser cleverly linked this intransigent, aggressive attitude toward the country's relations with a foreign power to a new era of nationalism and what soon came to be referred to as decolonisation. "We live today in a new age that is different from past ages, in which a new consciousness has been awakened among peoples, expressed in the new trend of nationalism, revival and liberation which cannot be stopped."[5] This spirit of the new age achieved full expression in two of Nasser's most interesting speeches delivered at the Azhar on 2 November 1956 during the Anglo–French landing in Port Said and in Port Said itself on 23 December 1956, the day after the final withdrawal of the Anglo–French expeditionary force from the Canal, the so-called Victory Day Speech. His clever fusion in these speeches of Egypt, Islam and Arabism was to become a favourite theme of his for the next decade. These two speeches also marked a consciousness of his new, wider Arab constituency, and an aggressive Middle Eastern policy directed against both his Arab enemies and the West. In the Azhar speech, he reminded his audience once again how Egypt was historically "a graveyard of conquerors and empires". Today, he told them, "we are fighting oppression and imperialism which is bent on destroying our liberty, humanity and self-respect." The allusion to honour and shame is clear. But then his suggestion that he was responsible for all Egyptians, in fact, that he was somehow "all of the Egyptians" is even clearer. "I have declared in your name that we shall fight and not surrender: that we shall not live a dishonourable life however long they persist in their aggressive plans."

Superficial explanations of Egypt's military collapse in Sinai, based on some extraordinary strategy, were compensated for by xenophobic scorn for the enemy personified in the then British Prime Minister Sir Anthony Eden. "What does Eden want from us? He wants to govern you, govern Egypt. He says he is against Abdel Nasser. You know why? Because Nasser refused to be his instrument. I represent the Egyptian people, not Eden's will."

And finally the climax of the speech with the punch line conjuring up the terrible past. "Eden wants to govern Egypt as in the past." The awful spectre of the past was always held by Nasser throughout this period, using the most vivid depictions of it, "in order to govern you from the British Embassy on the Nile". "The moment we refused and determined to remain independent and dignified, he [Eden] declared war on us . . . by deception and cunning."

Simplistic children's tales about the Egyptian air force's prowess in 1956 were linked to the myth of orderly withdrawal from Sinai.6 All this was necessary in order to construct yet another myth, that of Port Said. Inflating and magnifying odd and sporadic resistance to Anglo–French forces into a Stalingrad-like tenacious defence, Port Said became "the spirit of Egyptian independence and dignity . . . The honour of the Nation is indivisible . . . Port Said paid the blood tax for the whole of Egypt." A corollary myth, reassuring to a public whose armed forces had collapsed in Sinai while a foreign invader had already landed at the Mediterranean end of the Canal and was on its way to Ismailiyya, was that of offers of Arab help. There was solace in the weight of numbers the Arab nation disposed. "Why," Nasser asked "did the RAF bomb the transmitters of the Voice of the Arabs?" In any event, he triumphantly declared, all this was to no avail since Eden managed to get petrol supplies to the UK cut off by Arab producers, and turned both superpowers against Britain.

When I tell you our position after ten days is stronger than it was before, I know what I am saying. Arab nationalism has become a reality and a source of action after it had been a mere slogan . . . It has become the ideology of a whole region. The whole world supports us. Free men everywhere support us.

Here we have the magician who turned defeat into victory. But we also have a glimpse of Nasser's view of the outside world, including his obsession with Western perfidy. The essence of this view was one of conspiracy, distrust and deceit, so that despite the Port Said "victory" the struggle never ends, as the West's attempt to starve Egypt out will continue, as well as the war of nerves against what Nasser now claimed was Egypt's significant, symbolic role in a wider universal movement of liberation. "All these battles have one goal; to destroy the idea emanating from Egypt calling for liberty, independence and Arab nationalism." But he assured his audiences,

> There is no place here for spheres of influence. We shall not submit to anyone's influence or authority. We are free in our country to determine our policy, guided by our conscience. We are here then to celebrate victory in the war of nerves, economic pressure, . . . and isolation.

This was no less than a clear projection of the Egyptian David vanquishing the Anglo–French–Israeli Goliath. Using a combination of scorn and chauvinism, Nasser reminded his audiences, "You in Port Said of course know those 'Red Devils' [a reference to the British paratroops] well." He ascribed victory to the contrast between the past and present of Egypt. "Today Egypt is the property of its sons," he said, "not that of a particular group . . . not of the Khedive or royal family or a handful of landowners." His dexterity in evoking hazy pictures of past oppression and bitterness was great;

> It was only when we succeeded in giving Egypt back to all the Egyptians that we were able to achieve this victory and rout the great powers. I was confident from the start we would triumph over the great powers.

He reminded his audience through his contrast between past (e.g. 1882) and present that victory was also due to the absence of treachery. "Egypt was now purged of traitors, and therefore victory was possible." At the same time, he attributed the fall of Port Said and the ability of the Anglo–French force to land to a new kind of "regional" treachery, namely, the Israeli Trojan Horse with its attack in Sinai. "The battle of Port Said was that of Arab nationalism."

Within a year, in December 1957, Nasser was able to give Port Said a symbolic significance as constituting the historical moment of the shift in Egyptian and Arab policy, and make it a meaningfully epochal event for all small nations. "The battle for Port Said is an insurance policy for all small nations." But Nasser could never resist alluding to the dangers of Western agents amidst them. "The £162,500 they paid, I gift to Port Said," he hissed with scorn and sarcasm. But he extended his net wider; the tanks and planes were not attacking Egypt alone, because the same planes and tanks attack Cyprus, Palestine and other countries. Thus Egypt's confrontation with the Western powers was fused with that of all other countries.

The Permanence of Struggle

Nasser's promises were always coupled to the permanence of the struggle. The aims of the revolution were not simply dramatic, they were big. Conspiracy and sedition were the permanent enemies of the revolution, and these were repeated on every occasion with the confidential tone of the "inside dopester". "I'll tell you what really happened," Nasser would bellow at his audiences, an approach that was essential to his belittling the enemy and magnifying his own accomplishments. Thus Egypt had changed, he would remind his listeners, whereas the West remained unchanged, hankering after the past. "Where is Eden now, where is Mollet? They have disappeared. But the High Dam rises even higher," he shouted in his famous Aswan speech on 9 January 1963.

The theme of change was introduced by Nasser more forcefully in his speeches after the Syrian secession in 1961. After the submission of his National Charter and the widely publicised deliberations over it by a Congress of Popular Forces, Nasser took up this theme systematically in his speech of 24 September 1962. "Now I can tell you," he informed the Egyptian people, "we have a programme." The previous ten years had been spent trying to free the country from the shackles of the past. It was a period of transition. But the struggle had been more productive than that of the pre-1952 nationalists with their partisan differences, which gave birth to nothing. Nasser's revolution, on the other hand, had been creative, leading to a new stage of constructive action. But he equally emphasised the perpetual state of siege the country found itself in, attacked as it was from all directions; the Western powers over Suez, Israel and their Arab rivals in Syria and elsewhere. In communicating all of this, Nasser's technique of confidentiality, presumed frankness and openness became sharper. This was particularly observed with every turn in his fortunes and his need to try something new, as for example in presenting his Charter and the formation of the ASU. He confessed confidentially that he alone could no longer carry all the burdens of revolutionary change.

> I tried for ten years to retain the confidence of the people and took momentous decisions for the future of the country. My support and mainstay in all of this was my faith in Allah and confidence in the people of this republic. I experienced the weight and magnitude of this responsibility, and I assure you I would not wish it on anyone.

His real problem, however, was to justify the changes he had introduced in 1962 and why for ten long years it was not possible to introduce them. "Although our peasants still eat bread and onions, we cannot change this overnight." Still, that seemed easy because he had already designated the previous decade as one of struggle. Moreover, the old forces were stupidly and rigidly opposed to change, as for instance agrarian reform.

> But because you trusted me and had confidence in me— especially in 1956 which no one can forget—we were able to triumph over the enemy and the great powers. I, too, have tried to be worthy of your confidence. How? I worked twenty-four hours a day. I had no other preoccupation, no private life. All my life was my job. Just as before the revolution in the army, all my free time was devoted in preparing for it, because this was my conviction since a very long time.

Thus Nasser smoothly projected his role and his sacrifice, with allusions to his courage in the face of assassination attempts, including one arranged by King Saud of Saudi Arabia, in the cause of firmly establishing the Egyptian revolution within ten years. "The revolution is firmly established after ten years because it is not a revolution of one person [i.e. Nasser's], but of a whole people."

That is why, he explained, he could ride in open cars; "because I believe in the people".

Another important theme, that of affected modesty, comes through in Nasser's announcement of changes in economic policy, and political organisation in the 1960s. "It is not a shame for me," he confided, "to stand up before you and say we have erred in this or that. In fact, we are proud of our mistakes, because we learn from them." In any case, he was always on the side of the people. Proof of that was his expressed wish in 1962 to devote most of his time to the political organisation of the ASU, because

I believe the real protection of national action and the strengthening of the revolution which began on 23 July and the victories it achieved in the past decade lie in the success of our popular political organisation . . . that will supervise the work of the administrative agencies of state.

As usual, though, he was careful to issue his by now well-known warning against reactionaries and opportunists infiltrating the new ASU organisation. He admonished vigilance, but he also welcomed boldness, for he was tired of individual action. "Today", he said, "we want to put an end to isolated individual political action . . . we want group action." He retained his reservations about democracy. What he wanted to see in the ASU under the Charter was "true, healthy democracy, not like the one preached by reactionaries that is really the dictatorship of capital." After all, he protested, "This nation has given me far greater power than is normal for the president of a republic. I want to place this power under the disposal of a new vanguard." Ever pompous and didactic in his solemn announcement of the momentous nature of the ASU experiment, Nasser was able to gloss over all differences and disagreements as superficial and the result of necessary rapid change.

Egypt as the Vanguard of Arab Revolution

Ever since Suez, Nasser in his utterances tried to universalise the world-wide effects of the Egyptian revolution and the impact of his leadership and to suggest that the main reason for American and other Western opposition was this impact. Thus he linked the Egyptian struggle for independence with that for Arab unity and social justice. The arms deal with the Soviet Union broke the Western monopoly over arms supplied to the region: the nationalisation of the Canal was "a round fired in the battle of national dignity and Arab unity": the Aswan High Dam was a "round fired in the battle for modernization". Egypt, he told the General Congress of the National Union on 9 July 1960, had become the vanguard of Afro-Asian liberation, "Our nationalist revolutionary experience against colonialism made us emissaries of peace: our Arab revolutionary experiment against division and disunity made us partisans of Arab unity: our social revolutionary experiment against exploitation made us partisans of justice." And so Nasser tried to convince his Egyptian and Arab audiences that Egypt's example was a good guide for liberation movements everywhere. In so doing he reinforced the dignity and self-respect of the new Egypt.

Similarly, Nasser exploited the massive world news interest in him after 1955. Bandung, the arms deal and Suez pushed him on to the centre of world attention. This, in turn, dazzled and overwhelmed the Egyptians. He was therefore able to construct a myth of Egyptian greatness and world importance. Egyptians felt, "We are now a state in the Middle East led by a hero, and the hero is a leader of a new breed."[7]

Nasser's excursions into the realms of fantasy were now revived. He could also impress Egyptians with a "first time" in doing things —for their sake. Thus he described his dramatic action of going to Cairo Radio Station at 9 a.m. on 28 September 1961 to address them over Syria's secession from the union that morning.

It is the first time I go to the broadcasting station to speak to the people. I never did this before despite all the difficult situations that confronted us in the past. But today we all face a situation that affects the great aims for which we have struggled . . . This Syrian act endangers our national unity . . . Even during the Tripartite Aggression (1956) I did not go to the broadcasting station because I knew we all understood our sacred duty to defend our country. But I did so today because what happened in Syria today is more dangerous than what happened in 1956.

During this episode, Nasser's scorn and sarcasm, mixed with affected magnanimity, come through once more in his famous address to the Arab nation on 5 October 1961, in which he detailed and reviewed Egypt's awry and awkward relationship with Syria, and attacked the secessionists in Damascus. He decided to let Syria exist, that is why he did not take military action against the rebels.

Until now only five states have recognized secessionist Syria. I call them states after a manner of speaking. These are the last vestiges of the family of traitors in Arab history, residing in Amman, the government of Chiang kai shek which was expelled from China to Formosa, the fascist government in Turkey, the government of the American United Fruit Company in Guatemala, and the government of Israel's friend in Iran.

His use of histrionics on this occasion was at its best: "My consolation is that the Syrian people bade farewell with tears in their eyes to those coming back after being expelled from Syria."

Having defined the seriousness of the Syrian secession, Nasser linked it to the enemies of Egypt and the Arab nation. He proceeded later that day, in another broadcast at 7 p.m., to take the public into his confidence, by giving them the "details" of the situation. His use of the confidentiality technique was always effective. "I want you to know everything: I never hide anything from you." At the same time he magnified Egypt's role by identifying it as representative of Arab aspirations. In a Popular Rally the next day, 29 September, he argued how these aspirations were being thwarted by reactionary imperialist secessionists. He dramatically and sonorously informed Egyptians of his despatching of troops to Latakia. But he never told them what happened to them. Then he exonerated himself. After all, he did not wish the union with Syria: the Syrians pressed it on him, even after he advised them to move cautiously, beginning with an initial economic, military and cultural unity for five years. Finally, he dropped his bombshell; he confessed to the onerous burden of working with the difficult Syrians: how three-quarters of his time was taken up dealing with their squabbling. He reverted to the stab in the back theme; in 1948 the reactionaries, Abdullah of Jordan and Nuri of Iraq, had stabbed Egypt in the back over Palestine. Now it was the Syrians. But, he concluded, "this Republic is the citadel of Arabism."

The Rhetoric of Reconstruction

Nasser, the supreme political animal in Egypt at mid-century, insisted on projecting the image of himself as an anti- and non-politician. In fact, in his utterances on political parties, the difference between the healthy present and corrupt past underline his abhorrence of all politics—other than the personal kind. In accepting the presidential nomination in the National Assembly on 20 January 1965, he told the deputies, "I am not prepared today or tomorrow to play the role of a professional politician." He belittled politicians of the past and put forward, unsolicited, his own definition of politics under his leadership:

> Politics, brothers, no longer means stirring speeches [for a man who made so many]. Nor does it mean mere talk, stirring the sentiments of the people or jockeying for power as we used to see in the days of political parties, before the revolution. For any country that respects itself, politics means work, production . . . wages, prices . . . the transformation of society into a better one.

And a year later on 22 July 1966, he could claim, "Egypt today enjoys greater freedom than Britain which has been converted into an American colony to such an extent that it cannot express an opinion on any international issue without first . . . clearing it with Washington."

Between 1952 and 1956 the central ideas and themes of Nasser's speeches reflect also his main preoccupations in power; national independence (the resolution of the Anglo–Egyptian question) and the liquidation of the old order. Stated differently, he communicated the idea of emancipation from foreign rule and the need for national unity. Between 1956 and 1961 the emphasis turned to Arab nationalism and unity, Afro-Asian liberation and solidarity, non-alignment and generally Egypt's leadership role in a wider arena. This in turn entailed an active anti-Western posture, inter-Arab conflict and a greater Egyptian involvement in the affairs of other Arab states. It was during this period that Nasser introduced a whole new vocabulary into the Arabic political lexicon. Between 1962 and 1967 Nasser seemed to concentrate on the so-called restructuring and reorganisation of the Egyptian economy and society—the road to socialism. Thus the Aswan Dam became "the dam of dignity and self-respect . . . " After the defeat in the 1967 war, the theme of his speeches was one of reconciliation among Arab states, his new mandate for change at home and yet another reorganisation of Egyptian society and government.

The influence of Ahmad Hussein's rhetoric and idiom on Nasser's speech-making is apparent throughout his communication with the masses, equally in his earlier emphasis on themes of national independence, the release of Egypt's potentialities, the struggle against exploitation and imperialism as well as in the later attempted definitions of Arab socialism. Thus in 1949–51 Ahmad Hussein described "the socialism we support" as "national socialism".[8] Or, "our socialism is an expression of our nationalism." As in the later case of Nasser, Ahmad Hussein linked his socialism to cleansing not only Egypt but the whole Arab region of foreign influence, and of the Israeli menace.

> Europe and America oppose weak people. So long as there is a British soldier in Egypt, Iraq or Jordan, so long as there are British companies in Iran, so long as Pakistan is tied to Britain via the Commonwealth, so long as American imperialism is in the Arabian Peninsula, so long as the French occupy any part of Arab or Muslim lands, so long as the West continues to support Israel which it created, with iron and fire, and permits the dispersal of one million Palestinians who have been expelled from their homes and country . . .[9]

Ahmad Hussein also argued that the only way to dispel the Israeli danger and destroy that "strange mini state" was to adopt socialism. "Socialism, and only socialism, can guarantee the destruction of that state . . . which has come to threaten the peace and security of fifty million people, unless they accept humiliation under the power of American and European imperialism."[10]

Ahmad Hussein, even before Nasser, linked socialism with freeing Egypt from feudalist exploitation. He called for the redistribution of land and property in order to transform four million landless peasants into a productive force and limit land ownership to 50 *feddans*. It was the only way, in his view, of fighting imperialism.[11] He also called for national economic planning, necessary to guide industrialisation, the exploitation of mineral wealth and the construction of a high dam at Aswan.[12]

The potent mix of words with both secular and religious connotation was used by both men in their speeches, as much as the colloquial metaphor and sonorous neo-classical harangue. Nasser, the leader for example, was not a tyrant; "he represents the reality of Egypt." He was therefore to be found everywhile, like the "little Egyptian". "We are not going to create personalities," Nasser told a Cairo University audience in 1954. "The only acceptable authority is morality, events, necessity." Necessity and events were to be the source of law and the sole guide to the behaviour of the leader. But he also cleverly associated the people—or at least he only suggested it to them—in his responsibilities. "We", not "I", bridged this sharing between leader and masses. "We are not like some outgoing minister, but are here to accomplish the task together," Nasser told his audience a few weeks before Suez. "We are united in the fundamentals, and all have a share in our failures . . . We fought a revolution against injustice."

After the defeat in 1967, however, Nasser tended in his communication with the masses to lift himself above the problems, disputes and scandals that had erupted all around him—Amer, Badran, Salah Nasr. Now he was there to offer his unstinting service to the Egyptian people in sorting out the mess, in clearing out the "gangs of privilege", in rebuilding the armed forces, in reorganising the domestic political front in order to better confront the enemy. Thus his notorious resignation television speech on 9 June 1967 remained impersonal throughout, using the third person. Only at the end of his piece, he said, "I resign." In his place, he offered the Egyptians a trusted bureaucratic establishment lieutenant to succeed him in office. While assuming ultimate responsibility for defeat, he dextrously avoided personal identification with the Sinai débâcle: that remained an Amer-Badran failure.

A delicate game of equilibrium, rolling with the punch, followed on the pretext of putting the revolution back on a correct course. A relaxation of the emphasis on the personality of the leader, a give towards public participation in a reorganised political scheme and a desperate attempt to feign the diffusion of responsibility. After the student and worker troubles in February 1968, Nasser lamented on the 28th of that month, "What can I do if you are not prepared and ready! I cannot do everything. Even if I knew everything, how can I take a position for or against conditions . . . You must decide." Above all, he exploited the massive demonstrations on his behalf and for his return to power on 9–10 June for the purging of others. He asserted that these constituted a mandate from the people for change. In his famous 30 March 1968 Manifesto he could thus speak of a new "political-military ruling class" that ought to be dealt with by opening up participation in political life to the public. His old appeal to the people when in difficulty with his military constituency seemed to work. He demanded a reorganisation of the armed forces command in view of the Amer conspiracy. He emphasised the need for national unity after defeat in battle and therefore the right to impose a moratorium on divisive political activity. For as he claimed in his speech of 23 July 1967, the enemy (Israel) after all aimed at weakening and undermining the country's domestic front.

Like all charismatic types, Nasser preferred the spoken to the written word. Through verbal violence he could conjure up a sense of power while at the same time subsume and harness all forms of discontent into one mass organisation in order to gloss over class differences, antipathies and other kinds of antagonism. He could therefore overlook the need for institutional arrangements such as political parties. More important, this unstructured relationship to a public was the only one which allowed him to dominate. The potent combination of rhetoric creating a sense of power as well as unity over class divisions was grist to the political autocrat's mill. Yet even this assessment remains unfair when it is viewed out of context. Politics in Nasser's society—as well as in many others—is highly personal. Perhaps all politics everywhere is essentially that by nature. What did not occur—and Nasser was not willing to initiate it—is a movement to mitigate the highly personal character of politics by the introduction of institutional devices for its relative depersonalisation.

What emerges from the content and style of Nasser's speeches is the projection of his belief that he stood in place of formal institutional legality, whether this was expressed in a constitution or in political parties. Equally his conviction that Egypt in transition required a hegemonist in power—an estate manager, a *rayyes*—comes through clearly. In order to "modernise" Egypt, Nasser believed, like Muhammad Ali the Great before him, that it is necessary to impose a greater and wider servility on the country. In these circumstances, it was difficult for the mass of Egyptians to perceive the basic contradiction inherent for example in his post-1967 desire to coexist with other Arab régimes and at the same time press for fundamental change in Egyptian and Arab society. Nor were they able to appreciate the travesty of a purported socialist policy for the benefit of the people amidst a crushing administrative tyranny and glaring disparities between the privileged few and destitute many.

286   *Part IV El Rayyes*

Notes

1. Fuad Mattar, *Bisarāha 'an Abd al-Nasir* (Beirut, 1975), p.164.
2. *Hadhihi al-thawra*, p.72.
3. Ibid., p.93.
4. Abdel Moneim Shumais, *Al-za'im al-thā'ir* (Cairo, n.d.), pp.45–6.
5. Quoted in ibid., p.62.
6. Abdel Qadir al-Bindari and Najib Ilyas Barsum, *Thawrat al-hurriyya* (Cairo, 1961), pp.14–22. See also Nasser's interview with *Akher Sāa*, regarding the details of the 1956 Suez War, Cairo, 5 December 1956.
7. Bindari and Barsum, *Thawrat al-hurriyya*, p.27.
8. Ahmad Hussein, *Al-ishtirakiyya allati nad'ū ilayha* (Cairo, 1951), p.9.
9. Ibid., p.15.
10. Ibid., p.26.
11. Ibid., pp.18–19.
12. Ibid., pp.21–3.

CHAPTER 16

The Coming of the Despot

No sooner does the youth discover daring in himself and
strength in his muscles than he rushes to molest the trusting
and assault the peaceful; he imposes himself as the *ftewwa* of
the quarter—Naguib Mahfuz, *Awlad haritna.*

Nasser emerged from the shadow of anonymity in 1953–4. A certain
mythology about his youth and earlier career as a soldier and
revolutionary was hastily constructed.[1] That he was alienated from
his environment or even fellow-Egyptians there is little doubt. But
alienation alone is not an adequate basis of revolutionary behaviour.
This, in Nasser's case, is irrelevant anyway, since he was not a
revolutionary in the true, or accepted, sense of the term. He was,
however, a rebel.[2]

Nasser's rebelliousness must be viewed in relation to his background and life history before he came to power. In the light of that
one can argue that he tended to fuse personal with national
humiliation. The fusion was dramatically demonstrated in the Suez
affair, the break-up of the UAR in 1961 and the June 1967 war with
Israel. Heikal describes the nationalisation of the Suez Canal in
July 1956 as "Nasser's show".[3] As a *Sa'idi*, or Upper Egyptian, he
considered revenge against the exploiters of the country a sacred
duty. Once revenge had been taken, Nasser could relax and bask in
popularity and public adulation. Much of his presentation of
politics and its simplification for the masses in his public oratory
was as an act of revenge anyway.

The story of Suez is largely the story of the hatred between
Nasser, the Arab nationalist revolutionary, and Eden, the
sophisticated embodiment of a dying empire . . . In the end,
the Suez Affair became a personal business, a duel between
two men.[4]

Yet his act of revenge was nearly frustrated by the Anglo–French landing in Port Said. Fearing that his thunder as the miracle worker would be stolen, it is reported that he broke down and cried in Ismailiyya when the first British and French paratroopers dropped on Egyptian soil. It seems he never believed for a moment that the British would dare use force. The very fact that they did and that only American intervention prevented them from seeing their military operation through to its end rankled with Nasser. It detracted from his vaunted prescience and perceptiveness in the eyes of his followers, to whom he had promised plain sailing through the crisis.[5]

This fusion of personal and national humiliation, however, was not peculiar to Nasser. It was common among many of his fellow-countrymen, who revelled in his avenging them against past injustices perpetrated against them by their political masters at home and abroad. "He took away the power of the ruling classes. He nationalized their wealth. He made foreigners subject to Egyptian law. He gave Egypt back to the Egyptians."[6] His obsession with dignity and his fusion of personal with national humiliation at the hands of outsiders is reflected in a famous speech he delivered in Abnub, his family's native province, on 18 May 1954:

> I assure you that we have been getting ready, ever since the beginning of the revolution, to fight the great battle against colonialism and imperialism until we achieve the dignity the people feel is due to Egypt. At the same time, we are constructing in this fatherland a social revolution which aims at justice for its citizens, and we are trying to put an end to feudalism and the monopoly of capital.

Such fusion though was fraught with dangers, for it tended to promote distrust as the prevailing feeling in the conduct of affairs between individuals, subjects and rulers, and between states. It fostered instinct and intuition at the expense of a rational, or at least reasonable, assessment of events. It allowed Nasser, for example, to react prematurely and impulsively to unconfirmed, or unfounded, reports, as was the case in the miscalculation over the British reaction to the nationalisation of the Canal in 1956, or the case of American wheat shipments ten years later. More dangerously still, it rendered Nasser a victim of sycophantic aides who, in turn, had themselves made this fusion between personal and national humiliation, and thus often misled their leader about matters of national importance. The Abdel Hakim Amer conspiracy crisis and the subsequent trial of War Minister Shams Badran in 1967–8 supplied massive evidence of that practice. [7]

The dangers therefore of projecting personal humiliation on to the national and international levels, and those lurking in the motives of revenge were great indeed. In addition to distrust, secrecy and sycophancy, this projection also led to the practice of subversion abroad and the pervasiveness of fear and terror at home.

Clearly, though, Nasser's political "success" was unprecedented in the annals of recent Egyptian history. He appeared to elevate his vision of an Egypt locked in combat against the external forces of imperialism and Zionism, and the internal forces of reaction and privilege to an ideology, a myth of national regeneration. The magic of his will, sacrifice and single-mindedness was expressed in the kind of idiom the masses understood, and therefore they supported him. But it was not enough to bring everyone in line; The Citadel, Abu Zaabal, Huckstep Camp and Tura prison were therefore necessary centres of repression, so that the eventual assent of their inmates, if and when released, was from fear. The only choice open to these errant unfortunates was one of acclamation—like the rest of the crowds—or brutal repression. This in fact is the message of Naguib Mahfuz's short novel, *al-Karnak*. [8]

The romanticism of the Wafd at the end of the First World War excited the Egyptian masses with the prospect of national independence, and the facile equation of independence with democracy. The unpopular, elitist strong man, Ismail Sidqi, in 1930–3, desperately tried to impress upon the Egyptians the vital link between economic endeavour and political democracy. But he failed to excite the interest of the masses: he only provoked their anger and antagonism. Nasser, twenty years later, won them unquestioningly to his new "theology of justice" with his promise of political, economic and social democracy.

These portrayals suggest a link between Nasser's personal alienation and crisis on one hand and his perception of national problems on the other. His interest in history, for instance, was compensatory; he was attracted by powerful historical figures and grandiose schemes and projects. Heikal, as well as other Egyptian writers, reported Nasser's intense interest in the history of the unification of Germany under Bismarck, and his fascination with the Scarlet Pimpernel type of underground activity. [9]

Like Ahmad Hussein of Young Egypt before him, Nasser was able to communicate with the masses on a level of common distress, desperation and despondency. The hopelessness he shared with the *baladi* (lower-class native) was part of his charisma; obsessive, vengeful, passionate, vulgar. His rhetoric over crises like Suez and the Six Day War was riddled with disdain for reality, suggesting to his critics that he suffered from delusions of grandeur.

He pushed Egypt ahead, but soon let his fantasy take over, leading to the disaster of 5 June 1967 . . . From a *zaim* he turned into a prophet whom no one could criticize. He was all in one. In him were embodied all the national gains of Egypt ever since the country had a recorded history. Suez was the turning point. It led him to believe that revolutionary Egypt vanquished Imperialism and that had it not been for Nasser this would not have happened. Victory was his victory, protected by Providence. Everyone forgot Egypt was not victorious in 1956![10]

His world of fantasy was further expanded by the sycophantic obeisance of his entourage, consisting of courtiers and hatchet men. It marked the beginning of the Nasser cult: "His mother is the Nation, his father is History. He is the spirit of the Nation, hero of Arabism. He is vision, mind and wisdom. The man possesses extraordinary powers in confronting events and dealing with them."[11]

One Free Officer, a member of more than one government during the Nasser régime, reminisced;

The turning point was 1956. Many were opposed to the nationalization of the Canal. He insisted and won. After that, he considered himself and was viewed by the people as a miracle worker; no one could argue or dared disagree with him. He thought he was invincible. In 1959, for instance, despite the objections of his colleagues, he insisted on making an anti-Kassem speech in Deir al-Zor (Syria), saying that his direct appeal to the masses would automatically cause a revolution [in Iraq] . . . He never wanted anything or anyone to come between him and the masses. To this extent the ASU, for example, was never intended by Nasser to be a party. Furthermore, he would often by-pass his colleagues and ministers to get directly to the undersecretaries, heads of sections, even

lesser civil servants. This way he collected information he could
use against his colleagues. No one could prevail upon him,
for he pitted one against the other, spread his tentacles everywhere, used little paper, and dealt with various and sundry
confidentially, conspiratorially and face to face.[12]

The prominent writer, Tawfiq al-Hakim, described the relationship
between Nasser and the Egyptians as that of one who "had become
the idol, the worshipped of the people", and

> heaps of humanity without a mind or thought of their own,
> without an independent voice emanating from their gatherings.
> They became a collection of waving arms and applauding
> hands, and cheering mouths. And the Chief in his dominating
> presence, towering over them from his podium, spoke alone
> for long hours, interrupted only by the hysterical cries: "Nasser,
> Nasser, Nasser" . . . making it impossible to believe that any-
> one present could understand what was being said amidst that
> din. The larynx became the mind, but that did not disconcert
> the Chief. Rather a smile of approval was always traced on his
> lips.[13]

Then after the catastrophic defeat of June 1967, he projected himself
as the frail, erring human leader. How much could one man do,
surrounded as he was by the "centres of power,"[14] and cliques of
sycophantic advisers who prevented him from fulfilling his honest,
worthy intentions?

In the foreword to his book, Heikal asserted,

> it was the passion that he aroused among Arabs which led to
> his most important achievement; the linking of Egypt to the
> rest of the Arab world and the linking of the Arabs as an entity
> to the ideas and values prevailing in the world today.[15]

Needless to say, this linking of Egypt to the rest of the Arabs and
to the prevailing values of the world today had been going on for
some time before Nasser appeared on the scene, in fact as far back
as 1924.[16] Rather, as Heikal goes on to intimate, it was the furious
passion with which he projected Arab revenge on their enemies
which made Nasser a symbol of Arab aspirations and unfulfilled
hopes. The arms deal with the Soviet Union, Suez, opposition to

the Baghdad Pact, the union with Syria and other similar acts of defiance constituted the heady stuff for the miserable and deprived of Egypt and the Arab world.

All the same, this kind of passion-stirring charisma gave Nasser a translucent authority and a semi-divine sanction to his political perceptions and style. Building on the fears of the masses as well as their impractical salvationist expectations, he managed to neutralise even those few Egyptians who believed in some freedom or civil liberty under the rule of law. The story of the intellectuals, university teachers, writers and the press after 1956 at least suggests that these were willing to forgo and sacrifice the freedom of their conscience— some among them perhaps from a genuine conviction in the leader's abilities—by deferring all political judgement and decision to the *Rayyes*, the Chief. The widespread traditional political apathy and quietism of the masses was now extended and strengthened by the political conformism of the élite. [17]

From the way Nasser governed Egypt and the pattern of his relations with his associates and subordinates already described, it is plausible to conclude that he saw most problems in terms of conspiracy and intrigue. Therefore, he had to depend for his juggling and acrobatics on his instinct and intuition, and all this in order to weaken the position of others and strengthen his own. "When Nasser was dealing with any man," Heikal wrote, "he used to gather a collection of photos of him and study them, trying to assess his character . . ."[18] Dependence on instinct and intuition, coupled with suspicion and distrust, was also always shrouded in secrecy. If his personal feeling of humiliation was fused with the humiliation of the nation, his desire for revenge was equated with the act of liberating Egypt.

> The greatest impact on Nasser's personality and behaviour was his belief that Egypt cannot be delivered from her difficulties and cured of her ills except at his hands: that there can be no advance toward affluence or other goals unless he planned for it himself: that there can be no international role for the Middle East region unless all the Arab states adopted his programmes. He thus confined and assigned the execution of his plans to closed, secret agencies that were his instruments. He would not depend on or trust any others.[19]

Between 1957 and 1967 Nasser's position was unchallenged. His tremendous excess nervous energy handled all problems of state, even to the minutest detail. His great egoism and will guided all. None could oppose him. Anyone who dared or wished to do so had to live outside the pale, incarcerated or in exile; Abdel Moneim, Abdel Rauf, Rashad Mehanna, Muhammad Naguib, Khalid Mohieddin and, after 1964, Kamal el Din Hussein, Hasan Ibrahim and Abdel Latif Boghdadi among the more prominent ones. There were numerous others among the "lesser breed". He became in 1956 an historical figure whose egoism and will converged with the desires, fears and hopes of the nation. By a combination of demagogic genius and gifted political tactics he rendered his person supreme.

His seismic confrontation with the world in 1956 and 1967 reflected a furious will to power, a despotic tendency, an explosive craving and determination to prove himself. By then, his passion for histrionics ("Let them drink from the Nile") in 1956, or "If Israel wishes war, we say to her, 'Welcome, we are ready for you' " in May 1967), the massive effects of staged politics—Alexandria in October 1954 and July 1956, Port Said in December 1957, Republic Square, Cairo, in October 1961, national television and the mob in the streets in June 1967—were in full view.[20]

In times of disorientation, spiritual chaos and material deprivation, Nasser promised the salvation people craved. The few moderates among them had, or were willing, to bend the dictates of their conscience for the promised tomorrow, an abstract ideal of power and dignity. It was not all that difficult to do since a tradition of civil liberty which values the toleration of opposition as well as moral opposition to tyranny was lacking. At least the kind of experience with institutions that could have fostered it in the period from 1923 to 1952 was short-lived, confined to a relatively small section of the population, and dependent on a subordinate relationship with a foreign power.

Thus even for those few who had begun to escape the tradition of political quietism and shackles of old, they were, after 1952, forced back into them. The measure of legality that had been promoted over the preceding seventy years was discarded in favour of a despotism in which the word of the *Rayyes*, as the keeper of the nation's conscience, became law. One Egyptian chillingly described the erosion of legality and the undermining of the judicial process once the Chief's will replaced the law;

Nasser wanted me to trust and depend on him: I preferred to trust in the law . . . Ministers as a rule were dismissed: they

never resigned . . . From the very beginning I realized Nasser
could never forgive anyone who ignored his warnings or wishes
for he became used to their being taken as sacrosanct orders
. . . Nasser's control over the Security and Intelligence services
was complete; all the crimes or excesses committed by these
services were with his knowledge and approval, and not as he
tried to suggest that their conduct was contrary to his wishes.[21]

Later, as the leader of the Free Officer conspiracy, he came to
appreciate the utility of the Marxists' expertise in clandestine
organisation and political propaganda. In short, he managed by
1952 to forge links and "friendships" with diverse groups and
individuals of diametrically opposed political views, provided they
all worked for the destruction of the old régime. Yet his attitude
toward all of these was instrumental and tentative. From his
journalist "friends", like Abul Fath, Mustafa Amin and Ihsan Abdel
Quddus, he learned about the importance of propaganda and
determined, once in power, to bring all the media and the press
under state (i.e. his own) control, and harness them into his service.

Little wonder then that after his accession to power Nasser
preferred the duplication of functions in the agencies of the state,
and a "dualism of opposites" in running its affairs. Thus he created
multiple, overlapping intelligence services in order to keep members
of the RCC and later Cabinet Ministers and high government
officials under surveillance. He planted his own men, officers loyal
to his own person, in the offices of his Free Officer colleagues. These
kept him informed about their utterances and actions. He appointed
known rivals to the same duties and the execution of similar tasks.
He even pitted them against each other within the same agencies of
state. He controlled his diplomats abroad in more or less the same
way. He used Salah Salem against Khalid Mohieddin; to the former
he gave a morning newspaper, *al-Shaab*, to publish, to the latter an
evening one, *al-Masa'*. If the Sinai war of 1956 was a disaster for
the Egyptian army, members of his presidential and private office
spread abroad the idea that the head of the armed forces, Field
Marshal Abdel Hakim Amer, was responsible for it.[22] He even
used his special relationship with the people to intimidate his one
genuine constituency, the armed forces. In short, soon after 1952
and especially after mid-1954, Nasser treated his erstwhile officer
comrades as subordinates, and demanded total obedience—indeed,
subservience—from them.

Manifestations of this dualism were his occasional outbursts against a mindless, inefficient, lazy bureaucracy which ground the lives of the little people. In his oratorical harangues in popular rallies or television he would present this particular state structure as an albatross around his neck; if he could only reform, change, vitalise it . . . Therefore, he allowed extensive attacks on the sins of this bureaucracy in the press. Equally, he ridiculed to the people the hifalutin' abstract theories of the eggheads, whether in connection with the creation of a state political organisation such as the ASU, or the adumbration of an *ism*. Poised alertly and ever vigilant against these delaying, detracting encumbrances stood himself, the Leader, the Chief, the only authentic defender of the rights of the people against all constraints, including the law. He was the source of all national unity and inspiration for political advance. He did not therefore need a system, or institutions. On the contrary, he kept his government and administration in a state of flux, using it as a political weapon at his convenience. His associates, lieutenants, assistants and henchmen were all the creatures of his will.

Having been accepted first by the masses and then gradually by most of the élite as the keeper of the nation's conscience, institutional structures, legal rules and other regulative devices of the state and politics became, for Nasser, superfluous. Only he was sovereign. Thus the moment elements in the army would get restless over some aspect or other of his policy, he would appeal directly to his massive constituency in the streets. Or if diverse elements of the élite would try to exploit his attempts at creating a state political organisation (the ASU in 1962) in the hope of obtaining a measure of political participation, he would step in to veto their views and frustrate their plans on the grounds that he did not believe in political parties, which anyway only lead back to the old factionalism and national disunity.[23] He would reject notions of class struggle as alien and therefore disruptive of national solidarity. On the pretext of possible domestic strife being fomented by these "hare-brained intellectuals", bureaucrats and "godless ideologues," he would signal a wave of state repression whatever the price; e.g. in 1954, 1959–61, 1965 against the Ikhwan primarily, and 1967–8.

Nasser's capacity for dissimulation acquired greater scope in the miasma of competing state agencies he created. The complexity, terrifying power and corruption of these agencies were exposed only a year or two after his death, suggesting a narrow concern by Nasser with the seizure and retention of power that overrode all other considerations, including those of constructing a "new state and society".[24] "Power", Machiavelli wrote, "is not maintained with the same following that has helped to win it."

All of this further suggests that Nasser's relationships with others were always tentative, guided by his power needs and conditional upon his ability to dominate them. In this way, he was able to create a court, a retinue of mutually distrustful retainers and sycophants, most of whom lacked his passion for power. These arrangements moreover guaranteed his undisputed leadership. With only subordinates around him and no political groups to speak of between him and the unorganised masses, Nasser towered over everyone like a giant. Inevitably he alone could identify the country's enemies, absorb its various shocks and resentments, and provide the necessary transformation—or gyrations. With a subservient *gihaz*, or governing apparatus, Nasser balanced and dominated a near-anarchic network of competing and interlocking state organisations. Permanently improvising, he produced a Behemoth whose sense and consistency depended on his will. As one Egyptian put it,

> In a meeting a month before the declaration of the Republic [in 1953], Nasser was opposed to such a step . . . He was against politicians and parties, yet he plagiarized their ideas and programmes . . . He had no faith in the people . . . only in a first class governing apparatus.[25]

Nasser's need to dominate produced a perfect rapport, almost a pathological link, with the masses. In order to manipulate this vast, amorphous constituency he had to sway them by speech, and in order to do that he had, in turn, to address them frequently, either on radio and television or by staging huge rallies such as the annual ones in Port Said after 1956 or in the vast Republic Square in front of old Abdin Palace in Cairo. The repeated hypnotic incantation of "imperialism" and "agents of imperialism," "reactionaries," "revenge," "dignity and self-respect," "Zionism" and "Arabism" electrified the crowds which, galvanised by their charismatic leader, forgot their own misery. Perforce the speeches were long, the applause prolonged and the mass acclaim hysterical. In fact, in Syria in the winter and early spring of 1959, it was downright dangerous to life and limb to be caught in one of those rallies during Nasser's tour of the country—the UAR's Northern Region at that time.[26]

Even though Nasser's audiences may have lacked political conviction and, in fact, were deprived of any participation in the leader's choice of policies or their implementation, he nevertheless responded to their psychological need and euphoric feeling of being part of some momentous, dramatic time in history. Whatever and whomever the *Rayyes* scorned, derided or belittled, they did too, for he was catapulting them towards a new era, a new life. Though an unknown and ill-defined new epoch, it was the excitement of newness that overwhelmed the masses like a release from the burdens of the present—in fact, a substitute reality.

Not all Egyptians, incidentally, were eager or willing to submit readily to Nasser's leadership, especially when he demanded unquestioning loyalty and blind obedience. Evidence of this is not only the struggle for power within the Free Officer junta itself between 1952 and 1954, but also the intermittent yet persistent difficulties of the régime with a recalcitrant Muslim Brotherhood and many of the Marxists. Had it been otherwise, the pulverisation of political life as it existed before 1952 and the atomisation of society would not have been necessary. Nor would periodic purges of the officer corps have been a permanent feature of the régime. Somehow Nasser had to impose his undisputed hegemony over the country. Naguib Mahfuz, in his novel *al-Karnak*, referred to earlier, emphasises the impact of the questioning, doubting Egyptian's brush with Nasser's dreaded Mukhabarat, or intelligence and security services. It was one of such fear as to "cure" the Egyptian returning from interrogation or imprisonment of any notions of dissidence, and even independent thought or judgement. It paralysed him into a willing, or at least dissembling, minion.

It is for these and other reasons that Nasserism in Egypt at least had a limited political connotation. It referred to a phenomenon of personal charismatic leadership, not to a movement or ideology. Some Egyptians have described it as "modern pharaonism". All the public debates, writing and other discussions of a peculiarly Nasserite Arab socialist ideology in the decade 1960–70 must be seen as attempts by servants of the state—intellectuals and religious teachers —to come to terms with this overwhelming, dominating personality that was Nasser. After all, the Egyptian people, the masses, looked up to the *Rayyes*, the Chief, not to any political, social or economic programme with an ideological content or orientation. They followed Nasser's tone and style, not any specific or concrete ideas in the policies he put forward. The image they created and which he promoted was one of the Chief immovably on the side of the people against all comers—intellectuals, foreigners, bureaucrats, money-grabbers and others. He struggled continuously, selflessly and bravely, literally unto death, against the people's enemies at home and abroad. This perception of him was emotionally far more relevant to their miserable lives and inarticulate fears than any regulated political system. His idiom was their idiom, one of struggle, insecurity and uncertainty. The relationship was so personal, buttressed by the myth of the *Rayyes*, that it could not possibly have given rise to new political forms.

A recent monograph by a competent student of the Arab world argues that "Nasserism's leading and most damaging shortcoming" was "its lack of clarity and its perpetual vacillations."[27] In other words, a mixture of radical nationalist notions and socialism in terms of certain aspirations may conjure up images of what could be but without clarity and a systematic formulation of ideas these do not amount to an ideology. Only outside Egypt did Nasserism acquire the denotation of an Arab attitude to the world, and served as a convenient index for classifying Arab régimes and/or policies.[28]

Nasserism for Egypt meant an authoritarian "leader state" with an administrative apparatus for the execution of decisions which, in the absence of a clear ideology or other objective criteria, were taken by the *Rayyes*: in short, a despotism on the Nile. The organisation of the state, its policy and future were determined by his will. In such a state, with this type of ruler, the coalescence of an ideology could not be permitted: it always had to be postponed, even after the adoption of Nasser's National Charter in 1962. Commitment to an ideology would have cramped the Chief's style and limited his freedom of action—his arbitrariness.

This perhaps was an inevitable development after 1956 when Nasser had learnt how to manipulate, arouse and sway the people, either by his oratory or the dramatisation of "liberating acts"; the Stalingradisation of Port Said, the destruction of exploiting capitalists and feudalists, the defence of the revolution against reactionaries and Zionists. Thus he inspired confidence in the masses and mobilised their support. In this way, until 1967, Nasser remained close to the people. Yet paradoxically he was also distant from them, because he could not, would not, transform their rapport or sympathy with him into a vital or creative organised force. His rule remained wholly personal in character. He did not really create any new political forms, only a peculiar idiom, reminiscent incidentally of the Ahmad Hussein type of radicalism of the 1930s. In the meantime, his personal rule indirectly encouraged widespread corruption among his lieutenants.

Propaganda and his own personal exercise of power through a fluid though harsh administrative machine in the face of institutional chaos were more important, because they could be controlled, than any regularised or permanent system. In contrast to the pre-1952 period, however, the requirements of Nasser's personal rule did provide a new set of conditions for social mobility that could conceivably lead to changes in the future. So long as he lived any change had to be in favour of his power, not necessarily to the advantage of the community he appeared to have united. Thus he began his career in power with a dependence on the army, and ended it with a dependence on his secret state security organisation.

Notes

1. For example, *al-Musawwar*, Special Number, Cairo, August 1957; Abd al-Baqi Surur, *Jamal Abd al-Nasir, rajul ghayyra al-tarikh* (*Nasser, a man who changed history*) (Cairo, 1975); Saniyya Qara'a, *Haris al-majd, Jamal Abd al-Nasir* (*The guardian of glory, Nasser*) (Cairo, 1959); Abdel Qadir al-Bindari and Najib Ilyas Barsum, *Thawrat al-hurriyya* (Cairo, 1961); Abdel Moneim Shumais, *Al-za'im al-thā'ir* (Cairo, n.d.); Anwar al-Jundi, *Hādha huwa Jamal* (*This is Gamal*) (Beirut, 1960); Anwar al-Sadat, *Hāda 'ammak Jamal* (Cairo, 1975); Muhammad Rabī', *Shakhsiyyat Abd al-Nasir* (*The personality of Nasser*) (Cairo, 1966); Sulayman Mazhar, *'Imlāq min Bani Murr* (*A personality from Beni Murr*) (Cairo, 1963); and others. The Special Memorial Number, "Gamal Abd al-Nasir", published by *al-Hilal*, Cairo, November 1970 is in the same vein.
2. Muhammad Heikel commented on Nasser's rebelliousness as follows: "He was always a rebel, a characteristic which almost certainly stemmed from his reaction to the stern traditional views of his father who, as a post office clerk in Upper Egypt [*sic*], was a minor member of the Egyptian bureaucracy." When his mother died and his father remarried, "his world had fallen apart. From that moment on he was a confirmed rebel." *Nasser: The Cairo Documents* (London, New English Library, 1972), p.19.
3. Ibid., pp.115, 136.
4. Ibid., pp.115, 116.
5. Kamal al-Din Hussein, series of articles entitled "The Story of the 1952 rebels", *Rose el-Youssef*, Cairo, December 1975 – January 1976.
6. Heikal, *The Cairo Documents*, Foreword, p.viii.
7. See the transcripts of trial proceedings in *al-Ahram* and *al-Nahar*, February – September 1968, cited above.
8. Beirut, 1973.
9. Heikal, *The Cairo Documents*, p.21.
10. Hussein Dhu'l-Fiqar Sabri in *Rose el-Youssef*, 18 July 1975.
11. Muhammad Rabī', *Shakhsiyyat Abd al-Nasir*, pp.10–11.
12. Transcript of interview with Kamal el-Din Rifaat, London, 1972.
13. Tawfiq al-Hakim, *'Awdat al-wa'i* (Beirut, 1974).

14. A phrase common just before and after the Six Day War in the press and in Nasser's speeches, especially that of 30 March 1968, referring to the cliques of privilege in the new political élite.

15. Al-Hakim, *'Awdat al wa'i*, p.ix.

16. See Anis Sāyigh, *Al-fikra al-'arabiyya fi misr* (*The Arab idea in Egypt*) (Beirut, 1959); Ahmad Hussein, *Nisf qarn maa al-'uruba wa qadiyyat filastin* (Beirut, 1971); Sylvia G. Haim, *Arab Nationalism, an anthology* (Berkeley and London, 1962, 1976); and P. J. Vatikiotis, "kawmiyya", *Encyclopedia of Islam*, 2nd ed.

17. See P. J. Vatikiotis, "Al-muthaqqaf al-'arabi wa al-mujtama' al-hadith", *Hiwar*, Beirut, Vol.1, No.4, May 1963, pp.41–51; Louis Awad, *Al-hurriyya wa naqd al-hurriyya* (*Freedom and its critics*) (Cairo, 1971), and *Al-jāmi'a wa al-mujtama' al-jadid* (*The university and the new society*) (Cairo, n.d.) (1965?).

18. Heikal, *The Cairo Documents*, p.225.

19. Hussein Dhul-Fiqar Sabri, *Rose el-Youssef*, 18 July 1975.

20. See Chapter 15.

21. Ahmad Hussein, *Kayfa 'araftu Abdel Nasser was 'ishtu ayyāma hukmihi* (Beirut, 1973), pp.60, 94, 91 and 82.

22. Allusions to this practice are to be found in Sami Gohar, *Al-sāmitun yataallamūn* (Cairo, 1975) and Nāsir al-Din al-Nashāshibi, *Al-hibr aswad . . . aswad* (Paris, 1976). There is also evidence of precedents for the use of this tactic by Nasser, as in the instance of the publications by the Military Police in March–November 1954 designed to undermine the then President Naguib. Nasser's use of the régime's publishing organisation, *Dar al-Tahrir*, and its newspaper *al-Gumhuriyya* for similar purposes is reported too. See Ahmad Hamrush, "Shuhud yulio", *Rose el-Youssef*, Cairo, April 1977.

23. See *al-Tali'a*, Cairo, 1965. See also charges of Nasser's interference in the deliberations of the National Assembly already cited in Gohar, *Al-sāmitūn yatakallamūn*.

24. This impression is supported by the prolific effusion of "revelations" and "confessions" by key officials of Nasser's régime, such as those to be found in Hamrush, "Shuhud yulio".

25. Ahmad Hussein, *Kayfa 'araftu*, pp.30–5.

26. See *Khutab al-ra'is Jamal 'Abd al- Nasir fi'l-'id al-awwal lil-jumhuriyya al-arabiyya al-muttahida* (*The speeches of President Nasser on the first anniversary of the UAR*), Cairo (Kutub siyasiyya), No.99, Part II, March 1959.

27. Nissim Rejwan, *Nasserist ideology, its exponents and critics* (Jerusalem, 1974), p.181.

28. See Malcolm Kerr, *The Arab Cold War*, 3rd ed. (London, 1973), and "The Political Outlook in the local arena" in Abraham S. Becker, Bent Hansen and Malcolm Kerr, *The Economics and Politics of the Middle East* (New York, London and Amsterdam, 1975), pp.41–73.

PART V

The Personality of Nasser and his Impact on Egypt

CHAPTER 17

Nasser in the Mirror

Abdel Nasser is no more than a transient phenomenon that will run its course and leave . . . The operation is not one of a personality or concerned with me personally.—Nasser addressing a Congress of Arab lawyers at Kubba Palace on 8 February 1967.

Nasser's behaviour and personality were so contradictory at times that it is difficult to draw a composite portrait from the information available. His behaviour as a conspirator and ruler we have attempted to describe from the record of his rule, his actual policies and utterances. We also considered the little of his biography that we know in the context of the economic, social and political forces which influenced his generation. We must now turn to an examination of the fragments of comment by people who were close to him, worked with or for him, or suffered under him. In this way we may be able to approximate a composite picture of the man, and to finally hazard an assessment of his impact.

Physical Health

An important issue in the last ten years of Nasser's life was his health. It started to deteriorate in the early sixties and became progressively worse during the decade. The first rumours of his illness circulated in 1961 after the break-up of the UAR. It was not, however, until six to seven years later that most people learned of its nature and gravity. There were of course those few who knew of Nasser's diabetic condition not too long after the Suez war. Referring to Nasser's last exhausting meeting with Arab heads of state in Cairo in September 1970, when he brought about a temporary reconciliation between King Hussein of Jordan and Yasser Arafat, chairman of the Palestine Liberation Organization,

303

Muhammad Hasanein Heikal wrote, "He [Nasser] was already a sick man. He had suffered with diabetes since 1958 and, as a result of the disease, had developed an extremely painful arteriosclerosis condition in the upper legs."[1] Some Egyptian physicians reported that the type of diabetes finally diagnosed in the sixties (1964) by a professor of the Cairo University Medical Faculty was "bronze" diabetes. Whatever the nature of his condition may have been Nasser was in considerable pain throughout the sixties. In the summer of 1968 he underwent a course of hydrotherapy lasting several weeks in the Soviet Union to relieve the pain in his upper legs caused by arteriosclerosis. It is probable that he underwent similar treatment three years before that, in 1965. It is also likely he suffered his first, though mild, heart attack at that time. The attack he suffered in September 1969 was more serious, forcing him to take a complete rest from his office and duties for six weeks. It is true, as Heikal reports,[2] that even his family were not told about his true condition. His eldest son, Khalid, told this writer that the family learned about the seriousness of his father's condition only after engineers had installed a lift in their home at Manshiet el-Bakri, and when they connected it with the observation that his father had, two years earlier, stopped playing tennis with Salah Dasuqi[3] and other friends in the private court at the back of the house. Khalid Nasser, incidentally, also reported that his father dropped tennis altogether after the June 1967 war. Whether this was due to the burdens of office and pressure of work, to illness or both he was not certain. Anwar Sadat is reported to have said in October 1971 that Nasser in November 1967 "was quite ill. He suffered great pain and could hardly move his legs, which were semi-paralyzed. Nevertheless, he was at the peak of his mental clarity."[4] It appears too that for some years before that the family were not altogether satisfied with Nasser's old private physician, Dr El Sawi Habib's predecessor. Khalid recalls that whenever they broached the subject with his father he was always reluctant to change doctors, primarily because he did not wish to offend his old physician.

In any case, by 1965, Nasser's condition was serious enough for the government to seek the advice of specialists from the Soviet Union and the United Kingdom. Heikal mentions a team of experts headed by Dr Yevgeni Shazoff, then Soviet Deputy Health Minister and a prominent heart specialist. Mr Howard Hanley, a Harley Street urologist, was also consulted, since kidney trouble is not an uncommon complication in diabetics.

Medical opinion, however, is undecided and divided over the question of the effects of diabetes and its complications on the patient's mental faculties and emotional stability. One opinion is that the "consequences of such an illness in a statesman could be serious".[5] If diabetes is not properly controlled, "pain in the legs or discomfort in walking could occur with the arterial changes or the neuritis, which, though fortunately rare, may be serious accompaniments of diabetes."[6] It is argued by some that undue exertion, missing of meals, inability to keep to a rigorous diet leads to a more frequent condition of hypoglycaemia—low level of sugar in the blood. Some of its symptoms are fatigue, sleepiness and, in extreme cases, over-excitement and irrational behaviour due to mental impairment.

However, not only is it difficult to decide if any incapacity is linked to the illness, but also to assess the degree of that incapacity. As for Buerger's disease, for which Nasser was treated in the Soviet Union, it is a rare disorder, involving the absorption of iron into the liver, and causing complications in that organ. Patients are almost all male and tobacco smokers. The link of the disease to smoking is, some contend, very close. Nasser was a very heavy smoker, using at one point up to sixty cigarettes a day.

As for Nasser's two known heart attacks in 1969 and 1970, and the suspected one in 1965,[7] medical opinion has emphasised the association between great mental stress or exertion and coronary heart disease. Endocrinologists, cardiologists and other specialists, though, find no irrefutable scientific proof of a link between diabetes and its complications on one hand and mental incapacity or emotional disturbance on the other.

The limited information about Nasser's medical history that is readily available suggests he was physically a sick man by 1964 at the latest, and in considerable, constant pain after that. Regardless of the divided medical opinion over the connection between physical illness and mental health, especially in rulers, Nasser's physical condition is an important consideration for the study of his career. It is not invoked in order to condone or condemn his actions, or to detract from any of his accomplishments. Rather it is simply relevant. It is especially relevant in times and cultural settings where personal rule and personalised power—in some cases unlimited and unaccountable—are common phenomena. Persistent and painful illness takes its toll of any man, and sometimes reinforces whatever fears, predilections, prejudices, even fantasies he may have about

the world around him. Obsessions are not necessarily the manifestation of a psychotic condition. They may, however, reflect neurotic
tendencies.

Personality

An assessment of Nasser's personality is made more difficult by the
strength of one of its most particular traits. He was a master of
dissimulation and self-control, and very secretive. We can only
sketch the outline of the personality by reporting what his colleagues
and associates thought of him. Much of this material is contradictory, which itself reinforces the notion of dissimulation, but
much of it is revealing, allowing us the occasional glimpse of the real
character of Nasser.

Hussein Dhu'l Fiqar Sabri described Nasser's personality as
"strong and solitary; it does not interact, it reacts: it does not give
and take, it blends." Sabri went on to argue that Nasser put the
imprint of his personality on everything. Thus in a country where
privacy is difficult, Nasser managed to plan a military *coup* over a
period of two to three years in complete secrecy. To realise that is to
appreciate his bold, determined, patient and secretive personality.
As if in desperation, Hussein Sabri exclaimed, "What I know of
Nasser is of a personality that refused to be overwhelmed by others.
Hence he insisted on outmeeting and outpatiencing all, including
the notoriously dogged and rigid Left." [8]

Two other personal traits gave Nasser an advantage over his
colleagues. With every interlocutor he was able to affect a tone of
sincerity and strict confidentiality. When addressed about a
particular problem he maintained a poker face, giving the impression, though, that he approved of, or agreed with, whatever was
being said. "His behaviour was characteristic; when he spoke, he
uttered the best statements and sentiments possible. But when he
acted, he did exactly the opposite of what he said." [9]

It seems that until 1954–5, Nasser was a very good listener, and
a rare talker, loath to commit himself on anything. He watched
closely the weaknesses and incapacities of his officer colleagues. His
assessment of them was expressed graphically. Thus Anwar Sadat
was *al-bikbashi madbut* ("Colonel O.K."), Salah Salem was "Major
Balloon" who, when "pricked with a needle was found to be empty":
Hussein Shafei was "neither useful nor harmful and who, being
interested only in his moustache, hardly existed". He referred to
Zakariyya Mohieddin as *al-asfarawi*, "paleface". He derided Abdel

Latif Boghdadi's alleged fear during the clash with Naguib in February–March 1954, when he sought refuge with relatives. He equally scorned Zakariyya Mohieddin's retreat to his village, Kafr al-Sheikh, during those trying, critical times. He was amused by the story that Salah Salem trembled with fear in his car when driving over Kasr el Nil Bridge as the demonstrating mob screamed for the return of Naguib to power.

Ahmad Anwar, Commanding Officer of the Military Police in the early days of the Free Officer régime, who saw Nasser every morning and evening, noticed his "obsessive sensitivity and strong sense of dignity".[10] Another Free Officer, Amin Shakir, one-time Minister of Tourism, described Nasser's outstanding characteristic as "the strength of his nerves and his great ability to control them".[11] The obsessive sensitivity was also reflected in his dealings with other Arab rulers, especially Nuri el-Said of Iraq in the period 1954–6 over the Baghdad Pact, and King Faisal of Saudi Arabia over the Yemen. It seemed to prevent Nasser from considering compromise or co-operation for the sake of wider interests or issues. Instead it forced him into expensive and divisive policies. A touch of the irritability caused by his excessive sensitivity was illustrated in an episode in Damascus at the height of the first flush and euphoria of the union with Syria. Nasser was in the process of selecting the first UAR Cabinet. Shukri al-Quwwatli, the then Syrian President, objected to some of the Syrians who were being considered by Nasser for ministerial posts as being enemies of his National Bloc party. Nasser cut Quwwatli short by reminding him that now that he had been proclaimed the "first Arab citizen" he had no responsibility for the formation of the government, whereas he, Nasser, did. And, he added, that those who did not like the way he did things were perfectly free to leave the country. As for the opposition, he would gladly remind them of the people's courts and revolutionary tribunals the régime had used in Cairo in its early days to deal with the opposition in Egypt.[12]

A certain harshness and impatience were detected too in Nasser's dealings with interlocutors over major decisions. Thus, once he had made a decision, such as the nationalisation of the press in May 1960 ("I do not like what the newspapers write," he told the gathered editors and publishers), or the acceptance of the Rogers Plan in July 1970 over which one or two members of his government disagreed, he would brook no argument or dissent.[13]

Mixed with Nasser's professed seriousness of purpose was a

tendency towards triviality. One Arab journalist who went to see him early in 1957 after the Suez episode claims he asked Nasser, "What are your programmes now, Mr President?" Nasser shook with laughter, spread his open palm widely in the air and roared back: "By Allah, I don't know; am I a man of programmes?"[14]

The contradictions in Nasser's style and behaviour were extremely unnerving for many of his colleagues. Nasser in Cabinet meetings kept everyone on tenterhooks. Just before the meeting, as he greeted arriving Ministers, he would take one or another aside for a quick confidential word in his ear. Whoever the adversary or rival of that man was would be terrified. Then Nasser would open the meeting by soliciting the views of Ministers, or the submission of their respective ministerial recommendations. At the end, though, the Cabinet would go along with whatever he wanted or decided to do. The preliminary deliberations were an exercise of form; they were superfluous.

This style of behaviour in public implied that Nasser had very little time for the sensibilities or indeed the opinions of most of his colleagues. Some of his severest critics had felt this for a long time. Kamal el-Din Hussein, Hasan Ibrahim and Abdel Latif Boghdadi claim, "Nasser, even before the revolution, always confronted us with actions and decisions he took by himself without consultation." One such instance they recall was Nasser's plan to assassinate General Hussein Sirri Amer on 9 January 1952, a plan that was unsuccessfully implemented by himself, Kamal Rifaat and Hasan al-Tuhami. He had not consulted his colleagues on the Executive Committee of the Free Officers beforehand. Kamal Rifaat and Tuhami were members of the Free Officer movement in the army, but not members of the Executive. These same critics further claim that the divisions within the RCC began after the power crisis of March 1954. "Nasser inaugurated his rule as prime minister", they reminisced later, "by not convening the RCC regularly." When he asked for the RCC's dissolution after the promulgation of the 1956 constitution, he justified the move to his colleagues with his complaint that the RCC stood as an obstacle between him and the implementation of the various projects he had in mind for the benefit of the nation.[15]

Dr Abdel Wahab al-Burullusi, one-time Minister of Public Health (1968), on the other hand, wrote in September 1975,

Abdel Nasser was not a tyrant as some believe. He was considerate, polite, frank and decisive. He sought to understand what was being presented to him before he made a decision. If he were questioned about that particular decision he would think again, and try to convince the critic of his point of view, or even abandon his own altogether.[16]

Burullusi suggested that many Cabinet Ministers preferred ready agreement with Nasser to discussion or argument. He also denied that Nasser did not delegate. On the whole, he felt Nasser was a good listener. But he also alluded to the fact that Ministers were usually dismissed; they did not resign. More significant is Burullusi's general statement to the effect that if Ministers wanted anything done they had to go directly to Nasser. Nasser himself, according to Burullusi, always urged his Ministers, "I pray you to get in touch with me directly at any time for any important matter."[17]

Of course, Burullusi was not one of the Free Officers or RCC associates of Nasser. He was a medical doctor, a civilian. To this extent he had no axe to grind, and his testimony ought to be given weighty consideration. Hassein Dhu'l Fiqar Sabri, who claimed later that Nasser considered any criticism of specific cases of abuse in public institutions as "slanderous and conspiratorial", was the brother of Ali Sabri. Similarly, Nasser's three principal critics, Hussein, Ibrahim and Boghdadi, had, as original members of the Free Officer Executive and the RCC, possibly other aspirations. Their testimony therefore must be considered with some caution. Their overall assessment, however, to the effect that "the late Gamal Abdel Nasser loved being chief, and preferred to exercise sole personal rule," is accurate on two counts. First, it is an assessment shared by many others, both within the régime's governing élite, and by serious analysts outside it; second, it is an assessment borne out by Nasser's overt behaviour in power, his political style, and even his policies.

Fathi Radwan, another civilian, but, unlike Burullusi, a man who had been active in Egyptian radical nationalist politics since 1930, agrees with Nasser's critics. In the early days of the régime he had served as Minister of Communications; after 1956, Nasser appointed him Minister of National Guidance. He reports Nasser's impatience and irritability with Cabinet Ministers who would oppose certain projects initiated by the President's parallel state structure (his private office, the Liberation Rally or the National Union). He occasionally walked out of a Cabinet meeting in anger.[18]

Most informants agree that Nasser was not corrupt in the common sense of the term: he did not acquire the trappings of great wealth while in office. Recent polemicists assert Nasser received some $15 million from the Saudis. There is no way, at least for this writer, to establish conclusively if this story has any basis in fact. Nor do I think it is relevant. The more relevant observation in a régime that strikes one as Hobbes's "state of nature", in which the ruler's will is law, where no person is secure except at the pleasure of the ruler and life is turbulent and uncertain, is that the illicit receipt of funds from a variety of sources was widespread: so that even if Nasser received such funds, he was not the only recipient.

Some of Nasser's reported personal habits remind one of those of so many other autocrats. To be sure, in his youth and struggling days as an Egyptian army officer, Nasser was deprived of certain petty possessions. For instance, he liked ties, and owned about 250 of these, most of them gifts. He was also fond of cameras and cine cameras. Then, Egyptian men are partial to colognes and perfumes. Nasser was no exception: he owned scores of bottles. [19]

Clearly, though, Nasser was opposed to—in fact, scorned— luxury. He was no hedonist or *bon viveur*. His diet was simple; white native cheese, cucumber, tomatoes, rice and vegetables—a kind of *risotto*. He is not known to have given lavish parties in his home. No one has ever accused him of having purchased land, the favourite kind of property among rich and poor Egyptians alike, or other immovable property. His home in Manshiet el-Bakri was given as a residence to his widow and family after his death by a decision of the National Assembly and a Presidential decree. There was however some controversy in 1971 over the so-called "Fund for the Protection of the Revolution" deposited in Switzerland soon after the Free Officers came to power, which reputedly amounted to over 100 million dollars. [20]

It is fair to say that Nasser was not interested in money. Nor was he a collector of valuable possessions as, for example, art or jewellery. In fact, there is no indication that he was even interested in art or books. Newspapers were his staple reading, and the cinema his main form of entertainment. Heikal reported, and many Egyptians believed, that Nasser did not have any real enjoyment. The question is, was Nasser capable of enjoyment? Was the "viewing of three films consecutively in one evening" enjoyment or escapism? Incidentally, a gloomy seriousness in Nasser's earlier disposition is reported by the Commandant of the military academy in 1937–8, who wrote in 1957:

He was the most famous of the students in the class [1938]. He rarely smiled, but was balanced. He asked many questions, projected a strong personality, and was very conscious of his dignity. He was quickly promoted Squad Leader in the last five months of the course.[21]

To what extent, however, Nasser tolerated corruption among his lieutenants, relatives and governing apparatus is another matter. He must have been aware of the luxurious style of life adopted by several of his associates and members of his extended family. Most Egyptians have explained this as a reflection of Nasser's wish to have a hold over his subordinates, a form of blackmail which he could use as a pretext to dismiss them from office when it was in his interest to do so. One prominent instance was the case of Ali Sabri in 1969, who was accused of flouting customs regulations by importing luxury personal effects from the Soviet Union and elsewhere.[22] Basically, though, corruption among Nasser's courtiers and state officials flowed inevitably from the nature of his rule. He and his associates were not incidentally the first to introduce corruption in Egypt. The reason it became such a juicy topic of conversation and object of criticism was the fact that the Free Officers proclaimed repeatedly that they had grabbed power in 1952 in order to, among other things, cleanse Egypt of corruption.

More serious is the charge regarding Nasser's insistence on hegemony, his harsh treatment of colleagues or associates who disagreed with him, dared to resign their ministerial posts or refused to co-operate in some of his schemes. "He rejected the possibility of an alternative leadership to his own in Egypt or in the Arab Middle East," according to his critics Hussein, Ibrahim and Boghdadi.[23] He viewed Egypt's involvement in the Yemen after September 1962 as being crucial to the maintenance of his Arab leadership, especially after the break-up of the UAR. He even looked upon that involvement as a personal struggle between King Faisal of Saudi Arabia and himself.[24] Kamal el-Din Hussein suggests that Nasser's decision to act over the Yemen was primarily for the same personal reason:

In those days Abdel Nasser was concerned about his leadership. He told Gamal Salem, justifying his acceptance of the quick, precipitate union with Syria back in 1958, that it was the only way of covering up the regime's failure in dealing effectively with a million problems at home. 25

When Syria seceded from the union, Nasser blamed Field Marshal Abdel Hakim Amer for it. But only indirectly. He asked Amer to dismiss General Sidqi Mahmud of the air force, ostensibly for having failed to transport troops to Syria quickly enough. This caused the first serious rift between Nasser and his friend Amer. Also, in reorganising the government, Nasser formed a Presidential Council comprising all the old RCC members except for Khaled Mohieddin, Ali Sabri and Kamal Rifaat, as well as the civilians Nur al-Din Tarraf, Ahmad Abduh al-Shurabasi. The three critics assert that the new council, which was to be responsible for major policy in the country, was a way of demoting Amer and checking his rising influence in the armed forces. In fact, Amer opposed the formation of the council, and vehemently objected to the dismissal of his air force chief. But soon, the critics state, Nasser stopped convening the Presidential Council. It remained a timely and useful tactic in Nasser's manipulation of the rift between him and his friend Amer. 26

When Boghdadi submitted his resignation to Nasser on 16 March 1964, Nasser proceeded within a week to place his brother, Saad Boghdadi, under house arrest and sequestrate his assets. He also prevented Boghdadi's son-in-law from returning to the United Kingdom to complete his doctorate. When Kamal el-Din Hussein objected to Nasser's policy in the Yemen, his foreign policy *vis-à-vis* the Soviet Union in the mid-sixties, and his handling of the alleged Ikhwan conspiracy in the summer of 1965, Nasser had him arrested in October 1965.

Perhaps Nasser had evidence that his old associates like Hussein and Boghdadi were peripherally implicated in Ikhwan activities. There is no way of knowing if that was indeed the case. What is certain is the fact that they were never brought to trial before a military or other tribunal. Nor were charges of such involvement ever brought against them. Possibly their very disapproval and criticism of his policies were enough to constitute a threat in Nasser's mind. Thus on 25 March 1965 he announced yet another major reorganisation of the government. Its most prominent feature was the appointment of Amer as first Vice-President, Zakariyya Mohieddin, Hussein Shafei and Hasan Ibrahim as deputy Vice-Presidents. Sadat was president of the National Assembly. Nasser naturally considered his rule as standing for order against the known violent destructiveness of the Ikhwan. This view of his is in fact reflected in the exchange of letters between Kamal el-Din Hussein, from his relatively comfortable prison quarters near the Pyramids, and Field Marshal Amer.

Equally serious is the charge that Nasser lied to the Egyptians. It was not, for instance, until May 1967, that Egyptians learned for the first time that Israeli shipping had been using the Tiran Straits since 1956. But that is not uncommon practice among rulers, especially for domestic political purposes. What is both widely known and equally readily accepted is the fact that Nasser used terror as a political weapon against his unrepentant opponents on both the right and left of the Egyptian political spectrum. Acts of revenge, not terror, were mainly directed at more important critics and opponents within the establishment, including his erstwhile close officer associates and colleagues.[27]

Yet most Egyptians saw Nasser as one who

> signalled to the nation and it awoke; he signalled to the army and it moved; he signalled to the king and he departed; he berated Imperialism and it exited from the country, feudalism and it was smashed, political parties and they were dissolved.[28]

Or as another Arab commentator put it, his "merciless revenge on opponents and their victimization by his security apparatus" did not seem to "disfigure his public image or explode the myth [Nasserism]."[29] For many people, that is, Nasser still

> encompassed the nation, being endowed with an extraordinary power to face events and deal with them. The secret of his spirit consisted of faith, conviction, popular appeal, vision and wisdom. He thus fixed for this people a rendez-vous with destiny.[30]

Members of his immediate family at least knew him as a loyal husband and father, with simple lower-class Egyptian tastes, concerned with the future of the poor people: *el-nās el-ghalāba el-masākīn*, as he frequently put it, according to his eldest son. He lunched with them, if possible, daily between 2 and 3 p.m. at home. He quietly helped personally many supplicants, either from among his old officer colleagues or the common people. He was solicitous of the health and welfare of the families of his old RCC colleagues, especially those he had dismissed from office, and frequently telephoned to enquire about them. Even at the height of the crisis between himself and Abdel Hakim Amer in 1967, he urged his own family to continue their visits with Amer's family, suggesting that the break with his friend was not personal, but one for reasons of state.

All of this conjures up a picture of a gentle, reticent, unassuming family man, with little time for much diversion and a total dedication to the affairs of state. His occasional questioning by members of his family about particular events always elicited the response that he was anxious to improve the lot of the people. Nasser clearly did not discuss in any great length his political views or plans with his family. Nor did he have intimate friends during his eighteen years in power. His family even observed that whenever his father (their grandfather) would come to visit for any length of time, trouble was invariably instigated by his stepmother in Alexandria. This suggests that Nasser's relationship with his father, which had soured when his own mother died back in 1926, had not improved. And yet true to the characteristic ethos and values of Egyptian society, Nasser used members of his and his wife's extended family for sensitive, confidential tasks of state, and appointed them to certain senior posts. One case, for example, was his legal adviser, Muhammad Fahmi, the husband of his wife's niece.[31]

By all accounts Nasser had a happy home life. He was perhaps austere, whereas his wife lacked the glamour and sophistication of a First Lady. Loyalty to each other may have been a reflection of love and affection, or simply of mutual respect.[32] But that aspect of Nasser's life was quite separate from his public life and other activities, all of which were directed toward the seizure, exercise and retention of power as the sole ruler of Egypt at mid-century. The separation, even in a conservative Islamic society, is significant.

However others saw or knew him, it is clear Nasser had discovered early on in his drive for power that he could organise and manage a conspiracy, as well as control and subordinate his associates in it to his will. Later, he discovered, equally significantly for his career as an Egyptian ruler and Arab leader, that he could communicate with vast throngs and sway them by his oratory—in fact, elicit their admiration, fear and unqualified support. He could practically hypnotise them. To what extent he also hypnotised himself is difficult to say. Those close to him intimate that for a decade, between 1957 and 1967, he came closest to believing in the public image he and his publicists had constructed for himself. His severest critics and detractors emphasise their observation from the very beginning of the organised Free Officer conspiracy that Nasser insisted on being the supreme, unchallenged chief. In order to deal more adequately with this question, though, we need to know something about what Nasser thought of himself. And this kind of self-view is not readily known; Nasser left no notes, diaries or memoirs disclosing his innermost thoughts and feelings.

Within his own office, shielded from his numerous Ministers (Nasser usually formed huge Cabinets of between forty and fifty members) by a panoply of secretaries, private assistants and counsellors, Nasser conducted his state business face to face and largely by word of mouth. Although his autocracy may not have been distant from the people, it was very much a personal one. His contact with the people was earthily personal thanks to the use of the technical media: broadcasting and the press, which he nationalised in 1960, staged mass rallies and popular congresses. He would thus open his addresses by reminding his audiences of the point where he had left off when he last addressed them: "Ana kallimtukum . . . ", "Last time I spoke to you about . . ." The impression, to a great extent, depended on the medium.

Why Nasser behaved as he did in his public role is not therefore easy to explain, for it relates in part to the complex realm of motivation. His leadership was exercised with unlimited personal power. Was he ever interested in, say, constitutional office, in power defined by law and limited by the existence of alternative leadership, or solely in chieftaincy, *ri'āsa* and *za'āma*, as so many claim? He always boasted that he did not act, but only reacted to events as they occurred. Was he then a simple opportunist? Did he have long-term objectives, beyond that of power? Did his triumph over Naguib in 1954, his dramatic arms deal with the Soviet Union in 1955, his even more dramatic defiance of European power over the Baghdad Pact and Suez in 1955–6, his domination of the UAR in 1959–61, his "imperial" or "liberation" adventure in the Yemen in 1962–5, his construction of the High Dam at Aswan—a monument of Pharaonic proportions—all strengthen his conviction in his own intuition? Did they finally give him that feeling of infallibility and invincibility observed by so many of his associates after Suez? It is noteworthy that only after the Sinai disaster of 1967 did Nasser, for the first time in his life, complain of insomnia and admit of the need to take sleeping pills. Some allege that he also began to drink, but that is very doubtful.

In view of the disparity between Nasser's private life at home and his public behaviour as well as image, there are those who will infer a neurotic duality and detect a certain ambivalence in his personality. But in order to make anything of this inference with respect to his leadership of Egypt, one must be able to determine if Nasser was pathological. For all one knows—and given the scant evidence, one cannot really know for sure—Nasser may have unconsciously tried to resolve his personal conflicts and rectify the injustices of his childhood—and these, in his view, were many—by projecting them on to the old Egyptian establishment and the great powers of the world. It may even explain his inability to forge relations of equality with his colleagues, but instead insist on dominating them.

The fact, however, that the régime he led and dominated for eighteen years depended on the force of his personality and strength of his charisma is not necessarily an aberrant condition in the Egypt of that epoch. It is not a pathological phenomenon. There were, moreover, Egyptian rulers before him who achieved a similar style of dominant leadership—of autocracy or despotism. The state in Egypt is an overwhelming structure; he who controls it can attain immense power over society and dominate it. It is none the less true that seldom in the history of Egypt since Muhammad Ali had so much depended on one man's personality and person. Nasserism, after all, as the term itself implies, was Nasser himself—his vision, style and approach to power. Had it been something more, it would not have withered away or fallen into disuse—not to speak of abuse —so quickly after his death. In Egypt—indeed, in many countries— a forceful national leader, an autocrat or a despot, puts his own peculiar imprint on the state and the conduct of its affairs. Once he is gone, he is often soon forgotten. But it is the legacy of that imprint on the conduct of affairs which lingers on and constitutes a major problem for his successors.

As the first native Egyptian ruler and autocrat for several centuries, it was only natural for the people to embrace Nasser passionately. His despotism, if you will, even had a logical etiology and reasonable provenance in the 1940s in a country plagued and torn apart by domestic turmoil and disoriented by massive global changes. A study of Egyptian history therefore may explain in part the emergence and relative success of a ruler like Nasser. The study of Nasser's personality, on the other hand, may illuminate problematic areas in Egyptian history and society, but it does not constitute an adequate or satisfactory approach for the interpretation of Egyptian history.

Like Huey Long of Louisiana, Nasser perhaps ought to be judged, as V. O. Key argued, in terms of the pathological situation in which he arose, [33] and within the historical-political context of the Egyptian and Arab dilemma at mid-century. In a way he did stand for economic development and social justice. But his potential for achievement in these directions was threatened and ultimately undermined by his arrogance and lust for power, which prevented him from recognising the limits of his country's and his own capabilities.

Nasser was contemptuous of political parties and scorned institutions. His claim to legitimacy derived from his populist notion of a mandate from the people, as for instance, his famous "30 March" 1968 political reform programme, when he asserted the people had given him a "mandate for change". His idea of democracy is reminiscent of Huey Long's in Louisiana nearly fifty years ago:

> a leader gets up a program and then he goes out and explains it patiently and more patiently, until they get it. He asks for a mandate, and if they give it to him he goes ahead with the program in spite of hell and high water. He don't tolerate no opposition from the old gang of politicians, the legislature and the courts, the corporations, or anybody. [34]

He belittled the Egyptian past, and ignored the creative arts and culture of pre-1952 Egypt. He even created his own language in which he addressed the Egyptian people. To this extent he can be said to have given identity to an age.

Basically, though, Nasser preached the populist gospel of "every man a king", but only he wore a crown. Like the Greek colonels in Athens (1967–74), he assumed the role of surgeon in charge, putting the rest of the country in a plaster cast, because he knew best what was ailing it. In his revolt against the old order and its oligarchs, Nasser created a sense of crisis and an excitement of new opportunities. This dramatic quality about him was a source of fascination for the "better educated" at home, the alienated intellectuals in search of certitude and power, and the indulgent foreigners who proceeded to construct an elaborate mythology about him.

E. Victor Wolfenstein, an American student of personality and politics, tried in 1965 to apply Freudian psychology to a short study of Gandhi, Nasser and Lenin.[35] He enquired into the choice of political means for social change by examining the events in the lives of those holding differing views of legitimacy and the efficacy of violence. Specifically, he emphasised the influence of early life experience on later attitudes and behaviour. In Nasser's case he suggested a "desire to win applause" after losing his mother at an early age. Nasser blamed his father for his mother's death, which the old man had concealed from him. Uncle Khalil became for him a father substitute. Soon his whole view of the world was affected by this crisis in his childhood. There was a "congruence of personal crisis with the broader arena of Egyptian politics in the thirties". Nasser's "melancholy demeanor" and loneliness led him to notions of conspiracy and an admiration of old soldiers, such as General Aziz al-Masri and later General Muhammad Naguib—all of them substitute fathers.

What is suggested here is that Nasser's anti-paternal feeling made him identify with the lost or dead mother during a long period of disorientation. The implication is that Egypt became the dead mother that had to be resurrected—echoes of Ahmad Hussein's cry in 1933 for the resurrection of Egypt. If one accepts that the eighth to the thirteenth years in the life of a youth are a time of psycho-sexual development, one must also consider his ambivalent emotions.

Nasser's emotional needs, according to this analysis, were partially satisfied in the riots and demonstrations of the thirties, the political crucible provided by the Palace-appointed régimes. As an agitator for Young Egypt, he may have satisfied his desire for applause and the feeling that he was working for a benevolent personal authority against an evil alien force. Thus Egypt became Nasser's primary love object, and the British enemy the object of his hatred. Yet the authority of both objects had to be challenged and overthrown.

Nasser therefore greeted the Palestine War (1948–9) eagerly, anticipating victory and personal glory as "the militant defender of the fatherland". The defeat, however, led him to the realisation that he did not particularly like war ("the art of killing") and that Egypt had enemies both within (e.g. corruption) and without. She became the loved object to be saved from destruction; she became identified with mother. Even his involvement in desperate acts of assassination bothered him, especially when he heard the "voice of mother crying". His subsequent relationship with General Naguib reflects Nasser's ambivalent feelings towards a father figure, towards authority. Hence the initial compromises in 1952–4. Essentially, though, the loss of his mother left Nasser with a substantial burden of guilt. To this extent he also remained circumspect as regards limited violence in political action.

This kind of psychological personality analysis, however, may suggest the nature of the personal problems adolescents encounter in any society. It may even illustrate the peculiar problems of adolescents in the 1930s, or in times of widespread economic, political and cultural crisis. But it hardly constitutes a credible explanation either of Nasser as ruler of Egypt or of his and his fellow-officers' behaviour in power. The impact of their early political formation, their milieu and experience, coupled to Egyptian political tradition and the constraints of the Egyptian state, society and economy provides a more plausible and sounder basis for analysis and explanation.

Idol of the Egyptians

The paradox remains of Nasser at the head of a police state and yet the worshipped idol of the people; later of Nasser leading the country into socialism and yet surrounded by ex-officers turned into rich "princes"; and throughout his rule, of a president of a republic where no opinion could be expressed except that represented by the state, and in which no opposition was tolerated. It is on the other hand possible that Nasser himself was not responsible for the excesses of his régime. He was a very intelligent man, with a massive and overwhelming physical presence. Clearly, in order to determine once and for all the degree of his responsibility, a measure of public accountability is necessary to allow investigation and free enquiry.

The early combination, however, of a revolutionary tribunal in 1953 and a purification campaign aimed at the public humiliation of all known political leaders in the country and their destruction. If by this policy, Tawfiq al-Hakim commented twenty years later, the revolution intended to pre-empt any alternative sources of authority, to hit the big men with lesser ones, the scheme hurt the revolution itself when it consolidated its absolute power over the country. Al-Hakim goes on to reminisce ruefully,

> Abdel Nasser became the First Man in the country . . . loved by everyone, including those whose wealth he had expropriated . . . and the country became used to the rule of one man whom they loved and trusted. When the masses love, they do not

question or discuss . . . The beloved ruler became accustomed to unquestioned rule until an Iron Curtain fell between the people and the Absolute Ruler . . . We knew no more about the affairs of our country or those of the outside world than what he communicated to us from atop a high podium on some occasion or other. He would speak alone for hours on end words which showed us as heroes under his command, while the great powers about us appeared as pigmies. When he would forcefully tell a nuclear power that if she did not like what we did she could go drink the Nile, we felt proud . . . Confidence in our leader paralysed our thoughts.[36]

While on a visit to Cairo, the French writer Sartre asked al-Hakim why he did not write a book in defence of Nasser along the lines of the book Mauriac had written in defence of de Gaulle who had been attacked in *L'Observateur.* "In order for there to be a defence", al-Hakim replied, "there must be first an attack. No one attacks Nasser; no one in our country dares oppose his views." Perhaps, Tawfiq speculates,

> he overwhelmed us with his magic . . . and the hopes, dreams and promises which underlay the victories of the revolution which he repeatedly announced to us . . . with their pipes and drums, anthems, songs and films, which made us see ourselves as a great industrial state, leaders of the developing world . . . and the strongest military power in the Middle East.

After all, the fact of the idolised leader filled the television screen, towering over his audiences from the podiums of meeting halls, endlessly telling them tales of power and achievement, reminding them of "what they were and what they have become", without anyone contradicting him. "There was nothing else to do," Tawfiq asserts, "but to believe and applaud him."

Despite his emphasis upon the theme of idolisation, al-Hakim does not suggest that Nasser's rule rested solely on instant applause and extemporaneous cheering. Rather he points to Nasser's deliberate and careful management and organisation of this atmosphere, not to mention the sinews of state power. What Tawfiq tries to impress upon his readers is the fact that the revolution of the soldiers and the subsequent political style of Nasser as ruler of Egypt were not based on discussion.

Reflecting on the events of the Suez (1956) and Six Day (1967) wars and their presentation at home, Tawfiq asks, "Were bluffing and histrionics in the nature of Nasser?" It was bluffing that led to the crushing of Egypt in 1967, because of the mass self-deception exercised by leaders and followers alike ever since the non-existent "Stalingrad which was Port Said" in 1956. He then likens Egypt's military adventure in the Yemen to "collective madness". He quotes, for example, official communiqués during the Six Day War which had convinced him and many other Egyptians that Israel had been crushed by Wednesday 7 June:

It was clear to us that our forces would enter Tel Aviv by 9 p.m. on June 5 . . . It was rationally and logically impossible for us to believe that our army could be defeated so easily, because for years we had been told of its miraculous powers. On every national holiday of the revolution we witnessed its awesome parades, comprising the latest in armour, rockets with names like the "Conqueror", "Invincible" and "Victor;" units of troops called "Lightning" and "Thunderbolt", with their terrifying trot; paratroops dropping from the skies, scaling walls, tearing and eating snakes . . . Then we heard speeches about our air force which had no rival in the Middle East . . . for which we paid extra defence taxes . . . until it was whispered, "the revolution may have failed in all else, but it has built a powerful military machine . . ."

Yet none of us in Egypt questioned the truth of what we were told. Were we hypnotized by the man's magic; were we drugged? . . . Or was it the result of our complete confidence in a chief in whom we had placed all our hopes? Or had we become accustomed to this trance whereby the revolution rendered us no more than wireless receiving sets?

What is interesting about al-Hakim's characterisation of the relationship between Nasser and the Egyptians is the fact that he does not ascribe the shortcomings, failures or disasters of the eighteen-year-old military régime to the peculiarities of Nasser's personality alone. On the contrary, he puts forward the thesis of a collective, or national, psychology whose condition converged with the appearance of the idol—and magician. In his tract, al-Hakim repeatedly asks, "Where were people like myself, the leaders of thought . . .?"

In addition to Nasser's idolisation by the Egyptians, however, there are alternative lines of enquiry possible into the question of why it is that no one could disagree with, or oppose, Nasser effectively. Arthur Koestler could well be right when he argued that the extension of ideas of revolution, even revolutionary movements, from Europe to the East, "needed not intellectuals, but a ruthless and uncritically obedient bureaucracy", and that "bureaucracies in these circumstances do not aspire to attain new values but to climb to the top of the existing hierarchy."[37]

According to many informants already cited Nasser trusted no one, and yet he was idolised by the Egyptian and Arab masses. Perhaps in his suspicious and limited perception of the world about him, Nasser personified the view of the vast majority of his fellow-countrymen, especially the poor and miserable of Egypt. As for him, for them too there was the bogy of the exploiter, imperialism and the lackeys and agents of imperialism. Nasser's apparent unwillingness, for example, to countenance a sovereign Jewish political entity in the Middle East was shared by the majority of tradition-bound Egyptians as well as Arabs everywhere. Similarly, his unwillingness to allow the Baath party a free hand in governing Syria under the union with Egypt was due partly to his horror at the Christian Michel Aflaq, co-founder and leader of the party, coming to power over a predominantly Muslim country.[38] In these emotive tradition-bound matters the masses could totally identify with a man who personified and incarnated their frustrations, hopes and aspirations. There are those who will argue that this kind of *metendysis* was not a peculiarity of Nasser's personality but part of the Egyptian folk culture. Nasser, after all, took upon himself the whole burden of the national feeling of inferiority, not just his own. No one else among his original fellow-conspirators did; he grabbed it from the start, and the people came to know only him.[39]

Despite the country's vast bureaucracy, Nasser's expression of its emotional disturbances and needs took the form not of dramatic actions and genuinely radical policies, but of a dramatisation of them, regardless of how unheroic, inconsequential or routine they may have been. His very massive presence and visceral relationship with the native masses concealed the lack of solutions to perhaps insoluble problems. It could be said that he offered them comfort and the solace if not assurance of protection while the society rotted away. He made them feel great so that, as one Egyptian put it caustically, "whereas twenty years ago, we dared measure our progress by the standards of France or Great Britain to keep us on our toes intellectually, now we compare ourselves to the Libyans and Yemenis and think how great we are."[40]

Notes

1. Muhammad Heikal, *Nasser: The Cairo Documents* (London, New English Library, 1972), p.4.
2. Ibid., p.5.
3. A Free Officer and one-time Governor of Cairo.
4. Quoted in Musa Sabri, *Wathaiq harb oktobar* (Cairo, 1975), p.214.
5. Hugh L'Etang, *The pathology of leadership* (London, 1969), p.207.
6. Ibid., pp.207–8.
7. Other dates given for a suspected first heart attack are 1959 and 1961. There may well have been a history of heart disease in the family. Two of Nasser's younger brothers have died of it since.
8. *Rose el-Youssef*, Cairo, 18 July 1975.
9. Ahmad Hussein, *Kayfa 'araftu Abdel Nasser was 'ishtu ayyāma hukmihi* (Beirut, 1973), p.21.
10. Quoted in Nāsir al-Din al-Nashashibi, *Al-hibr aswad . . . aswad* (Paris, 1976), p.78, where it is also alleged Nasser eavesdropped on telephone conversations. The allegation was made by Salah Shahed, a senior presidential aide, explaining that Nasser was obsessed by the fear of betrayal.
11. Ibid., p.80.
12. Ibid., p.201. Moreover, Salah Shahed is quoted as saying, "Abdel Nasser did not respect a single Egyptian throughout his rule" (p.209).
13. Ibid., pp.128–31 and 169–70.
14. Ibid., p.81.
15. See Sami Gohar, *Al-sāmitūn yatakallamūn*. Abdel Latif Boghdadi has just published the first volume of his memoirs (Cairo, July 1977), which I have been unable to examine thoroughly. From the extracts I have seen published in *Rose el-Youssef*, June–July 1977, Boghdadi seems to have kept diaries on the Nasser régime.
16. *Rose el-Youssef*, 29 September 1975.
17. Ibid.
18. *Rose el-Youssef*, 18 and 25 August 1975.
19. Heikal in Fuad Mattar, *Bisarāha 'an Abd al-Nasir* (Beirut, 1975), p.180.
20. There was no way of checking out these reports. The practice by revolutionaries of establishing "funds for the protection of the revolution" is by no means an Egyptian peculiarity. The reports all the same did not persist for very long. There were similar reports about vanishing Algerian FLN funds in Europe a few years ago.
21. General Abdel Wahid 'Ammar, *al-Musawwar*, Special issue on Nasser, Cairo, August 1957.
22. But this surely was the pretext for the removal of Ali Sabri who had been under attack for some time before then. Heikal's dislike of him was common café talk and Heikal's press campaign against Ali Sabri was most probably inspired by Nasser. The latter simply believed that both his Arab policy and the need to move towards an acceptance of the Rogers peace plan required the demotion of Ali Sabri. See Fuad Mattar, *Bisarāha*, pp.100–2.
23. Sami Gohar, *Al-sāmitun yatakallamūn*, p.119.
24. Ibid., p.61.

25. Ibid., p.50.
26. Ibid., pp.55–9.
27. Ibid., pp.65–102. See also Kamal al-Din Hussein, series of interviews in *Rose el-Youssef*, December 1975–January 1976.
28. M. Rabi‘, *Shakhsiyyat ‘Abd al-Nasir* (Cairo, 1966), p.9.
29. Nashāshibi, *Al-Hibr aswad . . . aswad*, p.265.
30. M. Rabi‘, *Shakhsiyyat ‘Abd al-Nasir* pp.10–11.
31. At least one of his brothers and his uncle Khalil became deputies in the National Assembly.
32. A British medical specialist who was consulted by Nasser several times in the sixties reports that he was never introduced to Mrs Nasser. In fact, when he asked his patient if he wished him to explain his condition to his wife, Nasser simply refused.
33. V. O. Key, *Southern politics in state and nation* (New York, 1950).
34. Hugh Davis Graham (ed.), *Huey Long* (New Jersey, 1970), p.75.
35. E. Victor Wolfenstein, Centre for International Studies Paper, Princeton University, October 1965.
36. *‘Awdat al-wa‘i*. All quotations are from the original typescript, dated July 1972. The tract was published in book form in Beirut in 1974.
37. Arthur Koestler, *The Yogi and the Commissar* (London, 1964), p.78.
38. See comments by Heikal in Fuad Mattar, *Bisarāha*, pp.137–8.
39. See especially Jean Lacouture, *Nasser* (Paris, 1971).
40. A remark made to this author by an Egyptian writer in Cairo in November 1970.

CHAPTER 18

The Impact of Nasser: Interpretations

There is no better way of knowing a man's spirit, wisdom and will than when he proves it in public office, as ruler or lawgiver.—Sophocles, *Antigone.*

They cheer the victor whoever he is; they praise the strong whoever he is; they genuflect before the stick, and in this way they assuage the fear lurking in the depth of their souls.— Naguib Mahfuz, *Awlad haritna.*

Even granting Nasser's overwhelming charisma, the early actions and policies of his régime, as well as the bare outlines of political orientation underlying them, constitute a change from the past and reflect, however unclearly, certain cumulative social and economic changes in the country. To deplore Nasser's behaviour in power after his death and to reject his policies is one thing. To categorically deny a residue of their impact upon society is another. The Aswan Dam, for good or ill, is there; a public sector economy, however badly planned and administered, is still in place as the hallmark of national economic policy. Politically more significant, recruitment into the political class and governing élite from social groups excluded before 1952 continues under Nasser's successor. This is also the view of leading Egyptian critics of the Nasser régime.

Egyptian Assessments

Louis Awad, a prominent Egyptian writer and eminent scholar, is more circumspect and tentative than Tawfiq al-Hakim in his assessment of the Nasser régime and its impact on Egypt.[1] He disagrees with Hakim's explanation of Nasser's autocracy as deriving from an emotional, irrational relationship between Nasser and the masses of Egyptians. He suggests that people like himself and

Hakim never lost their consciousness during Nasser's rule. On the contrary, they were fully aware of what Nasser was doing. There is then an alternative explanation to the Nasser phenomenon, without shirking a wider responsibility among Egypt's educated élite for the kind of régime Nasser led. Dr Awad thus dismisses Hakim's thesis of Nasser as an idol, whose peculiar relationship with the people caused them to lose their consciousness, as a convenient escape from responsibility. He is not opposed, in principle, to socialism in Egypt, with its public sector economy and other features. A public sector economy, according to Dr Awad, was necessary; Egypt had no choice. Its success or failure however constitutes for him a proper area of criticism. He is thus critical of the failure to organise and administer it properly, and contends that the reason for the failure was Nasser's closed political system, his autocracy that was maintained by a "secret government", and the lack of public accountability or any other basic requirement of democratic rule. It is by an examination of this feature of his régime that Dr Awad seeks to assess Nasser's impact on Egypt.

Nasserism, as enunciated by Nasser, Dr Awad states, was a negative concept, referring primarily to the ending of colonialism. "All of Nasser's career", he writes, "was in the context of destroying this or that, not in creating something." Furthermore, the Nasser régime continued to use force even after it had attained its earliest two objectives, namely, the abolition of the monarchy and the destruction of the economic and political power of the land-owning élite.

It is difficult, Dr Awad argues, to judge the real or potential advantages of a closed system when elected public bodies or their representatives have no investigative powers. For example, between 1958 and 1966 loans to Egypt from the Eastern bloc countries for the Aswan High Dam and the industrial plan (excluding arms) totalled $1,334 million. In addition, loans from the Western countries during the same period amounted to $400 million. Total expenditure on the public sector of the economy from 1952 to 1966 was $6,000 million, in addition to another $4,000 million that accrued from the nationalisation of foreign assets in the country. How these huge sums of money were used, spent or deployed, Dr Awad asks, is very difficult to know. What, for instance, was the extent of technical and bureaucratic failure is equally difficult to establish.[2] Given the economic condition of the country and despite the two wars with Israel and the Yemen campaign, one must assume that the public sector was either not productive enough, or productive but subject to rampant venality and embezzlement, or productive but its fruits diverted to consumer purposes,[3] or again productive but eroded by the financial demands of wars. In order to begin to answer these questions, the public sector must be accountable to a popularly elected sovereign body such as a parliament. Under Nasser's closed system it was difficult to get answers. His so-called hidden government manned and supervised these activities by Nasser's gauleiters, who were responsible only to him. This inevitably destroyed the public service administering the public sector and gave further scope to the activities of the intelligence agencies.

Until 1962, the industrialisation of Egypt was not, according to Dr Awad, an aim of the Free Officer revolution. The Six Principles of the revolution enunciated in 1952 never promised that. The nationalisation of foreign interests in 1956–60 and other private native concerns in 1960–3, although constituting the "spinal cord" of the public sector, became the basis of a state capitalist, not a socialist, system. In fact, in 1952 the Free Officer régime hoped to improve industrial growth and development strictly with the aid of foreign, especially American, capital. And this, Dr Awad argues, was the régime's contradictory policy: it produced favourable legislation in order to attract Western capital, when at the same time it demanded the British evacuation of the Suez Canal. Moreover, foreign residents had been leaving the country in large numbers since 1946. Perhaps in a simple-minded way Nasser assumed that his suppression of the Communists in Egypt alone would attract US capital. When by 1956 this was not forthcoming he was forced on to the road to state capitalism. More serious is the distinction Dr Awad makes between socialism and Nasser's régime. In the former, profits are theoretically ploughed back into public welfare and services, and there is public control over the administration of the economy. Basically, though, it was Nasser's insistence upon allowing only those absolutely loyal to him, not necessarily competent or able, to supervise the public sector that ultimately undermined it, or at least rendered it less productive and inefficient. Then the long-standing Egyptian "bureaucratic disease" of overmanning compounded the difficulty.

Dr Awad avers that the 1956 constitution was the "first charter" of Nasserism. It had little to do with the revolution. The second was the famous National Charter of 1962, and the third and last the Manifesto of 30 March 1968. These were a sort of "social contract" between Nasser and the Egyptians, aimed primarily at the enemies of his rule. Thus the 1962 Charter did not promise Egyptians a well-defined economic, social and political system, only a vague kind of socialism with its trinitarian revolutionary slogan, "freedom, socialism, unity". "Our socialism was of the kind, as the popular saying goes, which crosses the Nile without getting wet." For example, it promised full employment without providing the basis for it. It rejected class interests, differences or struggle in the name of national unity, harmony and social peace, and Nasser remained the adjudicator of that peace.

Violence and repression characterised the régime of the Free Officers in its first two years. With his triumph over Naguib in April 1954, Nasser set on a course of "tyrannical autocracy". The revolution of the soldiers therefore was never transformed into a political system, but merely into one-man rule. The "hysteria of victory, the Zieg Heil", as Dr Awad calls it, began with Suez and reached its frenetic pitch when Syria united with Egypt in 1958. Thus Nasser, Dr Awad argues, was a romantic who had a romantic view of an Egyptian revolution. It is clear from his tract, *Philosophy of the Revolution*, that he considered himself a man of destiny, and viewed Egypt and the Egyptians as a nation and people of destiny too. He was in search of a role for himself in this pre-ordained destiny, and so was the nation. The romantic hero would lead the nation from the darkness into the light, since

> In Nasser's perception of the 1952 revolution we are then in a great romantic age, governed by a powerful irresistible mysterious force . . . or one controlled by compelling historical causes . . . a great romantic age in which reason is incapacitated and free choice impossible . . . an age in which all the roles are predetermined . . . awaiting only the appearance of the actors to play them.[4]

The actors appeared on 23 July 1952 in the form of the Free Officers. Nasser assumed the leading role in 1954. In 1956 he became the only hero, or protagonist. But from a mere dramatic hero he soon turned into a lifelike one. In short, Nasser considered his revolution to be an epochal event planned by history—and Providence.

Unlike Hakim, Dr Awad, however, also insists on judging Nasser's revolution on the soundness of its Six Principles, and on the success or failure of their implementation during the first ten years of the régime. In any case, three of these six principles were negative: the ending of colonialism, feudalism and the control of government by monopolistic capital. As for the other three, except for the concrete undertaking to create a national army, the remaining two—the establishment of social justice and a sound democratic life—were too general and no more than good slogans. The point is that Nasser never really promised Egyptians a specific economic and social system. Despite the socialist generalities and overtones of his 1962 Charter, Dr Awad remarks that in the end, "Nasser first liquidated democracy in Egypt, and later any socialism that may have existed in the country and the Arab world."

Self-sufficiency or autarky may have been one of Nasser's aims for the economic liberation of Egypt. But that is more like national socialism than socialism proper. A public sector was slowly forming before 1952. The creation of the National Council for Production in 1953 reflected the acceleration of this process. The massive nationalisation of foreign assets and interests in the country in 1956–60, mainly British and French, later Belgian and private Egyptian institutions such as Bank Misr, provided the basis of an expanded public sector. Dr Awad argues that just as foreign interests before that time provided the framework of a capitalist system in Egypt, their nationalisation from 1956 onwards served the same purpose for the new public sector economy. But these nationalised interests came to be owned by the state, not by the Egyptian public, whose savings were too meagre or non-existent to afford such ownership.

What is interesting, Dr Awad remarks, is that so long as the Nasser régime nationalised "the wealth of the *khawaga*", the foreigner that is, there were hardly any repercussions. No one objected, not even the Americans who, according to Dr Awad, secretly hoped to replace the ousted British and French. The nationalisations were considered by everyone to be patriotic acts. Once the régime, though, began to nationalise native industrial, commercial and financial institutions, beginning with Bank Misr, followed by the massive measures of 1961 and continuing through 1963–4, rumblings of an opposition were heard. The association of these measures with the charter's proclamation of a socialist revolution and the Yemen War provoked both inter-Arab conflict and foreign power rivalry. Dr Awad believes the trouble arose when Nasser sought to arouse the "Arab street" once again.

The main drift of Dr Awad's critique is that industrialisation became an aim of the Nasser régime only after 1962. Much of it had to be financed by foreign aid and loans, since there was hardly enough capital in Egypt to finance major industrial projects. In short, Nasser's new socialist programme meant no more than the outright ownership by the state of the means of production, a kind of state capitalism.[5] He also suggests that whereas Saad Zaghlul, leader of the nationalist movement after the First World War, managed to Egyptianise the administration, Nasser succeeded in Egyptianising the economy. He made further advances over the Wafd by promoting social security legislation. His terrible mistake in much of this, as Dr Awad sees it, was to liquidate the "foreign presence" in Egypt at a time when the country needed its expertise, skills and other talents. More disastrous was the fact that Nasser "demolished long-standing educational and cultural bridges between Egypt and the outside world . . . the teaching and learning of foreign languages died."

The fundamental disability which rendered the whole experiment lacking and soured it was a political one. Nasser was primarily concerned with the safety of his rule and security of his régime. Consequently when the needed public sector developed, he appointed trusted officers of limited education and experience to administer it. He also appointed officers to numerous other public positions. His closed autocratic political system permitted the extensive abuse of influence and power, especially in the public sector, while at the same time it was difficult to know exactly what went on inside it. The standards of public life in the administration of the economy and public services were, as a result, undermined. "Catching thieves in the public sector", as Dr Awad put it, "is more difficult than catching them in the private sector." Or "import controls in a closed autocratic system breed a rampant black market."

Another serious difficulty was Nasser's insistence upon "exporting the revolution". After all, Dr Awad argues, the principle of "liberation was the basis of Nasserism". In this process of liberation, however,

> Nasser's revolution and his regime destroyed some of the finer and sounder foundations of Egyptian society that had been constructed by Egyptians over the past 200 years as a result of their direct contact with European civilization: as for example democratic rights and freedoms, the separation of state and religion, of state powers, the supremacy of the law, the

sovereignty of the nation over government, freedom of political thought, expression and organization, work and choice.[6]

In the end, Dr Awad ruefully remarks, "Nasserism, after Nasser's triumph in Suez and his emergence as a charismatic leader of the Arabs, shook the faith of Egyptians in their national identity . . . and erased the name of Egypt by calling upon Egyptians to lose themselves in a greater political entity, that of the Arab nation extending from the Atlantic Ocean to the Gulf."[7] In fact, within Nasser's closed system, "Egyptian nationality took second place to 'revolutionary' nationality," and "with the deification of the state, the executive, legislative and judicial powers were fused, as well as the Fourth Estate of journalism. All four became the arms of the Chief in whom was embodied the will of the state."[8]

Yet Dr Awad insists the Free Officer revolution was the only kind of revolution possible for Egypt in 1952. Egypt's choice was one between that kind of upheaval or none at all. Dr Awad writes:

In my estimation, this revolution despite its traditional conservative origins was preferable to the preservation of the ancient regime . . . In spite of its shortcomings and lukewarm radicalism, blurred political and social vision, in spite of all its many fatal mistakes, it nevertheless succeeded in changing some of the main characteristics of Egyptian society for the better, but not in changing its basic structures.[9]

He seems to think that the revolution's and Nasser's own limitations derived from his and his colleagues', the Free Officers', background which was essentially that of the anxious, small middle class or petite bourgeoisie. In feeling, experience and vision these men were within the mainstream of the traditional conservative Egyptian spirit. Like Sukarno, Nkrumah, Ben Bella, Lumumba, Sekou Toure and others, Nasser too was a by-product of the Cold War. Things went his way between 1953, the end of the Korean War, and 1965. The decline set in after that for all of these leaders in the Third World, including Nasser. Nor did Nasser's conservative petit bourgeois suspicion, scorn and fear of the better-educated help him in clearly identifying the enemies of his revolution at home or abroad, until these shattered his régime in 1967. Instead he relied on his instinct, intuition and inspiration, "of which he was well endowed". Egypt, in short, was in need of an educated leadership beyond the limited confines of Nasser and his military-bureaucratic élite. Thus,

> Nasser preferred to export his revolution in order to avoid implementing it to its logical conclusion at home. First Arab nationalism and later Arab socialism were his escape from confronting the barefooted fellahin, the mainstay of the Egyptian countryside, the struggling working people, the mainstay of the Egyptian city, the millions of uprooted poor who belong neither to town nor country, just in the same way the Egyptian teacher tries to avoid teaching the children of the fellahin and workers because he is not rewarded as well as when he teaches the children of the Kuwaiti, Saudi or Libyan rich.[10]

In contrast to Tawfiq al-Hakim, then, Dr Awad concludes that Nasser's accomplishments were several: viz., agrarian reform, the Aswan High Dam and the creation of a public sector. It was his autocratic rule and secretive, closed system of government which prevented them from producing their full benefits. He does impute to Nasser, however, a more deliberate, calculated autocracy, thus rejecting Hakim's allusions to emotional predilections. But he concurs in Hakim's criticism of Nasser's Arab adventures. The "agitation of the Arab street", as Awad calls this policy, and the question of "Egypt's presence abroad" were disastrous policies. Nasser wasted his few political victories because he mistook his popularity in the Arab streets and with the Arab masses for military strength. Worst of all, in the name of national solidarity, Nasser atrophied the Egyptians politically and undermined their patriotism to the point that the word "patriotism" disappeared and was replaced by that of "nationalism". It is difficult not to infer from Dr Awad's critical piece his likening of Nasser and his régime to a Fascist type of national socialism. Its sterility after 1965 and its bankruptcy in 1967 suggest to him that the "Nasserite revolution" —like all other revolutions—had aged.

Dr Fuad Zakariyya was, until a few years ago, a professor of philosophy at Cairo University. He has since moved to the University of Kuwait. He has also been one of the most thoughtful, articulate, fair, calm yet incisive intellects of the Egyptian left. In the spring of 1975 he was invited by the Cairo weekly *Rose el-Youssef* to contribute a series of articles on the left's appreciation of Nasser and his régime.[11] The essence of Nasser's mistake, he wrote, lay in his style of implementing socialism in Egypt. It ignored the very essence of socialism, which is the control by the people over the means of production. Moreover, Nasser's socialism had no visible effect on the popular, i.e. lower, poorer classes of Egyptian society. Rather it expanded the more privileged classes tenfold without closing the gap with the lower ones. "The net practical result", Professor Zakariyya states baldly, was an "increase in the number of masters". He agrees with other critics that the Nasser experiment removed the sources of wealth and means of production from the control of the land-based élite and few capitalists in the country, and that it founded an industrial base that could become the basis of a socialist transformation in the future. "This overall picture", he concedes, "is correct, and I do not deny it. But I cannot accept its consequences so long as the transformation did not occur by any of the accepted criteria." What did occur in fact was "that the state . . . controls the means of production in the service [for the benefit] of its special elite and in order to get rid of the danger constituted by capital and productive means in the hands of a rival class."

Professor Zakariyya considers the absence of any public supervision over public funds the most serious charge against Nasser's régime:

Vast funds became available, beginning with the expropriated royal palaces . . . then those from sequestrated assets under custodianship, all of which passed into channels not all of which are known. Many cases of illegitimate enrichment appeared among people whose known incomes did not warrant their being rich. More revealing during this period was the condition in which public office itself had become a means to gain rather than public service. It is certain that many departments knew the details of these instances of the abuse of influence and power . . . but remained silent or covered them up.

"I cannot imagine", he wrote, "a socialist experiment in which the abuse of power is the rule and integrity the exception." But this, he goes on to explain, was the logical outcome of the absence of popular control, i.e. the accountability of public funds, and because the culprits relied on the so-called centres of power within Nasser's autocratic rule for their protection. Such exploitation of a crushed poor people like the Egyptians "is a crime, the perpetrator of which ought to be hanged publicly in the largest public square." Yet the cover-up was the rule, and continues to be so among those who insist on the unqualified defence of the Nasserite experiment.

Strong words perhaps, but significantly those of an Egyptian university professor who does not hesitate in stressing the deleterious effect of the Nasser régime on Egypt. He categorically asserts that Nasser's success over Suez and his consequent popularity in the Third World led him to pay, blithely and facilely, too much attention to foreign affairs while ignoring pressing problems at home. But this was not a national concern, required by or forced upon him by the Egyptian people. Rather he imposed it upon them, without proper discussion or planning. In the pursuit of easy popularity he spent too much money, even when every foreign adventure was a failure. His "revolution was one which oppressed all for the benefit of the ruling class above". In fact, the Nasserite experience comprised elements

> of oppression exceeding by far the legal limits for the protection of the revolution against a minority opposition. Consequently, Egyptian man emerged from this experience quite different from what he was at its beginning. At first, he felt he could speak, discuss and object, and that the country was his country, in which his opinion could be heard . . . But after the mass arrests, fear crept into him gradually. Fear led to negativism, hypocrisy and double talk. The Egyptian lost his ability to object, reject and protest, for terror was accompanied by an organised propaganda campaign aimed at there being only one opinion, and one point of view in the country . . . This inner destruction of the Egyptian's soul, personality and mind was one of the greatest disasters of the Nasserite experience.

Nasser, Professor Zakariyya believes, gave socialism a bad name among Egyptians. His so-called socialist régime did not give the simple Egyptian what socialism is expected to give any society. On the contrary, it acted against the humanity of the Egyptian. It even corrupted the so-called revolutionary élite, since "the quickest and easiest way of pulling out the claws of revolution from a revolutionary is to put in his hands money without accounting". The most dangerous phenomenon of the Nasserite experience was of a people who had come to accept an imposed double standard of behaviour, one for the governed and another for the governors, as a natural state of affairs. The inner rottenness of the soul occurred because

> the problem was not in the spread of oppression and privileged exceptions, but in the fact that the Egyptians became used to them to the point that they considered them as normal . . . The senses were numbed to oppression, the exception became the rule before which Egyptians could only surrender . . . Egyptians became spectators, robbed of all will and thought.

It is not only the study of Nasser's personality and his impact on Egypt that presents difficulties. The study of "Nasserism" as an ideology has even more serious limitations. Nasser himself always insisted he was a pragmatist, that he did not believe in grandiose theories or ideologies. All the same, he provided Egyptians with a kind of ideological weapon, namely, that of the struggle against capitalism, imperialism, reaction and Zionism. But this is not the same as providing them with an ideology. In fact this limitation is the essence of the Nasser phenomenon. Over and above so-called impersonal historical forces and sociological interpretations of his career, it was his personality, its will and the deliberate application of its perceptions which constituted Nasserism. Whatever economic and social interpretations one used to explain his régime, his state, the fact remains that it was above all, the expression of his peculiar political talent. If one were to ask the average Egyptian today, what is, or was, Nasserism, he would, beyond banal clichés, be at a loss for a reasoned definition of it. If one were to search for Nasser's message after his distinctive voice was silenced by death—i.e. after he ceased to manipulate the formula *vox dei vox populi*—one may find that little remains of his ideas, his views and especially his resentments.

It is incidentally understandable that many Westerners' view of Nasser tended to be ideological, even aesthetic. They saw someone imposing order on a proverbially conservative, lethargic people; someone defying his masters at home and abroad, a super-Egyptian and, later, a super-Arab; someone with a vision of a united Arab world, led by Egypt, secure and free of turmoil. Looked at even from a Hobbesian perspective Nasser appeared to be the absolute sovereign, the Leviathan, who provided peace, security and stability for the Egyptians after nearly twenty years of disorder and insecurity. What was overlooked was the fact that Hobbes' Leviathan was not meant to be arbitrary or tyrannical, for tyranny offers no escape from the fears and uncertainties of the state of nature, or Naguib Mahfuz's *Karnak*. It is only one of the forms that state might take, in which purges, expropriations, incarcerations at the ruler's will without due process of law become "daily, brutish and nasty" occurrences.

For some Westerners such abstract constructs as Arab nationalism and socialism had an appealing, promising ring about them. They implied independence, equality and social justice. Unfortunately, whatever the merits or drawbacks of these ideological expectations may have been, they soon became identified—indeed, fused—with Nasser himself, his personality and rule. Nasserism thus remained an instant ideological reference to the man's dominance over Egyptian and Arab affairs for at least a decade. It reflected his will and vision as the ruler of Egypt and leader of an Arab movement of liberation from alien control or foreign influence, as well as a collective Arab search of a panacea for their ills. Inevitably, a Western double standard of judgement became common which overlooked the fundamental autocracy of the Egyptian leader.

One suspects that Western observers and commentators were themselves disoriented by the rapid changes after the Second World War and the massive shift of world power from Europe to America and the Soviet Union. They were naturally attracted by the prospects of newness, the dawn of a new consciousness in any part of the world that might transform society "for the better". Nasser, at one point, was seen from this perspective: a radical nationalist, a popular, not a parliamentary, democrat, an Alcibiades cum Napoleon who would autocratically, but justifiably, modernise Egypt and unite the Arab countries in the cause of a more equitable and just society.

What Nasser really accomplished was to bring a new generation of Egyptians to power. From it his rule gave rise to a new "state class" of bureaucrats, technocrats, planners, media and propaganda experts, and a relatively privileged small group of industrial workers and small, land-owning peasant farmers. These were the main beneficiaries of his policies and, to this extent, they acquired a stake in the survival of his régime. Members of the military establishment, however, became at once its guardians and potential enemies. But Nasser did not provide this "state class" or the generation from which it sprang with a new conception of power. The ideological difference in this respect between the generations was never supplied. To the extent therefore that the new generation and the "state class" which arose from it have a vital interest in the kind of régime Nasser founded, their priorities will constitute a constraint upon the freedom of action of his successors for some time to come. It is in the sense of who partakes of, controls or exercises *state* power that Nasser founded something different, but alas not new, or that his régime represents a change from but not a break with the past in the history of modern Egypt.

Ahmad Hamrush, a leftist ex-Free Officer, currently a journalist, serialised in April 1977 in the Cairo weekly *Rose el-Youssef*,[12] excerpts from the projected fourth volume of his history of the 23 July 1952 revolution.[13] These consist of verbatim reproductions of his interviews with leading officer members of the old RCC, the Free Officer organisation and the Nasser régime. He calls them "Confessions by witnesses of the July revolution." They throw some light on Nasser's use of the military police and intelligence services in discrediting Muhammad Naguib, or undermining the authority of Abdel Hakim Amer among serving officers in the army. They are also instructive regarding Nasser's use of personal emissaries, appointees and special agents in seeking to "subvert" other Arab régimes. There is also an attempt by some of the interviewees who held key posts in the Nasser régime to rehabilitate the late Abdel Hakim Amer, whose relationship to Nasser had begun to go sour as early as July 1956. Thus Salah Nasr, the notorious Director of General Intelligence from 1957 to 1967, claims Amer protested to Nasser for his not informing him in advance about his intention to nationalise the Suez Canal.[14]

These "revelations" also allude to Nasser's ruthless pursuit of personal power. More significantly, they portray a typical eighteenth-century Mamluk-type of political environment, standard and morality. Officers in whatever capacity—in intelligence, the military police, regular army service, in government departments or in the administration of the public sector of the economy—were caught in the power plays of the very few members of the top leadership or ruling élite, such as the RCC, Nasser, Naguib and Amer in the earlier days of the régime, or the competing cliques around the supreme autocrat, the *Rayyes*, in its later days. These intrigued against each other, helped purge their own ranks, arrested and cashiered their colleagues. Alternatively, they protected and supported each other according to clique, army service, regiment, graduating class from military college and so on. Furthermore, most of them were of the same generation, having been born in the early twenties. Most interesting, unfortunately, in these "revelations" is the largely trivial nature of the inner deliberations and concerns of these groups. And it all suggests that the contest for power and advantage occurred at that top level and limited circle. The overwhelming majority of Egyptians, just as in the time of the Mamluks, remained patient, suffering spectators, unable to influence the contest, or for many of them to escape its arbitrary attention.

Retrospect

From 1930 to 1952 the political affairs of Egypt were in a continuous state of turmoil and crisis. But there was also a crisis in the lives of the young literate and aspiring Egyptians. To this extent Nasser's generation was as critical for recent Egyptian history as that of Lutfi el-Sayyid and Saad Zaghlul was for the period from 1906 to 1919. They shared in a world of collective beliefs, ideas of the period and spirit of the times centred upon extreme nationalism and the use of violence in political affairs. The Arab Middle East region as a whole was exposed to ideas from Europe and events leading to major shifts in world power not of their own making but which none the less affected them.

Inflation and unemployment plagued the Egyptian economy in 1951–2 just before the Free Officers grabbed power. Society was dislocated, if not quite uprooted. Nasser and his fellow officers did not quite reorient or redirect it. They primarily disrupted the old society by transforming its power hierarchy. They ousted the big landowners, the Egyptian land-based élite that had been created by the Muhammad Ali dynasty. In its place at the top of a new stratification they placed a military-bureaucratic élite of privilege, influence and power. At the same time, they expanded the salaried "state official class". A greater number of these was needed to run the administration and new public sector of the economy. To this extent the Nasser régime helped the growth of a state-created "middle class", consisting of bureaucrats, technocrats, skilled professionals and others.

Nasser's organisational ability and intuitive grasp of the possibilities in Egypt in 1949–52, as well as his noticeable charisma, first impressed a nucleus of ten to fifteen officers. A bond of comradeship, such as the one many of them experienced in their secondary school cliques, soon developed. With few exceptions—the Communists Yusuf Siddiq and Khaled Mohieddin and the Muslim Brother Abdel Moneim Abdel Rauf—the members of this cabal of officers were politically inexperienced. Anonymity in their conspiratorial activities was readily accepted in great measure because they were soldiers. Most of them, except perhaps for the Sabri brothers and Sarwat Okasha, were from modest backgrounds.

Brought up in a political culture characterised by the centralisation of power, they seemed to accept Nasser as leader of the clique (*shilla*) quite readily. The tragedy of course is that the closely knit nature of the clique did not lead later to the practice of consultation or collegial decisions. After 1956, not even his closest associates— Abdel Hakim Amer, Zakariyya Mohieddin, Ali Sabri, Anwar Sadat —could influence Nasser's decisions. For by then he had started to bypass them with a new echelon of appointed personal assistants: Hasan Tuhami, Sami Sharaf, Muhammad Heikal. By the 1960s, it seemed that none was able to withstand or check his relentless personification and concentration of power. How much the disasters in the Yemen and Sinai in 1967 were due to the steamroller effect of Nasser's paramount chieftaincy will not be known for some time yet.

Introducing a special Hilal publication,[15] Fathi Radwan described the July 1952 army movement as a "surgical operation". The soldiers had taken power in order to cure the ills of Egypt. Yet only five years later, in his speech on 23 December 1957, Nasser himself, basking in the glow of the Suez aftermath and his new political arrangements, declared, "The National Union is now the whole nation. Government is now by the people . . . There is no need for rules. Governments in the past were against the people. Today government is one—fused—with the people." The question, though, whether the 1952 military *coup* constituted a turn-about in Egypt remains difficult to answer unequivocally in the affirmative. What, however, can be said by way of a general conclusion about the Free Officer movement, the régime it founded and Nasser himself on the basis of this enquiry?

The Free Officers inaugurated a nationalist authoritarian régime which, under Nasser, set out to modernise Egypt in the only way he knew and preferred—perhaps the only possible way?—by decree. He launched industrialisation under a state-directed and -controlled economy. Egyptians after 1952 moved from some freedom under law to greater autocracy and servitude; from a degree of legality to almost plain arbitrariness. Arbitrary rule is, by definition, tyrannical. In practice, however, the equation is not that neat.

Nasser, a political romantic and radical autocrat, followed the collapse of a dynasty and the retreat of a foreign imperial power. He appealed equally to the dispossessed and insecure urban and rural masses of the country as well as to the alienated intelligentsia. He impressed upon them the overriding need for national unity, played on their sense of insecurity and convinced them of his ability to save Egypt. The autocrat, that is, was to be also the nation's redeemer. His despotic tendencies derived from his sense of personal and national humiliation, as well as his cultural and social background—and experience. The wider Egyptian sense of national humiliation in turn allowed them to develop further.

One of Nasser's most powerful weapons in increasing his power and maintaining his hegemony was the popular indictment of the Egyptian political past. Practically all so-called democratic experiments in the previous seventy years were emotionally identified in the minds of Egyptians with a foreign occupation and a steadily degenerating dynasty. Another powerful weapon was the psychological effect of Nasser as the first president of an Egyptian republic ever. Yet kingship had been a very old institution in the country. So was the tradition of one-man rule a venerable and durable one. It was therefore difficult for Nasser to escape their lingering force and attraction, albeit in a different guise.

The moderate elements in Egyptian society at mid-century were to be found among the few educated, Westernised, though disoriented, élites, including resident foreigners. Otherwise, the national ethic of the vast majority was traditionally authoritarian. It had barely been eroded by a thirty-year period of turbulent—and, in the end, unsuccessful—attempt at parliamentary democracy under the tutelage of a foreign power.

Unlike Napoleon, Nasser was not an "outsider". Nor was he a professional revolutionary like Lenin and Stalin, or a *déclassé* type like Hitler. He was very much an "insider" in terms of Egypt in the period from 1930 to 1952. He believed his own destiny to be tied to that of Egypt, or at least her national cause.

There was of course state terror under Nasser, but unlike totalitarian régimes, not mass terror. No modern ruler of Egypt has ever had to resort to mass terror; it is not necessary. The Mukhabarat was adequate enough an instrument of terror in producing the desired effect and results: fear, suspicion and distrust, the characteristics of an atomised society. Once citizens mistrust one another, they are rendered powerless for political action. As impotent subjects, they remain humble. Aristotle thought these were, or ought to be, the major aims of a tyrant.

As in all other instances of state terror, however, Nasser's régime too featured its fanatic bureaucratic dispensers of it: Salah Nasr, other chiefs and senior officers of the Mukhabarat. The extensive, frequent purging of the army, the trade unions, professional syndicates, the press and media provided Nasser with added levers of power for the manipulation of the country by his state machine. Even verbal opprobrium and violence, such as the branding of an individual or a group as reactionary, colonialist, exploiter or secessionist, was adequate terror, for it had the effect of finishing him or them off politically, economically and socially.

Nasser preferred a bureaucratic despotism to a personal one. At least that was the long-term effect of the 1952 *coup*. But this, in one way, was natural. Egypt's hierarchical, bureaucratic centralism had been one of the most durable in the world. What Nasser understood and used to his advantage was the fact that even such a monster was always entirely dependent on the despot. By its nature it is an instrument of despotism.

Nasser, however, was not a great tyrant. Rather he was a military-bureaucratic despot, a *rayyes*. Nor was he the only Egyptian about capable of self-deception: "We have not been beaten, only betrayed" (1967). He shared with his people a sharp sense of historic wrongs done to Egypt by outsiders: the Crusades, the British occupation, the creation of Israel. He felt the same sense of grievance and suspicion of being the victim of a world conspiracy against Egypt and the Arabs. In 1967, for example, it was the United States, according to him and the Egyptians, not the Israeli, air force that destroyed Egypt's air power in less than two hours. For the Arabs at large, Nasser was a romantic hero. He used the short-lived dynamic of revolutionary nationalism to attack his enemies and rivals to Arab leadership. Despite his support by the great powers, he got away with alternately attacking one or the other.

In his personal way of governing Egypt, Nasser was a bit like Mussolini of Italy. He perfected a balancing act between subordinates until no party, movement or other institutional arrangements really controlled the state or the army. It is noteworthy, for instance, that Nasser did not contemplate seriously the question of succession until two years before his death. Needless to say, his courtiers did. Rather Nasser, even in 1969, seemed content to manipulate his personal arrangements for control, consisting of a sort of praetorian guard (*al-gihaz al-tali'i*): the secret security services, the army, the bureaucracy, the media and a vague radical populist ideology expressed in massive, cumbersome institutions like the ASU.

From 1952 to 1954, Nasser indulged in what may be called "organisation politics". In 1954–6, he was almost wholly taken up by diplomacy, carving out a role for himself and Egypt in world affairs. Between 1957 and 1961, he concentrated on the "politics of Arabism", seeking to impose Egypt's leadership over Arab affairs in the region. After 1961, he was forced to consider ways of grafting a "political system" on to his personal power. On the whole, he failed. His attempt to reorganise government at home under a National Charter and use a vastly expanded public sector economy as the basis of a socialist régime produced meagre results. Alas, Nasser conceived the new leftist "ideology" as a mere appendage to his personal power, not as a substitute or a complement for it.

In the end he did not quite succeed in suppressing the realities facing him and Egypt. He even failed to provide novel or alternative ways of dealing with these realities. He thus failed to construct a world to his liking and according to his vision. He none the less inaugurated a new style of Egyptian and Arab politics, characterised by a fantastic ability at vilification, subsuming all possible concrete political action and discrete organisation in his *thawra*, his revolutionary syndrome. This way he managed, at least until 1967, to retain a phenomenal mass appeal while pursuing ever greater concentration of personal power. He proved unarguably that he was a "leader of the people", a *za'im*. What he failed to prove was that he was leading them somewhere. His "populist democracy" under a Ceasarist autocracy replaced even the semblance of law.

Yet it is not so much what Nasser himself specifically did or did not do that characterised his autocracy. It is the *gihaz*, the state apparatus, which he constructed that grew like Topsy and was let loose on an unsuspecting public to plague and tyrannise them. It soon acquired its own momentum and extended its tentacles so widely that no one could escape its sharp and often cruel attention. People soon became afraid to speak, let alone act.

As the leader of the Free Officer movement, Nasser aspired to liberate Egyptians from all kinds of disabilities and fetters, some of historical vintage, others of more recent origin. It is ironic that by his own behaviour at the summit and that of his subordinates in the state apparatus Nasser ended up by imposing on them even heavier shackles. Instead of freeing them for action, he immobilised them.

On balance, Nasser was an effective ruler of Egypt. The record of his concrete accomplishments in transforming the society and its economy, however, is mixed. He was not, that is, as efficient a ruler in getting things done. The belief he fostered among Egyptians that deliverance from foreign rule would bring untold benefits was not borne out by his performance. Instead, the socialism he introduced, consisting of the nationalisation and central planning of the economy, led to the greatest possible concentration of power over state and society in his hands. The ideology he proclaimed after 1962 supplied the semblance of a "scientific explanation" for his power. It had the added advantage of attracting support from the Soviet Union. Still, he managed throughout his rule to offer Egyptians attractive alternative images of self-respect, national dignity, identity and, occasionally, purpose.

In a recent biography of T. E. Lawrence, Professor John E. Mack suggested a link between Lawrence's search for redemption, his "egoism involved in assumption of responsibility", and his role in the Arab Revolt (1916–18). "When one person, who, because of exceptional abilities brought to focus on an unusual historical situation", he wrote, "has a chance to assume a powerful personal role, the opportunities for him to live out his personal needs and impulses in the service of those he is helping are very great indeed." [16]

Nasser in 1952 assumed the role of "enabler" in his dream to make Egypt independent of foreign control and transform her into a modern industrial state. His motivation and activity created a situation in which he could impose his will first on his fellow-officer conspirators and next on Egyptians at large. What Nasser's internal drives and personal purposes were is difficult to determine. That he was a historical figure in Egypt at mid-century is however a fair description. At least he acted out the part which his followers readily accepted of the restorer of Egyptian and Arab national dignity and the avenger of injustices against them.

Except for his tract, *Philosophy of the Revolution*, and his *Palestine War Memoirs* we have no other documentary evidence—letters, notes—by Nasser that can supply us with any clues about his consciousness of his self, his dreams or fantasies. He was clearly ambitious: he sought power and fame. He passionately pursued his "mission" of "liberating" Egypt and the Arab world. He became an Egyptian and Arab hero barely five years after usurping power by a military *coup d'état*. He became a legend during his lifetime.

Whatever Nasser's private purpose may have been, the public opportunity for the role he assumed was there. It arose at a time when Egyptians needed a hero. Whatever reservations one may have about Tawfiq al-Hakim's *Return of Consciousness*, in which he developed the theme of this desperate need of the Egyptians as illustrated by their idolisation of Nasser,

> Men need heroes in order to transcend the limitations and disappointments they experience in their everyday lives . . . But the *creation* of heroes depends upon the compliance of history, the coming together of special events and situations with unusual men . . . who take hold of these circumstances, force them upon their own actions and personalities, and transform them along the lines of their own dreams.[17]

His success in organising a military conspiracy and his subsequent triumph over Naguib suggested a determined, single-minded personality and forceful ruler.

There was no indication, however, at that time (1954) that he would become the "tribune of the people", the popular charismatic leader and hero of a wider Arab movement, however effective or ineffective the latter turned out to be. That really was an accidental, sudden development, a result mainly of the Suez episode of 1956. Followed so soon by the dramatic, short-lived union between Egypt and Syria, these two events gave Nasser a historical importance that he might not otherwise have attained. His actions and utterances, attitudes and postures during these crucial five years (1956–61) in a way defined his role and limited his subsequent freedom of action under less favourable circumstances after 1962. Politically and psychologically, Nasser, in the years of his declining popularity (1962–7), was a prisoner of that "golden age" of defiance and optimism.

His failure to be politically flexible, leading to the disasters of an ever more repressive police state at home and expensive adventurism abroad, derived partly from the idolised, charismatic experience of the 1950s. Nasser and Nasserism—the hero and the legend—were products of those "heroic" years. After 1962, Nasser had to contend with the traumatic impact of a series of disappointing, even shattering experiences, ranging from his rejection by the Syrians, Iraqis, South Arabians, North Africans and Africans to his humiliating military defeat in Sinai in 1967 and the resulting loud reprimand of his own people in 1968. His political recovery in 1967 was only partial and temporary: however hard he tried after that to infuse a new air of vitality into his régime, Egyptians on the whole simply no longer shared his vision. Whatever the mitigating circumstances, his performance had undermined his credibility and tarnished his image. His desperate pleas to be left to devote all his time and efforts exclusively to domestic political matters were of no avail. The bitter recriminations and purges within the group of erstwhile close associates—the Amer affair, the Shams Badran trial, the Ali Sabri scandal—tore asunder the charmed "family circle" of hopeful young officer-saviours. The glamour was gone. The washing of dirty linen in public exposed a festering malodorous cancer in the shape of a cynical, ruthless power clique. Undoubtedly, he suffered personally and yet he was compelled to live out the demands of his ambition and furious restlessness as well as those of his public image—and legend.

Nasser was, however, luckier with his erstwhile Arab enemies. He accommodated himself with them in a general atmosphere of forgiveness and co-operation, while he licked his wounds from his shattered Arab adventure. Most tragic was the wrecked state of his health. He died in September 1970 just as he was proving to his fellow-Egyptians once again that Egypt's primacy in Arab councils was still a reality, surrounded as he was in those last days of his life with practically all the heads of Arab states as his guests in Cairo. Nevertheless events in May 1971, less than a year after his death, highlighted the evanescence of his charisma, much like that of Sukarno, Nkrumah and Ben Bella after their departure from the political scene of their respective countries. One Egyptian may have characterised the Nasser interlude in the modern history of Egypt quite aptly when he wrote,

Nasser represents a phenomenon that has repeatedly appeared in the Pharaonic history of Egypt. A Pharaoh would ascend the throne in a transition period between getting rid of one foreign

influence and falling in the clutches of another . . . God have
mercy on you Nasser; you were a dictator, and it is inevitable
that dictatorial rule end in catastrophes and disasters.[18]

However one measures it, though, Nasser was a man of accomplishment. He rose from humble beginnings to the pinnacle of
power in his own country, and evoked a frenetic adulation by
millions of others outside it who spoke the same language and
worshipped the same god. His peculiar response to the needs of
Egypt at mid-century, as well as his own talent, enabled him to
reach power and, through his actions, affect the course of his
country's history. The proposition, therefore, that history occasionally pushes into prominence individuals whose personality, perhaps
nature, coincides with the critical historical moment may well be
valid. Clearly an extraordinary individual, Nasser, whatever his
personality traits, managed, in the context of epochal events, to
inaugurate a new phase in the history and fortunes of Egypt. What
the course and outcome of this phase will be it is still too early to
predict. But that it began partly as a result of the fusion between
Nasser's restlessness and disaffection on one hand and the condition
of his country at a given point in time on the other could be a
plausible hypothesis.

Notes

1. Louis Awad, *Aqni'at al-Nasiriyya al-sabaa* (*The Seven Masks of Nasserism*)
    (Beirut, 1975). All quotations are from this edition.
2. See the first part of Dr Awad's book and especially pp.45–88.
3. Galal Amin, *The Modernization of Poverty* (Leiden, 1974), hazards tentative
    answers to these questions.
4. Louis Awad, *Aqni'at al-Nasiriyya al-sabaa*, pp.46–7.
5. See also Galal Amin, *The Modernization of Poverty*, and P. K. O'Brien,
    The Revolution in Egypt's Economic System (London, 1966).
6. Louis Awad, *Aqni'at al-Nasiriyya al-sabaa*, p.111.
7. Ibid., pp.111–12.
8. Ibid., p.113.
9. Ibid., p.109.
10. Ibid., p.118.
11. See *Rose el-Youssef*, Cairo, 14 and 21 April 1975. All quotations are from
    these two articles in the series.
12. 4, 11, 18 and 25 April 1977, "Shuhud yulio" ("Witness of July 1952").
13. Vol.1: *Qissat thawrat 23 yulio, Misr wa al-'askariyyun* (*Story of the 23 July
    revolution, Egypt and the military*), 1973; Vol.2: *Mujtama' Abdl al-Nasir
    (Nasser's milieu)*, 1974; Vol.3: *Abd al-Nasir wa al-'arab* (*Nasser and the
    Arabs*), 1976.
14. See also Mahmud al-Gayar, "The men who killed Marshal Amer", *Rose
    el-Youssef*, 5 January 1976.

15. *Kitab al-Hilal*, No.71, February 1957.
16. John E. Mack, *A Prince of our disorder, the life of T. E. Lawrence* (Boston, 1976), p.198.
17. Ibid., p.216.
18. Ahmad Hussein, *Kayfa 'araftu Abd al-Nasir was 'ishtu ayyāma hukmihi* (Beirut, 1973), p.147.

CHAPTER 19

Nasser, an Alcibiadic Cameo

Go on boldly, my son, and increase in credit with the people,
for thou wilt one day bring them calamities enough.—Timon
addressing Alcibiades. Quoted in Plutarch, *Lives*.

Gamal Abdel Nasser dominated the Egyptian and Arab political
scene from 1957 to 1967: from his Suez "victory" to his humiliating
Sinai defeat. His career impressed many people in the world; yet
his true admirers among sophisticated Egyptians and Arabs at large
were few. He inspired hope in the deprived, underprivileged masses
of the Arab countries, and planted fear in the hearts of the privileged
few. Political leaders in Europe, Africa and Asia alternately admired,
resented and mistrusted him. The superpowers alternately wooed and
opposed him.

Early on in his career the Americans, in their boundless enthusiasm
for "poor boys from the sticks who do well", relished the way he
battered the British Lion, and saw him as the Bismarck the Arabs
needed and had been waiting for. Later they found him to be an
undependable Arab quarterback. The Russians, for their part,
showered him with arms, money, medals and praise in line with
their more aggressive global policy. Like the Americans, they
considered him the strong Arab ruler upon whom to anchor their
policies for the rest of the Arab Middle East. At great cost, however,
they discovered what an expensive "paper tiger" he was, and by
1970, even before his death, they began to look for alternative
arrangements with other Arab rulers in the Middle East and North
Africa. British journalists adopted him after the Suez fiasco as the
whip with which to flagellate themselves and their fellow-countrymen
for the expiation of all the sins the "Ingleezi" had committed against

the "Wog" since 1882. The Israelis considered him the major obstacle to a peaceful coexistence with their Arab neighbours. Whatever diverse feelings he evoked, Nasser, above all, mesmerised a good part of the world in a brief but eventful career.

There was only an Egyptian Nasser; there is no generalised Nasser. He was not at any time and any place; he was in Egypt. When he appeared in Egypt is just as important to understanding the kind of political experience he constituted for the Egyptians as the fact that he was Egyptian. The Nasser phenomenon and episode had therefore to be viewed in the evolutionary context, the time perspective of Egyptian history in order to understand the way in which Nasser developed any peculiar characteristics as a political leader. The Arab states had not yet developed in 1952 the calibre of leadership and level of political organisation adequate to cope with their problems. Their heritage from the distant past and their experience from the more recent past under foreign control, combined with a poverty associated with agricultural economies only recently mitigated by petroleum and other industry, had habituated their peoples to a norm of non-participation in political life. Nasser inevitably—and perhaps detrimentally for Egypt—came to be universally accepted as a great Arab leader. In part, this recognition was readily given in the hope that he would make a difference in the Arab world: that he would inaugurate something politically new: that he would be the architect of a new foundation. Thus, for millions of Egyptians, after 1956, he was a miracle-worker.

Unlike Zaghlul, founder of the Wafd party, and his successor Nahhas before him, Nasser in Egypt came closest to being a Kingfish, to borrow a political epithet from the American South. Zaghlul may have dominated the Wafd party and, when he was Prime Minister, parliament too. Nahhas never dominated the Wafd. Both of these leaders of the largest political party in modern Egyptian history may have been populists, but only Nasser knew how to use populism in its thoroughly native import. He appeared to the people as the virulent xenophobe, the skilled politician most readily identified with the poor downtrodden rural and urban masses, the rabble-rousing anti-Establishment man, the affable demagogue who welded together a fanatically loyal following to his own person; the captain who constantly rhetorically enquired of his team if he had kept faith with them and they hypnotically yelled back in unison in the affirmative. He earned the admiration of the little man because he knew how to stay free of delaying, cumbersome political institutions like parties and legislatures; in fact, he formed and elected his own, and erected a structure of political power which, though native in its provenance, was at once terrifying and paralysing. He became the champion of the people in dramatic fashion—and at the great cost of the people—against sinister imperialist and diabolical Zionist interests. All agreements he may have reached with outside powers were not of a compromising nature, because he claimed— and the people, for a long time, believed him—that these were on his own terms.

It has been essential therefore to explore the necessary ingredients for the construction of a political portrait, perhaps only a cameo, of Nasser and his generation. One of these is the environment in which Nasser acquired his earliest political ideas, preferences and prejudices. This environment, with its prevailing political climate, also affected the formative years of his fellow-conspirators and closest associates in power after July 1952. It transmitted both to Nasser and his generation the *Weltanschauung* which was to constitute the basis of their political style and behaviour when in power. It was very much an Egyptian perspective, generated by the peculiarities of the country's political and economic experience in the years from 1930 to 1952. In fact, contemporaries of Nasser who were born say, between 1917 and 1922, who were thirty in 1948 or in their early thirties between 1948 and 1952, constitute a "generation" in historical terms, and particularly in terms of modern Egyptian history.

Needless to say, the ways in which Nasser perceived the problem of governing Egypt, as these can be inferred from a quick recapitulation of the Free Officer movement, his "alliances" and conspiratorial arrangements with others in the pursuit of power are crucial to an understanding of his personality as a leader. So is his social and economic vision of a new Egypt; and his bid for the leadership of the Arab states in the Middle East. Inexorably linked to that is his handling of the conflict with Israel. A depiction of Nasser's view of the outside world is also an important source for understanding his behaviour. Finally, an examination of Nasser's political legacy to Egypt and, by extension, to modern Arab political history could illuminate several areas of his actions, his behaviour while in power and serve as a measure for an assessment of his leadership.

A political portrait of Nasser therefore had to be sketched against the background of modern Egyptian history. Without access to official state papers, its colours had to be mixed from a collation of Nasser's utterances with his actions—at least, overt actions— throughout his career. Any evaluation of him as a ruler and political leader must also be partly based on the response and reaction of his own people to his leadership, as well as to his demise, and partly on his legacy, if any.

Unlike Lenin, Sun Yat-sen, Trotsky, Stalin, Mao, Mussolini, Hitler or Atatürk, little is known of Nasser's political activities before he emerged as a successful uniformed conspirator. In any case, these were not extensive or important. He did not undergo the prolonged dangerous experience of arduous underground political education and ideological formation. Membership of the Young Egypt Society in the 1930s and participation in student demonstrations, though an expression of sympathy with a nationalist cause or opposition to a government policy, are not comparably intense political involvements.

Lenin, Trotsky, Mao, even Stalin, showed great capacity for political thinking, ideological proselytisation and practical political organisation long before they attained their positions of power. Mussolini was an accomplished, albeit controversial, journalist before his Fascist March on Rome. Atatürk was a successful military man, one of Turkey's best generals, a national hero of the Great War, a *ghazi*—a conqueror of infidels—and the saviour of his country from foreign invasion. Nasser's few brooding letters to his schoolmate Ali Hasan al-Nashar, resurrected after his coming to power, reveal nothing extraordinary about their author beyond the expression of disaffection and despair with his own and his country's lot, feelings which were shared widely by Egyptian youth of his generation.

Nor did Nasser possess the "audacious vision of the future" which a man like Trotsky did. He was not a revolutionary ideologue or a profound thinker who sought a rational critique of phenomena. Significantly, he was not by upbringing, interest, temperament or experience a man who had or wished to have a connection with physical things. Besides a limited experience as a soldier with weapons, he had none with the plough of the peasant farmer or the machine of the industrial worker. In fact, in an overwhelmingly rural country, Nasser had hardly ever lived in the countryside, except very briefly when he attended school at Khatatba. Like many other Egyptians, including political leaders, his connection with physical things was extremely limited. The countryside, with its teeming peasants, was something to be romanticised—and used politically.

Like so many of his contemporaries and eventual lieutenants in power, Nasser was a product and member of that swarming amorphous monster, the city, the urban milieu of Egypt without genuine urbanites. It provided him with his earliest political notions and prejudices, as well as his perceptions about himself, his country and the world. The packed, French-modelled, intellectually debilitating curriculum of the secondary school (*thānawiyya*), the odd political demonstration in the streets of Cairo or Alexandria organised by the Young Egypt Society, the National party, or the Wafd comprise his early political education and almost sum total of his cultural formation. Military academy offered him entry into what, at that time, was a relatively exclusive club.

In a way, these gaps in Nasser's formation proved an asset, not a hindrance, to his later pursuit of power. Free of the doubts which are engendered by a more direct, or close, and thoughtful brush with the encumbrances of one's physical and intellectual environment, Nasser could single-mindedly concentrate all his efforts on his drive for power, at a time when most of his contemporaries were driven towards the bland routine existence of bureaucratic pursuits or aspirations. His lack of any deep intellectual directing principle, ideological commitment, or even concern with the disabling qualities of a harsh and cruel environment proved to be a blessing when rationalising later his flexible tactics in the pursuit of his singular objective. Even the very detachment from his own family from an early age, a separation which occurred after the death of his mother and his father's almost immediate remarriage, and then later his own marriage to the quiet, self-effacing daughter of a merchant were all clear advantages in his concentration on his political goal. They enabled him later to devote all his energies to the Free Officer conspiracy. This single-minded devotion is partly responsible for the subsequent belief of the Egyptian masses that Nasser was indeed extraordinary, and their acceptance of him as a charismatic leader.

When Nasser was at the peak of his popularity in the years from 1956 to 1960 some, outside the Arab world, were inclined to compare him with Atatürk of Turkey. There was an apparent dynamism in both men, "a relentless drive and didactic imperiousness". Yet the two men, when viewed as national leaders, could not have been more different, and the contrast between them in retrospect is quite sharp.

Atatürk was a military genius, a great soldier. He had been involved in conspiracies and secret revolutionary activities against the Sultan early in his military career, in Salonika, Monastir and elsewhere. He had none the less been a brilliant cadet and, later, staff officer. Nasser had none of Atatürk's military competence, experience or prestige. In fact, the record of his military career is undistinguished. Until 1948 he remained a careful, cautious and circumspect officer. They shared two characteristics. Both came from humble backgrounds. They both possessed a great capacity for hard work under tremendous pressure, wearing down everyone around them. Nasser, however, did not share Atatürk's weakness for drink, gambling and women.[1]

Both men experienced a temporary adulation by people outside their own respective countries, Atatürk in the 1920s and Nasser in the mid and late fifties. The appeal of their Davidian prowess against the white, Christian European Goliath was brief but intense.

> Wherever there was massed hostility to the imperial nations of the West men looked up expectant to Mustafa Kemal, believing that a champion had arisen. They saw in this Moslem general, who had defeated all the might of Europe, the spearhead of their advance towards freedom from the white man and the Christian. The Soviets were urging him on . . . From all sides came invitations to become champion of the East against the West.[2]

The parallelism with Nasser's image and popularity at home and abroad, especially the wild Arab response to it after the Suez affair in 1956 and the union of Egypt with Syria in 1958, is uncanny. It did not matter, at the height of exhilarating nationalist passion and euphoria, that Nasser had not won a military victory.

Atatürk in 1922, however, recognised the limits of his victory, and forced his people to exchange a nationalism territorially centred in and limited to Anatolia and part of Western Asia Minor for the more romantic and greater Ottomanism and Islamism of old. Nasser, by contrast, in 1956, did not exhibit similar circumspection. "After the tribulations of the nation there was no evidence of greatness which lay in the knowledge and acceptance of the narrow limits" of Egypt's opportunities. Nasser's pedestrian lack of political perceptiveness after 1956 in contrast was disastrously brought home to the Egyptians and the world in 1967.[3]

Without the army Nasser in 1952, like Atatürk in 1919, would have been politically nobody. He too had to proceed cautiously towards his objectives, dissimulating his real intentions along the way. Like Atatürk, Nasser was to eventually consolidate his own personal power and dominant position over the opposition of his erstwhile closest associates. He was equally, if not more generously, blessed by a society in which the masses of the population cared little for politics. He had ample scope—at times, good reason—to exercise, develop and ultimately master a supreme demagogic ploy regarding the outside world: at first, there were imperialists, later there were neo-imperialists and reactionaries, and always Zionists and Israelis.

Whereas the creation of the structures which were to give Nasser total control over the state proceeded at an ostensibly measured pace—a republic, a presidential form of government, a single-state political organisation—most of the opposition was dismantled by drastic and punitive economic measures. The potentially more dangerous opposition (e.g. the Muslim Brotherhood, the various Communist groups, army officer cliques) was dealt with more harshly, and often brutally. Fortuitously and to Nasser's advantage, the society was on the whole alienated from most of this opposition, so that its decimation, neutralisation or destruction elicited no consequential reaction. In these circumstances, it was difficult for the people to detect, at that early stage in Nasser's career (1952–7), any streak of ruthlessness or cynicism in their leader's character or behaviour. Even though some had detected in him a lack of sentiment that could affect his political steadfastness or his consuming ambition for power, they none the less ascribed it to circumstances, the requirements of office, and the needs of his difficult revolutionary task in Egypt.[4]

For a long time, Egyptians accepted Nasser as evidence of an evolutionary breakthrough in Arab political leadership. As a phenomenal political mutation, they felt he needed time to adjust to and cope with the environment. It was not until the aftermath of the Six Day War in June 1967 and the events in Egypt eight months after his death in May 1971 that a shattering traumatic realisation of Nasser's cynicism occurred. Simple and sophisticated Egyptians alike asked, for example, how could Nasser allow the demise of his closest friend and collaborator, Field Marshal Abdel Hakim Amer?

(They did not know then that Nasser and Amer had been at odds for nearly ten years.) How could he allow a "Mafia" of his immediate lieutenants such leeway to terrorise Egyptian society while at the same time obscenely enjoying the privileges of a new *apparatchik* class in power? Apart from having his opposition hanged, Atatürk, forty years earlier in Turkey, signed his close friend Aref's death warrant. Nasser, one could plead in mitigation, only signed Abdel Hakim's arrest warrant. How novel or immoral, though, was this kind of ruthlessness in the cultural values of the Egyptian or Turkish society which had been transmitted over scores of generations? Despotism's original home, after all, lay in Mesopotamia and the Nile valley.

How strange, for example, or extraordinary ought one to consider the hysterical mob's chanting outside the National Assembly on 9 June 1967, when Nasser had tendered his resignation, "Record, Record, O Sadat, we have specifically chosen Gamal." (Arabic: *"Saggil, Saggil yā Sādāt, ihnā khtarnā Gamāl bidhāt."*) Or their chant outside Nasser's residence in Manshiet el-Bakri, on the same day, "O Gamal, light of our life, you're leaving Egypt and going where?" (Arabic: *"Yā Gamāl, yā nūr el-ayn . . . sāyib masr u rāyih fein?"*)

Dia' al-Din Dawud, a leading member of the executive committee of the Arab Socialist Union (ASU), who was later imprisoned for his part in the 14 May 1971 conspiracy against President Sadat, emphasised in the piece he contributed to the Special Memorial Issue of *al-Hilal* (November 1970) on President Nasser, the late President's "faith in the masses". "I recall," he wrote, "when we were discussing his statement of reforms on the 30th March [1968], how Nasser always asked: 'what do the masses want?' " Any critical study of Nasser must, in turn, ask, what does this mean, if anything at all? Masses are amorphous and a notoriously elusive political category, favoured by ruthless despots and dextrous demagogues. In 1967, for instance, the ideologue of the Syrian National Social Party (ex-Parti Populaire Syrienne) published a collection of articles under the title *Masses and Disasters*,[5] criticising the haphazard character of all Arab revolutionary movements in the 1950s and the absence of substantial, impersonal political institutions. The torrent of soul-searching, self-critical (though not necessarily genuinely intro-spective) Arabic writing in the period 1965-8, much of it penned by erstwhile political and military leaders, equally deplored the political vacuity of Arab revolutionary movements.[6] In the face of such self-confessed *malaise*, the student is bound to question the accepted popular image and hagiography of leaders in the Arab Middle East.

Nasser claimed he had a vision about the kind of Egypt he wished to build. He was also a political being with an immense appetite for power and inordinate ambition. But were his abilities commensurate with his vision? Was his vision credible? Was he a statesman? How new was his New Order for Egypt?

"There is nothing more difficult to carry out than a new order of things," Machiavelli opined in the sixteenth century; "nor more doubtful of success." [7] Yet if one follows Machiavelli, Nasser came to power in Egypt with a great advantage. The kind of government he took over was in the tradition of the Turk, not of the Frenchman: "having conquered it, it would be very easy to hold it," because "it is governed by one ruler, the others are his servants . . . as ministers by his grace and permission, they assist in governing the realm." [8]

Throughout his career, Nasser appears to have acted on the premise that "nothing causes a prince to be so much esteemed as great enterprise and giving proof of prowess": [9] the nationalisation of the Suez Canal and other foreign-owned enterprises and property in Egypt which supplied the basis of the country's new public sector economy, the building of the Aswan High Dam and other projects of industrialisation, the policy of revolutionary Arab nationalism and socialism in the struggle for the leadership of the Arab states.

Nasser has been described as a pragmatic ruler to the point of cynicism. What may have not been adequately recognised is the source of his cynical pragmatism, which was clearly rooted in the experience of his formative years (1930–6), his brief career as an army officer on active duty in the years from 1938 to 1952. Unlike other Arabs, the Egyptians are not Manichean in their view of the world. They do not make a stubborn, categorical distinction between good and evil. They are more supple and flexible, and one would assume that a more open, pluralist political order is not excluded from the variety of their experience or spectrum of capabilities. What has always militated against this and in favour of rule by powerful princes has been their apathy and the sapping of their will which derive from demographic profusion and suffocating human propinquity, as well as the intractable social and economic problems these conditions generate. It was often phantasmagoric release from these conditions that they craved, not formulae for methodical hard work. Nasser recognised these disabling conditions in his country. The recognition, in turn, became another source of his cynicism.

The lasting influences on Nasser's formation derived from the *Weltanschauung* of the lower ranks of the petite bourgeoisie in the Egypt of the inter-war period. His educational and cultural preparation was therefore shallow because it was limited to these formative influences. Apart from his apparent charisma, however, he had an instinctive grasp of the political in the Egyptian context. Habituation in violent, albeit futile, political activity as a student, born of personal frustration as well as despair over social and economic conditions in his country, engendered in Nasser an ultimately counter-productive view of politics: that of secrecy, distrust and conspiracy. His seemingly genuine desire to transform his country for the greater benefit of his fellow-Egyptians was dissipated by this permanent attitude and conduct when in power, which tended to undermine all public endeavour.

Because of his conservative upbringing, Nasser felt shame and disgrace in a cataclysmic, depressing way. The shame and disgrace and, in Nasser's view, dishonourable record of Egyptian politics in the years from 1930 to 1936 were compounded by the humiliation of the Egyptian crown and army at the hands of the British in Cairo in February 1942 and of the Israelis in the Palestine War of 1948–9. His *Palestine War Memoirs*, conveniently published soon after the Israel army raid on the Gaza Strip in February 1955, clearly reflect Nasser's desire to exonerate the army and seek out the "real culprits" of Egypt's humiliation.

Whether as a Machiavellian "prince" or an Islamic *amir*, Nasser was very much in the Egyptian and Near Eastern tradition of rulership. A soldier of humble origin and social background, he acceded to practically unlimited power in the governing of Egypt. Almost exclusively interested in power, Nasser was consumed by politics and what Miles Copeland popularised as "the game of nations",[10] or what his colleagues and Muhammad Hasanein Heikal have called "the contest of wills".[11] It is widely accepted that his interest in power was not from dubious motives or for corrupt purposes, but for the pursuit of a vision consisting basically first, of restoring Egypt's autonomy, and second, of transforming its society into a strong modern industrial state. "All Egypt's ills", he is reported to have said once, "whether economic, social or political, derive from the fact of foreign domination." Or "The English are the root of all evil in Egypt", a slogan first made popular by Ahmad Hussein and the Egyptian officers' mentor General Aziz Masri. Be that as it may, within five years of seizing power, Nasser, the man who overthrew the monarchy, became the uncrowned monarch of Egypt. Herodotus at least thought that Egyptians are unable "to do without a king for long."[12]

In modern times, Egypt experienced three epochal transformations. The first, under Muhammad Ali the Great (1805–9), an Albanian soldier of fortune; the second under British occupation (1882–1922); and the third under Abdel Nasser, a native Egyptian soldier. Muhammad Ali ruthlessly forged the basic structures of a modern state. His main instruments were the army and the great number of imported European advisers and mercenaries. The British pro-consuls in Cairo introduced the appurtenances of a modern fiscal and judicial administration. They also made Egyptian agriculture more efficient and productive, and completed the incorporation of the Egyptian agricultural economy into the European market economy and patterns of trade. Their principal instrument was the bureaucracy, assisted by British advisers. Nasser in 1952 overthrew the *ancien régime* of the monarchy (thus putting an end to the dynasty founded by Muhammad Ali) and the brief pluralist political experiment (1923–52) by a *coup d'état*. He then proceeded to create the bases and framework of a popular despotism with which he claimed he wanted to transform Egypt economically, socially and politically. Like Muhammad Ali a hundred and fifty years before him, Nasser's principal instrument for the projected transformation was the army and imported advisers provided by a patron super-power, the Soviet Union. He made the army the vanguard of his revolution and the main source of a new technocratic-military state bureaucracy.

On the surface, Nasser possessed the painful intensity of the puritan, who is certain of the righteousness of his vision and way of salvation. At the same time, his secular view of power, given the reality of his country's condition, was forcefully clear: "In those states which are governed by a prince and his servants, the prince possesses more authority, because there is no one in the state regarded as superior other than himself."[13] He believed in the creative role of the hero in the seven-thousand-year-long history of his country: Menes, Ramses II and his generals, the Caliph Omar,

Saladin and other Mamluk soldier-princes, the tragic peasant-soldier Orabi, the fiery nationalist leader of schoolboys Mustafa Kamil, the native lawyer-intellectual father of the modern independence movement Saad Zaghlul—some men of the sword, others men of the pen.

Intuitively, deeply conscious of this eminent heritage, though not quite rationally understanding its complexities, Nasser showed an instinctive feeling for the essence of Egypt's political history. Despots have invariably ruled the country who, in most cases, have also been soldiers; and for a long time, foreign soldiers. Excluding periods of direct foreign occupation or control, Egypt prospered under benevolent, popular despots. Alternatively, her people suffered great misery and privation under malevolent, incompetent despots. With the exception of thirty years (1923–52), the primacy of the military, the political domination of the country by soldiers, in modern Egyptian history, and since the nineteenth century in an uneasy alliance with technocrats and bureaucrats, is too well-known to be argued. In his policy, however, the soldier Nasser, turned popular despot, exhibited a sense of the possible and practicable and a contempt for aspiring politicians among his fellow-countrymen as well as other Arabs verging on the callous and cynical. At the same time, he seemed possessed by the desire for greatness: "Of all men who have been eulogized, those deserve it most who have been the authors or founders of religions; next come such as have established republics or kingdoms."[14]

The Egyptian nation and its unity had been formed over a very long history. Creating, or building, a nation, therefore, was not one of the problems which Nasser faced. Nor was his task one of constructing a modern state in the technical-formal sense of the term. That had been accomplished by Muhammad Ali and his successors, and developed further by the British when they controlled Egypt. Nasser's task rather was that of transforming its economic foundations and the components of its social relationships. And that entailed a drastic change in the arrangements for national power, as well as the introduction of new values and perceptions. It is too early to say definitely whether Nasser accomplished either or neither. On balance, despite a promising beginning he appears to have failed.

In a practical sense, Nasser accepted unequivocally the need for state central control, planning and direction of the country's economic resources—a kind of state capitalism—especially water which, for millennia, has been the mainstay of its existence and survival. Egypt, that is, still needed an autocrat, a *rayyes*. He also recognised the overwhelming orientation of its society roughly since AD 650 towards Islam, and its inexorable link with the Muslim East, or at least Muslim South West Asia, which evolved since that time. As a military-civilian leader, Nasser was therefore very much in the tradition of Egyptian political history. The heroic model of soldiers turned rulers, princes and even dynasts was too boldly encrusted in the annals of Pharaonic, Greek, Roman, Muslim Arab, Mamluk and Ottoman–Turkish Egypt to be ignored.

On the evening of 9 June 1967, after the defeat in the Six Day War, Nasser resigned the presidency. On the morrow, Nasser was again President of Egypt by public acclamation in the streets—some would say by mob furore. One of the more talented short-story writers and dramatists in Egypt today wondered whether he should laugh or cry. What was it that attached the Egyptian masses so deeply to their leader? Did they wish him to stay on because they believed he was the best leader they had, or could hope for? Was he the best, most articulate exponent of their resentment against decades of native and foreign exploitation? Was he the embodiment of their generation's revolution? Or did they want to force him to stay on and face the consequences of his disastrous adventurism: a way of inflicting mass punishment on him? Was the miserably poor average Egyptian indulging his intuition against the gambler who took his money away, played the horses and lost? There are those who claim that in any event the average Egyptian probably had no wholly free choice in the matter; for those in control of mass state organisations, such as the ASU and the security services, helped to organise *in part* the massive demonstrations on behalf of Nasser on that day for their own purposes. They hoped, for example, to bring him under their control and so erode his power.[15]

Or how is one to describe the phenomenon of four million mourners in President Nasser's funeral on the first day of October 1970? In addition to shock over the sudden loss of their leader and the void he was leaving behind—feelings of an orphaned nation— was it also a panegyric of thanksgiving, a festive mass release from an overwhelming presence over their lives? Were the mourning millions in the streets on that day expressing a close attachment to their father-leader? Or were they making certain he was finally out of the way?

Sorrow, mourning, release, relief: a combination of all these disparate feelings crowded upon Egyptians high and low during those three days between the evening of 28 September when Nasser died of a heart attack and 1 October, the day he was laid to rest in the forecourt of the mosque he had planned and built.

What were their fears and hopes of eighteen years of Nasser's rule, which began with a quietly efficient, almost bloodless, seizure of power in the early hours of 23 July 1952? Those up early that morning heard the first communiqué of the Revolution read in the name of the Free Officers by a colonel of the Signal Corps, Anwar Sadat, the man who was to succeed Nasser as their President in October 1970. They had been promised a "new deal". Some believed they had been given it by 1 October 1970; many more believed they had not. Others still argue that the promise was too fantastic to be fulfilled by any one ruler in Egypt. All Egyptians, however, were left a most difficult legacy to continue with.

Whatever the feelings of the Egyptians towards their departed President, one thing was certain. Fifteen years of Nasser's revolutionary régime did not resolve any of the perennial problems of their country. The population on the Nile increased relentlessly. The galloping rise in the birth rate (2.5 per cent per annum) seemed to neutralise all the economic "triumphs" of the régime, whether under its state capitalist or Arab socialist schemes. A new privileged class just as extravagant in its consumption and rather incompetent in the more equitable distribution of national wealth succeeded in spreading poverty more evenly and "modernising" it.[16]

Overpopulation, illiteracy, unemployment and underemployment, malnutrition and undernourishment were some of the problems which faced Nasser's Egypt; the same as those which faced the Egypt of King Faruq eighteen years before that. The rate of illiteracy remained at around 75 per cent and the *per capita* income at about £E75 per annum. Lacking solutions to such, often hopelessly complex problems, Nasser could claim that at least he imparted into more Egyptians than ever before a national consciousness, and pursued a dynamic, ambitious and grand foreign policy. Yet neither of these constituted an original contribution, for one could make an equally good case for national consciousness among Egyptians in 1919, 1936, and 1946 or 1951. As for an ambitious, dynamic foreign policy one need only refer to the more successful power-seeking adventures of Muhammad Ali in the Sudan, Arabia, Syria and the Eastern Mediterranean; to the imperial aspirations of his grandson, the Khedive Ismail, in Africa; or even to Fuad's and Faruq's ill-conceived, unrealistic ambitions for Muslim pre-eminence among an increasing number of new Arab states. Actually, under Nasser the Egyptians found themselves involved in three wars, two against Israel and one against other Arabs in the Yemen; their army was destroyed; 20 per cent of their territory—all of Sinai—was lost; and the Israelis advanced to the east bank of the Suez Canal.

What did the régime of the Free Officers mean for Egypt and the Egyptians; what kind of political experience did it constitute for them? Was their leader, Nasser, different from rulers of Egypt before him, and if so, in what ways? Did he have a great vision for the liberation of his people from their millennial misery, and if he did, why was he so devoid of original policies usually associated with what Westerners call statesmen? Was he a reforming hero, or simply another despot on the Nile, full of bluff and histrionics, and in whose eyes was he the one or the other, or both? There are no easy answers to these questions. What, however, emerges from the Nasser political experience is that prolonged, complex and proliferating conspiracy within a small, closed circle of associates in power breeds contemptuous indifference in the mass of spectators. Without institutions, power tends to be so remote from the people as to be ineffective as a socially and politically creative or transforming force. It remains purely a repressive one.

The testimony, for example, of Ahmad Kamil, Director of Egyptian Intelligence until 13 May 1971, before the State Prosecutor in the trial of the accused conspirators against President Sadat, shows the overriding and abiding preoccupation of President Nasser's élite with domestic conspiracy. It establishes what has always been suspected, namely, that Nasser's régime rested essentially on three crucial structures of state power: the army, the bureaucracy and the secret security and intelligence services. All the so-called state, or single, political organisations, such as the ASU and its predecessors (the National Union and the Liberation Rally) were no more than adjuncts of this troika of state power, as well as further arenas for the more extensive and elaborate play of secret security arrangements. They were never meant to be political institutions for the limitation and accountability of public power.

The Nasser revolution, one has often been reminded, was one of hope. The American journalist, C. Wilton Wynn, an early admirer of Nasser, argued in his book *Nasser of Egypt, the search for dignity,*[17] that Nasser gave back to the Egyptians their dignity and self-respect when he successfully defied their erstwhile Western masters. To assert this is to assume all Egyptians lacked dignity and self-respect in the past. It is to argue that Egypt had no national history before 1952.

Nasser assumed that all Egyptians shared his underlying explanation of the national problem: that all the ills Egypt suffered were due to foreign domination. Hence his earliest policy priority of "complete independence", which in his view involved a total national struggle that would bring Egyptians of all classes together. Yet in eighteen years he monopolised the "struggle". Whatever the degree of his success or failure in it, it did not vindicate his theory about Egypt's ills. These remained as serious as ever. Perhaps in pondering over the political meaning of Nasser for Egypt at mid-century, one may be better advised to recall Huey Long of Louisiana (bearing in mind the differences in environment, talent and education between the two men and instances) rather than Oliver Cromwell of England.

Nasser, on the contrary, was a model Egyptian ruler for the reasons suggested in this quest of constructing his political portrait. His perception of politics, power and governing did not differ drastically from that of his predecessors. Moreover, it was formed and nourished by the continuity of a specifically Egyptian tradition and culture.

> The man deserves neither glorification nor denigration, for he lived his life and played his role in the life of Egypt as an absolute ruler. He was not the first absolute ruler in the history of Egypt. Nor will he be the last, for the Egyptians among peoples are the most inclined toward such rulers . . . transforming them into tyrants . . . Egyptian rulers are doomed in fact, however good their intentions . . . if their rule is of long duration . . . to end up as tyrants.[18]

The man therefore who, in less than a generation, became the oracle of Egypt's destiny and of Arab revolution at mid-century, was a soldier by chance, a politician by instinct and a conspirator by ability and inclination. He contributed little to soldiering or politics. But he elevated the more native art of conspiracy to new

technical heights. At the end of the day, however, he was by formation, tradition and force of circumstances an Egyptian despot. The
monstrous structure he controlled—the Egyptian state—tends to
transform any well-intentioned ruler into a tyrant, *unless he is
prepared to limit its and his own powers.*

Notes

1. On Atatürk, see H. C. Armstrong, *Grey Wolf* (London, 1932), and Lord
   Kinross, *Ataturk* (London, 1965). Remarks about Nasser's working habits
   were made to the author by his eldest son and several of his Free Officer
   colleagues and Cabinet Ministers.
2. Armstrong, *Grey Wolf*, p.218.
3. On the blunders leading up to the Six Day War in June 1967, see Malcolm
   H. Kerr, *The Arab Cold War*, 3rd ed. (London, 1971), and Walter Z. Laqueur,
   The Road to War (London, 1968). See also General Salah al-Din al-Hadidi,
   Shahid 'ala harb sabaa wa sittin (*Witness to the 67 War*) (Beirut, 1974).
4. See Chapters 16–18 above, and reference to excerpts from Tawfiq al-Hakim,
   '*Awdat al-wa'i* (Beirut, 1974).
5. Henri Hamati, *Jamahir wa kawarith* (Beirut, 1967).
6. For example, Munif al-Razzaz, *al-Tajriba al-murra* (*The bitter experience*)
   (Beirut, 1967); Salah al-Din al-Munajjid, *A'midat al-nakba* (*The pillars of
   disaster*) (Beirut, 1967); Saad Jumaa, *al-Mu'amara wa maarakat al-masir*
   (*The conspiracy and the battle of destiny*) (Beirut, 1968); Sadiq al-'Azm,
   Al-Naqd al-dhati baad al-hazima (*Autocritique after the defeat*) (Beirut, 1968);
   Nasir al-Din al-Nashashibi, *Safir mutajawwil* (*Roving ambassador*) (Beirut,
   1968); Sami al-Jundi, *al-Baath* (*The Baath*); and many others. Cf. Elie
   Kedouri, *Arabic political memoirs* (London, 1974).
7. Machiavelli, *The Prince* (The Modern Library 1940 edition), p.21.
8. Ibid., pp.15–16.
9. Ibid., p.81.
10. Miles Copeland, *The Game of Nations* (London, 1969). One could make a
    case for a wider pattern of so-called caesarist autocracy, not uncommon in
    the Mediterranean basin.
11. Fuad Mattar, *Bisaraha 'an Abd al-Nasir* (Beirut, 1975).
12. *The Historian* (Penguin Classics), p.160.
13. Machiavelli, *The Prince*, p.15.
14. Machiavelli, *The Discourses* (The Modern Library 1940 edition), p.141.
15. See the testimony of Ahmad Kamil, Director of Egyptian Intelligence, in
    the investigation of the Ali Sabri conspiracy in May–June 1971 as reported in
    al-Nahar and *al-Anwar* of Beirut, September 1971. Cf. Muhammad Jalal
    Kishk, *Madha yuridu al-talaba al-misriyyin* (Cairo, 1969), published on the
    heels of serious student disturbances in November 1967 and February 1968.
    Kishk argues that the people would not countenance a Nasserite régime
    without Nasser; they preferred Nasser without Nasserism. A report has
    circulated since that time that Muhammad Fa'iq, Minister of Information
    at the time of Nasser's resignation, was set upon by the crowds outside the
    President's home on 9 June, because they mistook him for Zakariyya
    Mohieddin, the man Nasser had designated as his successor in his televised
    resignation speech. There is, incidentally, a slight resemblance between the

two men. Nasser's eldest son told this writer that this incident did occur. See also Sami Gohar, *Al-sāmitūn yatakallamūn* (Cairo, 1975), for allusions to it.

16. See Galal A. Amin, *The Modernization of Poverty* (Leiden, 1974).
17. Cambridge, Massachusetts, 1959.
18. Ahmad Hussein, *Kayfa 'araftu Abdel Nasser was 'ishtu ayyāma hukmihi* (Beirut, 1973), p.9.

CHAPTER 20

Conclusion

> Every man who has seen the world knows that nothing is so useless as a general maxim. . . . few indeed of the many apothegms which have been uttered from the time of the Seven Sages of Greece to that of poor Richard have prevented a single foolish action.—Lord Macaulay, *Critical and historical essays*.

In this book we have tried to set out how a variety of influences upon Nasser from a young age through a short military career produced certain qualities in him that enabled him to become what he was and do what he did. As we have, so far, no recorded evidence of his inner motivation, we had to rely partly on his words and actions in assessing the kind of Egyptian ruler he was. We have tried to reconstruct a portrait of his strengths and weaknesses, his perceptions and attitudes, his likes and dislikes. Above all, we have tried to trace, if only in outline form, his impact on others and particularly on his own country and the wider Arabic-speaking community. To be sure, we have at the outset emphasised the forces, influences and relations that shaped and moved him; that is, the sources of his perceptions, attitudes, beliefs and political style, and tried to relate these to his subsequent actions and utterances, as well as events. In short, we have tried to suggest what and who Nasser was by describing what he said and did. In doing so, we have etched him against the background of the wider political canvas of his generation, for we have argued that he was its prototype, and that his portrait is the mirror of a whole generation.

Commenting on the T. E. Lawrence phenomenon, Elie Kedourie wrote in 1956, "The consequences of his actions have touched numberless lives, and yet their motives were strictly personal, to be sought only in his intimate restlessness and private torment."[1] He went on to describe Lawrence as an "agitated and forceful personality".[2] Much of this is true of Nasser too. How much of it exactly is impossible to say. Despite the adulation of the masses and the tedious attention of the media and world press, Nasser was and remained an intensely private and secretive man; so private and secretive that even his own immediate family knew little about him.

Nasser did not correspond with individuals in a private capacity. He did not leave behind any diaries or notes where he might have revealed his thoughts, tastes or other interests beyond those of governing Egypt. These matters constitute a major dimension of a life and, in Nasser's case if they formed any part of his life, they are not documented. Hence the inference, or suspicion, that his sole preoccupation was with power.

To some extent our attempt to construct a political portrait of Nasser and his generation may be viewed as a study in political power and, in this particular case, personal power. But political power is an elusive concept, especially when it refers to the control of men. Since man is not an inanimate object or dumb creature of nature, but one endowed with reason and plagued by feeling, political power is a difficult category to measure precisely. Nor is it the sole category in political study. The emphasis therefore on Nasser's hegemony and monopoly of power should not suggest that we equate politics with power. Despite his inordinate preoccupation with power even Nasser—and his associates—had to be considered from the perspective of their environment. Their personality traits, preferences and values are seen as only one, though an important, element in the total setting. Whatever values and vision they may have had in their declared objective to transform Egyptian state and society are therefore set out. But Nasser in particular was also found wanting in achieving this objective because he prevented for nearly twenty years the struggle of ideas which is very much an aspect of politics. Instead, he confined himself to a struggle for and manipulation of power.

According to Montesquieu's typology of rule, Nasserism was a form of despotism. A single person governed without regulation or accounting. "Every man was" more or less "afraid of every other man." Nasser exercised his power through the control of the traditional means of coercion, that is the army, the police, the bureaucracy and the courts. Since he also felt he had to attract popular support and secure a mass base both for his attainment of power and its retention, his rule was a personal one, a "caesaristic autocracy". But he aspired to more than simply making himself supreme; he originally sought power as the means for transforming his country into a modern industrial state. The fact that he did not succeed—the main reasons for which failure were set out in this book—does not make him into a totalitarian dictator. That in any case was not necessary in Egypt at mid-century.

Yet by 1967 Nasser's personal rule did verge on the totalitarian. A state based, however inadequately or inefficiently, upon the rule of law had been transformed into a police state. There was a change from a shabby pluralist régime to one of the concentration of power in the hands of a single ruler. There were also the repeated unsuccessful attempts to construct a single state political organisation. At the same time there were serious efforts to create a "mass" culture and society, while there was a constant reliance by the state on terror.

The drift towards totalitarianism, however, was arrested because, among other reasons, Nasser could not completely eliminate the division between state and society. He did of course eliminate the one between state and government. Even though the state was permeated by his power, his failure to create a monopolistic state political organisation prevented the development of a totalitarian system. Perhaps in his persistent opposition to it (for he feared the potential challenge to his concentration of power) Nasser unwittingly served his country well by saving it from a kind of totalitarian development or fate.

Finally, our attempt to project a political portrait of Nasser and his generation focussed on the political formation, behaviour and rule of the Free Officers, their personal background and peculiar environment, and the emergence of Nasser himself as the sole charismatic ruler of Egypt.

Our early references to a generation of alienation and anxiety are relevant to the consideration of how the Free Officers behaved when they attained power. But they are also relevant on a broader scale when Nasser emerged as a charismatic leader in examining why and how masses of Egyptians were prepared to follow him blindly for at least a decade. If they identified with him, why did they? It seems that in following him they hoped for deliverance from all kinds of anxieties, fears and disabilities. They concurred in his ascription of their ills to specific individuals and groups within their country, and to certain foreign powers outside it. Nasser adumbrated for them a set of abstract principles, vague hopes and aspirations which were difficult to realise or put into practice. But the people readily adopted them as the new myth of their impending liberation. Conversely, the myth sustained Nasser's power. History for the Egyptians at that particular juncture was not only a romance with Nasser as its hero, but very much a conspiracy, too. Like the Calvinist view of Cromwell in the seventeenth century, Allah sent Nasser, the "secular redeemer", to overthrow the exploiters and the tyrants. But Nasser's authoritarianism did not produce socialism in Egypt, only a new tyranny rooted, some would argue, in ancient Oriental despotism. What the Nasser experience may have taught the Egyptians is that every political order is based on anxiety and alienation. One man's gain is often another man's loss. Without necessarily subscribing to Machiavelli's or the Greek dramatists' pessimistic view of the nature of man, we must accept the reality that no political order, however well designed or well intentioned, can eliminate human anxiety, alienation and antagonism. It is always dangerous to invest it with any transcendental significance or to expect from it spiritual fulfilment. Redemption and salvation in this life have eluded man since time immemorial. Revolution, as we ought to know by now, does not always—in fact, rarely—produce new men, only new faces. Only a more pragmatic and less dogmatic approach to politics can perhaps spare man the excesses of an autocrat, be he demagogic, charismatic or otherwise.

Notes

1. Elie Kedourie, *England and the Middle East* (London, 1956), p.105.
2. Ibid., p.88.

Index

370